Splendid Survivors

Splendid Survivors

San Francisco's Downtown Architectural Heritage

prepared by
CHARLES HALL PAGE & ASSOCIATES, INC.
for
THE FOUNDATION FOR SAN FRANCISCO'S
ARCHITECTURAL HERITAGE

text by
Michael R. Corbett

A California Living Book

Published by California Living Books. The San Francisco Examiner Division of The Hearst Corporation. Suite 223, The Hearst Building, Third and Market Streets, San Francisco, California 94103.

Library of Congress Catalog Card No. 79-63454
ISBN: 0-89395-037-8 (cloth)
ISBN: 0-89395-031-9 (paper)

Cover Photo: by Hal Lauritzen, Grant Avenue, 1979
Title Page Photo: by Gabriel Moulin Studios,
                  Grant Avenue, 1948.

Printed in the United States of America

TABLE OF CONTENTS

The Survey

FOREWORD

"San Francisco, the gateway to the Orient, was a city of good food and cheap prices; the first to introduce me to frog's legs à la Provençale, strawberry shortcake and avocado pears. Everything was new and bright, including my small hotel."

In his autobiography, Charlie Chaplin thus recalls his first visit to California, in 1910. His observations are unremarkable, to be sure, but how eagerly we who are fascinated by San Francisco read these words, as we read everything we can lay hands on about the mysterious City That Was. We keep trying to solve the riddle that haunts us all our lives: what *was* there about Old San Francisco that made it so special in the eyes of the world? Why did this small city, pulsating at continent's end under a cocoon of fog, capture and fire the imagination of sophisticates who had been everywhere? If there was real magic, where did it go, or is it still in the air; and if it has vanished indeed, how responsible are we who came in the wake of the myth-makers?

Will Irwin, a respected observer who knew the pre-fire-quake city as well as anybody, insisted to his death that something intangible, some mystical quality, vanished in the flames of 1906. "There was only one San Francisco," he often said. "The city that arose after the quake was quite another thing." To him and a few others, the new city looked, felt and even smelled different, but he must have been judging too harshly, for generations of San Francisco lovers were yet to come, Charlie Chaplin among them. In the sea gulls scream, chunk-chunk of ferryboat paddles, naughty giggles in upstairs rooms at the St. Germaine and Blanco's and slap of cable on what Gelett Burgess called "The Hyde Street Grip"—in these things and more, the magic seems to have endured long after '06.

The city has many lives but few golden ages and most of us suspect, not without hard evidence, that this is not one of them. We stare at the ancient, flyspecked, yellowing photos of cobbled streets long gone; we gaze at the almost foreign faces of yesterday's San Franciscans, looking for the key. In their photos, they look solid, stolid, not particularly dashing. Yet they must have had style in profusion; one has only to read the lavish menus of circa 1910, the accounts of glittering balls, the stories of escapade and scandal to know they were a rare, crazy lot. Pampered, poised forever on an earthquake fault—no wonder the San Franciscan had a reputation for living fast to die young and beautiful.

Golden ages. They came in waves, inundating the young city, spreading its fables. Abandoned sailing ships in a Gold Rush harbor whose boundaries long since have been filled in. Gaslights and lamplights, fleas and sand, cobbles, cables, cobwebs and the clatter of carriages in and out of imposing courtyards. Golden ages of garish mansions on Nob Hill (how nouveaux the rich and how rich the nouveaux) and the old Palace Hotel, with one thousand items on the menu daily and ten thousand bottles of the finest French wine gathering dust in the cellars. Golden age of snobbish Gertrude Atherton, Jack (London) and George (Sterling) and a Bohemia of candlelight and Dago red (you could say Dago then) on Nannygoat Hill, the free souls wearing hand-loomed clothes and Indian turquoise jewelry, singing their way to Marin each weekend on the gingerbread ferries, the beautiful boats of extravagant proportion.

From the testimony, there was still magic in the twenties, described so warmly by Charles Caldwell Dobie, illustrated by the filigree etchings of E. H. Suydam. Still a smallish town, maybe six hundred thousand people, but hardly any of them commuting, all of them very much involved with the life of the place, ruled indulgently by a Sunny Jim of loose rein and looser reign, a few tall buildings going up here and there, but always, more by accident than design, in the right places. "The Quality City" was one of San Francisco's least inspired slogans, but the quality was very much there. You still get the sense of it in the Flood Building lobby, at the Merchants Exchange, in the solid, built-for-the-ages exteriors of the old St. Francis and Fairmont.

The Saroyan-Sam Spade city—perhaps that was the last of it, as far as storybooks are concerned, but there is no way to give up on San Francisco, once you have fallen under its spell. You keep looking for the magic, and now and then, when the wind and the light are right, and the air smells ocean-clean, and a white ship is emerging from the Golden Gate mist into the Bay, and the towers are reflecting the sun's last rays—at moments like that you turn to the ghosts and ask, "Was this the way it was?" and there is never an answer . . .

Herb Caen
Columnist, *San Francisco Chronicle*

EDITOR'S NOTE

It was Gerald Adams who first heightened our awareness of the process of landmarking. As an urban affairs writer for the *San Francisco Examiner* and a former *California Living Magazine* staff writer, he explained, through articles and discussions, its relevance not only to San Francisco but to urban preservationists throughout the nation. So it is not surprising that we turned to him when assessing the research and conclusions in this book in terms of its value in the public arena. In other words, "What does it all mean?" and "Who cares?" Here are the answers to those questions as well as the fundamental reasons for publishing *Splendid Survivors* under the California Living Books imprint:

In the 1960s San Francisco gained national prominence as a city that cared so much about its past it encouraged imaginative recycling of buildings. Old red-brick factories along the waterfront were turned into the now-famous Ghirardelli Square and the Cannery. An old icehouse was transformed into an outstanding decorators showroom edifice (appropriately called the Icehouse) and an entire neighborhood blossomed into the Jackson Square Historical District, an interior design center of beauty and renown. Since that time, however, inflation, building speculation and the demand for office and retail space in downtown San Francisco have forced the destruction—complete or pending—of several major buildings.

Monuments of the past, confronted by forces of development, can only be saved if they are sufficiently appreciated and understood for their historical and architectural values. In the age of taxpayer rebellions and the already legendary Proposition 13 tax-limit initiative, public agencies are often too strapped for funds to perform the research functions necessary to determine the heritage value of an old building. Clearly, the private sector has to provide what government formerly handled. By means of the data collected here, San Francisco and the portions of the public that care about fine traditional architecture and history now have the definite information needed to evaluate what remains and the knowledge to determine which structures should be saved. This volume, therefore, is more than just a permanent souvenir of past eras in architecture. It is an invaluable piece of research as well as a sourcebook for all those interested in urban revitalizing and the landmarking process—a book that has relevance not only in San Francisco but in any city that cherishes its past as well as its present.

Harold I. Silverman
Director, California Living Books; Associate Editor, *San Francisco Examiner*

P.S. Architectural sophisticates throughout the nation have enthusiastically greeted this book. Here is a sampling of their comments:

San Francisco has been a prodigy from the moment it rose from the shores of Yerba Buena Cove in 1849. Water-bound and light-washed, enormously wealthy, tolerant and cosmopolitan, it has, for good and bad, been a civic theatre of fantasy. Its constricted site and wealth combined to create a concentration of buildings expressive of the city's dominance of a vast hinterland. Until recently, San Francisco's downtown remained relatively intact while other U.S. cities experienced redevelopment and "renewal" resembling wartime bombing raids. However, the process of homogenization that is turning San Francisco into Everycity has been accelerating since World War II.

Splendid Survivors should provide an invaluable service to anyone who loves San Francisco and who cares about the quality and texture of urban life. It goes beyond the individual "landmark" structures to consider *all* the visible components of the downtown fabric; from the alleys, squares and monuments, to the lampposts and clocks. The book teaches one to see not only isolated buildings, and the extraordinary richness of architectural detail, but also whole ensembles which make walking through downtown so endlessly enjoyable.

It is very late, but still, as Lewis Mumford wrote in 1963, "not yet too late." We must remember what has been lost and reconsider, very seriously, what survives. But to do so, we must see, and this book is about seeing. "When San Franciscans have convinced themselves," Mumford concluded, "that they need not accept the demolition of their city . . . they may collectively devise the political controls that will bring a halt to cataclysmic finance and catastrophic engineering." I sincerely hope this book will help us to see to that end.

Gray Brechin
Architectural Historian, The Foundation for San Francisco's Architectural Heritage

This splendid appreciation of historic San Francisco architecture is a landmark in urban literature. Everyone who prizes old buildings will admire this book as a guide to entire streets of architecture that up until now were almost unknown. The book's unprecedented importance is that it goes beyond individual buildings and teaches us how to build cities. Such a large overview of the urban environment marks a tremendous step forward for the preservationist movement. The authors' sure grasp of timeless architectural values and their systematic approach enables us to appraise buildings and neighborhoods in a way that is truly new for preservationists. Here is a *critical* planning tool, a precise and reliable comparative technique, that should be employed by all cities.

Only in the past generation have large numbers of Americans, after sad experience with bulldozers, learned that one way to build cities is to save them. Yet the pure preservationist position—that of 'save everything'—had many obvious weaknesses. Highly charged with emotion, at times wildly self-righteous, it was more a secular faith than a rational creative attitude towards environment. Societies as sure of aesthetics as Periclean Athens and the Paris of St. Louis had powerful cultural criteria, developed over generations if not centuries, to determine what should or should not be kept. In modern industrial society such sureness about architecture and urban design evaporated in a crucible of cultural confusion and parvenu affluence often mistaken as progress. It is no accident that *Splendid Survivors* arose in a place like San Francisco which has so much to cherish, but nevertheless has in a short space of time, since the 1950s really, lost so much. In the forefront of the struggle to stop wanton devastation have been San Francisco Heritage and enlightened designers and planners such as the office of Charles Hall Page who learned on the battlefield, as did the whole preservationist movement, and in some ways learned best when they lost. At last they are beginning to hold their own, if not yet to win. But the struggle goes on.

No less than 790 buildings downtown and many more at its fringes have been rated here according to their discernible architectural and historic virtues or—and this is equally crucial—their lack of them. Soon, thanks to this new method, a steadier kind of environmental politics should supplant the bitter confrontations that presently exist. This book can do much to educate all of us. By its very nature urban education is an on-going process. The authors recognize this by stating that their verdicts, like the inventory itself, are not final, can never be final. They invite additions and corrections. Perhaps in another generation we shall know what to keep, what would be urban insanity to destroy; for that we owe a public vote of thanks to Heritage and the authors of this book.

Allan Temko
Architecture Editor, *San Francisco Chronicle*

Since its inception, "Heritage" has emerged as one of the foremost urban preservation organizations in the United States. The reason for this pre-eminence is apparent in this publication, *Splendid Survivors: San Francisco's Downtown Architectural Heritage*, for here they have provided the community with a well-documented tool which will be of tremendous value for both short- and long-range planning. The general public and those officially charged with planning will now be in a position to have the basic factual information at their finger tips, so that the old and new can be more closely and meaningfully intermingled. The quality of research, analysis and judgment revealed in this inventory decidedly marks it as an ideal that other urban communities in the United States can emulate.

David Gebhard
Director, University of California at Santa Barbara Art Museum

San Francisco is one of America's liveliest cities and one of those most heavily impacted by new development, development not always sympathetic to its special meanings. Buildings collected into cities are like friends or possessions we gather around us to support our sense of identity in the universe, our sense of who and where and when we are. By creating visible time and place, architecture buttresses us against the void. A city is a clearing in the wilderness, a campfire at night. If too many of its ties to the past are cut, we begin to lose the sense of where we are in time; if there are too many spatial discontinuities, we lose the sense of place.

The preservation movement grew powerful because so many people were seeing these meanings fade from their environments. A book like this one, moving far beyond the retention of individual "historic" buildings to a consideration of the meaning and value of an urban environment as a whole, is most welcome. Its attempt to create and articulate standards of value for buildings and other urban places is much needed, especially since so little of this kind of work has been done for downtown commercial areas.

Robert Campbell
Practicing Architect, Cambridge, MA; Architecture Critic for the *Boston Globe*

A major hindrance to productive discourse between redevelopers and preservationists, especially in downtown districts, has been that they are hardly ever talking about the same things—the same buildings, perhaps, but different priorities and value scales. Preservationists are most vulnerable on the point that they come into the situation too late, with too little firm information. Since developers and redevelopers are not noted for making their plans known far in advance of the demolition schedule, confrontations over issues of land clearance, with landmark buildings in danger, have invariably found those who argue for some degree of continuity in their downtowns at a severe disadvantage.

Splendid Survivors overcomes the disadvantages with the kind of information that has almost always been lacking in emergency confrontations over commercial district land use and design. It cuts through nitpicking stylistic distinctions to set up architectural evaluations in categories that city officials and redevelopers can respect and understand. Its criteria are no less pointed because of this and are considerably more applicable, given the mixed and richly improvisatorial character that crosses stylistic disciplines and is, in fact, a major vital force in American architecture.

The book is not only a valuable manual of San Francisco's unique abundance of commercial architecture but also a yardstick with which other communities can gauge their success at understanding their own heritage. Its methodology is readily transferable to any downtown.

George McCue
Retired Art and Urban Design Critic for the *St. Louis Post-Dispatch*

Most American cities have recycled downtown every generation. San Francisco is no exception. Competition among cities for the tallest building still goes on with apparently the same fervor that powered the Gothic cathedral builders. And it doesn't seem to puzzle us much that a variety of establishments proclaim their longevity over the door while repackaging their physical image every so many years. Another prevailing attitude is that the users of buildings are always inside. Yet those who experience those buildings everyday from the sidewalk or from windows across the street are also users. The amenity of old-shoe comfort, of everyday familiarity has not yet had its day in court. Buildings are not animate objects; they are molded by forces largely invisible and unapproachable.

Splendid Survivors puts the people in the street in possession of the kind of knowledge needed to judge whether the old should be exchanged for the new. Not only are the buildings described and chronicled, but the city's physical ups and downs are presented in historical context. This kind of popular appraisal of downtown is long overdue. Getting to know downtown, however, should not be a moral burden. Looking at buildings is fun because architectural details, like window displays and gardens, have eye appeal. Only experimental knowledge can help us evaluate our environment. Furthermore, we must acknowledge that this question of evaluation is neither new nor easily answered.

Sally B. Woodbridge
Architectural Historian, Writer and Lecturer

Most architectural guidebooks are content to praise old buildings that soon after become buried in the wake of blind change. Realizing that the fullest value of architecture resides in its continuing presence, this book does not stop at the point of passive appreciation. Through methodical evaluation of architectural and urban qualities, it passes beyond antiquarianism and aesthetics into the realities of an ever-changing downtown.

By giving public officials and private developers a professional assessment of the comparative importance of older downtown structures, this inventory can assist them in weighing the cultural impact of new construction and aid them in formulating alternatives to the removal of important buildings and streetscapes. Conversely, where a development proposal stubbornly flies in the face of its urbanistic responsibilities, it could provide the public and its elected representatives with a foundation for informed opposition to the undertaking.

This guide ought to be consulted by those who contribute to the growth of downtown, since it can help shape the city's evolution in a manner that is far more satisfactory than reliance on economic considerations alone. Similarly, its purpose and methods can provide a useful model for other major cities, since the issue it addresses is not unique to San Francisco but is as widespread as urban change itself.

John Pastier
Architectural Critic and Educator

PREFACE

Until relatively recently, concern for the environment focused on the protection of natural resources—air and water quality, land conservation and wildlife preservation. As interest in the environment has intensified, a broader and more sophisticated understanding of environmental quality has emerged to encompass natural *and* man-made factors that make up our environment. Underlying this expanded concept is a recognition that buildings and neighborhoods should be preserved for reasons that go beyond historic or architectural significance. A "sense of place" and one of cultural continuity are increasingly accepted as genuine needs in urban American society. Equally widespread is the growing recognition that the quality of life in urban areas is intimately related to a hospitable environment. Conserving our built environment, particularly those older elements that are often more gracious and humane in terms of scale, texture, and design, is now a priority in almost all urban revitalization programs.

We are, indeed, beginning to see many advantages in reusing old buildings, whether or not they are historic. Older structures are often better constructed, with quality workmanship and features that, in today's market, can only be duplicated at a prohibitive cost, if at all. Many old buildings were designed for their native climate, having thicker walls and windows that open, and they make maximum use of both natural light and ventilation. By comparison, the hermetically sealed environments built in the 1960s and 1970s are now seen as highly wasteful. Besides potential operating efficiencies, the long-range energy costs of renovation versus new construction argue strongly for the former. This advantage reflects the savings in energy that come from reusing existing materials. Heavily labor-intensive rehabilitation contributes to this edge compared to energy-intensive new construction.

San Francisco's downtown commercial center still retains much of the historic scale and character that has helped make it the favorite city of millions of people. Architecturally, historically and culturally the most diverse part of the city, the downtown is also subject to the greatest development pressures. One of the major factors in the destruction of irreplaceable buildings has been a lack of information. In most cases, there was or is no great awareness on the part of owner or developer of an older building's broad public value; and by the time the public value is perceived and asserted, a project has often progressed too far to be changed or abandoned. Identifying buildings and structures that are important enables planners and developers to take these resources into account in the planning and development process from the outset, rather than after plans, commitments and initial steps have been made.

This inventory identifies and documents significant buildings, building groups, streetscapes, and selected urban design elements. Buildings are graded and priorities for conservation indicated. It will be an important tool in the city's landmarks program, environmental review, zoning and development questions, and future planning efforts. Moreover, the inventory should make all of us more aware of the civic riches we have inherited. The uses of the inventory to the City of San Francisco are generally applicable to any city or town.

1. City Planning: San Francisco's officially adopted Comprehensive Plan asserts certain "fundamental policies for conservation" in the section on Urban Design. The introduction to that section states—"If San Francisco is to retain its charm and human proportion, certain irreplaceable resources must not be lost or diminished . . . Past development, as represented both by distinctive buildings and areas of established character, must be preserved." The application of these policies has been weak and inconsistent because the specific resources they apply to either have not been identified, or have been identified too late in the development process. The inventory provides clear identification and documentation. Liaison during the inventory process with the City Planning Department assures the relevance and usefulness of the inventory to city planning efforts, policy making, and programs.

2. Landmark Designation: Since the City of San Francisco adopted a Landmark Ordinance in 1967, only about one hundred buildings in the entire city have been designated (twenty of these in the city's only historic district) due to lack of staff necessary to do the research and analysis upon which designation must be based. Only seven of these are located in the downtown business and commercial district. Furthermore, landmarks designation has proceeded on an ad hoc building-by-building basis, rather than by evaluation of the whole. The inventory will provide priorities and detailed information the Landmarks Board can readily adopt into case reports.

3. Environmental Review: California's Environmental Quality Act requires local governments to review and analyze proposed public and private projects for their effect on the environment. This applies in cases of proposed demolition of historically and architecturally significant structures. Until this inventory was made, there was no detailed, organized, and evaluated information on environmentally significant buildings in downtown San Francisco. The inventory will serve city decision-makers as an organized data base for use in assessing the impacts of proposed development projects on our great yet limited historic and architectural resources.

4. State of California Inventory of Historic Resources: The inventory will be used by the California State Office of Historic Preservation in the compilation of a state-wide inventory of properties "possessing historical, architectural, archaeological and cultural value" pursuant to the National Historic Preservation Act of 1966.

5. Procedures Manual: A *Procedures Manual* is being developed to document the criteria, evaluation process, organization and methodology used in this project. This will be available for subsequent efforts elsewhere.

6. Public Awareness: The success of any conservation effort ultimately depends on an informed public that can make government responsive and accountable. Perhaps the single most important use of the inventory is to help conserve San Francisco's downtown environment through awareness, appreciation and understanding.

Robert Berner
Executive Director, The Foundation for San Francisco's Architectural Heritage

ACKNOWLEDGEMENTS

The preparation of this volume was supported in part by funds from the Arts and Architecture division of the National Endowment for the Arts, the California Office of Historic Preservation through the National Historic Preservation Act of 1966, the Wallace Alexander Gerbode Foundation, the Louis R. Lurie Foundation, and the Edwin W. and Catherine M. Davis Foundation. Contributions were received from Alice C. Russell and Richard and Helen Tavernetti.

Grateful acknowledgement is made to the following for permission to reproduce copyrighted material: to Tom Moulin of Gabriel Moulin Studios for use of a number of very fine photographs; to E. H. Wilder of *Architect's Daily Reports* for permission to reproduce illustrations from the *Architect and Engineer* and the *Pacific Coast Architect*; to the San Francisco Architectural Club for permission to reproduce an illustration from their 1909 *Yearbook*; to the *Architectural Record* for permission to reproduce two illustrations; and to the *Chicago Tribune* for permission to reproduce a drawing from *Tribune Tower Competition* of 1923.

In addition, acknowledgement is made to the Bancroft Library at the University of California at Berkeley, and to the Special Collections Room at the San Francisco Public Library for use of photographs in their collections. We are also grateful for the use of photographs by John W. Procter from the Florence M. Procter collection, and by Stanley H. Page from the collection of Charles H. Page.

Essential to the project was the availability of the following collections: The Bancroft Library, the Environmental Design Library and its Documents Collection at the University of California at Berkeley; the Stanford University Library; the Mechanic's Institute; the California Historical Society; the State Library in Sacramento; and the San Francisco Public Library and its Special Collections Room.

As in any project of this kind, this inventory was accomplished with the generous assistance of many institutions and individuals—so many that we can do little more than list them here.

Randolph Delehanty, Joan Draper, and Jeremy Kotas served on the inventory review panel and each contributed immeasurably to the project, from its organization to reviewing drafts of the text. We are equally indebted to Richard Longstreth who developed the system used in the Architectural Classifications section of this volume.

Harold Kalman gave freely of his ideas which appear in *The Evaluation of Historic Buildings, A Manual*, published by the Canadian Government in 1978. We also appreciate the assistance of the Director of City Planning, Rai Okamoto, and his staff.

Dan Gregory contributed in conversations about downtown San Francisco architecture, and Peter Svirsky shared his extensive knowledge of zoning and related matters. Both of them read portions of the text, as did Peter Culley.

For his unique knowledge of downtown San Francisco and its architects, freely shared, we are indebted to Charles Pope. Susan Harrison donated a great deal of time looking at buildings in the secondary areas.

Conversations with Reyner Banham, John Beach, Sara Holmes Boutelle, Steve Levin, Norton Meyer, Francisco Mujica, Thomas K. Procter, and Alan Rudy gave us important information about a variety of topics.

We are indebted to Ward Hill for the donation of his time, to Heritage volunteers Stephanie Turkington and Dale Copland for typing the State Historic Resources Inventory Forms, and to the Y.W.C.A. for sending us Bill Hobson for the summer of 1977.

In addition to the above, we wish to express our thanks to many individuals, real-estate offices, architectural firms, public agencies, and building managers who helped us gather information for the inventory.

Finally, public thanks to Joan McDermott for her support of this project are long overdue.

Michael Corbett
Charles Hall Page & Associates, Inc.

INTRODUCTION

SCOPE AND PURPOSE

The purpose of this volume is to make widely available the results of Heritage's downtown architectural inventory, and to provide a historical context within which the results of the inventory can be interpreted.

The inventory seeks to recognize the architectural and other cultural resources of downtown San Francisco, to educate the public to their importance, and by doing so to protect them and the qualities they establish from destruction.

The inventory has involved a comprehensive survey of 790 parcels within the central business district of downtown San Francisco. Each parcel has been photographed, described, researched, and evaluated. The evaluated results, which constitute the bulk of this volume, and are the most important product of the project, are intended to provide an objective basis of information on which public and private development decisions can be made in the future.

More than a list of potential historic landmarks or a narrow "preservation" document, the evaluated inventory is intended to serve as a planning document. The inventory will achieve its goals, not necessarily if the most important buildings are declared landmarks, but if, by more subtle means, the qualities of the area are preserved. The objective is not "preservation" in the narrow, traditional sense, but preservation in its most enlightened sense, when it ceases to be the goal of some special-interest group and becomes the proper goal of the entire city. The goal is not preservation; the goal is the city. The means is preservation.

As a document for public education, it is hoped that the sections of introductory text will serve to make downtown San Francisco's architecture better understood, and that the survey sections will serve as a guidebook to the downtown area. As in other cities all over the country, San Francisco's "non-Modern" downtown architecture has long been neglected by historians who viewed it as a stumbling block in the development of Modern Architecture; and it has been actively deprecated by Modernist architects and critics who saw it as

reactionary. It is hoped that this volume can help restore an appreciation of this architecture for San Franciscans.

A secondary but not insignificant objective in this inventory is to serve as a model for other cities contemplating similar survey/inventory projects. Most previous model inventories, such as those for College Hill in Providence, Rhode Island, in 1959, and for the Vieux Carré in New Orleans in 1968, have dealt with predominantly small-scale, residential areas. None have dealt with the predominantly 20th-century downtown area of a major city. As the preservation movement has matured and gained in acceptance, its proponents have been able increasingly to concern themselves with politically sensitive areas. Certainly none are more sensitive than the central business districts of prosperous cities like San Francisco, where land values are so high and so much is at stake economically in development decisions.

The methodology of this project is treated briefly on the following pages, but is available in greater detail from Heritage in a separate technical report.

HISTORY OF THE PROJECT

By the mid-1970s, predictions of accelerated growth of new construction in downtown San Francisco were widespread. San Francisco Planning and Urban Renewal Association (SPUR), the Chamber of Commerce, and San Francisco Tomorrow were only a few organizations which made these predictions. Many landmark-quality buildings had been lost in recent years and the traditional character of the downtown area was, although still largely intact, on the verge of irreversible change. Clearly, if these predictions for continued growth were accurate, many more fine buildings would be lost and the character of the area would continue to be eroded.

It was clear to those who were involved in the lost fight to save the Alaska Commercial Building and in the campaigns to save the Fitzhugh Building and the City of Paris, which were then getting underway, that one of the major obstacles to preservation of downtown buildings was the absence of any public agreement about which buildings were important. Developers objected that complaints of preservationists came too late, that they had no previous knowledge of the significance of buildings they proposed to demolish, and that by the time they found out they had already committed large amounts of time and large sums of money on new projects.

It was with this background that Heritage decided in 1975 to seek funding for a downtown architectural inventory. Over the next two years, grants were sought and accepted from the National Endowment for the Arts, the State Office of Historic Preservation, the Wallace Alexander Gerbode Foundation, the Louis R. Lurie Foundation, and the Edwin W. and Catherine M. Davis Foundation, and contributions were received from individuals.

Under the terms of the grants, along with an inventory of downtown San Francisco's architecture and other cultural resources, Heritage was obligated to submit State Historic Resource Inventory forms for eligible resources, to determine eligibility of resources to the National Register of Historic Places, and to publish a report in order to make the results of the inventory widely available and to make its methods known as an example for other cities.

By March 1977, enough money was in hand to begin the project. Charles Hall Page & Associates, Inc., an urban planning and architectural firm specializing in historic preservation, was hired as the consultant to carry it out at cost. Originally scheduled to take about one year, the ambitious scope of the project and preparation of this volume doubled the project time. The survey itself was completed in the fall of 1978.

PROJECT BOUNDARIES

The boundaries of the project area fall into two categories: the primary areas (Financial District, Retail District, and Market Street District) in which a comprehensive inventory was conducted of all 790 parcels; and the secondary areas (South of Market East, South of Market West, Civic Center, Tenderloin, and Nob Hill) in which a survey of several thousand parcels was much more selective.

The outside boundaries of the primary areas include office, commercial and institutional buildings built before 1945 as well as adjacent newer buildings which were thought of as being "downtown." Strictly residential areas were excluded as were non-residential areas (such as Jackson Square, the Civic Center, and Chinatown) which had already been surveyed or were in the process of being surveyed independently. A few boundary decisions were necessarily arbitrary.

Secondary area boundaries were drawn to include areas linked by: proximity to the primary areas; a predominance of brick, reinforced-concrete, and steel-frame buildings; a shared pool of architects with the primary areas; and listing in the same sources used in the project for researching primary areas.

The boundaries chosen for the primary areas were a compromise between the necessary and the practical. Two adjacent areas should be given priority in any expansions of this inventory: the area south of Market and east of Third Street; and the large triangle of land bound by Market, Franklin, and Clay Streets, as these areas have become increasingly subject to the expanded development pressure of downtown growth.

SAN FRANCISCO BAY

FINANCIAL

NOB HILL

RETAIL

MARKET STREET

TENDERLOIN

CIVIC CENTER

SOUTH OF MARKET EAST

SOUTH OF MARKET WEST

● PRIMARY SURVEY AREA
● SECONDARY SURVEY AREA

5

METHODOLOGY

This project has consisted of four major tasks: field survey, research, evaluation, and report preparation. These tasks are discussed below with the idea that such discussion may be useful to those who wish to know the strengths and limitations of the project, in order better to use its results. This discussion should also be useful to other cities planning similar projects. A more complete discussion is available separately from Heritage.

FIELD SURVEY

The field survey of the primary areas was undertaken in three stages: an initial survey of buildings; a second survey of urban-design elements including streetscapes, civic art, and other street furniture; and a third survey to identify potential historic districts. Field survey forms were prepared with the assistance of the Department of City Planning for the surveys of buildings and urban-design elements, each one designed to record largely predetermined, descriptive information. Both the buildings and urban-design elements and their surroundings were described on the survey forms. Photographs were taken of all buildings and urban-design elements, and at least one photograph was attached to each survey card. These surveys were carried out by a planner and an architectural historian, one of whom doubled as a photographer. The initial survey of buildings took about five months. The second survey of streetscapes and urban-design elements took about six weeks. The third survey of potential historic districts, which was built upon the results of the previous surveys and based on National Register criteria, took about two weeks.

The less formal survey of secondary areas took place after all research was completed, and was guided by that research and the 1976 Architectural Inventory of the Department of City Planning. For the most part the research merely augmented the findings of the 1976 Architectural Inventory. In other cases the research focused attention on buildings not identified in that survey. There were also some cases where new buildings were identified as significant on visual criteria alone. This task took about two and one-half months.

RESEARCH

Research was carried out for two purposes: to document the inventory and to prepare the historical introduction to this volume. In documenting the inventory, research was intensive for primary-area buildings and less so for secondary-area buildings. Resources for both groups of buildings were the same. The objective of this research was to establish construction dates, architects, design alterations, construction technology, and other relevant historical information.

The most important sources consulted were old Sanborn Insurance Co. maps for their information on construction types; the Realdex at the City Hall which provided a reliable date of original building permit applications; various photographic files; other files such as those from the Junior League Survey that resulted in *Here Today*; and, most importantly, the *Architect and Engineer* and other regional architectural periodicals. This information was found at the State Library in Sacramento; the San Francisco Public Library, especially in the Special Collections room; the Bancroft Library and the Environmental Design Library with its Documents Collection, at the University of California at Berkeley; the California Historical Society; and the Mechanics' Institute.

Altogether about six months were spent on the research, largely carried out by the same planner and architectural historian who conducted the field survey.

EVALUATION

Introduction

One of the most significant aspects of an inventory is the method of evaluation used for buildings and other cultural resources. An effort has been made in this inventory to evaluate the buildings, urban-design elements, and historic districts on the basis of explicit objective criteria in order to arrive at results which will be widely accepted as valid. In addition, for the inventory to succeed, its results must be in a form which can be readily understood by political leaders, public agencies, private real-estate and business interests, and the general public.

Objective systematic evaluation systems are still rejected by many preservationists and architectural historians in England who feel that the aesthetic qualities of architecture cannot be quantified. In the United States, however, despite some honest questioning among preservationists, such systems

SAN FRANCISCO DOWNTOWN INVENTORY
EVALUATION SHEET

Address_____
Name_____

A. ARCHITECTURE
1. Style _____ E VG G FP
2. Construction _____ E VG G FP
3. Age _____ E VG G FP
4. Architect _____ E VG G FP
5. Design _____ E VG G FP
6. Interior _____ E VG G FP
B. HISTORY
7. Person _____ E VG G FP
8. Event _____ E VG G FP
9. Patterns _____ E VG G FP
C. ENVIRONMENT
10. Continuity _____ E VG G FP
11. Setting _____ E VG G FP
12. Landmark _____ E VG G FP
D. INTEGRITY
13. Alterations _____ E VG G FP

Evaluated by _____ Date _____
Reviewed by _____ Date _____ Approved ☐ See Comment Sheet ☐
Reviewed by _____ Date _____ Approved ☐ See Comment Sheet ☐
Reviewed by _____ Date _____ Approved ☐ See Comment Sheet ☐

STATUS
Inventory Group: _____
City Landmark Status: Listed ☐   In process ☐   Potential ☐
SHRI Status: Listed ☐   Eligible ☐
National Register Status: Listed ☐   In process ☐   Potential ☐
Historic District Status: City ☐ SHRI ☐ National Register ☐
                          Potential ☐ Eligible ☐
Site of Opportunity ☐   Property Endangered (date) _____

have become increasingly acceptable and reliable over the last 20 years.

Harold Kalman, whose book *The Evaluation of Historic Buildings, A Manual* (published in 1978 by the Canadian government) provides the basis for the evaluation system used in downtown San Francisco, has helped clarify the legitimacy of such systems through a useful analogy between evaluating historic buildings and the grading of fruit or meat by government agencies. He points out that as long as there are objective, widely acceptable criteria used in such evaluations, and as long as they are consistently applied, there is widespread agreement on the part of the public as to what, for example, a Grade A orange is, and why it is more desirable than a Grade B orange. The same ought to be able to be said of evaluation systems applied to architecture.

Despite the resistance of some preservationists, these objective evaluation systems have long been not merely acceptable to political leaders, city planning officials, real-estate developers, and others in positions of influence over land use and development, but they have been almost demanded by them in their hesitancy to work with anything less systematic. In this demand, apart from the reliability of such systems, is the real justification for their use. If the preservation inventory is to be more than a study to be filed away, and if it is to be of practical value in realizing the goals of preservation, it must respond to the realities of modern political and economic decision-making processes.

The objective evaluation system was first used in the pioneering College Hill Demonstration Study in Providence, Rhode Island in 1958. Based on a pre-established set of criteria, each building was given a numerical score for Historical Significance, Architectural Significance, Importance to Neighborhood, Desecration of Original Design, and Physical Condition. The scores were totaled and the total scores grouped together as Exceptional, Excellent, Good, Fair, and Poor.

In subsequent uses of this evaluation method, refinements were made both in order to meet the particular circumstances of different cities and also to improve the basic system. The most important refinements occurred in the Vieux Carré Historic District Demonstration Study in New Orleans in 1968, and in the survey of the Gastown and Chinatown districts of Vancouver in 1970. The system used here marks a further refinement of these previous efforts.

The System Explained

The evaluation used in downtown San Francisco consists of two parts: rating of each building, urban-design element, and historic district against pre-established criteria; and review of the ratings by an independent panel of experts.

The criteria used in the evaluation, as in any inventory, are specially designed to fit the needs of the particular circumstances of this project. They are based, however, on the guidelines of the National Trust for Historic Preservation, and on the criteria of the National Register of Historic Places and the State Historic Resources Inventory. The particular form that they take follows the model suggested in *The Evaluation of Historic Buildings.* Like criteria used in previous inventories, these are divided into broad categories of Architectural Significance, Historical Significance, Environmental Significance, and Design Integrity. Unlike the criteria used in most previous inventories, however, these are designed so that each criterion can be evaluated separately.

CRITERIA

Criterion	Ratings

A. ARCHITECTURE

1. STYLE
Significance as an example of a particular architectural style, type, or convention.

E Especially fine or extremely early example if many survive; excellent example if few survive.

VG Excellent or very early example if many survive; good example if few survive.

G Good example.

FP Of no particular interest.

2. CONSTRUCTION
Significance as an example of a particular material or method of construction.

E Especially fine or extremely early example if many survive; excellent example if few survive.

VG Excellent or very early example if many survive; good example if few survive.

G Good example.

FP Of no particular interest.

3. AGE
Of particular age in relationship to the periods of development of buildings in the area.

E Built between 1889 and April 1906.

VG Built between May 1906 and 1930.

G Built between 1931 and 1945.

FP Built since 1945.

4. ARCHITECT
Designed or built by an architect or builder who has made a significant contribution to the community, state, or nation.

E Of particular importance to the history of the community, state, or nation.
VG Of considerable importance.
G Architect or builder identified and known, but not of particular importance.
FP Unidentified or unknown.

5. DESIGN
Architectural quality of composition, detailing, and ornament measured, in part in originality, quality as urban architecture, craftsmanship, and uniqueness.

E Excellent.
VG Very good.
G Good.
FP Fair or poor.

6. INTERIOR
Interior arrangement, finish, craftsmanship, and/or detail is/are particularly attractive or unique.

E Excellent
VG Very good.
G Good.
FP Fair or Poor.

B. HISTORY

7. PERSON
Associated with the life or activities of a person, group, organization, or institution that has made a significant contribution to the community, state or nation.

E Person of primary importance intimately connected with the building.
VG Person of primary importance loosely connected, or person of secondary importance intimately connected.
G Person of secondary importance loosely connected.
FP No connection with person of importance.

8. EVENT
Associated with an event that has made a significant contribution to the community, state, or nation.

E Event of primary importance intimately connected with the building.
VG Event of primary importance loosely connected, or event of secondary importance intimately connected.
G Event of secondary importance loosely connected.
FP No connections with event of importance.

9. PATTERNS
Associated with, and effectively illustrative of, broad patterns of cultural, social, political, economic, or industrial history, or of the urban development of the city.

E Patterns of primary importance intimately connected with the building.
VG Patterns of primary importance loosely connected, or patterns of secondary importance intimately connected.
G Patterns of secondary importance loosely connected.
FP No connection with patterns of importance.

C. ENVIRONMENT

10. CONTINUITY
Contributes to the continuity or character of the street, neighborhood, or area.

E Of particular importance in establishing the character of a distinguished area.
VG Of importance in establishing or maintaining the character of a distinguished area.
G Compatible with the character of a distinguished area.
FP Incompatible with the character of an area.

11. SETTING
Setting and/or landscaping contributes to the continuity or character of the street, neighborhood, or area.

E Of particular importance in establishing the character of the area.
VG Of importance in establishing or maintaining the dominant character of the area.
G Compatible with the dominant character of the area.
FP Incompatible with the dominant character of the area, or unimportant.

12. LANDMARK
Significance as a visual landmark.

E A structure which may be taken as symbol for the city or region as a whole.
VG A conspicuous and familiar structure in the context of the city or region.
G A conspicuous and familiar structure in the context of the neighborhood.
FP Not particularly conspicuous or familiar.

11

D. INTEGRITY

13. ALTERATIONS

Has suffered little alteration and retains most of its original materials and design features.

E No changes or very minor changes.

VG Ground floor remodeled, cornice removed, or minor alterations which do not destroy the overall character.

G Overall character changed, but recognizable through removal of major cornice/parapet, alteration of upper floors, or gross alteration of any major element.

FP Altered beyond recognition.

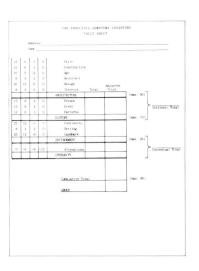

Rating

For each building and urban-design element, each of the 13 criteria within the four major categories was rated on a four-level scale on the Evaluation Sheet. Each criterion is rated Excellent (E), Very Good (VG), Good (G), or Fair/Poor (FP). Space on the evaluation sheet by each separate criterion is used to explain briefly each rating, providing a permanent record of objectively based judgements.

Scoring

Each of the separate criteria was assigned a progression of numerical values that corresponded to the four-level scale of ratings. The choice of ratings for each criterion was always the same (E, VG, G, FP), but the numerical values varied. In other words, an E rating for Design was worth 25 points, but an E rating for Construction, a relatively less important criterion, was worth only 12 points. Once rated, the ratings could be translated into numbers on the separate Tally Sheets. Ratings and numbers were kept separate in order to emphasize the primacy of the ratings, the functions of numbers as mere tools of the process, and to avoid prejudicing the process itself.

Once the ratings were translated into numbers, the numbers were totaled (points for alterations were subtracted), producing a composite score. The composite scores were then placed into four tentative categories of value—A, B, C, and D—pending confirmation by the independent outside review. A- and B-buildings were both of National Register eligibility, with A-buildings of higher significance and of first priority for City Landmark status. C-buildings were of contextual value. D-buildings were of minor or no importance.

Outside Review

After the Consultant completed the in-house evaluation of buildings and urban-design elements, three independent outside professionals were invited to review the results. The reviewers were Randolph Delehanty, an urban historian at Heritage, with specialized knowledge of San Francisco and its architecture; Jeremy Kotas, an architect in the Urban Design section of the San Francisco Department of City Planning, who was responsible for the Department's citywide 1976 Architectural Inventory; and Joan Draper, an architectural historian particularly familiar with San Francisco's post-fire architecture, formerly at the University of California at Berkeley, and now an Assistant Professor in the School of Architecture at Montana State University.

The procedure used in the week-long formal review was a systematic one designed to reinforce the objectivity of the evaluation, and to clearly explain any adjustments made. The three evaluators were asked to look at the files on each building and urban-design element, and either to confirm or reject the evaluations given for individual criteria and the resulting final inventory group (e.g., A, B, C, or D). Afterwards, adjustments were made to the ratings in view of these comments. All comments became part of the permanent files.

FINAL EVALUATION

Following the outside review, the range of the four summary categories of value was adjusted, and put into final form as follows:

A. Highest Importance—Individually the most important buildings in downtown San Francisco, distinguished by outstanding qualities of architecture, historical values, and relationship to the environment. All A-group buildings are eligible for the National Register, and of highest priority for City Landmark status.

B. Major Importance—Buildings which are of individual importance by virtue of architectural, historical, and environmental criteria. These buildings tend to stand out for their overall quality rather than for any particular outstanding characteristics. B-group buildings are eligible for the National Register, and of secondary priority for City Landmark status.

C. **Contextual Importance**—Buildings which are distinguished by their scale, materials, compositional treatment, cornice, and other features. They provide the setting for more important buildings and they add visual richness and character to the downtown area. Many C-group buildings may be eligible for the National Register as part of historic districts.

D. **Minor or No Importance**—Buildings which are insignificant examples of architecture by virtue of original design, or more frequently, insensitive remodeling. This category includes vacant buildings and parking lots. Most D-group buildings are "sites of opportunity."

NOT RATED: Buildings which have been built or suffered insensitive exterior remodelings since 1945.

Interpretation of Scoring System

It is important to recognize that the scoring system used in this inventory is a planning tool which is more complex than its final evaluation rankings might suggest. The final evaluation rankings are only summaries, and when questions come up about the future of a building or district, the entire evaluation must be looked at both for the ratings of its separate criteria and for evaluators' comments. This is particularly important for buildings that rank below the A-group, which might score so well in one category that they merit special consideration. Even for D-group buildings, there are some which, although in the lowest category of "objectionable or unimportant" buildings, are rated VG for continuity, and possess certain desirable characteristics which might be enhanced by remodeling, or re-established in a new building. These latter fall into the category of "sites of opportunity," discussed below.

It is important also to recognize the purpose of translating the numerical scores into four summary groups. To allow the numbered scores to stand by themselves would suggest a preciseness about them which is not warranted. With this system it is not possible to say, for example, that an 86-point building is necessarily better than an 81-point building. It is only possible to say that the buildings within a certain range are better than those within a lower range. Finally, it is not possible to use the final evaluation rankings without reference to the ratings of individual criteria and to the full explanation of those criteria. In other words, it is not enough to refer only to the Evaluation Sheets for any one building, and, for example, to a VG rating for Design, without seeing what that rating means under the full criteria.

Post-1945 Buildings

Buildings built since 1945 were not evaluated in the inventory for a variety of reasons. Most importantly, most post-war buildings are so different from those which were built previously that they are not amenable to evaluation in the same terms. A few could have been so evaluated, such as the old Home Insurance Building at Kearny and California, or Frank Lloyd Wright's V. C. Morris Store on Maiden Lane, but they were exceptions.

Some buildings remodeled since 1945 ended up with D-ratings if they were of no interest and could be considered unfortunate alterations of earlier designs. All new buildings and the most significant remodelings were listed as "Not Rated," and most of these appear in the survey section of this volume.

RELATIONSHIP TO THE CITY LANDMARKS PROGRAM, THE STATE HISTORIC RESOURCES INVENTORY, AND THE NATIONAL REGISTER OF HISTORIC PLACES

One of the principal areas in which this inventory is likely to be useful is in determining the relationship of individual buildings to the various levels of public governmental recognition. With the protection provided by such recognition, these relationships are extremely important both to preservationists and developers.

City Landmarks

Because there are no detailed criteria for City Landmarks in San Francisco, it is difficult to state with any authority the relationship between this inventory and the City Landmarks program.

Under Article 10 of the City Planning Code, entitled "Preservation of Historical, Architectural and Aesthetic Landmarks," almost any A- or B-group structure and many C-group structures would appear to be eligible for City Landmark status. Because recommendations for Landmark status are made by the Landmarks Preservation Advisory Board to the City Planning Commission and the Board of Supervisors, without more explicit criteria initiation of Landmarks designation is largely up to the discretion of the Landmarks Board. Thus, the results of this inventory could be used as the basis for establishing priorities for Landmarks designation downtown. A-group buildings would be of highest priority, B-group buildings of second priority, and C-group buildings, should any be deemed eligible, of last priority. Of those 16 downtown buildings so far designated landmarks, all have been A-group buildings. One B-group building, the Holbrook Building, has recently been recommended for designation by the Planning Commission to the Board of Supervisors.

In addition to the recognition it entails, City Landmark status can involve a prohibition against demolition or alteration for up to one year after application is made for a demolition permit.

State Historic Resources Inventory

As a condition of funding of this project by the State Office of Historic Preservation, 374 individual buildings, eight historic districts, and four thematic groups were found to be eligible for the State Historic Resources Inventory under the State's criteria. Inventory forms were filled out for these buildings and submitted to the State. No downtown San Francisco structures were previously listed.

The State Inventory is a list of cultural resources considered valuable to the State and to individual localities. Listing on the State Inventory carries no explicit protection; however, it does cause the provisions of the California Environmental Quality Act to come into play when a listed property is threatened by a state-funded project.

The categories of California Historical Landmarks and Points of Interest carry with them additional recognition but no additional legal protection.

National Register of Historic Places

The National Register of Historic Places, maintained by the U.S. Department of the Interior, is a list of cultural resources which are significant in architecture, history, and culture to the nation, the states, and individual localities. Listing on the National Register carries with it a degree of protection against federally licensed or funded projects. It affords no protection against strictly private enterprises, and thus has limited legal usefulness in downtown San Francisco. Properties listed on the National Register are eligible for a variety of grants and loans, and for tax relief under the Tax Reform Act of 1976.

Tentative eligibility of cultural resources in downtown San Francisco to the National Register was determined as a condition of funding by the State. Altogether, 172 buildings (including those already listed)—all A and B buildings—were found to be eligible. In addition, eight historic districts and four thematic districts were found to be eligible.

Although the criteria of evaluation of this inventory were not exactly those of the National Register, by definition buildings in inventory groups A and B are eligible. In addition, C-buildings within historic districts would be eligible should an official historic district be designated.

Presently, there are six individual downtown-area buildings, Lotta's Fountain, and the Cable Cars listed on the National Register. Two other buildings (the Hallidie Building and the Bank of America at 552 Montgomery) are National Historic Landmarks, in addition to being on the National Register, and part of one district, the Civic Center Historic District, is on the National Register. National Historic Landmark status involves greater recognition but no additional legal protection. Recording by the Historic American Engineering Record (HAER) involves more thorough documentation but, again, no additional legal protection.

Tax Reform Act of 1976

Under the Tax Reform Act of 1976, significant incentives are provided for the preservation of buildings held for income which are eligible for the National Register or within historic districts and/or designated as local landmarks under ordinances certified by the Secretary of the Interior. Although such certification has not been made at this writing, action by the City pursuant to an inventory such as this could provide the basis for implementation of the provisions of the Tax Reform Act.

The major provisions of the Act are that rehabilitation costs of a certified historic building held for income purposes can be written off over 60 months, or the improved property can be depreciated at an accelerated rate. Subsequent legislation extends this preferential treatment to lessees of 30 years or more in addition to fee owners.

Additional tax reform legislation in 1978 clarifies some of the language of the 1976 Act, but also adds an attractive alternative in the form of an investment tax credit. Buildings 20 years old or older, regardless of their historic value, may be rehabilitated under this legislation with the owner entitled to a one-time tax credit of 10% of the improvement cost.

NEW CONSTRUCTION—SITES OF OPPORTUNITY

Far from being opposed to new construction or remodeling downtown, Heritage eagerly supports sensitive new projects in the right places. To this end, a number of "sites of opportunity" are identified in this inventory. A "site of opportunity" is a site (a vacant lot or a parking lot) which could be built upon, or a building which could be replaced or remodeled. While most D-group buildings (located in the files, but not listed in this volume) could be considered "sites of opportunity," a few examples will better illustrate the meaning of the term.

Foremost among downtown remodeling "sites of opportunity" are the Chronicle and David Hewes Buildings, two very fine older buildings, which were covered with removable veneers about 1960, and which could probably be easily restored to an approximation of their original appearances. Both buildings are good examples of once stylish remodelings which now appear dated, and whose original design would, ironically, look both cleaner and more in tune with the times.

D-group buildings such as 239 Grant and 101 Kearny, which are in potential historic districts, could be remodeled to the great enhancement of their surroundings.

Chains like Casual Corner, whose standard storefronts are terrible, could take a hint from McDonald's whose recent downtown designs have been more appropriate to their locations.

The Orpheum Theater on Market Street, with its bare concrete back walls that face the Civic Center, could be a more compatible neighbor for the Civic Center if those back walls were painted with a giant mural of a monumental classical building or some other suitable subject. Plans for covering these walls in the same Spanish Gothic ornamentation as the front facade were part of the original project, but a disagreement over whether the Orpheum Theater or the City would pay for carrying them out was never resolved.

MAINTAINING THE INVENTORY

Although every effort was made to research each building thoroughly, the possibility exists for many buildings whose architects are still unknown, or for which additional research might turn up new information, to rise in the rankings. The files of the inventory will be available to the public, and the public is invited to contribute new information to them. The inventory should not be considered completed, but should be updated and corrected as new information is available.

OUTSIDE PARTICIPATION

The goals and methods of the project were presented to various downtown area leaders in two public meetings in September 1977. The purpose of these meetings was to increase awareness of the inventory and its uses among those individuals and groups who were in decision-making positions about future development downtown. Representatives from the business community, real-estate interests, government agencies, and public interest organizations attended. Following a suggestion at one of those meetings, they were followed up by a series of three project reports sent out to 200 individuals and organizations in the business, real-estate, and political communities, which further explained the inventory and its goals.

Role of the Department of City Planning

From the beginning it was felt that the goals of the project could not be fully realized without the support and cooperation of the San Francisco Department of City Planning. In view of Heritage's goal of completing a project which would be useful to the City as more than a program for landmarks designation, it was essential that the Department of City Planning be involved in the planning of the project and in the reaching of its conclusions.

The mundane but fundamental task of designing forms to be used in the various field surveys was accomplished with the help of the Director of City Planning and his staff. A staff member served in the outside review of the evaluated inventory. The results of the Department's 1976 Architectural Inventory were used as the basis for the secondary-area inventory in this volume. And, the Departmental staff assisted in the formulation of Final Evaluation definitions. In addition, the City Planning Commission passed a resolution of support for the conduct of the inventory in June 1977.

PRODUCTS

The principal products of this inventory are this volume, a separate technical report, and voluminous files on the buildings of downtown San Francisco.

The technical report, available from Heritage, describes and criticizes the methodology of the inventory and the evaluation process in greater detail. It is intended for two audiences: the preservation and planning professionals in other cities who are interested in a detailed model of an inventory to serve as an example for similar projects; and for anyone in San Francisco who wants to know in greater detail how the results were arrived at.

The files of the inventory should be useful in both preservation and research efforts in San Francisco in the future. They will be accessible to the public at Heritage.

The files fall into several categories. Most important are the files of the survey itself. For the primary areas there is a file on each building or site. Each file includes, at a minimum, an Architectural Survey Form with a paragraph, a Supplementary Data form, an Evaluation Sheet, and a Tally Sheet. Most files also include an Evaluator's Comment Sheet, photocopies of articles and photographs about the building, and miscellaneous notes from a variety of sources. To supplement these files, there are other files of demolished buildings which originally stood in the primary areas, and of projects which were never built.

A second major set of files includes specific information, mostly from architectural periodicals, on several hundred buildings in the secondary areas. These are supplemented by two lists of names of buildings in the secondary areas: one organized by street and the other organized alphabetically.

A third major set of files, the architect's files, includes a separate folder on each architect who worked in downtown San Francisco. The folders contain indexes to all the buildings by each architect which fall within the boundaries of the survey area. Some files also contain additional biographical information and photocopies of general articles on architects and their work.

A last set of files on buildings includes information gathered on San Francisco buildings outside the downtown area. These are not extensive or exhaustive for any one area, but include much about Chinatown, for example, which initially was to be part of this project but was abandoned when a separate inventory was begun there.

Like the building files for the primary areas, there are files on urban-design elements such as streetlights, clocks, civic art, fountains, and plazas, with field survey forms, photographs, research information, and evaluation forms on each.

Finally, there are files of Environmental Context forms, with photographs, field descriptions, and annotated maps of all streets in the primary areas.

SUMMARY & CONCLUSIONS

The Phelan Building, ca. 1920.

Final Evaluations

● A Buildings

● B Buildings

● C Buildings

The following tables summarize the final evaluations of this inventory, and the relationship of those evaluations to the National Register, the State Historic Resources Inventory, and the City Landmarks program.

SUMMARY TABLES

Final Evaluations

Buildings	Totals
A (Highest importance)	102
B (Major Importance)	170
C (Contextual Importance)	279
D (Minor or No Importance)	124
NOT RATED (Post-1945)	115

Urban-Design Elements	
A (Highest Importance)	17
B (Major Importance)	8
C (Contextual Importance)	5
D (Minor or No Importance)	0
NOT RATED (Post-1945)	40

Districts	
Historic Districts	8
Thematic Districts	4

National Register Eligibility (tentative)

Buildings	
A- and B-groups	272

Urban-Design Elements	
A- and B-groups	25

Districts	
Historic	8
Thematic	4

State Historic Resources Inventory

Buildings	
A- and B-groups	272
C-groups within potential districts	102
	374

Urban-Design Elements	
A- and B-groups	25
C-groups within potential districts	4

Districts	
Historic	8
Thematic	4

City Landmark Priorities

Buildings	
1st priority, A-group	
2nd priority, B-group	

Urban-Design Elements	
1st priority, A-group	
2nd priority, B-group	

Districts

Priorities should be established on the basis of significance, degree of endangerment, and acceptability to the public. On the basis of significance, the Grant Avenue District would receive the highest priority. On the basis of endangerment, the Market Street loft District would receive the highest priority. On the basis of public acceptability, perhaps the Powell Street or Grant Avenue Districts would be first.

CONCLUSIONS

The results of this inventory, summarized above, point out in detail the architectural and other cultural resources which together make San Francisco's downtown among the most attractive and vital in the United States. The high quality of this area is due to its many fine examples of the architecture of the late 19th and early 20th centuries, and, more importantly, to its rare cohesiveness. This cohesiveness is the result of its having been built in a relatively short period of time after the earthquake and fire of 1906, and to the shared attitudes of its architects and clients toward architecture and the city.

In the years since World War II, the cohesiveness of downtown San Francisco has been gradually eroded. San Francisco is fortunate that its downtown has not suffered to the same degree as most other American cities during these years at the hands of Redevelopment, new construction, highway builders, and other needs of the automobile. However, changes have already occurred on an immense scale, and in the face of the current building boom downtown, its quality and cohesiveness are precarious. If the desirable features and qualities of this area, which are so widely admired and which are given more precise definition in this volume, are not protected now, it will soon be too late. Downtown San Francisco will be more like parts of Houston or New York, or any number of other cities, than like the San Francisco of the recent past.

While the results of this inventory are closely keyed to the various levels of official recognition which are available, such as the National Register and the City Landmarks program, it is not the purpose of this volume to suggest that the City or any organization should embark on a wholesale campaign to have them so recognized. It is the purpose of this volume to point out those features and qualities which deserve recognition so that intelligent planning and decisions can be made about building projects in the future. Clearly, growth and change will continue to occur; it is essential, however, that it be guided in a manner that will be least destructive to the traditional character of the city.

The guidance of future growth can be accomplished in a number of ways. Because of downtown San Francisco's booming economy, tremendous land values, and requirements for continuing functional efficiency, the great range of traditional preservation tools is of limited usefulness here. Those traditional tools already in existence or of potential application in downtown San Francisco are enumerated below. (1) Maintenance or adaptive reuse of existing buildings under private initiative is already going on and is the single most important tool available for preservation downtown. (2) Density transfers are allowable under the planning code, but they have not been widely used. However, they are of great potential value under modified conditions or under a more liberal and complex development rights transfer scheme. (3) Minimum maintenance laws and (4) facade easements are two instruments of preservation which have not been used downtown but which might be. (5) City Landmarks and other categories of official recognition have of course been and will continue to be, but, while they are important tools, they cannot be relied upon alone. Not all of the buildings and features downtown which deserve to be protected are of landmark quality, and, just as importantly, landmarks are too diffuse to be effective in protecting qualities that usually involve relationships between buildings as well as the buildings themselves. (6) Special use districts or

traditional historic districts are sufficiently comprehensive to answer whatever shortcomings exist in any of the other preservation tools by themselves, but, except in limited cases, it seems probable that such districts downtown would meet great political opposition.

While all of these traditional tools are helpful, they are not enough, and must be supplemented by greater public recognition of the issues involved, and by comprehensive City policies. A major document already exists which can and should provide the framework both for conservation and new development downtown. The Urban Design Plan, adopted in 1971, sets forth strong and unequivocal policies for preservation of landmark quality buildings, and of more general qualities of urban character. In addition, together with the bonus system and height and bulk regulations, it provides guidelines for new development. In view of the findings of this inventory, the policies of the Urban Design Plan can and should give rise to strengthened policies for new development downtown, and the bonus system and height and bulk regulations should be re-examined for the impact they have on preservation of the character of the city.

Preservation in downtown San Francisco is a difficult but important problem. No other major city has attempted comprehensive preservation efforts in its central core, but few if any cities have so much to lose in the failure to do so. Traditional tools of preservation must be supplemented with increased public awareness of the qualities of the area and the issues at stake, and with renewed attention to the provisions of the Urban Design Plan. The alternative, changing to emulate the formlessness and facelessness of most of urban America, is one that San Francisco can ill afford.

HISTORICAL BACKGROUND

INTRODUCTION: INSTANT CITY

In the unusual circumstances of its emergence during the Gold Rush, San Francisco has been called an "instant city."[1] In 1849 it grew from a small village of less than 1,000 people to a booming metropolis of 20,000. By the time the transcontinental railroad arrived in 1869, it was the premier city of the Pacific coast and had grown larger than much older places such as Buffalo, Washington, Newark and Louisville. By the turn of the century it had become the 11th largest city in the country.

Then, in 1906, the earthquake and fire destroyed the heart of San Francisco in the worst disaster ever to befall a major American city. Three years later it was substantially rebuilt—for the second time San Francisco was an instant city.

Downtown San Francisco today is essentially the instant city which reappeared in the aftermath of the fire, and which developed in the 25 years from 1906 to 1931. Nevertheless, the street grid, parceling, patterns of ownership and use, construction technology, and architectural ornamentation—in short, the various aspects of the urban landscape—all have their roots in the pre-fire period.

San Francisco is one of those many American cities whose downtown came to a certain level of maturity in the 1920s after an extended but continuous development since the 1880s. Like so many others, it entered that period a visually chaotic Victorian city of largely traditional construction and uniform height of three to five stories. And, when that period was brought to a close by the Depression, it was a modern city, transformed by the height of its buildings and the imagery of an urban architecture that had come to this country from Europe and dominated building styles during those years.

The American city that resulted from that great period of growth represented the high point of urbanism in our history. Despite their frequent scorn for the details of its architecture and its economic reason for being, early Modern artists and architects were widely inspired by the physical form of this early 20th-century city. It was a city that had an organic feel about it in its unplanned order, harmony and integration of parts, texture, and coloration. And the height of its buildings, the technology that made that height possible, and the ornamental wrappings of the buildings themselves, all contributed to the romance and attraction of the image.

San Francisco was one of the most beautiful of the cities of this era, largely because it was built almost at once. The period was profoundly influenced by the City Beautiful Movement, an aspect of the widespread municipal reform efforts of the time in planning and architecture. The combination of the nearly total building of the downtown between 1906 and 1931 and the influence of the City Beautiful Movement created a city that was architecturally very cohesive, and, in a sense, the fullest flowering of that great age of city-building. New York's financial district was taller and more dramatic, Chicago's Loop covered a larger area, and other cities were distinguished in other ways, but no other city had the unified image of downtown San Francisco that was entirely the product of modern times.

The city that was completed in 1931 lasted about 25 years through the Depression, War, and recovery with very little change. But, in the late 1950s, there began to develop a new city within the old that had little or no relationship to what had been built before. From that time to the present a freeway has nearly encircled the downtown, federal Redevelopment projects have cleared large areas and rebuilt one of them, and huge new skyscrapers of an unprecedented size and scale have greatly altered the character of the place. If downtown San Francisco had been invaded by another planet the juxtapositions between the city of 1930 and the post-war city could not be more jarring.

These changes have resulted in the loss of irreplaceable architectural landmarks, in addition to the erosion of the character of this uniquely cohesive city. Despite a growing awareness on the part of both the public and the city government of the importance of the existing city and its architecture, many fine buildings are currently threatened as San Francisco enters the biggest building boom downtown since 1906.

The essay which follows is an attempt to characterize the physical changes of the city as they have developed since the Gold Rush.

---

(1) See Gunther Barth, *Instant Cities: Urbanization and the Rise of San Francisco and Denver* (New York, 1975) for a full discussion of San Francisco as an instant city. See also Charles Lockwood, *Suddenly San Francisco: The Early Years of an Instant City* (San Francisco, 1978) for a more recent use of the term.

Map of San Francisco, 1852, showing O'Farrell survey and extensions.

GOLD RUSH SAN FRANCISCO

Gold Rush San Francisco was established on a street grid whose dimensions had been crudely defined by the Mexican era settlement around Portsmouth Square. In 1839 a few streets were laid out around the Square and, in 1847, Jasper O'Farrell conducted a proper survey, correcting the grid, and extending it over a great area of unsettled land. At the same time, O'Farrell laid out Market Street from the ferry dock in a line to Twin Peaks, parallel to the road from the Bay to Mission Dolores. South of this line he laid out larger blocks of four times the size of those in the original grid.

As the instant city boomed and began to occupy the grid, it was extended to the west beyond Larkin Street and to the east over landfill in shallow bay waters. This landfilling began almost simultaneously with the Gold Rush and was largely complete by the 1880s. The process of landfilling accomplished two immediate purposes. It created land where it was in great demand in a city where land has always been in short supply, and it provided a place to dump sand from street grading and the leveling of sand dunes and hills that had blocked Market Street, Second Street, and other areas.

The original commercial district around Portsmouth Square spread north at first to the area we now call Jackson Square, but very quickly it shifted south toward its present location. As the city grew the commercial district expanded, displacing houses, and as it expanded it specialized, forming distinct sub-areas. The first sub-area was the financial district which settled near the corner of California and Montgomery streets by the 1860s. Warehousing was concentrated on the landfill closest to the bay. Retailing, which first coalesced near Portsmouth Square, shifted to lower Kearny Street in the 1860s and 1870s and afterwards spread gradually west toward Union Square.

The first buildings in the Gold Rush city were tents and wooden shacks made from dismantled ships. Sometimes ships themselves were pulled up on dry land or left at shallow anchorage which was filled as the shoreline was extended; doorways were cut through the hulls of ships and the ships were occupied as buildings. Also, prefabricated houses were brought around the Horn in sailing ships from New England. Construction was simple, and if there was any ornamental dress to these first buildings, it was often mildly Greek Revival, or, sometimes, Gothic Revival in derivation. After the city had been burned down a number of times, in 1853 an ordinance was passed requiring everything in the commercial district to be built of brick. Although this didn't stop the fires completely, it helped, and it permanently altered the appearance of the area.

Looking down Sacramento Street in 1856 at San Francisco's small scaled, predominantly brick commercial district.

VICTORIAN SAN FRANCISCO

As San Francisco grew, the two- and three-story brick city of the 1850s shifted in its ornamental references from predominantly Greek Revival among new buildings to predominantly Italianate. The quality of some of this early architecture was surprisingly high, as well-trained architects had been among those who had come from all over the world to San Francisco in the Gold Rush and like others had turned to their past occupations when they became disillusioned with mining. The abilities of some of these architects, together with the inherent qualities of the prevailing ornamental treatments of the period, produced a number of fine old buildings and at least a few handsome groupings of buildings along the more important streets.

In the late 1850s and 1860s newly available structural cast iron was used to open up the facades of buildings, either by lessening the amount of brick needed, or as all cast-iron fronts. In the 1870s ornamental references began to change from Italianate to Second Empire, characterized by a more exuberant variation of Italianate ornamentation and a massard roof. Facade compositions grew increasingly wild as the emphasis in design was placed on ornament. The characteristic busyness of the Second Empire Style began to erode the stately restrained harmony of the Italianate city. From that time to the end of the century the disharmony would only increase as the variety of architectural treatments multiplied. Eastlake, Renaissance Revival, High Victorian Gothic, and the persistent Italianate and Second Empire Styles were all common sources of ornamentation. The closest thing today to the character of Victorian downtown San Francisco is in the 400 block of Ninth Street in Oakland, with its three- to five-story, elaborately ornamented, bay-windowed buildings that still retain a rich mixture of commercial, residential, and office uses.

By the end of the 1860s the overall height of the downtown area had begun to rise to its Victorian era average of three to five stories. This unofficial height limit was broken only by the seven-story Palace Hotel in 1875 and, to a lesser extent, by the Baldwin Hotel in 1877. Together with the spires of churches, Selby's Shot Tower, and a few tall smokestacks, these hotels constituted the skyline of the Victorian city. At the same time, they represented the first dramatic examples of the change in scale that resulted from assembly of lots into large parcels, a process which had already begun but which would not make widespread radical changes until after 1900.

Italianate streetscape. Looking down Sacramento from Montgomery, 1865.

25

The most forward-looking Victorian building in downtown San Francisco was the Palace Hotel of 1875. In its scale and technology it was years ahead of other buildings of its time. It was of a size that would not generally be matched until 1901-1906. Although extremely well built of brick with iron reinforcing, it did not represent a significant structural advancement, but it was far advanced in the use it made of newly available mechanical systems. It was one of the earliest buildings in San Francisco with a passenger elevator, and the first to utilize the potential of the elevator for building higher than the norm of the period. Its heating, lighting, and plumbing systems were not so much innovative in their basic technology as in their size and complexity. While not dramatic advances from a current viewpoint, these were of tremendous importance at the time, and essential to the subsequent development of large modern buildings.

In spite of its technological sophistication, the Palace was quintessentially Victorian in its ornamental treatment, with its ill-proportioned facades and multitude of small detail on an immense mass. Thus, along with the technological progress it represented, the Palace was also a major contributor to the eclectic and untidy character of Victorian downtown San Francisco.

Union Block, Pine and Market, in 1888. Richly ornamented facades appear to be cast iron.

Below:
View from Howard Street, 1880s, showing the huge increase in scale introduced by the Palace Hotel.

duce more skyscrapers. In addition to the availability of the technology, the skyscraper came to San Francisco when it did because the downtown area could not expand outward anymore. More bayfill was impractical, there were hills on several sides and existing neighborhoods that wouldn't dislodge. Also, there was a limit to the distance a commercial district could spread without losing its advantages as a centralized business area. The only logical way was to go up. The Chronicle Building was 10 stories high, only three more than the Palace, but it represented a quicker and more efficient way of reaching that height.

Above:
Hotel Pleasanton in 1890. A typical large building of its period in its multitude of small ornamental details.

MODERNIZATION

In the midst of what was perceived by visitors to be the increasing visual disharmony of 19th-century San Francisco, several developments occurred around 1890 which were part of a process of modernization. The terms "modern" and "modernization" mean simply the taking advantage of the current ideas and technologies of the time and responding to current needs. They have nothing necessarily to do with Modern Architecture, which had virtually no impact in downtown San Francisco until after World War II. Most late 19th- and early 20th-century San Francisco architects considered themselves to be modern, although their architecture was invariably and unapologetically historicist. To be modern among most local architects meant to be aware of new technological developments in the "architectural" treatment of buildings, but never to make a show of being innovative for its own sake.

Modernization of downtown San Francisco's architectural and urban landscape proceeded in two parallel and often united areas of development: technology and imagery. The Palace Hotel has already been mentioned as an early and important example of technological advancement. The next step would come with the Chronicle (690 Market) and Mills (220 Montgomery) Buildings. But in its imagery the Palace did not represent an important advancement, and the Chronicle and Mills Buildings with their Romanesque ornamentation belonged to a stylistic mode that was not popular for very long. The first important building in the modern imagery which would remake downtown San Francisco after the fire was the Hibernia Bank (1 Jones) of 1891, in which the new technology was also utilized. After this time, generally speaking, the development of technology and imagery proceeded together, to the extent that the only buildings outside of Jackson Square to survive the fire of 1906 were "modern" buildings.

With the Chronicle Building of 1889 the iron- and steel-frame skyscraper was introduced to San Francisco and the West. The first skyscraper brought with it a true skyline, and the technology to pro-

Montgomery Street from Market, 1885, showing the typically eclectic and disorderly visual character of the Victorian city.

Chronicle Building (1889) in 1901, before additions. The city's first skyscraper.

The skyscraper first came to San Francisco at the corner of Third, Market, and Kearny Streets because it was the busiest intersection downtown. Third Street was the main route up from the Peninsula. Market Street was then, as now, the principal artery of the city and the focus of its public transportation. In an age when printed newspapers were the primary source of news and information, newspaper offices were a natural gathering place for the city. All the major newspapers would be located at that intersection within a few years, and it would not decline as one of the focal points of the city until the advent of radio and television and the diminished importance of newspapers. It was appropriate that San Francisco's first skyscraper would be for a newspaper.

The Chronicle Building, and the Mills Building of two years later, were both designed by Burnham and Root of Chicago, one of the leading architectural firms in the country at the time. Both were Chicago School versions of the Richardsonian Romanesque in ornamental treatment. Such treatment had been greeted as a suitably restrained response to the prevailing visual chaos of the 19th-century city and quite a few examples were built here. However, most were built before the steel frame and its rudimentary fireproofing came into common usage, and therefore most perished in 1906. Among the most prominent examples that

were lost were A. Page Brown's Donohue and Sharon Buildings, Meyer and O'Brien's Crossley Building, T. Patterson Ross's California Hotel, and G. W. Percy's Academy of Sciences Building.

Much more important in imagery for the future city, and the counterpart to the modernism of the structural features of the Chronicle and Mills Buildings, were the buildings sometimes lumped together as the American Renaissance and first represented here by Albert Pissis' Hibernia Bank of 1891. The American Renaissance was a broad movement in the arts during the late 19th and early 20th centuries which saw American culture as the heir of the European Renaissance, and which sought to revive and maintain "Renaissance" ideas. In architecture it traditionally encompasses the Second Renaissance Revival, the Classical Revival, and the Beaux-Arts Classical Styles. Willis Polk, who was a leader in this local "Renaissance," called the Hibernia Bank the most beautiful building in the city. It was widely admired from the day of its completion and it remained one of the favorite buildings of the local architectural community for many years. In its literate use of classical motifs, its rich yet ordered composition, and its consciousness of its place in the city, it was the first local representative of a new approach to architectural design that would shortly come to dominate new construction.

The Hibernia Bank and A. Page Brown's Crocker Building (demolished) of 1892 both preceded the World's Columbian Exposition in Chicago of 1893, which popularized the stylistic modes of the American Renaissance to which they belonged, and, more importantly, a new vision in America of what the city could be.

The Hibernia Bank and the Chicago Exposition were both early examples in the United States of the influence of the Ecole des Beaux-Arts in Paris (see section on Architects and Education). Because of the lack of opportunities for an architectural education in this country many Americans had begun attending the Ecole. They returned far better trained than their colleagues who had never left, and they brought with them new attitudes toward architecture and a new sensitivity to the city.

As the most powerful expression of the teachings of the Ecole des Beaux-Arts of its day, the Chicago Exposition spawned the City Beautiful Movement. At the height of the chaos of Victorian urban America, the Chicago Exposition, with its group of monumental, classically derived buildings around a central lagoon, presented a vision of order, beauty, and magnificence. The City Beautiful Movement sought to recapture those qualities all over the country.

In San Francisco, the City Beautiful Movement had a particularly powerful appeal and influence. As in other cities, after 1893 the overwhelming new architectural "styles" in San Francisco were those of the American Renaissance. But whereas many cities were tantalized by the City Beautiful Movement, few could finally boast of a City Beautiful plan by Daniel Burnham, a monumental Civic Center, a world's fair in the image of Chicago's, nor, indeed, nearly so thoroughly a Beaux-Arts commercial district.

During the rest of the 1890s, although little building actually occurred in downtown San Francisco, the City of Paris, the Ferry Building, the Emporium, and the Call Building all fell within the tradition of the American Renaissance and promoted the image of the City Beautiful. Between 1901 and 1905, another 19 major buildings which survive totally or in part today were constructed, all of them in the imagery of the American Renaissance and furthering the concept of the City Beautiful. Those significant pre-fire buildings which survive in some form are as follows:

Crocker Building (1892), Post and Market, ca. 1904.

1872	756 Mission Street	St. Patrick's Church
1889	690 Market Street	Chronicle Building (remodeled)
1891	220 Montgomery Street	Mills Building
1892	1 Jones Street	Hibernia Bank
1895	The Embarcadero	Union Depot and Ferry House (Ferry Building)
1896	199 Geary Street	Spring Valley Water Works Building (City of Paris)
1896	835–865 Market Street	Parrott Building (Emporium)
1898	703 Market Street	Call/Spreckels Building (Central Tower)
1901	400 Montgomery Street	Alvinza Hayward (Kohl) Building
1902	979–989 Market Street	Hale Brothers Building
1902	116 New Montgomery	Rialto Building
1902	704 Market Street	Mutual Savings Bank Building (Citizens Savings)
1902	71–85 Second Street	Wells Fargo Building
1902	101–105 Market Street	Aetna (Young) Building
1902	108–110 Sutter Street	Bullock and Jones Building (old French Bank)
1903	700 Mission Street	Aronson Building
1903	465 California Street	Merchant's Exchange Building
1904	602–606 Mission Street	Atlas Building (remodeled)
1904	301–345 Powell Street	St. Francis Hotel
1904	870–898 Market Street	Flood Building
1905	1125 Market Street	Bell (Embassy) Theater
1905	1095–1097 Market Street	Grant Building
1905	222–226 Jessie Street	Station C, P. G. & E.

1905	445 Bush Street	Pacific States Telephone & Telegraph Co. Building
1905	301–305 Grant Avenue	Myers Building
1905	201 Grant Avenue	Shreve Building
1905	381 Bush Street	J. E. Adams (Alto) Building

The following major buildings were proposed or under construction:

1906	233 Geary Street	Butler Building (remodeled)
1906	201–209 Post Street	Head Building
1906	234–240 Stockton Street	Shroth Building
1906	673–687 Market Street	Monadnock Building
1906	166 Geary Street	Whittell Building
1906	240–244 Kearny Street	Marston Building
1906	301–345 Powell Street	St. Francis Hotel addition
1906	690 Market Street	Chronicle Building addition

Thus, from 1890 on, most big new building in downtown San Francisco was of a very different character from that which preceded it. The scale of these new developments was much bigger—a skyscraper was at city-scale rather than street-scale—and it was visible from a wide area, not just from its own street or intersection. And in ornamentation, these new buildings were treated with a scale of detail that befitted their size. By 1906 there was a lot of new building downtown, but still it was only a scattering in the vast Victorian city around it. Certain areas, like the intersection of Third and Market Streets where the Chronicle, Call, and Citizens Savings Buildings still stand (although the Chronicle and Call are both altered) and the stretch of Market in the vicinity of the Emporium and Flood Buildings, had concentrations of these new buildings that set them apart from the old city, but they were the exceptions. Both the height and the imagery of

this new architecture were giving the downtown a new look. From a distance it had a vigorous skyline, and from the street it was obvious to anyone which buildings were the modern ones. They were larger in size and scale. They were still richly detailed, but far more restrained than the Victorian buildings around them. Although few could have detected the difference, they were also mostly steel-frame buildings with at least a rudimentary attempt at fireproofing.

By the end of the 19th century there was less construction under way in downtown San Francisco than at any time since the 1860s. But by 1905, a census of "fireproof" buildings in the United States (these are roughly translatable into steel-frame buildings) showed there to be a comparable number in San Francisco to other cities, and as many under construction as anywhere else, "population considered." In the April 1906 issue of the *Architect and Engineer*, the last issue before the earthquake and fire, an editorial on "The Skyscraper in California" observed that San Francisco rivaled New York and Chicago in the number of its skyscrapers, taking relative population into account, and that two-thirds of San Francisco's skyscrapers had been built in the previous five years.

By 1906, the central business district had grown and continued to shift to the south and southwest from its original location around Portsmouth Square. The central business district was smaller than it grew to be afterwards but not much different in the organization of its key parts from the present day. The financial district was centered at Montgomery and California Streets, insurance companies were located along Sansome, warehousing was to the east on landfill, Kearny was a transitional area, and Grant Avenue was the heart of the shopping district, with a secondary shopping area out Market between Fourth and Sixth Streets.

In the promising period just before the earthquake,

bold steps were being taken by the city's leaders to insure a proper image for San Francisco's future. In 1904 the Society for the Improvement and Adornment of San Francisco was formed under the leadership of former Mayor James D. Phelan. The Society invited Daniel Burnham, the leading City Beautiful Movement planner in America, to provide the city with a plan. He had laid out the Chicago Exposition in 1893, been a leader in the revival of L'Enfant's plan for Washington in 1901, planned the Cleveland Civic Center, and would later do a plan for Chicago, and for Manila and the summer capital of Baguio in the Philippines.

Burnham's plan for San Francisco was ready in 1905. It called for practical improvements such as street lighting, major reservations of land for parks, and, most ambitiously, new boulevards cut through the city, as in Paris, in the general pattern of concentric circles connected by spokes to the center of the city. The spokes were to converge at Van Ness and Market where a great Civic Center of public buildings would be erected. The boulevards would be lined with trees and punctuated with civic art. Various nodes would be singled out for special treatment, but, apart from the boulevards themselves, the grand buildings that were to give substance to the plan were to be erected by enlightened private interests. The plan was a source of great public interest and admiration and was endorsed by the Board of Supervisors just before the earthquake.

THE WHITE HOUSE

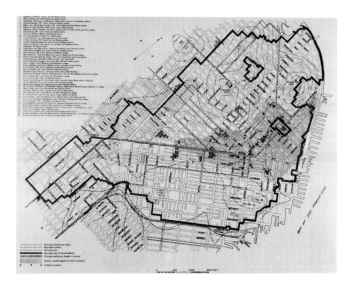

Map showing the boundaries of the area that burned after the 1906 earthquake.

EARTHQUAKE AND FIRE

Despite the availability of the recently published Burnham Plan, and its endorsement by both the City and the architectural community, there was never really any serious chance of its being implemented after the fire. The central idea of the Burnham plan had been "beautification" but with the city in ruins, beautification was the last thing on most people's minds. On April 17, 1906, San Francisco was the major city in the West. It was in the midst of a building boom downtown, and its future looked bright. The Burnham Plan itself was evidence of the city's prosperity, culture, and promise. But by April 22, after the smoke had cleared, all that remained of the city were the shells of two-dozen-odd salvageable buildings among thousands. Not even streets or property lines were visible as everything was buried under ash and rubble. The anxiety which that vision provoked among citizens who saw their homes and jobs destroyed, and among real-estate investors and business people whose fortunes and futures were suddenly uncertain, was tremendous. There were very real fears of a financial panic.

For the Burnham Plan to have been implemented under the best of circumstances, the whole-hearted support of the business community would have been essential. For a prosperous business district to be sliced by diagonal avenues and opened up by great plazas would have demolished profitable buildings and businesses, and altered the relationships of others to the city—a risky business before the fire, but unthinkable in its aftermath. Where $500 million worth of buildings and property stood one day, suddenly there was only vacant land whose only value lay in its potential to be built upon. There was no guarantee that the insurance companies would pay on claims, or even if they did, that the city could be rebuilt at all. And if it was to be rebuilt, no one could say that the heart of the financial and prestige shopping districts would not shift and that property that was once valuable for its location wouldn't suffer a

Lower left:
Downtown San Francisco on fire after the 1906 earthquake.

Below:
Illustrations from the Burnham Plan, 1905.

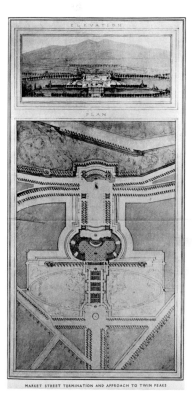

MARKET STREET TERMINATION AND APPROACH TO TWIN PEAKS

San Francisco after the fire.

Construction around Union Square in 1907.

great loss in the new city. There was much reason for anxiety, and, for those people who were in a position to rebuild, the only sensible course of action was to re-establish the old city in order to re-establish the pre-fire value of the property.

Thus, the new city was built on the same street and property lines as the old. Burnham was wrong, as he prepared to implement his plan, in thinking that the city was now a clean slate. Publicly owned street lines and privately owned lot lines still existed —both invisible, but of greater importance than the buildings themselves in shaping reconstruction.

RECONSTRUCTION

The reconstruction of San Francisco was an astonishing accomplishment to all who had seen the devastation—and to the country at large. By August 1907, a year and three months after the earthquake, 6000 buildings had been completed and 3000 more were under construction. In three years, by 1909, the city was considered rebuilt. Although there were still vacant lots downtown, it was largely built up, including many new large buildings. The shells of the devastation were no longer in evidence, business could be carried on normally, and to the first-time visitor there was little that was likely to suggest the recent disaster. San Francisco was for the second time an instant city, but this time of a different order. Whereas 20,000 people arrived on a barren peninsula in one year in 1849, this time a thoroughly modern city of skyscrapers arose out of the ashes—from devastation to a city of national prominence in three years.

Despite rebuilding on the same street and property lines, the character of the new city was very different from the old. Except for a few blocks in Jackson Square, every vestige of the Victorian downtown was destroyed. The only survivors of the fire were buildings which had been somewhat incongruous in their old settings. These survivors had been harbingers of the future, and belonged to stylistic modes and philosophies of architecture that would be entirely compatible, if not indistinguishable, from the buildings of the new city. Only the Chronicle and Mills buildings brought the outmoded Romanesque into the new era, but in every other respect they were also modern. The only other visible clue to the past was the survival of stone facades on older buildings; afterwards nearly everything was clad in terra cotta. Underneath the facades of post-fire buildings were structural changes, but they had only the most rare and obscure effects on exterior expression.

Despite the abandonment of the Burnham Plan, there was a sense in which the City Beautiful to which Burnham aspired was still realized, albeit in altered form. (Parts of the Burnham Plan would later be realized in the western parts of the city and in the street lighting of the post-fire and Panama-Pacific International Exposition years.) While there was a premium on rapid reconstruction, still the design of individual structures was carefully worked out. The local architectural profession was dominated by former students of the Ecole des Beaux-Arts in Paris (see Section on Architects and Education), or of its methods in this country, and was overwhelmingly given over to the ideals of the City Beautiful Movement. Under these influences there was a widely shared belief in the possibilities of architecture to transform the image of the city to one of classical order and grandeur which would leave the eclectic chaos of the Victorian city behind. The new city's image would suitably express the rightful place of San Francisco among American cities, and the place of American cities in the world. This was a vision which was shared among clients and the general population, and was a highly significant aspect in the realization of the city that was built.

The expression of the architecture which resulted was tempered by practical requirements and the eccentricity of significant numbers of local architects and their backgrounds. Despite extensive student work with imaginary, impractical exercises among Beaux-Arts architects, these and others were able to make the transition to buildable architecture. While the Ecole des Beaux-Arts provided the basis for the "beauty" of downtown San Francisco's post-fire architecture, its response to function, and, indeed, often the articulation of its facades, was akin to that of the Chicago School. Functional planning of office floors, light wells, mechanical services, and skeletal treatments of facades followed the Chicago model and sometimes carried that model even further. In 1908, an article in the *Architect and Engineer* observed that whereas Chicago and New York tended to frame storefronts with masonry piers, in San Francisco there was an effort to "get as much glass up as possible." This architecture responded to the needs of business to the extent that it could accommodate frequent changes in height or program even after construction had begun.

Just as the non-Beaux-Arts architects subscribed to many Beaux-Arts principles, so even San Francisco's Beaux-Arts architects saw their function as largely a response to the practical. In describing the work of Lewis Hobart, a former student at the Ecole, an article in the *Architectural Record* in 1909 effectively synthesized these two strains of influence:

These edifices range from two to twelve stories in height, and are occupied for all kinds of business purposes. But no matter what their height and pur-

The reconstructed city. Looking east on Market from Powell, 1915.

pose, they are stamped with certain common architectural characteristics. The designer has not allowed his interest in 'architecture' to interfere with the planning of thoroughly useful and serviceable buildings. They are all of them plain, unpretentious structures with no superfluous ornament and no irrelevant 'effects'. The utmost care has been taken to secure good light to the tenants of the stores and the offices, and the amount of window space in each of the several buildings has been carefully adapted to the service, which the different floors were designed to perform. Salesrooms intended for display of goods required and received more window space than mere offices. But frankly as the architect accepted conditions of that kind, and careful as he was to avoid architectural superfluities and irrelevancies, he has nevertheless managed to keep his facades both substantial and interesting in appearance. The piers are always solid enough and the reveals deep enough to give the buildings a certain dignity. The horizontal divisions of the facade are both well distributed and well tied together. The little ornament used is of the right kind and is applied in the right place. The lack of pretension in these buildings never becomes equivalent either to commonplaceness or insignificance.

Unexecuted project for a site on Third Street near Mission by L. C. Mullgardt, 1911.

*Fredericks Building, 1910.
The 2-story glass commercial base
is surmounted by a 5-story
"architectural" top.*

The criticisms which would later be made of the architecture of this period as not honestly expressive of its structure and function, were, in retrospect, frequently beside the point in the task of city-building. A building such as the Fredericks Building (298 Post), an excellent and very typical example of San Francisco's commercial architecture of the period, had a glass base surmounted by a three-part composition of implied masonry. Apart from the purely functional rationale for "getting as much glass up as possible" to provide maximum storefront display space, there was an "architectural" rationale for this as well. The two-story base was designed for a commercial store and the "masonry" superstructure for offices. The functional disparity of the two is evident in their frequently being served by two sets of elevators. The glass base displayed merchandise and was expressed differently from the differently used upper stories. The glass storefront was the practical, changeable base that could change its window displays or even its whole design with each passing style without altering the essential character of the building, while the historicist upper levels would maintain the permanence of the public facade to the city, literally above the whims of fashion. This approach expressed the more complex functions of buildings at a time before single-use structures became the rule. That this was an extremely practical approach for a commercial architecture which was bound to undergo remodelings is amply demonstrated. The ground floors of the retail district have been remodeled countless times since the area was built, yet it retains its essential cohesiveness and original appearance. The buildings which have suffered the most through lower-level remodelings are those like the Financial Center (405 Montgomery) or Kemper (417 Montgomery) Buildings in the financial district, whose integrally architectural bases, formerly treated as masonry rather than glass, have been "modernized."

As for the "honest" expression of structure, steel-frame buildings have always been clad in fire-proofing and the steel has never been exposed (except in very recent experiments such as 1 Liberty Plaza in New York). The treatment of any cladding, whether metal, glass, stone, terra cotta, brick, or anything else, is a question of style. The decorative treatment by post-fire San Francisco architects of terra-cotta curtain walls in classically derived or other historicist imagery was a matter of response to historical traditions, symbolic needs, and an attitude toward urbanism. The approach of the architects of the post-fire city, then, was extremely practical, and capable of expressing both symbolic and functional requirements of complex buildings in a way that later architecture could not do.

The impact of hundreds of buildings like the Fredericks, with active commercial ground floor areas, and symbolic images of the permanence, grandeur, and culture of the city above, was to create an extremely vital urban ensemble, almost infinitely rich in its varied textures and individual expressions, yet held together in an aesthetic whole by a shared, urban-based view of architecture.

The architecture of the post-fire period followed local prototypes largely if not entirely established in the immediate pre-fire period. Beyond the predominantly classical imagery of the Ecole des Beaux-Arts and the City Beautiful Movement, individual models were suggested by, among others, the Merchant's Exchange (465 California), the Emporium (835–865 Market), the Call Building (703–705 Market), the Kohl Building (400 Montgomery), the Rialto Building (116 New Montgomery), the Butler Building (233 Geary), and the St. Francis Hotel (301–345 Powell). Although the expression of these buildings is in part derived from that of the Chicago School, as noted above, and in those buildings that follow the example of the Rialto Building by Meyer and O'Brien, the dominant influences were D. H. Burnham & Co.'s post-Chicago-School work, exemplified by the Merchant's Exchange, and the less structural and more historicist work that came out of New York. The work of McKim, Mead, and White was perhaps the most universally admired of outside architects among San Francisco designers, and their Phoenix Building in New York was probably the single most prevalent model.

There were few major new buildings in the immediate post-fire period that diverged from these models. At the same time, however, in the wholesale rebuilding of the city, there were a great many buildings that were still built with load-

*Lower right:
Merchant's Exchange (1903),
ca. 1907. A prototype for many
later buildings downtown.*

*Below:
Unexecuted project by Ross and
Burgren, 1908.*

bearing brick walls and therefore were not modern in the same sense that most larger buildings were. While they still shared the broad ornamental and compositional treatment of the larger buildings, most of these were much smaller—usually two or three stories—and were evolutionary examples of traditional local types. A few even retained the image of late 19th-century commercial buildings in the Italianate mode.

If there was one place where the theory and practice of this post-fire city came together, and which still expresses those values almost as clearly as at that time, it is along Grant Avenue and the cross blocks of Geary, Post, and Sutter. One observer in the *Architect and Engineer* went so far as to call Grant Avenue the greatest architectural street in the world. While perhaps a little overenthusiastic, the statement does speak well for the pride local architects felt in what they had done, not only on Grant Avenue, but in the burned district as a whole. Not only had the city rebuilt and recovered financially in three years, but it had done so with great style. With Grant Avenue it is possible to see just how the uncoordinated efforts of disparate architects with a shared view can achieve a fine aesthetic composition.

Looking up from the great assemblage at the foot of Grant, the street is characterized by large areas of glass framed in classical ornamentation; each side of the street is a two-dimensional facade of roughly uniform cornice level, massing, color, material, and style which is punctuated at intervals by taller and otherwise more imposing buildings. The small but rich, plastic, granite-clad architectural forms of the two banks at the foot of Grant serve as suitably monumental entrance gates and anchors to the group. The Phelan Building (760–784 Market), also at the foot of Grant, and the pair formed by the Head and Shreve Buildings at Post (all by William Curlett), the Myer's Building at Sutter, and Ernest Coxhead's Telephone Building (333 Grant) near Bush, the principal tall buildings along the street, are spread out along the few blocks of the retail district that ends with the narrowed entrance to Chinatown at Bush, giving each more emphasis and the street more vitality. The Shreve and Head Buildings face each other at the center of the group, one a pre-fire example clad in granite, and the other a post-fire example clad in terra cotta of the same type of mixed-use commercial building. The bronze storefronts of the Shreve Building and the carved stone walls of the Shreve and Telephone buildings add elements of permanence and richness to the generally flat facade of the street. And the Telephone Building, near the end, like the Eleanor Green Building (51–55 Grant) near the foot of Grant, provides a playful composition of overscaled classical details, which in this case is both richer and more interesting as an individual work of architecture than most of the buildings of the area. The Abrahamson (311–319 Grant) and Phoenix (220–228 Grant) Buildings, with their

Grant Avenue, ca. 1948.

simple facades of immense square windows on opposite sides of Grant are the most elegant expressions of the basic texture of the street. The White House, with its curving corner and continuous monumental superstructure over a glass base, is a superb work of urban design which unites the two finest streets in the area, Grant and Sutter. The whole group is diverse yet unified, and its effect is enhanced by the particularly pleasing relationship of the width of the streets to the height of the commercial bases, and to the buildings themselves. As much as any place outside the Civic Center, this was the City Beautiful.

As the city was rebuilt after the fire, the conservatism of the reconstruction was manifest in the maintenance of pre-fire patterns. By 1915, the new downtown covered almost 50% more area than the pre-fire downtown, but its organization was similar. There was of course some shifting around, but largely in the way of accelerating patterns which had begun before the fire. For example, the financial district was reconstructed almost in place. The warehouse district, which had been undergoing displacement by the expanding financial district to the east, shifted south. The retail area moved somewhat west, taking over Union Square and reaffirming the area around Powell and Market as a second major retail center. Hotels moved entirely out of the financial district to the area west and south of Union Square. The only significant new patterns were the establishment of a distinct theater district on Market Street beyond Fifth, and an area of private men's clubs west of Union Square.

John Galois Building (ca. 1910), Sutter east of Grant, by G. A. Applegarth. An example of a characteristic glass-front building, demolished for the Stockton-Sutter garage.

Aerial view of San Francisco, 1922.

As for the skyline, in the immediate post-fire period, due to a severe height limit, there were no new buildings as tall as several in the pre-fire period. Buildings such as the Call, which was long since completed, or the Humboldt (783–785 Market) and Whittell (166 Geary) on which construction had begun before the fire, were allowed to be rebuilt although they were above the new height limit. But there was no planning of new buildings whose height was greater than one and a half times the street width until the height limit was removed in March of 1907. At least one project, the reconstruction of the Hearst Building (691–699 Market), was greatly altered by the height limit. Nevertheless, the skyline was greatly augmented in the post-fire period by the number of new buildings of about 10 stories, and the square footage of downtown buildings increased greatly. Among the most prominent of this period were the Royal Globe Insurance, the Newhall, the Argonaut, the Post Telegraph, the Metropolis Trust and Savings Bank, the Phelan, the Commercial, the David Hewes, the First National Bank, the Kohler and Chase, the Heineman, the Standard Oil, the California Pacific, and the Adam Grant Buildings. As before the fire, San Francisco maintained its position as one of the leading American cities in the number of its skyscrapers, but even without a height limit after 1907 the cautiousness of local builders after the earthquake produced a remarkably low skyline. In 1913, when the 55-story Woolworth Building was com-

pleted in New York, the tallest building in San Francisco was still the 1898 Call Building with its 15 office floors and six-story dome.

In retrospect, the earthquake and fire of 1906 might be called a fortunate catastrophe. As a result of the devastation San Francisco was transformed more easily than most from a Victorian to a modern city. Inefficiencies in the organization of the business district were relatively easily overcome. In a very short period of time there was a large increase in the number of modern "fireproof" buildings and in the amount of floor space downtown. As in the case of a war, the crisis of the fire and tremendous demand for construction helped develop certain local industries, notably steel, lessening reliance of the local economy on eastern producers. The fact of the earthquake itself resulted in lower heights of buildings than other major American cities, creating a compact but relatively open and humane downtown. Not least, it resulted in an unique architectural cohesiveness.

PANAMA-PACIFIC INTERNATIONAL EXPOSITION/CIVIC CENTER

In celebration of its recovery—and in order to secure the trade that would soon be coming through the Panama Canal—San Francisco began planning the Panama-Pacific International Exposition (P-P.I.E.) for 1915. In the area west of Union Square this meant construction of large numbers of apartment hotels in the years 1913-1915 in anticipation of the great numbers of visitors who would come. These were buildings which would serve as hotels but could be easily converted to permanent residences after the Exposition was over.

Although the Exposition would be in the Marina district, entirely outside of the burned area, the spirit which produced it was strongly related to the same spirit which rebuilt the city, which had recently reformed the city's politics, and which would begin planning the Civic Center as a permanent symbol of recovery and the city's new status.

In 1907, Boss Abe Reuf, the last and most powerful of the corrupt political bosses, went to jail, and his cohort, Mayor Eugene Schmitz, was removed from office. They were followed in power by a succession of reform-minded mayors, including, from 1911 to 1930, James Rolph, Jr. Rolph had been elected on the platform "Forward San Francisco." He was a vice-president of the P-P.I.E. Company, and an advocate of the Civic Center. Under Rolph, the corruption and the devastation of the recent past would be left behind.

The P-P.I.E. would be the celebration of the recovery from the fire and the symbol to the world that San Francisco belonged in that world class of cities, like Chicago, which could afford to stage such a lavish spectacle and which had the cultured tastes to do it in the right way. The P-P.I.E. was to last less than a year, and like previous American expositions, be dismantled. Built largely of lath and plaster on light steel, iron, and timber frames, the Exposition was in the image of the Chicago Fair and the visionary student work of the Ecole des Beaux-Arts. Called the City of Domes, its grand ex-

hibition buildings were grouped around courts with names like the Court of the Universe, the Court of the Four Seasons, and the Court of Abundance. The Exposition was largely planned and built by the most prominent of the city's architects, most of them former students of the Ecole des Beaux-Arts and all central figures in the rebuilding of the city after the fire. There were also buildings by some of the nation's best-known architects, brought here to add national stature to the Exposition and its architecture.

In the same period, the same local circle of architects planned the Civic Center as a more lasting gesture of the city's recovery and its new stature among cities. The link between the two was evident in the philosophies of design, the architects, politicians, and promoters who were involved, and, concretely, in the construction of the Exposition Auditorium in the Civic Center by the Exposition Company. The Exposition Auditorium was intended to be both a permanent reminder of the Exposition (at that time no buildings, not even the Palace of Fine Arts, were contemplated to last beyond the term of the Fair) and a boost to completion of the Civic Center. The Exposition Auditorium was, in fact, the first building finished in the Civic Center, and the only one completed before the Exposition began. The City Hall was opened about a month after the Exposition closed.

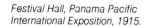

Festival Hall, Panama-Pacific International Exposition, 1915.

Bird's Eye View of the Civic Center. Plan as adopted, 1912.

Influential Second Prize winner, Chicago Tribune Tower competition, 1922, by Eliel Saarinen.

Below right:
Pacific National Bank Building, 1930, the O'Brien Bros. and Wilbur Peugh; demolished for the Bank of America World Headquarters.

Below:
Russ Building, 1927.

1920s

After the P-P.I.E., building activity diminished as the World War got underway in Europe, and did not resume in earnest until 1919 when the war was over. The Robert Dollar Building (301–333 California), by Charles McCall, was the first major new building after the war and was considered at the time to have inaugurated the boom of the 1920s.

There were building lulls during the 1920s, mostly due to materials shortages, but the boom continued largely unabated until the Stock Market Crash of 1929 and it did not finally exhaust itself until 1931.

In the early 1920s there were a number of sizable new office blocks but most were massive—like larger versions of the Merchant's Exchange Building—and did not produce a markedly different skyline. Then from 1925 to 1927, as the Pacific Telephone Building (134–140 New Montgomery), the Hunter-Dulin Building (111 Sutter), and the Russ Building (235 Montgomery) were completed, the

character of the skyline changed dramatically. The old downtown was pierced by graceful towers that seemed to set back or taper as they rose, or, in the case of the Hunter-Dulin, presented an elaborate and picturesque roof to the city. These buildings were followed by the Sir Francis Drake, 450 Sutter, the Mills Tower, and the Shell Building, all picturesque additions to the skyline, and later, in 1938, by the remodeled and enlarged Call Building. The results of the boom were so dramatic that it was worth noting in the *Architect and Engineer* in 1927 that many people with offices in the newly completed Russ Building could remember when there were shacks on its site.

After the early 1920s, when so many buildings were designed not merely with the massing of the Merchant's Exchange but with many of its ornamental and compositional details, there began to be a significant shift in the image of the city's new architecture. First and most important was the Pacific Telephone Building of 1924 by Miller and Pfleuger. The Pacific Telephone Building was the first of many in San Francisco to follow the example of Eliel Saarinen's highly influential entry for the Chicago Tribune Tower Competition of 1922. The Saarinen design responded far better than the winning entry to a variety of new concerns among architects nationwide who had begun to question the validity of the traditional compositional and ornamental treatment of tall buildings. The Telephone Building rose in setbacks, in an attenuated reference to the architecture created by New York's widely influential zoning law of 1916. Its lines were vertical in order to express the verticality of the skyscraper, and its terra-cotta ornamentation, although somewhat Gothic in feeling, was entirely invented. The Russ Building, the old William Taylor Hotel (100 McAllister) near the Civic Center, the Pacific National Bank (demolished), and the Shell Building all followed the example of Saarinen's design and the Telephone Building. Other tall buildings, like the Hunter-Dulin, were more traditional in expression but equally powerful additions to the skyline.

Although there were fewer buildings constructed downtown during this period than in the post-fire boom, they tended to be larger, and their overall impact on the skyline was very great. Their height, shapes, and concentration tended to give the downtown area the exaggerated appearance of an eccentric man-made hill. Although bigger and often representing very new attitudes to composition and ornamentation, these new buildings were out of the same tradition as their post-fire predecessors, and their effect on the urban qualities of the city was a positive one. Most of these buildings were by the same architects that designed the post-fire city and although they might work in a different stylistic mode—the Moderne (an umbrella term for a family of related decorative treatments including Art Deco, Zig Zag Moderne, and Streamlined Moderne)—they still held a belief in the importance of the relation of an individual work of architecture to the city. The Moderne was still largely based in Beaux-Arts ideas of planning, composition, ornamentation, and urbanism, although its specific ornamental references were largely from new sources.

While the boom ended with the Crash of 1929, projects in progress were completed as late as 1931. Among the most interesting and significant were Miller and Pfleuger's 450 Sutter and their Pacific Coast Stock Exchange (301 Pine). Although the impact of these buildings on the city landscape was not great either in themselves or by their influence (because they were completed at the beginning of a 15-year building hiatus) they were extremely well received both here and in other parts of the country.

The interior of the Stock Exchange Club in the Stock Exchange buildings foreshadowed work by Pfleuger and others in the San Francisco schools and WPA projects of the 1930s, but had little impact downtown. 450 Sutter was an image remembered across the United States when building resumed in earnest in the 1950s, but found few clear offspring, unless San Francisco's Bank of America Tower, and

the Pacific Mutual Building (now under construction at 505 Sansome) might be considered such.

During this period downtown San Francisco increased greatly in area, expanding down Market Street to the Embarcadero, west of Union Square to Taylor Street, and out Market to Eighth. The westward movement was largely in the growth of the apparel-shopping district, in the establishment of a district of women's clubs, and in the relocation of medical offices to the area west of Union Square. Eastward expansion was due principally to growth of the financial district. Altogether, the 1920s were a time of centralization of activities in the city which accounted for much of the growth in the downtown area.

1930s

In the 1930s, the downtown landscape was altered principally by remodeling—most of it with an unfortunately disruptive impact on the cohesiveness of the city—by architects who were otherwise out of work. By this time, the Beaux-Arts generation which had rebuilt the city after the fire was older and no longer so dominant. Younger architects who were attracted to Modern architecture didn't have the same reverence for the city. While the Moderne skyscraper, or small, terra-cotta-clad Art Deco structures such as Omar Khayyams worked quite well in the Beaux-Arts city, the plain, stuccoed, horizontal, streamlined work typified by D. D. Stone's remodeling of Bond's at Kearny and Post was totally out of place. Although there was some attempt to justify this new approach on aesthetic grounds, the most pervasive reasons were changing fashions, the desire for clean new images in the midst of a depression, and economics. The latter reason was summed up by Vincent Raney in an article in the *Architect and Engineer* on the remodeling of the Atlas Building (602–606 Mission):

> In times of depression when the building industry is at a low ebb and when property owners are too conservative to invest in new structures, arguments for modernizing old buildings have a responsive appeal, and the opportunities for the architect to develop his business loom encouragingly. If he can convince the owner how he may place his property on a paying basis, the architect is certain of a commission that will at least tide him over until bigger things develop.

Major changes downtown occurred in 1937 when both the Golden Gate and Bay Bridges opened, bringing fleets of traffic into the area every day, and signaling the end of ferry service and the functional significance of the Ferry Building. All this new traffic led to congestion, new parking garages, and a flurry of transformations of parks to landscaped roofs of underground parking garages. In the 1920s new garages had been built

which blended with the existing fabric of the city. The Financial Center Garage (351 Bush), the Palace Garage (111–127 Stevenson), and the Musto Garage (569 Post) are all good examples that managed to serve their unpleasant but necessary functions without visually disrupting the city. But in the late 1930s attitudes to design changed and new garages were not so compatible. It became profitable to tear down otherwise viable structures for parking lots and gas stations.

*Golden Gate International
Exposition, 1939.*

In 1939, in an attempt to help bring the city out of the Depression, and in celebration of the opening of the bridges, the Golden Gate International Exposition was held on Treasure Island, a man-made extension of Yerba Buena Island in the Bay. Again, Beaux-Arts architects were involved in the planning of the Exposition, including Arthur Brown, Jr., and George Kelham, but it was the technological imagery of the 1930s which characterized its architecture. The plan of the 1939 Exposition was again Beaux-Arts, and much of its architecture was as impressive in a different way as that of the Panama-Pacific International Exposition, but its influence on design in downtown San Francisco was considerably less. The 1939 Exposition took place in the middle of a great lapse in building, and the stylistic modes of its architecture were neither those of the pre-Depression nor the post-war periods. A minor spurt of remodelings between 1939 and 1941, which was stylistically inspired by the Exposition, was almost uniformly disastrous.

From the end of the 1920s boom in 1931 until 1946 there was virtually no building downtown. The new Bohemian Club (625 Taylor) was built in 1934. In 1936 the 10-story Kemper Building (417 Montgomery) was built, reputedly the first major office building in the United States since the Crash. And, in 1941, the old American Trust Building (300 Montgomery) was remodeled and enlarged by the Bank of America.

The World War II years themselves saw nothing new downtown. Thus, at the end of the war, the character of downtown San Francisco was almost exactly as it had been at the close of the building boom of the 1920s.

San Francisco skyline, 1927.

POST-WAR

1945–1963

Throughout the late 1940s and most of the 1950s, building was sluggish but steady. The period saw the last of the traditional architecture that had dominated the city in the past with such structures as Macy's addition of 1948, the large addition to the Standard Oil Building at 225 Bush in the same year, the addition to the P. G. & E. Building at Market and Beale in 1949, and the Home Insurance Building (now Fireman's Fund) at California and Kearny in 1950.

It was also architecturally a transitional period which saw the last gasps of the Moderne in such buildings as the Cahill Building at 320 California (1946), the Equitable Life Building at 120 Montgomery (1955), and the Wells Fargo Building at 464 California (1959). There were several openly Modern buildings including I. Magnin's (1947), 350 Sansome (1952), 530 Kearny (1957), 320 Market (1957), and the Occidental Life Building at 550 California (1960). The best of these was Wilbur Peugh's International Style Pacific Mutual Life Building at California and Kearny (1954). The influence of South American Modernism was evident in the IBM Building at 340 Market (1956), in the remodelings of the Chronicle (now American Savings) and David Hewes (995–997 Market) Buildings, and in the Continental Insurance Co. Building at 160 Pine (1956) and the California Union Insurance Co. Building at 244 Pine (1957), both interesting designs by Hertzka and Knowles.

The most active architects of the period were Hertzka and Knowles, and the old firm of Meyer and Evers and their successor firms, Ashley & Evers, and Ashley, Keyser, and Runge.

Although a few buildings of this period retain some interest today, and although there was not a lot of building, still, the 1950s was a time when the hard-earned cohesiveness of the downtown area began to be eroded at an accelerated pace. The new building of this period belonged largely to a new tradition which was not an outgrowth of that which preceded it, but rather marked a dramatic watershed in the development of local architecture. At the same time, however, all of these changes were accomplished within the traditional fabric of the city. Buildings were built to lot lines and although not always in scale with surroundings by virtue of scaleless facades, they were generally of traditional height, color, and massing so that whatever negative impact they had was largely limited to their immediate surroundings and not thrust on the entire neighborhood or the city at large. The worst effect was perhaps the tendency to build single-use structures without so much as a bank at the ground level to generate pedestrian activity.

As the city's architecture changed so also did other environmental features. As traffic increased, more garages were built, and buildings were torn down for parking lots, including one of the great architectural and historic monuments of the city, the Montgomery Block. The New Orpheum Theater on O'Farrell was torn down for a parking garage. Streetcar and cable-car lines were replaced by diesel buses. Civic art which had long occupied downtown intersections was moved to Golden Gate Park because some considered it to be a traffic hazard. A proposal by Mario Ciampi and the Department of City Planning in 1963, the Downtown General Plan, called for wholesale separation of vehicular and pedestrian traffic with raised plazas connected by elevated walkways over the street. Planning was begun for the Embarcadero Freeway, and for the Redevelopment projects at Yerba Buena Center and Golden Gateway (out of which would later be separately developed Golden Gateway and Embarcadero Centers). And, the Hall of Justice on Portsmouth Square was torn down by the Redevelopment Agency on a site which would later be developed with the environmentally disastrous Chinese Cultural and Trade Center and Holiday Inn. The period saw the spread

of the idea that there was something basically inadequate about the traditional city which only radical departures could rectify.

Then in 1959 and 1960 a small crop of architecturally distinguished new buildings was completed that signalled an even greater departure from the patterns of the past. The John Hancock (255 California), Bethlehem Steel (100 California), Crown Zellerbach (1 Bush), and International (601 California) Buildings were all widely admired expressions of the Corporate International Style. They were all at a scale which was compatible with the existing city, and in the case of the International and Crown Zellerbach Buildings, they introduced welcome elements of color that were theretofore largely absent. The most significant break that these buildings made with the past, however, was in the altered relationships of two of them to the city. In the case of the Bethlehem Steel Building, but much more strikingly in the case of Crown Zellerbach, for the first time in San Francisco's history, new buildings were not built to lot lines and the traditional street walls created by buildings built shoulder-to-shoulder over the previous 50-odd years were lost. While previous post-war buildings had been just as Modern, these were the first to abandon the lot lines and follow the newly stylish, anti-urban image of the tower-in-the-park which had been put forth by Le Corbusier in the 1920s and first executed in New York only in 1958 with Mies van der Rohe and Philip Johnson's Seagram Building. While these first few incarnations of that ideal may have been, as many people said at the time, ''refreshing'' in their openness and in the relief they provided from the congestion of the city, the tower-in-the-park has proved to be an unfortunate prototype as its image has multiplied all over downtown and transformed the landscape from a thoroughly vital and urban place to a sometimes disharmonious landscape of jarring juxtapositions which is no longer traditionally urban in character.

Above:
Embarcadero Freeway (1959).

Lower left:
New Orpheum Theater (1909) by Lansburgh and Joseph. Demolished ca. 1955 for a parking garage.

Below:
Aerial view of the Crown Zellerbach Building and Plaza (1959).

43

*Bank of California Tower (1966)
and the Bank of California (1906).*

1963-1975

The building lull of the early 1960s, brought on by the recession of the late 1950s was broken in 1963 by construction of the 33-story Hartford Building (636–650 California), which, for a short time until completion of the Wells Fargo Building (2–44 Montgomery) in 1966, was the tallest in the city. For a variety of reasons, the Hartford Building was the first to stir up significant public opposition, which through the rest of the decade was part of nearly every major project.

Building activity then increased to a peak around 1969-1971 and tapered off again by 1973. Along with the Hartford Building, the Wells Fargo, Mutual Benefit Life, Aetna, Bank of America, Embarcadero One, Union Bank, Transamerica, Pacific Insurance Co., Metropolitan Life, and Tishman Buildings, all brought a monumental new scale to downtown San Francisco.

As in other American cities, tall buildings no longer tapered gracefully to the sky; rather, they were set down without regard for the scale or texture of their surroundings. Functionally, they no longer responded to the complexity of conditions that a building like the Russ had handled so masterfully. They were built without awareness of their impact on pedestrian life, and they created great shadows and winds. In their frequent incorporation of "plazas," they established an entirely new urban landscape that was anti-urban in its openness and denial of the proximity of buildings and activities that gives cohesiveness and a sense of community to the city. With the Mutual Benefit Life, Union Bank, Metropolitan Life, Tishman, and the first new Standard Oil Buildings, a whole swath of lower Market and California Streets was transformed into an immense wedge of monolithic blocks set in a paved sea of streets and plazas. The urban lessons of the great Moderne buildings of the late 1920s, which provided light and air by setting back from the street but maintained the quality of the street at ground level, were ignored. The few very fine designs like the Hong Kong Bank Building (160–180 Sansome) of 1965, and the Bank of California (430–444 California), distinguished by a sensitivity to their surroundings, were the exception during these years.

Mutual Benefit Life Plaza (1969).

Apart from the aesthetic damage this period of growth did to the city, obliterating the almost organic quality of the man-made hill formed by the earlier skyline, the unprecedented scale of change created its own opposition. Noisy public campaigns opposed new highrises, succeeding to the extent that some projects were modified and others abandoned (most notably the U.S. Steel Building in 1971). The whole subject became an issue in local elections, culminating in the height limit initiatives of November 1971 and June 1972. The argument was made that there were serious social, financial, and aesthetic costs to the city incurred by the growth of highrises.

Although both initiatives were defeated, the proponents of the height limits made respectable enough showings to demonstrate sustained widespread local concern about these issues. This concern about downtown had taken a different form in the 1968 approval by the voters of the Market Street Beautification Project.

Meanwhile, throughout the 1960s the Department of City Planning and the City developed policies and implemented programs which both responded to the problems associated with highrises and helped to shape the impact they would have on the city. The entire downtown area had been uniformly zoned for commercial purposes since zoning laws were enacted in San Francisco in 1921. But there were no other controls on development until 1960 when maximum Floor Area Ratios (FARs) were established in an effort to limit the size and impact of new buildings. (The FAR is the "ratio of the floor area in each building to the land occupied by it.") Because the FARs of 1960 were so high as to be virtually meaningless, pressures from the public and the Department of City Planning led to lower FARs in 1964 and the beginning of a downtown zoning study. Completed in 1966, the downtown zoning study resulted in rezoning of the downtown into four areas, each with a different maximum FAR, and proposed the "bonus system" which was adopted in 1968. There were also provisions adopted in the same year, which have not been used extensively, for the limited transfer of development rights between adjacent properties.

With the adoption of the city-wide Urban Design Plan in 1971, downtown development was guided by many specific policies which spoke to detail, scale, proportion, texture, materials, color, and building form among other things. In addition, height and bulk controls were established. These were in force on an interim basis until adopted outright in 1972. Under these regulations maximum height limits were established in each of the four downtown zoning districts, with the highest limits in the office district where they rose from 300 feet at the edges to a maximum of 700 feet at the center. Bulk was determined by a simple formula that measured diagonal and horizontal dimensions. Maximum bulk could not exceed the average bulk of neighboring buildings. Because of the lead-time involved in most highrise developments the first building which fully conformed to these regulations downtown was the Standard Oil Building, not completed until 1974. Buildings in progress like the Metropolitan Life and Tishman Buildings were modified somewhat in light of the new regulations but were not controlled by them.

About the time these regulations were adopted the project review section was set up in the Department of City Planning, formalizing a recently implemented practice, to work with developers from the earliest stages of projects in interpreting the bonus system and the height and bulk limits, and in working for the greatest public benefit of urban design and bonus features. Similar functions were served in different areas by the involvement of the Department of City Planning staff after the environmental review system was established. Together with increased use of the long established power of discretionary review, all of these new functions meant significant growth in the influence of the Department of City Planning during this period.

A related development which has not been used extensively downtown, but could potentially have a major effect on new development, was the adoption of a landmarks ordinance and establishment of the Landmarks Preservation Advisory Board in 1967. During its stormy first years the Landmarks Board failed to recommend for designation such important endangered buildings as the Alaska Commercial Building; and others of its designations (such as the City of Paris) were overturned by the Planning Commission and the Board of Supervisors. Altogether only ten buildings have been declared landmarks downtown to date, with several others pending.

In the private sector, organizations such as the Downtown Association, the Building Owners and Managers Association, the Chamber of Commerce, SPUR, the AIA, San Francisco Tomorrow, and San Francisco Beautiful sought to influence the policies of the Department of City Planning toward growth and development. The Foundation for San Francisco's Architectural Heritage sought to supplement and assist the Landmarks Board.

Under the bonus system, a new building was restricted to a lowered FAR unless it incorporated certain previously established features, such as rapid transit or parking access, multiple building entrances, sidewalk widenings, plazas, upper-floor setbacks, and observation decks. In return for these features, considered public benefits, the building was granted an increased FAR, and could therefore be made larger. Although buildings such as the Bank of America and Aetna Life Building responded to the provisions of the bonus system, they were begun before it took effect. Among the first buildings completed under the bonus system were the Mutual Benefit Life Building (1 California) of 1969, the P. G. & E. Building (77 Beale) of 1970, and the Union Bank (50 California) and Pacific Insurance (100 Pine) Buildings of 1972.

Standard Oil Building (1975), the first building downtown which conformed to the height and bulk regulations.

Mutual Benefit Life Building (1969), one of the first buildings completed under the bonus system.

Above:
Union Trust Co. Building (ca. 1905) by Clinton Day, about 1955. Demolished ca. 1964 for the Wells Fargo Bank Building.

Upper right:
Fireman's Fund Insurance Co. Building (ca. 1909) by Lewis Hobart. Demolished ca. 1966 for Great Western Savings Tower.

Right:
Intersection of Post, Montgomery, and Market Streets, ca. 1910.

The building boom of these years was brought about by the continuing growth of the Bay Area and by the attractiveness of San Francisco as a headquarters city for major corporations. It was also fed by the promise of BART which would accommodate the residents of outlying suburbs who were expected to be employees in the highrises. BART was approved by the voters in 1962 and finally appeared toward the end of this boom in 1972. With the freeways, BART, and Redevelopment, the period was marked by huge infusions of public money. And this new public role, together with the characteristic private involvement of the period, were both at a scale previously unknown in the downtown area.

With so many new public mechanisms and private interest groups concerned with downtown development, this boom was also under many more controls than previous growth periods. Nevertheless, despite the policy of the Urban Design Plan and the influence of height controls, major new construction did not move significantly south of Market Street during this period. It got little farther than a line of very big buildings on the south side of Market Street itself at the tail end of the boom. This line is a fitting rival to the often cited example of Sixth Avenue in New York as representative in its enormity and scalelessness of the failure of architecture and planning of the period.

Despite the very real losses that occurred, in view of the amount of building that went on San Francisco was lucky to have lost as few truly significant buildings as it did. For the most part, these new buildings grew up in a ring around the heart of the old financial district, largely preserving its character, at least as viewed from the street. (From the city's hills, the Bay Bridge, or across the Bay, the old downtown was hidden by new construction.) The most serious losses of individual buildings in this period were the Fox Theater, the California Theater, the Pacific National Bank, the Mercantile Trust Building, the Liverpool and London and Globe Insurance Building, the Fireman's Fund Building, and a concentration of fine old structures at Post, Montgomery, and Market Streets. A. Page Brown's Crocker Building, a very fine Renaissance-detailed flatiron of 1892 was replaced by the Aetna Building and Crocker Plaza, and Clinton Day's Union Trust Co. Building was replaced by the Wells Fargo Tower at 44 Montgomery. Together with the Crocker Bank at 1 Montgomery, whose tower had been remodeled in 1960, the Hobart Building, and several less distinguished but important supportive neighbors, this must once have been one of the finest ensembles of commercial architecture in the United States.

In addition, the "post-Modern" stylistic treatment of many of these buildings, which is partly in response to the past insensitivity of Modern Architecture to the city, has results which are at least less offensive, even if infrequently successful to the degree they could be. More variable shapes and facade treatments characterize the majority of these buildings. Some have gone even farther in their responsiveness while at the same time achieving greater expressiveness as architecture. Buildings like the California First Bank Building (370 California), which is vaguely historicist, aware of the traditional compositional and textural qualities of its neighbors, and altogether more multi-dimensional in the levels at which it communicates, are a great advance beyond such behemoths as the Tishman Building. While Skidmore, Owings and Merrill have led the way with several interesting buildings, including the California First Bank Building and the Shaklee Building (under construction), urban and architectural disasters by other architects, like that at 180 Montgomery, with its crude detailing and clumsy and insensitive proportions, right in the heart of the financial district, are also going up.

Still, despite its more congenial nature, and the promise of a more sensitive architecture, this current boom has destroyed a number of fine buildings, most significantly the Alaska Commercial and Fitzhugh Buildings, but also including George Kelham's Balboa Building and G. Albert Lansburgh's E. F. Hutton Building. Worse, the number of significant buildings that are endangered by pro-

Above:
One Market Plaza (1976), the enclosed mall is an alternative to the previously ubiquitous plazas.

Upper left:
California First Bank (1977) by Skidmore, Owings, and Merrill.

1975 to Present

Since the recession of 1973-1975, building has resumed again at a pace not equaled since the period of recovery after the 1906 fire. At this writing there are 11 highrises under construction or recently completed and six more proposed including at least three very large buildings. This most recent boom has differed from that of the late 1960s and early 1970s, although it has continued to follow the earlier pattern that ringed the old financial district with new buildings. Up to this point most of the latest crop have been smaller and of a higher design quality. Adoption of height and bulk controls in 1972 and changing styles have meant alternative solutions to the unfortunately routine plaza concept of the recent past. Now such new ideas as the enclosed mall that links the new Southern Pacific Towers (One Market Plaza) with the old Southern Pacific Building, the pocket plaza at the new Shaklee Building (under construction at 444 Market), and the general tendency once again to build to the lot lines, are all serving to ameliorate some of the bad effects of new highrises on the old city. Federal, state, and city requirements for environmental assessment have at least brought some of the negative effects of highrise development into sharper focus, even if their effectiveness as instruments of change is questionable.

Alaska Commercial Building (1908) by Meyers and Ward. Demolished in 1975 for the California First Bank Building.

Downtown from the Ferry Building Tower, 1978.

Shaklee Building, under construction 1979.

posed projects is startling: the old Borel Bank, Sutro and Co., 1 Montgomery, the Foxcroft Building, 1 Sansome, the Holbrook Building, the City of Paris, the old Aetna Building, Breen's, a block of fine buildings on Market between Sixth and Seventh Streets and a host of lesser supportive structures. The danger which downtown San Francisco faces now is different than in the early 1970s. With so much new construction under way or proposed the question may no longer be how best to control it for the preservation of single buildings, but how to avoid the near total destruction of the traditional fabric, image, and character of the city.

As the intersection of Post, Montgomery, and Market was the greatest localized casualty of the last

boom, so the greatest loss this time promises to be Union Square. After 20 years of remodelings and new construction, the traditional character of Union Square is greatly diminished. The loss of the Fitzhugh Building and the probable loss of the City of Paris will erode this character further, to be replaced by buildings which do not respond to the demands of a great urban space.

A less specific but potentially equally disastrous development is in the enforcement of the so-called parapet ordinance which requires achoring or removal of cornices and other projecting pieces of buildings which might fall in earthquakes. The co-operation of the Department of City Planning, the Department of Public Works, the AIA, Heritage, and property owners has helped find ways to reinforce and save many of these architectural elements, but others will be lost in spite of these efforts.

On the other hand, the current boom period has seen the first preservation achievements down-town as preservation interests have become more sophisticated and as the City and the public have become more concerned. Certain features of the Urban Design Plan, and the 1976 Architectural Inventory conducted by the Department of City Planning have been two important developments in these efforts. The Jessie Street Substation (222–226 Jessie) and the Aronson Building (700 Mission) are the most visible successes of recent preservation efforts but there are many others that are less public which result from the decisions of private property owners to maintain or renovate old buildings or to reinforce parapets. The Southern Pacific Building, the St. Francis Hotel, the Fairmont Hotel, and the P. G. & E. Building, each with a new tower behind the old building, are all prominent examples of private decisions for preservation. At a smaller scale, another example is the imaginative replacement of a deteriorated terra-cotta cornice on the Royal Globe Insurance Co. (201 Sansome) with copper which will weather to blend with other features of the building.

Looking ahead, with the existing bonus system, current height and bulk restrictions, and existing market pressures, San Francisco can expect continued losses of landmark buildings and erosion of the character of its older areas unless priorities for preservation of buildings and groups of buildings can be established. New growth must be guided to sites of least potential destructiveness and greatest benefit to the city's economic vitality and architectural character. Such is the purpose of this survey.

ARCHITECTS AND EDUCATION

Education

As San Francisco's architecture underwent modernization during the period 1880 to 1930, so also did the architectural profession. In 1880 there were few professionally trained architects in San Francisco. Many of those that were here had been trained in Europe. Of those trained locally, some began by attending engineering school, but most either apprenticed with established architects, or they were builders who at a certain point declared themselves to be architects as well. Terms of apprenticeship varied so much that there was no large or consistently trained body of professional architects.

In the United States at large, architectural education was hardly any better. The first architectural school in this country had not been started until 1868 at MIT, and there was a widespread recognition that a better system of architectural education was badly needed. Then, during the last quarter of the 19th century, as increasing numbers of Americans returned from study at the Ecole des Beaux-Arts in Paris, there began to be a revolution in architectural education.

The Ecole des Beaux-Arts was a nationally supported school which offered rigorous training in architecture, painting, and sculpture. It was open to anyone, regardless of nationality, between the ages of 15 and 30. (Julia Morgan was the first woman to enter, in 1898, but women were never in very great numbers there.) The Ecole was not a school in quite the same sense as an American school. The Ecole itself was a place where lectures were given, where there was a library, and a vast collection of drawings, photographs, and models of the great architecture of the past for study. But most of the education actually took place outside the grounds and the jurisdiction of the Ecole in a number of private *ateliers*, or studios, in which large numbers of students of all ages and levels of experience worked on problems. The problems were defined by the Ecole, but were carried out under the supervision of a *patron*—himself a former student of the Ecole and usually a former Grand Prix de Rome winner. The *ateliers* were typically high spirited groups where the younger students were helped by the more experienced and where all pitched in to help an experienced student finish a major project. The camaraderie of the *atelier* was, in fact, one of the more memorable aspects of the education and one which former students often sought to re-establish in their own practices.

After passing rigorous entrance requirements, students worked up from the Second Class to the First Class, learning drawing, modeling, composition, history, construction, stereotomy, descriptive geometry, mathematics, and perspective.

If there was a single overriding goal, it was to learn "the fine art of composition." There was no prescribed pace or time limit for advancement, but it took a minimum of 16 months to get out of the Second Class. The average stay among French students was about six years, and somewhat less for Americans who had frequently already graduated from college in the United States. After 1867, diplomas were granted to those who completed certain requirements—which many students simply never bothered to fulfill until after 1887 when the diploma attained a new respectability. Even then, the diploma was less important to many students, particularly Americans, than simply having attended the Ecole and learned by its methods.

The course of study consisted of a number of assignments based on two primary types of problems. The most basic was the *esquisse*—the sketch —in which the student was given a few hours to sketch out a solution. The second type was the *projet rendu* which began with an *esquisse* that was afterwards to be transformed into finished draw-

Palace of Horticulture, P.-P.I.E. Preliminary study, ca. 1914, by Bakewell and Brown. Drawn in the manner of an esquisse.

ings over a two-month period—without altering the basic concept of the *esquisse.* The *projet rendu* took the form of plans, elevations, and sections. It was typically executed in an ink wash, often colored, and, particularly toward the end of the 19th century, of very large dimensions—up to 20 feet or more in length. The subject matter was invariably some generalized, monumental fantasy, on the order of "An Atheneum for a Capital City" or "The Principal Staircase of the House of a Sovereign." Quite apart from their educational intent, these projects were frequently very beautiful and impressive drawings that could stand on their own.

The Ecole produced students who were extremely accomplished draftsmen. Their designs were typically based in the classical architecture of Greece or Rome, or the Italian or French Renaissance. They were symmetrical in composition, based on logical, axial, and hierarchical planning, and they were intended to be expressive in elevation of the functions and organization of the interior. Very importantly, the style or character of a design was to be suitable to its purpose and its place. Buildings were often planned in groups and the effect of any one part on the whole was considered extremely important, an aspect of the training that led naturally to a concern for the role of architecture in the city.

American students went to Paris at first largely because there were so few ways to gain an architectural education in this country. When they returned they established *ateliers* on the Parisian model all over the United States. Many former Ecole students established sections within their own offices which functioned as *ateliers* for young draftsmen. Among them were the extremely important firms of H. H. Richardson and McKim, Mead, and White, both of which helped train architects who later came to San Francisco. Still others returned to establish university programs in architecture. After World War I the Ecole began educating fewer Americans as our own opportunities for architectural education improved, largely on the Beaux-Arts model. This model remained the most pervasive in the United States through the 1940s.

The first Beaux-Arts trained architect in San Francisco, or for that matter in the United States, may have been Peter Portois who arrived during the Gold-Rush period. Despite a few fine designs, his influence and that of the Ecole appear to have been quite limited locally. More important was the later and better known wave of Beaux-Arts architects beginning with Albert Pissis and Bernard Maybeck. Pissis did the first significant "Beaux-Arts" design of this period—the Hibernia Bank of 1891. Maybeck was extremely influential in the 1890s as an educator. In 1894 he started teaching a drawing class at the University of California and in the same year he offered private lessons in his home to a group which later became extremely important in San Francisco and elsewhere—John Bakewell, Edward Bennett, Arthur Brown, Jr., Harvey Wiley Corbett, Lewis Hobart, G. Albert Lansburgh, Julia Morgan, and Loring P. Rixford. All later went to Paris to study and seven of the eight returned to the Bay Area where they continued the tradition begun by Maybeck—both as architects and educators.

Maybeck was also the first Director of the Architecture Section at the Mark Hopkins Institute of Art in 1895, and in 1898 he was formally appointed Instructor of Architecture at the University of California. This department was based on the Beaux-Arts model, although it was altered to fit an American university setting. After the turn of the century, like their counterparts in other cities, returning Ecole students established *ateliers* in San Francisco, mostly under the auspices of the San Francisco Architectural Club which had been established by young architects who typically aspired to an education in Paris. Arthur Brown, Jr., and George Kelham ran two of the more prominent *ateliers.* The Architectural Club held periodic exhibitions of student work, as did the University of California Architecture Department. Later, in 1907, a local Beaux-Arts Society was established.

Thus, it is clear that by 1906 there had recently emerged in San Francisco both a structure for acquiring a Beaux-Arts-style education and a sizable body of architects who were either trained in Paris, in the eastern United States under this system, or locally. In 1900 there were five Beaux-Arts architects in San Francisco. By the time of the earthquake there were at least 13 former Ecole students in the Bay Area. Altogether there would be over 25 who established practices in San Francisco. Their influence, and that of the Ecole through others who had learned its methods, dominated the architectural scene up to the Second World War. Increasingly, after 1910, University of California graduates, with their modified Beaux-Arts training, became prominent locally. With virtually no building downtown from 1931 to 1947, it was these architects who almost exclusively built the pre-Modern downtown.

Those San Francisco architects who attended the Ecole des Beaux-Arts, their approximate dates of attendance, *atelier*, and status upon leaving, are listed below, as far as the information is known. Beaux-Arts architects from other cities who built in San Francisco but never established offices here are not listed. A few architects whose attendance seems certain but whose names have not appeared in various published lists of official Ecole students are marked with an asterisk (*). Three others who were reported to have attended but for whom the evidence is shaky are marked with a question mark (?). One explanation for these unofficial or unlisted students may be that they studied at an *atelier* connected to the Ecole without formally enrolling.

George A. Applegarth	1902-06	Laloux	diploma
John Bakewell, Jr.	1895-1900	Gaudet/Paulin	diploma
John Albert Baur	1897-1901		diploma
Edward H. Bennett	1895-1901	Gaudet/Paulin	diploma
Arthur Brown, Jr.	1897-1901	Laloux	diploma
Charles Henry Cheney	1907	Deglane	diploma
Robert D. Farquhar	1896-1901	Pascal	diploma
Edward L. Frick	1914	Laloux	
Henry H. Gutterson*	1907-10		
Chandler I. Harrison	ca. 1914		
William Charles Hays	1898	Laloux	
August G. Headman*	after 1907		
Henry Hedger	1902	Redon	
Lewis P. Hobart	1901-03	Deglane	
John Galen Howard	1891-93	Laloux	
Albert Henry Jacobs	after 1905		
George Kelham	1896	DuMonclos	
Gustave Albert Lansburgh	1901-06	Pascal	diploma
John D. Lofquist*		Paulin	
Kenneth MacDonald, Jr.*	ca. 1900-06	Pascal	
Ralph Bernard Maybeck	1882-84	Andre	
Julia Morgan	1898-1900	Chaussemiche	
Warren Charles Perry	1908-		
Albert Pissis	1872-74	Gaudet	
Peter Portois (?)	before 1849		
James Reid (?)	ca. 1847-62		
John Reid, Jr.	1906-09		diploma
Loring P. Rixford	1899-1901	Laloux	
Frank T. Shea (?)	ca. 1875-90		
Eldridge T. Spencer*	ca. 1920s		
Carl I. Warnecke*	after 1907		
Charles Peter Weeks	1893-	Laloux	
Ernest E. Wiehe	1919-		

While the tradition of the Ecole des Beaux-Arts provided the dominant influence on local architecture downtown from the turn of the century to the Second World War, it was not entirely through the Beaux-Arts system of education. Many architects established before the fire had learned by apprenticeship or in other ways, as did an increasingly smaller number of younger architects. But, regardless of training, the architects of the post-fire era, almost without exception, were united in their endorsement of the City Beautiful Movement, which was itself an outgrowth of Beaux-Arts ideas in this country. The ideals of the City Beautiful Movement (see Urban Development section) were transmitted in professional journals and the increasingly numerous and influential professional societies.

While stressing the influence of the Ecole des Beaux-Arts on San Francisco's commercial architecture, it is also important to recognize other influences. Indeed, there appears to have been some tension in the local profession between locally trained architects and those who studied in Paris or on the East Coast. This tension was embodied in the formation of the San Francisco Society of Architects in 1913, in opposition to the locally dominated San Francisco Chapter of the AIA. Among non-Beaux-Arts architects, the most significant strains of influence are perhaps best represented by two architects whose point of view helped temper the abstract intellectual quality of the French Beaux-Arts, and by another movement which found few strict adherents downtown but which nevertheless had a detectable impact.

Frederick H. Meyer was born in San Francisco, the son of a cabinetmaker. He received no formal education but learned from his father and from his work as a draftsman in a planing mill. These experiences provided him with an appreciation for fine craftsmanship and detail, and an ability to solve the practical problems of developing commercial building types. Meyer was one of the few local architects who is known to have visited Chicago and been influenced by the planning and design of skyscrapers there. After such a visit in 1902 he designed the Rialto Building with his partner Smith O'Brien, following Chicago models for flexible interior planning and for facade design which was expressive of its internal organization. The Rialto Building was an important prototype for the later work of Meyer and O'Brien and others.

Frederick H. Meyer in 1909.

As an architect who represented influences other than that of the predominant Beaux-Arts, Meyer was also typical in his wholehearted embracing of the City Beautiful Movement. He was one of three architects who oversaw planning of the Civic Center, San Francisco's purest embodiment of the City Beautiful Movement, and he was a frequent entrant in competitions for monumental civic buildings around California.

Another principal strain of non-Beaux-Arts influence is ably represented by Bernard J. S. Cahill, an Englishman who practiced architecture in San Francisco beginning in 1891, but who was most influential as a writer and critic after 1900. Cahill had been trained by apprenticeship, the traditional English manner, which typically produced more practically minded architects. By working while learning, architects were provided with a greater appreciation of functional requirements than their Beaux-Arts counterparts, the focus of whose educations was learning composition. Moreover, the English emphasized the eye-level perspective drawing of a building in its context as a means of presentation and communication of design ideas. Some observers called this a more honest means of presentation than the Beaux-Arts emphasis on plan, elevation, and section, or bird's-eye perspective without context. At any rate, it tended to produce designs that translated better into real architecture. It minimized the tendency to lose a vast symmetrical composition on a narrow street, and it tended to produce somewhat more eccentric work.

Cahill purveyed these attitudes both explicitly and implicitly in his writing. He was the editor of the short-lived but excellent *American Builder's Review* and a long-time writer for the *Architect and Engineer*. He was a proponent of what he called "provincialism" in California architecture, the idea that local architects should respond to local cultural and environmental conditions, that San Francisco architects were as good as those in the East, and that it was wrong to bring Eastern architects here or to invite them to participate in local competitions. At the same time, Cahill was a great believer in City Planning and the City Beautiful Movement, and was in fact author of several plans for the San Francisco Civic Center including the one which was actually executed.

Lastly, many architects of the period received at least some training from schools of art, arts and crafts, or industrial arts where they came into contact with the Arts and Crafts Movement. This was a local offshoot of the English Arts and Crafts Movement which had come to the United States in the late 19th century and flourished here in the work of such designers as Gustave Stickley and the Greene Brothers. Like the Ecole, the Arts and Crafts Movement stressed competence in drawing but also placed great emphasis on the quality of craftsmanship and materials, and the importance of all the arts as adjuncts of architecture.

Although typically associated only with domestic architecture, the Arts and Crafts Movement was extremely influential on a broad range of architects of the period. For that matter, many of the same architects who designed Beaux-Arts office buildings downtown did shingled Arts and Crafts

cottages as well. There is a sense in which the City Beautiful and the Arts and Crafts Movement were two sides of the same coin. The typically rustic imagery of the Arts and Crafts Movement is uncommon downtown, but the concern for materials and craftsmanship that it taught is widespread. Some of the best interior design in downtown San Francisco was by Arts and Crafts designers, notably Arthur Mathews who worked on the Mechanic's Institute, Savings Union Bank, and Bank of California, among others.

The Profession

The mid-19th-century American architect typically worked alone or with a partner and a few draftsmen. The architect knew the prevailing style of the day and very basic, universal technologies of brick and wood-frame construction. Plumbing, heating, and other auxiliary services were not so difficult that they could not be understood by the same person who did the designing, and their effect on design was minimal.

By the time of the San Francisco earthquake, however, the profession was in the throes of change. With most large new construction requiring a knowledge of steel, a sophisticated grasp of foundation engineering, at least a rudimentary knowledge of concrete, and a facility with a whole world of new mechanical systems, an architect could no longer get by so simply.

The average size of architectural offices grew tremendously. There grew to be increasing specialization within them to the point that some members ceased to design at all, but became supervisors. The principal architect himself had to become "more of an executive and less of an artist." An article in the *Architect and Engineer* on steel buildings in 1907 said that a designing firm needed an architect, civil, electrical, mechanical, structural, sanitary, and operating engineers, a purchasing agent, a construction supervisor, and an accountant. The architect himself clearly no longer had the same relationship to a finished building that he had in the past.

Just as this upheaval happened in the architectural profession, so also it happened among builders. Again, whereas a builder who knew masonry and how to build in wood could previously do almost anything asked of him, now separate, specialized fields grew up around concrete work, steel erection, and all the various aspects of modern construction. With so many unrelated specialists on a site, the process of building grew far more complicated. At first there were delays due to lack of coordination, and, immediately after the fire, a terrible lack of skilled labor in San Francisco. At the same time, with already existing trades like brick-layers who were in less demand, there were strikes and other labor problems. Out of this disorder arose the general contractor bringing relative harmony and efficiency to the building process again.

As the nature of architectural practice changed, so did the make-up of the whole profession. Beginning with the local chapter of the AIA in the 1880s and accelerating after the turn of the century, professional societies played an increasingly large role in establishing standards of the profession and in increasing business. In 1901 California was the second state to institute the licensing of architects. Between that time and 1907, the positions of State Architect and San Francisco City Architect were created, and the whole issue of public architecture was put on a more regulated, potentially less corrupt basis.

Civic Center Plan of 1899 by B. J. S. Cahill. The realistic perspective of this drawing and its practical proposal to use existing buildings (the Hibernia Bank, 7th and Mission Post Office, and old City Hall) were hallmarks of the English approach to design.

Illustration from the Pacific Coast Architect *on the occasion of a visit of a group of architects to the P-P.I.E. in 1915.*

Visiting Architects Stimulate Chapter Unity.

By SYLVAIN SCHNAITTACHER

VISITING AND LOCAL ARTHITECTS, THEIR WIVES AND FRIENDS GATHERED IN SAN FRANCISCO
Read from left to right, top row—No. 1, M. M. Bruce; 2—D. D. Kearns; 4—Austin Allen; 5—Herman Barth; 6—Edward Stoltz; 7—Walter Parker; 8—Herbert Mainzer; 9—Frederick Reese; 12—J. A. Drummond; 15—R. S. Hirschfield; 22—C. Swain; 23—Will Shea;   24 A. E. Doyle.   Seated—2—G. Page; 5—E. Garden; 6—T. J. Welsh; 7—E. J. Kraft; 8—D. C. Day; 9—Scofield; 10—Sylvain Schnaittacher; 11—Morgan; 12—Fenner; 13—Mrs. Fenner.

Above:
McCreery's Building (1876),
310 Pine, in 1888. The front of this
building appears to be cast iron.

Along with the changing nature of the profession, the position of the architect in society changed also. Prior to the widespread professionalization of American society, the architect stood out more prominently. He was part of a relatively small body of well-educated people which was relied upon in situations for which we now have separate professions. In the post-fire period, when organizations like the Bohemian and Olympic Clubs were extremely important in the city, architects were prominent members. In 1907, when a vacancy appeared on the Board of Supervisors, Loring P. Rixford was appointed to the position. Architects served on the committee for the reconstruction of the city after the fire, and on the general planning boards of the Panama-Pacific and Golden Gate International Expositions.

Architects had influence as individuals partly because they shared a common and respected attitude to questions of design. Beginning in the 1930s, as the attraction of the Modern Movement began to be felt and as artistic divisions appeared in the local profession, that influence waned.

CONSTRUCTION

Construction Prior to 1906

After 1853, when wooden buildings were banned from San Francisco's central commercial district, the basic building type in the downtown area was a two- to three-story masonry structure of brick or, occasionally, stone, with a timber-framed interior, wood floors and partitions, and an asbestos-covered wood roof. Brick walls were sometimes clad in stone and often stuccoed and scored in imitation of stone. Granite was sometimes used as a foundation material on solid ground, but natural stones were not often used for walls. Unreinforced load-bearing masonry walls were the universal structural system until the local availability of structural cast iron after 1855 increased the number of design alternatives. At first iron columns were used only in place of interior timber columns and to open up ground-floor storefronts of small commercial buildings, permitting larger glass areas for better display and lighting. Both of these building types are still in evidence in Jackson Square.

In the 1860s similarly constructed buildings with load-bearing brick walls at the side and rear were opened up on their street facades with self-supporting cast-iron fronts. These cast-iron fronts could be molded and stamped in any style desired. They had the advantage of requiring less labor to build and were therefore less expensive; and because they were structurally much less massive, they were mostly glass and admitted more light. As the downtown area became more

Upper right:
Appraisers Warehouse, built 1874,
demolished 1940 for new
Appraisers Building. An excellent
example of brick masonry
construction.

Above:
East side of Sansome between
Bush and Pine in 1870. Brick build-
ings with cast-iron ground levels.

densely built and the average building height increased to three to five stories, the problem of light in the lower floors of buildings became more acute and the value of cast-iron fronts more apparent. Short of the full cast-iron front, iron was also utilized in buildings of a more traditional facade expression in which the street facade was relieved of its structural role (which was entirely transferred to the side walls) and reduced to carrying its own weight. With the use of iron columns and beams the ground floors could be turned to glass storefronts and upper floors clad in a lighter masonry than a full load-bearing wall would require. In this manner, the facade would suggest a traditional masonry wall but in fact allowed more light with less material.

Still, up to the time of the 1906 earthquake, the predominant building method downtown was brick masonry with iron or timber interior columns. Although iron had advantages of lightness and cost over brick as a facade material, it did not perform as well in a fire, buckling and sometimes bringing buildings down with it in heat that a well-built brick wall would withstand. In the 1870s and 1880s these brick buildings rose to a fairly uniform height of three to five stories over the entire downtown area.

Apart from the question of need, the size, proximity, and configuration of buildings in this period were limited not so much by structural limitations as by the lack of adequate mechanical systems. Elevators and other systems such as electric lights, heating and air circulation, plumbing, water supply, and telephones were all less visible but essential elements in the development of relatively tall, densely packed buildings. Although no research has been done on this aspect of San Francisco's architecture, judging from the impact of the Palace Hotel (1875) it seems plausible that the Palace marked major advances in mechanical technology. Passenger elevators were probably in use prior to its composition, but not for more than a few years. Electric lights were introduced at the Palace as soon as they were available in 1877, and telephones were first used in 1880. Because no previous building in San Francisco approached it in size and complexity, its heating, ventilation, and plumbing systems were immensely more sophisticated than anything that was built before.

Among the major changes that occurred in the character of 19th-century buildings were those resulting from increased mass and density, rather

Palace Hotel (1875). It incorporated major advances in mechanical technology.

than simply construction technology or function alone. As parcels were assembled and larger buildings built on larger lots, the use of light courts either centrally or peripherally became widespread. Peripheral light courts were frequently aligned with counterparts in adjacent buildings, increasing the amount of light that a building could admit by itself.

After the Palace Hotel, the next major advance in structural and mechanical systems in 19th-century San Francisco was marked by the Chronicle Building in 1889. It was designed by the important Chicago firm of Burnham and Root, and introduced a new world of possibilities to local architects.

The Chronicle Building was the first skyscraper in the West. It was built on an iron and steel frame with self-supporting walls of sandstone and brick, and it was fireproofed in the most advanced manner then known in Chicago, by cladding the metal frame in hollow terra-cotta tile and constructing floors out of hollow-tile arches. it was equipped with passenger elevators and the necessary me-

chanical services for a tall building, including heating, ventilation, and plumbing which posed special problems that had not previously been encountered in San Francisco.

The Mills Building, completed in 1891 by the same firm, was a more up-to-date example of a modern skyscraper, entirely steel frame with self-supporting walls. It was built around a central light court, with continuous corridors on all floors that opened onto offices on each side—each suite of offices having access to a window on either the street or the light court. The clarity of the plan and the openness of the light court were widely admired and copied.

The first use of a curtain wall on a steel skeleton in San Francisco is not known for certain but may have been the City of Paris Building in 1896. At any rate it is the oldest still in existence. (The curtain wall was an important structural advance, developed in Chicago in the 1880s and still in use today. Unlike a traditional masonry wall, it carries neither its own weight nor that of a building's floors, but instead is hung from each floor of a steel or concrete skeleton, like a curtain.) The Call Building of 1898 was another early example of the type and was later singled out as the best constructed building to survive the earthquake and fire. From the first use of the steel frame until the time of the earthquake in 1906, the steel frame underwent minor structural refinements for better wind bracing, but these refinements were based on conditions encountered in places like New York and Chicago, and did not specifically take into account the possibility of earthquakes. Just before the earthquake,

the Humboldt Bank Building and the Whittell Building were braced with lattice girders, a method which allowed greater use of glass at the corners of buildings by alleviating the need to cover diagonal corner bracing with masonry.

Also with the Whittell Building came the first use of pneumatic tools. As buildings got bigger and building technology more complicated, and as average financing and building costs rose to previously unheard of levels, speed of construction became a prime consideration. Construction equipment and tools were essential elements in rapid construction, and advances in these areas were as important in the development of modern buildings as the more visible features of the finished products. A related development was the standardization of the production of steel and other building products, resulting in materials of reliable strength and predictably regular sizes and shapes.

Another equally important factor in the speed of construction was labor and the way it was organized. The period just before and after the earthquake was a time of readjustment in the local labor force. Old unions resisted new technologies and laborsaving devices. And, with the vastly increased scale and complexity of new projects, there was costly and time-wasting disorder in the coordination of diverse trades. This disorder was largely resolved in 1912 when the Sharon Building on New Montgomery was constructed under a general contractor who was responsible for coordination of all the workers on the project.

n the few years before the earthquake, the typical modern "fireproof" building was a steel-frame structure with brick curtain walls clad in stone or trimmed in stone or terra cotta. The favored stone was a gray sandstone from Colusa, California. The steel in most of these buildings was protected with a cladding of hollow-tile blocks, or, sometimes, of wire lath and plaster. Floors were hollow tile and partitions were hollow tile or lath and plaster. Ceilings were suspended lath and plaster.

The best constructed of the pre-earthquake buildings had reinforced-concrete floors and their steel skeletons were clad in brick or concrete. The whole question of fireproofing, long a major concern, gained considerable urgency following a destructive fire in Baltimore's business district in 1904.

Despite claims to the contrary, however, there really were no "fireproof" buildings in San Francisco, as the earthquake and fire amply demonstrated. There were, as there are today, only more or less fire-resistant buildings. The earthquake itself did relatively little damage to structures; it resulted in universal bracing of steel-frame buildings against earthquakes and favoring of certain types of foundations, important but not revolutionary developments. On the other hand, the terribly destructive fire had two very great and far-reaching effects on construction in downtown San Francisco and elsewhere: the virtual abandonment of stone as an exterior building material in favor of terra cotta; and the enthusiastic adoption of reinforced concrete, both for fireproofing and for cladding of entire buildings. Natural stone had spalled badly in the intense heat of the fire, whereas terra cotta performed much better as an exterior material. Reinforced concrete, when it was of good quality, was thought to be an excellent material against the dual menace of earthquake and fire. The fire also sparked some very far-sighted, but seemingly fantastic proposals for steel-frame skyscrapers to be sheathed entirely in wire glass, as proposed by a Boston architect, and steel plates in the case of the Whittell Building. But these ideas were lost in the rush to rebuild both safely and conservatively.

REINFORCED CONCRETE AFTER 1906

Concrete had been known to the Romans, but had been forgotten and only rediscovered in the early 19th century. The discovery that concrete could be reinforced with iron or steel and transformed into a single structural material which had the advantages of each of its constituents occurred in France in 1849. The first reinforced-concrete building was the Arctic Oil Works (now demolished) of 1888 in San Francisco, by Ernest L. Ransome.

Reinforced concrete was used here in early work on the sea wall, in the foundations of the Ferry Building, in the Alvord Bridge in Golden Gate Park and in scattered other industrial and utilitarian structures.

Many scattered reinforced-concrete buildings had appeared around the United States and Europe, and it had begun to be used in bridges, dams, and other works of engineering, but nowhere in the world was it accepted as an everyday building material until after the 1906 fire. Even where its technology was known and its constituent elements were available, its use was retarded by superstition, conservative building laws, and bricklayers' unions.

At the time of the fire, apart from its use as fireproofing and for floors in big buildings, reinforced concrete was used structurally in downtown San Francisco in two places: it formed part of the interior structure of an annex at the rear of the Academy of Sciences Building on Market Street, and it was being used in a new Bekin's warehouse at 13th and Mission streets which was under construction at the time. While both structures survived, the Bekin's warehouse provided a particularly striking display of the value of reinforced concrete in a fire, remaining unharmed in an area that was otherwise totally destroyed and had been judged to be one of the hottest areas of the fire. Although very little used, reinforced concrete was the subject of major articles and much debate in the local architectural press in the months before the fire.

In its early years, concrete was rarely left exposed and never expressed as concrete. There were, instead, elaborate efforts to make concrete look like masonry. Traditional ornamentation was sometimes precast or poured-in-place, and walls were stuccoed with a cement finish. More commonly, however, a concrete structure was clad in brick or terra cotta, resulting in buildings that were visually indistinguishable from steel-frame or masonry structures. Another frequent combination of these methods involved the use of concrete curtain walls on steel-frame buildings and a brick or terra-cotta veneer.

Reinforced concrete enjoyed great popularity in San Francisco from the few years after the fire to the early 1920s. It was used to a lesser extent up to the 1950s but, except in the case of parking garages and small buildings outside the downtown area, not much after that time. Labor costs, the weight of concrete, and earthquake-influenced building codes have made it too expensive, in most cases, to build large buildings of reinforced concrete in San Francisco today.

TERRA COTTA AFTER 1906

Like concrete, terra cotta had been known for centuries, but had only recently been revived as an architectural building material. It had been widely used in Chicago as a fireproofing and decorative material since the fire there in 1871, and it had first been brought to prominence in San Francisco by Chicago architects with the Mills Building in 1891. Its first use as an exclusive material for exterior facing of a large building was on the Reliance Building in Chicago in 1895, but outside of Chicago it was never commonly used as an exterior cladding until after 1906. Detroit's Majestic Building of 1896, New York's Bayard Building of 1897-98, Philadelphia's Bellevue-Stratford Hotel of 1902, and San Francisco's Bullock and Jones Building of 1902 (remodeled in 1907 for the French Bank), were a few of the scattered examples around the country before the San Francisco earthquake and fire. As in the case of reinforced concrete, the use of terra cotta was the subject of articles in every issue of the *Architect and Engineer* in the months before the fire, but it was still little used as an exterior cladding. Then after the fire it suddenly came into common use, immediately replacing stone as the favored material for important buildings. One of the most striking examples of its new popularity was its use on the Head Building of 1909 by William Curlett, across the street from the sandstone-clad Shreve Building of 1905, also by Curlett.

Thus, after the fire there was immediately a great deal of reinforced-concrete construction of whole buildings, and vastly increased use of it in fireproofing, floor slabs, curtain walls, and foundations. An article in the June 1907 *Architect and Engineer* stated "It is safe to say that there never before has been near as much work of this character going on in any one city at one time." The article listed 78 reinforced-concrete buildings which were constructued in the burned district in the first year, including such major structures as the Sheldon Building, the Pacific Building, the West Building, and the MacDonough Building. Interestingly, these buildings were said to be predominantly by little known architects and built for small landowners.

It was a number of years before the technology of reinforced concrete was very well understood. In the meantime many buildings were constructed with wholly inadequate amounts of reinforcing material or of reinforcing material that was not efficiently designed, while others were built with far more reinforcing than was needed, to the extent that the reinforcing steel almost became structural steel cast in concrete. For fireproofing it became common to completely encase structural steel in concrete, which some people erroneously referred to as reinforced-concrete construction. In the few years after 1906 there were several well-publicized failures of reinforced concrete, although none of them were in San Francisco.

Terra cotta was actively promoted by manufacturers and manufacturers' associations in the period after the fire. It was said to be better in a fire than stone, it was lighter than stone and resulted in savings in structural steel and more rentable floor space, it was very quickly attached to a building, it was easily cleaned, and it could be made to look like anything—including the stone it replaced.

The use of terra cotta reached its peak in the 1920s when such giants as the Pacific Telephone Building, the Russ Building, the Hunter-Dulin Building, and the Shell Building were entirely clad in it. After the 1930s its use declined to the point where it has been almost entirely replaced by aluminum and precast concrete. For a brief period around 1960, enameled metal panels, such as are still commonly used for gas station walls, were in vogue. By the 1960s terra cotta was distinctly less economical than other materials; laborsaving advances in its production and design have resulted in a small resurgence in its use but are unlikely to make it competitive in the long run. The Standard Oil Building of 1975 is a recent major example of a terra-cotta clad highrise, with a terra-cotta veneer attached to lightweight concrete backing.

STEEL FRAME

The steel frame, developed in Chicago in the 1880s, has been refined but little changed in principle since that time. The typical steel-frame building of the immediate post-fire period in San Francisco was thus essentially the same as a steel-frame building today. While bracing methods are different now, and consequently buildings are more earthquake resistant and can go higher, they are still rectangular cages of steel columns and beams on which are hung curtain walls. The development of field welding and the rigid frame in the 1950s have replaced all previous forms of bracing. Floors, then and now, are reinforced-concrete slabs. Steel is typically fireproofed now with gypsum cement rather than encased in concrete, but the principle is the same.

The major differences between the earliest steel-frame buildings and those of the present are in the size of buildings, the tremendous advances made in mechanical systems, the production of steel, and exterior cladding materials. Buildings today are less likely to be clad in stone, terra cotta or brick and much more likely to have skins of aluminum, glass, or some form of precast concrete. The Bank of America is an exception with its Carnelian-granite exterior. The new Hibernia Bank Building (under construction) will be the first building in many years to be clad in brick. The usually high quality of precast concrete in the San Francisco area, such as in the California First Bank and other recent Skidmore, Owings, and Merrill office buildings, is a local phenomenon, apparently due to the availability of materials and the survival of an industry which did plaster work in the 1920s and has been able to translate its techniques into the production of precast concrete.

Left:
Steel frame of the Financial Center Building under construction in 1926.

Far left:
Mills Building (1891). Detail of terra cotta ornamentation. The earliest prominent use of ornamental terra cotta in San Francisco.

MECHANICAL AND ORGANIZATIONAL ADVANCES
SINCE 1906

In the period after the fire there were well-developed, reasonably efficient, and widely available mechanical systems which were universally used in the rebuilding of the city. These systems were partly powered by electrical and steam sub-stations of the Pacific Gas & Electric Co. However, many buildings had their own generators and steam plants, and some sold excess electricity to nearby buildings. Every large building required a basement to house mechanical equipment including generators, boilers, blowers, and elevator motors.

Water was delivered in public water mains but was stored in roof-top tanks to maintain consistent pressure throughout each building. Whereas the fire greatly accelerated the universal acceptance of electricity for lighting, there were still gaslit buildings downtown in the years after 1906.

As before the fire, there was a continuing tendency to assemble parcels into larger lots for larger buildings. Up to the First World War, most buildings continued to have light wells as before, so that apparently more massive buildings were still broken up inside. By the 1920s, however, still larger buildings with improved ventilation and other mechanical features that permitted greater floor areas were commonly built with wings to the rear and sometimes simply as uninterrupted masses.

In 1927, the Russ Building was a prominent example of the former plan, and the Shell Building of the latter. The increasing height of buildings such as the Russ also required intermediate mechanical floors to achieve maximum efficiency of duct size, water pressure, and other mechanical services. By the 1930s long-available high-speed elevator equipment which operated from the roof rather than the basement was universally used.

After World War II, the shapes of buildings were entirely freed from the need to admit natural light and air by advances in lighting, heating, air-conditioning, and ventilation technology. Not since the 1950s has a major building been constructed in downtown San Francisco with windows that would open. (The Pacific Mutual Building, now under construction, will have openable windows.) Today, modern highrise buildings are totally removed from reliance on daylight or climate in maintaining working conditions.

Hobart Building, under construction in 1914. Its short building time was called "a practical demonstration of the value of a preconceived scheme of construction."

OTHER BUILDING METHODS SINCE 1906

Despite the lessons of the fire, the urgency of rebuilding resulted in large-scale duplication of pre-fire building methods. While steel and reinforced concrete were the overwhelmingly predominant structural materials for large or otherwise important buildings, most small buildings were still being constructed as they had been since Gold-Rush times. Most of these small buildings, ranging up to about six stories, were of brick-masonry construction with iron or wood interior columns and front facades of glass set in iron frames. These iron frames were either exposed or, more commonly, clad in brick or terra cotta. The major difference in this later generation of iron-front buildings seems to have resulted from advances in the production of plate glass, which could make much bigger sheets than in the 1860s. A large sheet of glass, roughly seven feet square, which was common in the years 1905-1912 and resulted in a characteristically open grid of big windows, particularly in the retail area, may have been the largest commonly available size in this region.

By the First World War, everything downtown was being built in steel or reinforced concrete and these small brick buildings were no longer built.

ARCHITECTURAL CLASSIFICATIONS
System developed by Richard W. Longstreth

In the last 15 years, traditional stylistic terminology in architecture has been called into question by the work of cultural geographers and scholars in related fields, including Henry Glassie, Pierce Lewis, Fred Kniffen, James Deetz, and others. Terms like Greek Revival, Gothic Revival, Italianate, Eastlake, and Queen Anne have been shown to be insufficient in discussing common houses (and by implication, other building types) whose most important characteristics are typically associated with plan, local building methods and materials, massing, composition of elements, and other features which can be clothed in a variety of historicist wrappings. These non-historicist features often develop local or regional characteristics which persist through several "stylistic" periods. Thus, the same house type in a particular locality might be Gothic, Eastlake, or Queen Anne, depending on the year it was built.

Despite the obvious opportunities for application of these insights in an age of increasing nationwide interest in historic preservation and ordinary architecture, and the development of techniques for their use, they have not yet been widely brought to bear on historic preservation surveys.

The last 15 years have also seen a vastly increased interest in the subject matter of this inventory: the academic, eclectic, non-Modern commercial architecture of the 20th century. Like the ordinary architecture of houses, this architecture has generally continued to be discussed in traditional stylistic terms, but not very successfully. (Winston Weisman has written "A New View of Skyscraper History" in *The Rise of an American Architecture*, pointing a way out, but it is restricted to skyscrapers.) It is simply not very useful or revealing to refer to the Hallidie Building, for example, as being Gothic Revival, or to the Palace Hotel as Second (or later) Renaissance Revival, or to any of the buildings of the period with all their variations as Commercial Style. Moreover, with the birth of the skyscraper and the development of new technologies for new building types, together with the influence of the Ecole des Beaux-Arts, traditional stylistic terminology is simply inaccurate, given the use of those terms in the past. Rather than "revivals," the use of historicist imagery on the commercial buildings of turn-of-the-century San Francisco was eclectic in derivation and composition, and it was thought of not as an attempt to recreate the past but as modern in inspiration and execution.

As in the case of the cultural geographers who have worked primarily with houses, it seems far more effective to derive a terminology for 20th-century academic architecture by a descriptive method—by working with the characteristics of the architecture in question, whatever they may be, rather than applying old terms that arose more properly to describe older architectures.

In the system used here, an attempt has been made to devise a way of talking about downtown San Francisco's architecture which is derived from the buildings themselves. The emphasis in the system is on facade composition, because under the influence of the Ecole des Beaux-Arts, the architects who built downtown San Francisco were taught composition first and foremost as an approach to design.

The benefits of this system would seem to be in the accurate synopses of the characteristics of buildings which can be grouped and compared. The drawbacks appear to be in the nature of a complex set of building types which, to be described accurately, must be described in more than a few words. While useful for scholars, this produces difficulties in its full form, in the context of an inventory which will be used by the general public, in not providing a single term of reference.

The full system as it was developed is described in an appendix to this volume. However, because of the purposes of this inventory and its principal intended audience, the full system does not appear in the text of the inventory, but rather its most salient aspects are extracted for each building, notably, in every case, the compositional format. The fully worked out description for each building is in the files of the survey. Examples are at the end of the appendix.

Primary Areas

Each entry in the primary areas is keyed to a map at the beginning of its area (Map I, Map II, Map III, Map IV).

Buildings listed in the National Register of Historic Places and as City Landmarks are indicated as follows:

NR   National Register
NRp National Register listing pending
NRD within a National Register District
NRDp National Register District listing pending
CL   City Landmark

Hale Brothers Department Store, ca. 1915.

Market Street District

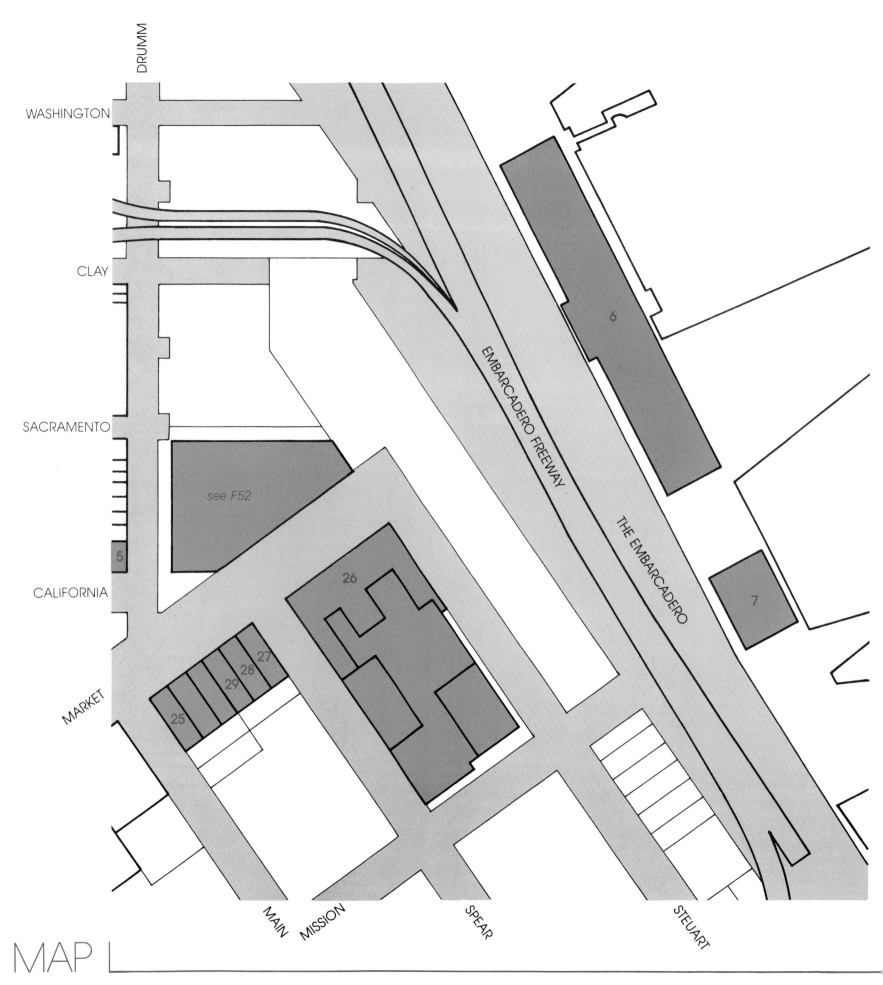

WASHINGTON

DRUMM

CLAY

SACRAMENTO

see F52

5

CALIFORNIA

MARKET

25

29

28

27

26

6

7

EMBARCADERO FREEWAY

THE EMBARCADERO

MAIN

MISSION

SPEAR

STEUART

MAP L

MAP II

67

MAP IIL

MAP IV

69

MAP V

HYDE

LEAVENWORTH

JONES

TAYLOR

GOLDEN GATE

McALLISTER

FULTON

MARKET

EIGHTH

MISSION

SEVENTH

12

96

102

24

110

97

98

100

103

101

99

113

105

104

106

107

108

109

111

112

208

476

114

115

116

118

117

MAP VI

71

M1 MAP II
22 Battery Street
NE corner Bush at Market
Postal Telegraph Building
Lewis Hobart
1908

Built for the Postal Telegraph and Cable Co., this is one of several post-fire structures for the Crocker Estate by Lewis Hobart. The building is highly visible from Market Street, and since the demolition of the Imperial Building, is the last in the very fine group of major buildings on Bush Street. In composition, a three part vertical block with a stacked shaft and Renaissance/ Baroque ornamentation. A broad projecting cornice was removed when the top story was added. The ground level has been remodeled in a manner sympathetic to the rest of the building. Steel frame construction.

A

M2 MAP II
77 Beale Street
SE corner Market
Pacific Gas & Electric Co.
Bakewell and Brown
1925

A major downtown landmark by virtue of its design, its location, and its history. Built for the Pacific Gas & Electric Company, it was enlarged in the style of the original by Frick, Weihe, and Kruse in 1949, and was connected to a modern highrise tower by Hertzka and Knowles in 1971. The building forms an imposing pair on Market Street with the old Matson Building next door, which terminates the view down Pine Street. In composition, the building is a three part vertical block with an attic story and a giant order in the upper zone. The giant order is surmounted by freestanding urns above the entablature. Other notable details include symbolic references to P. G. & E. in the sculptural group over the entrance by Edgar Walter and ram's head keystone masks over the ground level arcade. The deep foundation and advanced mechanical features of the steel frame, terra cotta clad structure were the subject of an article in the *Architect and Engineer* in 1925.

A

M3 MAP II
1 Bush Street
at Market
Crown Zellerbach Building
Hertzka and Knowles; Skidmore, Owings, and Merrill
1959

One of several high style designs of the late 1950s and early 1960s built in downtown San Francisco. This one recalls Lever House in New York by the New York office of Skidmore, Owings, and Merrill in its coloring, wall treatment and massing of the slab. This was the first San Francisco building to be built in a plaza, abandoning the time honored urban tradition of building to the lot lines.

NOT RATED

M4 MAP II
1 California Street
at Market
Mutual Benefit Life Building
Welton Becket and Associates
1969

The heart of San Francisco's version of the new downtown American urban landscape, characterized by towers rising from the center of windy paved lots euphemistically referred to as plazas.

NOT RATED

M5 MAP I
16 California Street
NW corner Drumm
St. Clair Building
Nathaniel Blaisdell
1908

A three part vertical block with differentiated end bays and Renaissance/Baroque ornamentation. The cornice has been removed. A good example of the simultaneous interest at the time in progressive technologies and traditional stylistic images. A reinforced concrete office building on a concrete foundation, the beams and girders reinforced with the unit truss, a type of prefabricated reinforcement which is placed directly in concrete forms. The unit truss was designed for rapid and uniform placement of reinforcing. Ornamentation on this building is poured-in-place concrete. Walls are 17 inches thick with hollow cores, designed "to achieve a massive appearance." An important corner anchor to the last older group of buildings in this area.

C

Interior before remodeling.

M6 MAP I
The Embarcadero
foot of Market Street
Ferry Building
originally Union Depot and Ferry House
A. Page Brown
1895-1903

A long-time symbol of the city, built as the Union Depot and Ferry House, a ferry terminal which also held state offices. Now rudely walled off by a freeway. Designed by one of the city's most important pre-fire architects, few of whose major works survive. The supervising architect was Edward R. Swain who completed the project after Brown's death. Once the transportation hub of the city, where 170 ferry boats a day brought commuters and transcontinental railroad passengers to the foot of Market Street and where the city's streetcar lines ended. Use declined when the San Francisco-Oakland Bay Bridge opened rail lines on the lower level in 1939. After ferry service ended in 1958, the building was completely remodeled inside and at the rear and some of its windows were altered on the main facade. The skylit galleries that ran the length of the building were floored-in to create more office space.

Although built over mud and water, the building withstood the earthquake of 1906 with damage only to the tower, due to its foundation of concrete pilings. The foundation represented a pioneering use of reinforced concrete many years before it began to be widely used. The tower, which like the rest of the building was steel frame with self-supporting sandstone walls, was strengthened after the fire and reclad in reinforced concrete painted to match the sandstone base. The structure was also one of the first steel frame buildings in the city. The

design of the building with its long arcaded base recalls Shepley, Rutan, and Coolidge's South Boston Station; its central tower is modeled after the Giralda Tower of the Cathedral of Seville. The ornamentation of the base is derived from Roman sources. In composition, a pavilion with flanking wings. The Port Commission is now seeking a developer to rehabilitate the structure and restore its usage to a more lively and appropriate character for one of the city's major landmarks.

A NR; CL

M7 MAP I
The Embarcadero
foot of Mission Street
Agriculture Building
originally U.S. Post Office
A.A. Pyle, State Department of Engineering
1914

Built as a U.S. Post Office but long known as the Agriculture Building following its transfer to the U.S. Department of Agriculture about 1930. In the years after the building opened, 98% of the city's mail passed through it. Designed by the State Department of Engineering because it fell under the jurisdiction of the State Board of Harbor Commissioners. In composition, a modified palazzo with Renaissance ornamentation. The building is an excellent example of its type, and particularly notable for its detailing. Dark red brick laid up in Flemish bond with light mortar is set off by artificial stone piers and entrance surrounds made of ochre colored cement. Patterned brick work around windows and in second tier panels is unusually well done. The dark brick with its light pointing, ochre piers and courses, copper cornice, and red tiled hip roof, exhibit a sensitive use of color. Steel frame construction built on the reinforced concrete bulkhead wharf.

A NR

M8 MAP II
45 Fremont Street
Skidmore, Owings, and Merrill
1976

A good example of the 1970s interest in a building's skin, as opposed to the earlier interest of modern architecture in structure.

NOT RATED

M9 MAP II
50-60 Fremont Street
architect unknown
1907

A rare survivor of a 19th-century type in a two part vertical composition with Renaissance/ Baroque ornamentation. Segmental arched windows and a central gabled parapet recall the commercial Italianate style once common in San Francisco and other California cities. Remarkable also for its intact cast iron ground floor storefront. Once occupied by the Yawman Erbe Manufacturing Co., now evidently vacant and ripe for an imaginative reuse project. Brick construction with iron posts on the ground floor and wood posts above.

B

M10 MAP IV
2 Geary Street
NW corner Kearny at Market
architect unknown
1908

A small but important building at what was, for a long time, the prime intersection in the city. Recently refurbished by Robert Hagman and Associates for Fidelity Savings. At the time of the remodeling a "spite wall" was removed from the rear of the property, exposing windows in the adjacent L-shaped structure at 10–12 Geary. A two part vertical block with skeletal articulation and Renaissance/Baroque ornamental references. Steel frame construction.

B

M11 MAP IV
10-12 Geary Street
Schmidt Building
architect unknown
1908

An L-shaped building in a prominent location that wraps around a small corner building and actually has a wider frontage on Kearny Street. This building and its corner neighbor together provide as graphic an illustration as any of the effect of lot lines and property values on the historic shape of San Francisco architecture. If the corner building filled the L, the visual impression would be of two separate narrow buildings of different widths. As it is, the building demonstrates the reality of so many older structures which consist of a thin veneer of "architecture" applied to a building squeezed into an irregular lot. Although Modern architects characteristically criticized this practice, its success in creating an urban architecture is unmatched since the advent of the Modern Movement. In composition, a three part vertical block with Renaissance/Baroque ornamentation. Reinforced concrete construction.

B

M12 MAP VI
42 Golden Gate Avenue
NW corner Taylor at Market
Golden Gate Theater
G. Albert Lansburgh
1922

A fine example of a theater building designed to take advantage of its location at a major Market Street intersection. Its two major facades meet at an angled corner surmounted by a profusely ornamented dome which culminates in a flag pole on a base of fish. The domed corner is the focal point of the intersection. The building is a three part vertical composition with arcaded, terra cotta clad base and capital sections setting off a brick shaft. A diagonal string of balconied windows distinguishes the Golden Gate Avenue facade. Ornamentation is predominantly Renaissance/Baroque in derivation but also draws on Moorish and Spanish Colonial Revival models. The interior has been divided into three theaters and remodeled. Steel frame construction.

A

M13 MAP IV
1 Grant Avenue
NW corner O'Farrell at Market
Security Pacific National Bank
originally Savings Union Bank
Bliss and Faville
1910

Originally the Savings Union Bank of San Francisco. An example of what the *Architect and Engineer* called the first period of Bliss and Faville's work, characterized by an "enthusiasm for the antique" and an interest in the work of McKim, Mead, and White, in whose office both architects had apprenticed. Its greatest importance lies in its function, together with the Wells Fargo Bank across the street (M66), as a gateway to Grant Avenue, and together with the flat-iron Phelan Building (M67) and other immediate neighbors, as part of a splendid group of contemporary designs. This gateway to Grant Avenue is altogether, perhaps, the best of the remaining older Market Street intersections, and a suitably grand entrance to a street which comes closer than any other to embodying the ideals of the City Beautiful Movement. In composition, the building is a modified temple derived from the Roman Pantheon. Its steel frame is clad in granite and surmounted by a reinforced concrete dome. The main Grant Avenue facade is formed by a pedimented Ionic temple front with a bas relief of Liberty by Haig Patigian. The bronze doors representing "the historical succession of races in the State" and the interior furnishings are by Arthur Mathews.

A

M14 MAP V
1 Hallidie Plaza
SW corner Eddy and North Fifth
Skidmore, Owings, and Merrill
1973

NOT RATED

M15 MAP III
631 Howard Street
foot of New Montgomery
William Volker Building
George Kelham
1929

A handsomely detailed industrial loft structure located at the important terminus of New Montgomery Street. A two part vertical composition with Art Deco detailing. Reinforced concrete construction.

C

M16 MAP II
16-30 Jessie Street
NE corner Ecker
One Ecker
original architect unknown
1906

A handsome brick warehouse building, renovated in 1972 by Arthur Gensler and Associates. The steel X-bracing of the renovation is visible through upper level windows, and at the opened-up ground level. Part of a group of massive industrial structures on a network of narrow mid-block alleys. Brick construction with iron posts.

B

M17 MAP II
40-48 Jessie Street
NW corner Ecker
architect unknown
1913

A reinforced concrete industrial warehouse.

C

M18 MAP III
57 Jessie Street
Thomas Davis
1929

A remarkable survival of a metal diner built on this site in 1929 and still serving lunch. The designer was Thomas Davis, a man who built and sold similar structures up and down the coast from San Francisco. Another of his diners survives as part of a larger restaurant called the Grubstake at 1525 Pine Street. The building was reputedly placed on a lot which had been "lost" until a claim was filed and the deed taken by the first owner of this diner.

C

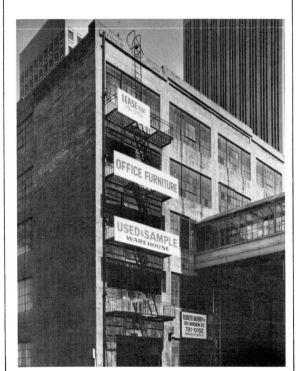

M19 MAP III
64 Jessie Street
architect unknown
1924

A very handsome reinforced concrete industrial warehouse with skeletal articulation of the Jessie Street facade and well-proportioned openings glazed in industrial sash.

B

M20 MAP III
96 Jessie Street
NE corner Anthony
architect unknown
1909

A steel frame warehouse clad in brick, in a two part vertical composition. Ornamentation makes vague reference to Renaissance sources in the corbeled courses.

C

M21 MAP IV
163-165 Jessie Street
SW corner Annie
Hess Building
C.A. Meussdorffer
1912

A reinforced concrete loft building in a two part vertical composition with skeletal articulation and Renaissance/Baroque ornamental references. Unusual fenestration, flush with the wall and pulled away from the center. Originally built for the California Demokrat.

C

M22 MAP IV
167-179 Jessie Street
Hotel Jessie
architect unknown
1912

A handsome facade on a reinforced concrete hotel bulding in a three part vertical composition with differentiated end bays. Ornamentation is Renaissance/Baroque. Threatened by Yerba Buena Center.

C   NRp

M23 MAP IV
222-226 Jessie Street
Yerba Buena Center
Pacific Gas & Electric Co., Station C
Jessie St. Substation
Willis Polk
1905, 1907, 1909

The finest and the first of a number of designs by Polk for P. G. & E. substations in northern California. These widely publicized designs served as prototypes for work by other architects for the same company. Such "beautification" of industrial structures was an aspect of the City Beautiful Movement. The design of this building was a 1905 remodel of an 1881 structure which burned in February 1906 and again in April of 1906. It was rebuilt in 1907 and enlarged in 1909. The building is a steel frame and reinforced concrete structure with a steel truss roof. Its main brick facade is a modified vault in composition, with Renaissance/Baroque ornamentation in cream colored, matte glazed terra cotta. Its finest feature is a sculptural group over the smaller of two main entrances consisting of four cherubs with gourds and garlands of fruit beneath a torch. The facade sets up a tension between carefully wrought, sometimes delicate terra cotta ornament and a vast wall of rough red industrial brick. Until demolition of adjacent structures for Yerba Buena Center in recent years, this grand facade was hidden on a blind alley in the middle of a block of taller buildings. This building was initially slated for demolition, as well, but now figures prominently in plans for revitalization of the area.

A   NR; CL

Left: Pacific Gas & Electric Co., Station C. Entrance detail.

M24 MAP VI
1 Jones Street
NW corner McAllister at Market
Hibernia Bank
Albert Pissis
1892, 1905, 1907

The oldest and one of the finest of San Francisco's uniquely superb collection of modified temple form banks. Also one of the best designs for the numerous irregular Market Street intersections. Built as a narrower structure along Jones in 1892; the building was enlarged to its present size in 1905 and was rebuilt after the fire. It is the earliest surviving building in the city in the strictly classical idiom, a style that did not sweep the country until after the Chicago World's Fair held the year after this bank was completed. The building was widely admired among local architects of the day. In composition, it is a hybrid of a modified temple form and a variety of Baroque elements, notably the domed entrance corner and the fine entrance stairway. Its steel frame is clad in carved granite. Its interior is a richly detailed space dominated by a large stained glass dome. The building occupies its Market Street corner with unusual control. Its columned sides present rich textures to the street. The copper crowned entrance dome provides a focal point which is simultaneously the most massive part of the building and a 2-story open entranceway.

A

M25 MAP I
9-23 Main Street
SE corner Market
Bay Building
architect unknown
1909

A three part vertical block, skeletal in articulation with Renaissance/Baroque ornamentation.

C

M26 MAP I
1 Market Street
Southern Pacific Building
Bliss and Faville
1916

A major Market Street landmark, long prominent as the first large building visible to Bay commuters leaving the Ferry Building, located at the end of the important view down California Street. Also one of the earliest major corporate headquarters buildings in the city. In composition, a three part vertical block with differentiated end bays and Renaissance/Baroque ornamentation. A steel frame building with brick curtain walls and glazed terra cotta details concentrated in the arcaded base and the giant order beneath the cornice. The building is crowned with a small tower, following the example of the Merchants Exchange Building. The interior was designed with wide corridors for the noon hour rush, and flexible partitions for changing work patterns.

Rather than demolish its fine old building for a new one, in 1976 the Southern Pacific Company (with the Del Monte Corporation) completed a pair of towers at the rear of the block. They are designed by Welton Becket and Associates, called One Market Plaza and are connected to the old building by a glazed mall. Although not so successful as architecture, the planning of the project included the consideration of urban values and has resulted in a complex which is more beneficial to the city than most recent Market Street office developments. Rather than another empty plaza, the complex includes a more realistic generator of pedestrian activity in its mall, and at the scale of the city, its pair of towers are among the most attractive of the existing recent crop south of Market on the skyline.

A

M27 MAP I
101-105 Market Street
SW corner Spear
Young Building
later Aetna, now Seaboard Building
Kenitzer and Barth
ca. 1902, rebuilt 1906

A 1902 building which was widely admired for its survival of the earthquake. Damage was largely confined to the brick walls, while the foundation, innovative concrete floor design, and steel frame were unharmed. Designed by a firm, both of whose members were important pre-fire era designers. Only a few of Herman Barth's once numerous downtown designs survive. Although essentially a two part vertical block, the composition here is more complex than most, with a successful integration of larger and smaller orders. Rich terra cotta ornamentation, particularly in the spandrels, pier capitals, and in the frieze, is derived from Renaissance/Baroque sources. Site of the proposed Federal Reserve Bank.

B

M28 MAP I
115-121 Market Street
Lincoln Hotel
architect unknown
1913

A steel frame residential hotel in a variation of a three part vertical composition. Modified Renaissance/Baroque ornamentation. Site of the proposed Federal Reserve Bank.

C

M29 MAP I
125-131 Market Street
architect unknown
1911

A two part small commercial block with skeletal articulation of the facade and Renaissance/Baroque ornamentation. Brick construction. Site of the proposed Federal Reserve Bank.

C

M30 MAP II
215 Market Street
SW corner Main
Matson Building
later Pacific National Life Assurance Co.
  Building
Bliss and Faville
1921

Part of a very fine pair with the old P. G. & E. Building (M2) which forms an important part of the now interrupted Market Street wall, and terminates a grand view down Pine Street. A steel frame structure richly clad in polychrome glazed terra cotta in a three part vertical composition. The typically superb detailing of Bliss and Faville is rarely better than in this building. Its columned ground floor with central arch and arcaded upper zone are especially fine. The rusticated texture of the shaft and the open tower of the roof recall similar features in many San Francisco buildings beginning with the Merchants Exchange. The classically derived interior at the ground level was partially remodeled with meaningless references to the first Bay Area tradition in the 1960s. The maps of Hawaii on the elevator door recall the building's first owner, Matson Shipping Lines, and the fact that most if not all of Hawaii's Big Five corporations once had their mainland headquarters here. The building is now occupied by P. G. & E.

A

M31 MAP II
320 Market Street
gore of Pine and Market at Davis
Ashley, Keyser, and Runge
1957

NOT RATED

M32 MAP II
333 Market Street
SW corner Beale
Gin Wong and Associates
under construction 1978

Part of the Bechtel/Metropolitan Life block. Designed by the project director of the St. Francis Tower for William Pereira in 1972, now on his own.

NOT RATED

M33 MAP II
340 Market Street
NE corner Front
IBM Building
Meyer and Evers
1956

NOT RATED

M34 MAP II
425 Market Street
SW corner Fremont
One Metropolitan Plaza
Skidmore, Owings, and Merrill
1973

Part of the Bechtel/Metropolitan Life group. A small, shadowed, and cold plaza needlessly separates this building from its Market Street neighbor.

NOT RATED

M35 MAP II
444 Market Street
NW corner Front
Shaklee Building
Skidmore, Owings, and Merrill
under construction 1978

NOT RATED

M36 MAP II
525 Market Street
SW corner First
Tishman Realty Corporation Building
John Carl Warnecke
1973

An immense blockbuster without scale clues, without any gesture to the city beyond a perfunctory little sliver of a plaza. The worst of the "new Market Street" buildings.

NOT RATED

M37 MAP II
540-548 Market Street
gore of Market, Sutter, and Sansome
Flatiron Building
Havens and Toepke
1913

One of the best of several fine buildings by this firm, and one of several fine flatirons on the gore blocks created by Market Street's diagonal intersection of the original grid of the city. A steel frame building with skeletal expression of the facade, lightly ornamented with Gothic detail except at the cornice which projects out from the wall and drops like a curtain, foreshadowing the Hallidie Building's cornice. In composition, a two part vertical block. It relates to the remaining older buildings on Sutter, to the longer street facade on Sansome, and to its Market Street block as far as the Hobart Building.

A

M38 MAP II
550 Market Street
architect unknown
1908

A two part small commercial block with skeletal articulation of the facade and restrained Renaissance/Baroque ornamentation. Reinforced concrete construction.

C

M39 MAP II
554 Market Street
architect unknown
1907

A two part small commercial block with skeletal articulation of the facade and modified Renaissance/Baroque ornamentation.

C

M40 MAP II
555-575 Market Street
Standard Oil of California
Hertzka and Knowles
1964, 1975

A pair of office towers built eleven years apart to the same design, surrounded by small and useless plazas. The fenced garden between the towers, by Theodore Osmundson and John Staley, is very pretty to look at. It was closed to the public several years ago after being repeatedly vandalized. The buildings are the result of the continuing expansion of the Standard Oil Co. to the south from its old headquarters at 200 Bush Street. The smaller of these two towers was finished in 1964, the larger in 1975. Both are clad in terra cotta above a granite base.

NOT RATED

Sutter Street facade.

M41 MAP II
560 Market Street
architect unknown
1907

An unfortunate remodeling of the Market Street facade of this building has destroyed (or merely obscured?) the fine design which still exists at the rear of the building on Sutter Street. A hybrid composition of an enframed pavilion with a giant order above what was, presumably, originally an enframed window wall. The recessed wall of the facade, behind piers and columns, is an unusual and expensive device which loses rentable floor space but gains a three dimensional quality often lacking in what is generally an architecture of facades. The graceful columns carry a foliated frieze whose cornice has been removed. Reinforced concrete construction.

B

M42 MAP IV
562-566 Market Street
Chancery Building
Willis Polk
1923

The ultimate background building in a rusticated terra cotta facade which reflects the same treatment on the Finance (M44) and Hobart (M45) buildings up the street. In composition, a three part vertical block with Renaissance/Baroque ornamental references. Reinforced concrete construction.

B

M43 MAP III
579-581 Market Street
Stacey's
White and Herman
1948

The only building left on Market between First and Second under 22 stories. A 1907 brick structure, remodeled in 1948, with alterations to the ground floor by John Bolles in 1959.

NOT RATED

M44 MAP IV
576-580 Market Street
Finance Building
Willis Polk
1923

In material, design, and detail, a six story extension of the Hobart Building next door, and part of the larger group on this block which also includes the Chancery (M42) and the Flatiron Building (M37). A two part vertical composition with restrained Renaissance/Baroque ornamentation. A reinforced concrete structure clad in terra cotta.

B

M45 MAP IV
582-592 Market Street
foot of Second
Hobart Building
Willis Polk
1914

A

From just about any point of view, one of the most successful tall buildings ever built in San Francisco. Located on a mid-block site, it manages to relate both to the diagonal of Market Street in the positioning of its tower and to the north of Market grid in the shape of its base. Its glass commercial base was designed to play the mundane role that should be retained by any street level space in a commercial area. Its rusticated shaft gives the building an urban character that links it in an anonymous but pleasing texture to its neighbors. And the tower gives it a particular romantic quality that distinguishes it from anything else in San Francisco, or from any other American skyscraper. The tower is the building's finest feature in its distinctive oval-with-flat-sides shape, dense terra cotta ornamental detail, corbeled cornice, and two-leveled tiled hip roof. Its expression of the soaring quality of the tower is certainly less literal than that of New York's Woolworth Building (1913), which was considered the last word on the subject at the time, but it is just as successful in another way. The tower long stood out on the skyline of the city and, although now dwarfed in height, is still a conspicuous land-

mark in its neighborhood and from Second Street, the location from which it was designed to be viewed.

In composition, the building is a three part vertical design with highly inventive use of Renaissance/Baroque ornamentation. In construction, the building is steel frame with reinforced concrete floors, walls, and roof. Its construction was accomplished in the remarkable time of eleven months, a record which, according to the *Pacific Coast Architect*, "occasioned much comment and some criticism, it being alleged that it was constructed in a reckless manner, one critic expressing the opinion that no greater crime against the public had ever been committed." In the end, however, the building was constructed on time and under budget and served as "a practical demonstration of the value of a preconceived scheme of construction." The particularly fine glass base of the building managed to survive until about the time this survey was begun, when it was grossly remodeled in a glaring white marble by Financial Savings and Loan.

M48 MAP IV
601-605 Market Street
SW corner Second
Santa Fe Building
now West Coast Life
Wood and Simpson
1917

A three part vertical block with a later two story
addition. Ornamentation is 18th century English
in derivation. According to the *Architect and Engineer* a few months before completion, "The
conflict between art and economy, which is
always present in a commercial building, was
particularly acute in this case, but by careful
study and by reason of certain innovations
in construction the architects were able to
produce what gives promise of being a distinguished and convenient building, while keeping the cost at a very low figure." Interior costs
on the first four floors, which were occupied by
the Santa Fe Railroad, were not so low, due to
marble, hardwood, and ornamental plaster
finishing. A steel frame building with lattice
girders and brick curtain walls, with a marble
base and terra cotta detail elsewhere.

B

M49 MAP IV
609-611 Market Street
architect unknown
1914

A two part vertical block, skeletal in expression,
with restrained Renaissance/Baroque ornamentation. Its cornice has been removed. Steel
frame construction.

C

M50 MAP IV
613-615 Market Street
architect unknown
1907

A two part small commercial block with skeletal
expression of the facade and an elaborate
Gothic panel across the top. An appropriately
scaled neighbor for Hoffman's Grill next door.
Brick construction.

C

M51 MAP IV
619 Market Street
Hoffman's Grill
architect unknown
1913

A long-time San Francisco restaurant, established nearby in 1891 and in this building since
1913. An enframed window wall with handsome
brick work and a metal and stained glass marquee. Ornamentation is vaguely Romanesque.
The original interior includes a great carved
wood bar and tile floors. Brick construction.

B

M52 MAP IV
621 Market Street
architect unknown
1920

A two part small commercial block with skeletal
expression of the upper section and restrained
use of Renaissance/Baroque ornamentation.
Reinforced concrete construction. Relates in
scale to Hoffman's Grill. As part of a small commercial group it adds vitality to a generally
more serious area.

C

M53 MAP IV
623-631 Market Street
SE corner New Montgomery
Metropolis Trust and Savings Bank
later Merchant's National Building
L. B. Dutton
1907

Another design by George Applegarth for the office of L. B. Dutton. Located at an important corner on Market Street at New Montgomery. A three part vertical composition with Renaissance/Baroque ornamentation. The steel frame is clad in stone at the base with terra cotta above, and the largely glass facade has "the merest skeleton" for maximum natural light. The base is characterized by a massive Doric order. The old mullions of the tall arched bays of the shaft have been replaced with aluminum to the detriment of the design. A fine cantilevered clock at the corner is discussed in the Urban Design section of this volume.

B

M54 MAP IV
633-665 Market Street
SW corner New Montgomery
Sheraton Palace Hotel
Trowbridge and Livingston
1909

Originally just the Palace Hotel, the post-fire successor to William Ralston's 1873 Palace. The first Palace building was the center of San Francisco's social life and the image of luxury throughout the West.

The finest feature of the present building is its magnificent skylit Garden Court, an example of Parisian opulence equal to almost any contemporary space in Paris. The exterior is certainly less exuberant but nevertheless quite successful in its creation of a warm textural element along Market and New Montgomery streets. In composition, the building is a three part vertical block with differentiated end bays and restrained Renaissance/Baroque ornamentation. The steel building was constructed in 1909 with additions in 1915, 1919, and 1925. The architect was the important New York firm of Trowbridge and Livingston who sent George Kelham to San Francisco as supervising architect on this project. After completion of the hotel, Kelham stayed in San Francisco and opened his own office. Leonard Schultze, later of Schultze and Weaver, was also involved in this project. Warren G. Harding died here in 1923.

A   CL: Garden Court only

M56 MAP IV
673-687 Market Street
SW corner Annie
Monadnock Building
Meyer and O'Brien
1906

A well-constructed steel frame building, under construction at the time of the fire and rebuilt rapidly afterwards. At the time of the fire, construction proceeded according to the current design, except for the west end which was pending purchase of a building that was in the way. This suggests something of the haste and occasional rapaciousness of the period. A two part vertical composition with an attic, skeletal in articulation, with restrained use of Renaissance/Baroque ornamentation. It was referred to by the *Architect and Engineer* as a typical business block. The design of the facade is the result of an effort to maximize natural lighting of offices. The facade treatment is similar to that of the Rialto and Galen buildings by the same architects who had been influenced by office planning and its effect on composition in Chicago. Also, like many buildings of its day, the Monadnock Building was constructed around a large central light court. Inside, it followed the model of the Mills Building with its continuous corridors. These corridors were originally finished in Spanish mahogany and Colton marble.

B

Chronicle Building, ca. 1910, with additions. Before remodeling.

M57 MAP IV
690 Market Street
Chronicle Building
Burnham and Root/
   remodeled by Hagman and Meyer
1889/remodeled 1962

Underneath the bland 1962 remodeling lies one of the great architectural treasures of San Francisco. Originally an example of a Romanesque Chicago School design by one of Chicago's most important architectural firms, it was sensitively enlarged twice by Willis Polk. The building was the first iron and steel frame building in the West and the city's tallest at the time it was built—the same year that New York City saw its first steel frame skyscraper. The building was built as the headquarters for the *San Francisco Chronicle* and was one of the major landmarks of "Newspaper Angle"—the intersection of Third, Kearny, and Market streets where the Examiner and Call Buildings were also located.

The present outer skin of the building appears to be a thin veneer of enameled metal porcelain panels that has left the original facades intact and could be easily removed. The restoration of this building, one of the most important buildings in the city, would be a great civic gesture, comparable in its own way to its original construction which was intended and accepted as an object of beauty and a source of pride. Restored to its original appearance, this would be a strong "A" group building.

NOT RATED

M55 MAP IV
660 Market Street
Lewis Hobart
1924

A steel frame terra cotta clad office building that forms a part of the Market Street wall. In composition, a two part vertical block with modified Gothic ornamentation. Ground floor remodelings have respected the storefront arcade.

B

M59   Call Building, ca. 1902.

M58 MAP IV
691-699 Market Street
SE corner Third
Hearst Building
Kirby, Petit, and Green
1909

The second headquarters building of the *San Francisco Examiner* on this site, replacing A. C. Schweinfurth's earlier design which was destroyed in the fire. As constructed, the present building is a greatly scaled down version of the original design by the New York firm of Kirby, Petit, and Green. That design called for a larger building with an elaborate upper zone that recalled Schweinfurth's building, to be surmounted by a colossal, overscaled clock tower. As it is, the building is a two part vertical composition with differentiated end bays. Ornamentation is modified Renaissance/Baroque, referred to as "Mission Style" by the *American Architect* in 1908. The building is a notable example of post-fire "fireproof" and earthquake resistant construction. Its foundation is a rigid steel grillage covered in concrete. Heavy plate girders under each column make the connection to the steel frame of the building itself. It is the only one of the three newspaper buildings standing at this corner which still functions as newspaper offices. The angled corner of the facade follows the lot lines and helps give definition to "Newspaper Angle," once the heart of the city.

B

M59 MAP IV
703 Market Street
SW corner Third
Central Tower
originally Call/Claus Spreckels Building
Albert Roller
1938

A 1938 remodel of the Reid Brothers' 1898 Call Building, one of the finest skyscrapers ever built in San Francisco. The old Call Building was a domed tower that the prominent local critic, B. J. S. Cahill, called the "handsomest tall office building in the world." It inspired many local design imitations, only one of which, and perhaps the least literal, was built—the Humboldt Bank Building. As important structurally as it was architecturally, the U.S. Geological Survey, in its post-fire report on the condition of buildings that survived said, "The design of this steel work is well worthy of study by anyone interested in such structures. It is probably, on the whole, the best designed piece of such work in the U.S." The original structural engineer was Charles Strobel of Chicago, the inventor of Z bar columns.

Ironically, the strength of the structure was partly responsible for the remodeling. Because the structure could support it, when additional space was needed in the mid 1930s, the dome was removed and six floors of offices were added. An article in *Architectural Record* on the new design was entitled "Economic Forces Prove Stronger Than Earthquakes." The new design created a Moderne tower, set back at the upper levels in a manner that recalls the 1931 design of the Irving Trust Co. in New York. The best feature of the new design was its lobby of curving glass brick walls, now obscured by wood paneling, but possibly still intact.

B

M60 MAP IV
704 Market Street
foot of Third Street
Citizens Savings
originally Mutual Savings Bank Building
William Curlett
1902, 1906

A pre-fire skyscraper which was not severely damaged and was rebuilt by its original architect in 1906. One of the most distinctive older buildings in the city, in a three part vertical composition with Renaissance/Baroque ornamentation. The design is distinguished by the mannered rustication of the base and a high, red mansard roof with elaborate dormers and copper cresting. It is prominently located near a major intersection and at the foot of Third Street, the historic southern approach to downtown. The steel frame is clad in limestone. The corner addition was built in 1964 in a complementary manner that made references to the historic forms of the older structure, notably its mansard roof, dormer, cornice, and floor levels. Architects of the addition were Clark and Beuttler, with Charles Moore and Alan Morgan associated architects.

A

M61 MAP IV
715-719 Market Street
Morris Plan Co.
Bliss and Fairweather
1940

A 1940 remodel of the 1906 Kamm Building by Bliss and Faville, altered again in 1950 by Hurt, Trudell, and Berger. The 1940 design transformed some of the building to garage space, entered from the rear. This is a three part vertical composition with Moderne references. The steel frame dates from before the fire.

C

M62 MAP IV
721 Market Street
Bliss and Fairweather
1940

A 1940 remodel of a 1907 building. The remodel by Bliss and Fairweather relates to the Morris Plan Co. Building next door. In composition, a two part small commercial block with skeletal articulation of the facade and Moderne references.

C

M63 MAP IV
722-742 Market Street
Bankers Investment Building
Frederick H. Meyer
1912, 1918

A two part vertical composition with the later addition of an attic. Terra cotta ornamentation is derived from Renaissance/Baroque sources. The steel frame structure is fireproofed with concrete and has reinforced concrete floors, roof, and curtain walls. The building forms an important part of the street walls on both Market and Geary streets. The ground floor storefront arcade has been remodeled.

B

M64 MAP IV
725-731 Market Street
Bancroft Building
Cunningham and Politeo
1908

The third Bancroft Building on this site, built by Hubert Howe Bancroft who operated his famous historical publishing company in the building's predecessors. The design for this building developed from an elaborate reinforced concrete structure with a dome and a fanciful parapet, to a 12-story version of the present building, to the present brick building of only six stories. In composition, it is a three part vertical block with end bay articulation. Ornamentation is modified Renaissance/Baroque. Part of the Market Street wall. Together with the Carroll and Tilton Building next door, important as a framing device for the entrance to Yerba Buena Center.

B

M65 MAP IV
735 Market Street
Carroll and Tilton Building
Willis Polk
1907

A handsome stacked composition with a progression of orders that resembles Albert Pissis' 1908 Rosenstock Building (R28) and recalls Polk's own pre-fire Bare Building. With the Bancroft Building next door, it flanks the wide entrance to Yerba Buena Center. At the same time it relates to the important intersection of Market, Grant, and O'Farrell across the street. A brick building with Renaissance/Baroque ornamentation.

B

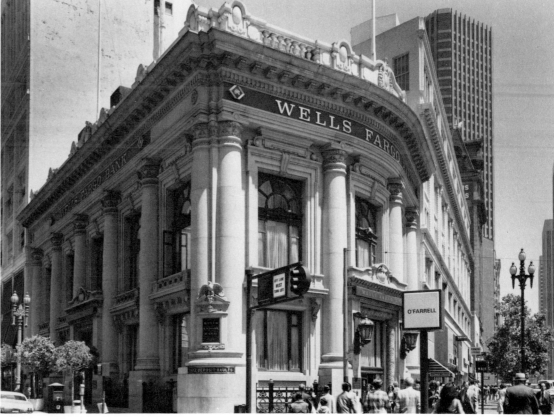

M66 MAP IV
744 Market Street
NE corner Grant
Wells Fargo Bank
originally Union Trust Co.
Clinton Day
1910

The winning design in a competition for the Union Trust Co., at an extremely important Market Street intersection. A competition entry was also submitted by Frederick Meyer. Together with Security Pacific Bank across the street (M13) and the Phelan flatiron (M67) on Market, this forms probably the best of the remaining Market Street intersections. The two banks in particular serve as an imposing gateway to Grant Avenue.

In composition, the building is a modified temple without a pediment. Ornamentation is derived from classical antiquity. Its layered facades have carved granite ornament setting back to dark iron window framing. This treatment adds a rich textural element to the design which suitably enhances its prominence in an area where most buildings are more two dimensional in effect. The curving Market Street facade further enriches the building's relationship to a complex intersection. The classical interior is faced in white marble with gold highlights. The Wells Fargo Bank signs have been sensitively integrated into the original design. A steel frame building.

A

M67 MAP IV
760-784 Market Street
gore of Market and O'Farrell at Grant
Phelan Building
William Curlett
1908

A new building on the site of a pre-fire Phelan Building. A "fireproof" steel frame structure with metal windows and glazed terra cotta exterior cladding, originally designed to carry an additional ten stories. In composition, a three part vertical block with Renaissance/Baroque ornamentation on a large flatiron with a rounded corner. The "architectural" composition rests on a 2-story glass commercial base, the ground floor of which has been entirely remodeled. The second floor of this base is still a well-lit continuous indoor shopping street.

An extremely important building in its several contexts—as part of the street wall on Market and O'Farrell streets, as part of the "gateway group" to Grant Avenue and perhaps in the future to Yerba Buena Center, and as a major element in the larger context of the Grant Avenue retail area. Viewed from Bush Street, Grant is punctuated by two Curlett buildings at Post (the Shreve and Head buildings) and terminated by a third, the Phelan. After the immediate post-fire rebuilding period, Curlett moved his practice to Los Angeles. This structure was built by James Duvall Phelan, Mayor of San Francisco from 1897 to 1902 and U.S. Senator from 1913 to 1919.

A

M68 MAP IV
783-785 Market Street
Humboldt Bank Building
Meyer and O'Brien
1906

Under construction at the time of the earthquake, but entirely destroyed. Then redesigned and rebuilt with the most advanced structural system available. The steel frame was one of the first locally to be braced with lattice girders. The building is clad in sandstone at the base with terra cotta above. Of the several domed towers designed for San Francisco following the model of the Call Building of 1898, this is the only one which was built. Although not nearly as literal a copy as most of the other designs, this also follows the general model as a three part vertical block capped by a dome, with Renaissance/Baroque ornamentation. Ornamental detail is concentrated at the base with its rusticated stonework and carved lions, and in the dome which has been red, white, and blue since the Bicentennial in 1976. It was originally gray in imitation of sandstone.

The design of the building is actually a long narrow slab. Its ornamental tower at the street and glazed walls of the cut-away light well behind represent again the attitude of post-fire architects who built under severe practical and economic constraints, but always with the city in mind. This building was designed in anticipation of large-scale adjacent construction which would hide the rear slab and leave only a narrow street front exposed. The logical expression of this narrow street front was seen to be a tower. Rather than dishonest design as Modern architects long claimed, this two-faced approach responded to a more complex set of problems than is now even taken into account. The ground floor banking hall was altered in 1920 by Smith O'Brien, by that time in his own office, with the addition of bronze, marble, and ornamental plaster.

A

M69 MAP V
790 Market Street
NE corner Stockton
Grodins
Bliss and Fairweather
1937

A pallid remodeling of Albert Pissis' fine old Roos Brothers store of 1907. Now a two part composition with Moderne ornamental references. The second level interior has recently been remodeled for the Northern California A.I.A. headquarters by Sandy and Babcock. Brick construction with iron columns.

C

M70 MAP IV
799 Market Street
SE corner Fourth
Roos Atkins
Burke, Kober, Nicolais, and Archuleta
1968

A modern department store with blank walls to accommodate "modern merchandising methods" which require storage space at the perimeter of open sales floors. This resembles Macy's additions on Union Square, architect unknown. Built on the site of the old California Theater by Albert Henry Jacobs.

NOT RATED

M71 MAP V
800-830 Market Street
gore of Market and Ellis at Stockton
West Bank Building
C. F. Whittlesey
1908

A remodeled reinforced concrete flatiron building which still retains much of the character of its original design by C. F. Whittlesey. Whittlesey had worked for Sullivan in Chicago and was a strong proponent of reinforced concrete construction and of the use of color in architecture. A two part vertical composition with Gothic ornamentation on a skeletal facade, clad in cream colored terra cotta with spandrels over mezzanine arches "in the hottest red you ever heard about." Forms a rare pair of Whittlesey buildings with the Pacific Building across Market Street.

B

M72 MAP V
801-823 Market Street
SW corner Fourth
Pacific Building
C. F. Whittlesey
1907

Reputedly the world's largest reinforced concrete office building when built, and one of the most literal examples of the influence of Louis Sullivan in San Francisco. A three part vertical block with differentiated end bays. It recalls Sullivan's Carson Pirie Scott store in the convergence of its two skeletal facades at a round corner bay, and in the setting of the principal facades above a 2-story glass base. The building is embellished in Sullivanesque terra cotta ornamentation.

The most striking feature of the building is the distinctive color scheme which was the source of controversy in its day. The ground floors are clad in red tile, the shaft is green tile, and the whole is trimmed in cream terra cotta with occasional vermilion highlights. Whittlesey explained his reasons for the colors in the *Architect and Engineer:* "Because the climate of our city is decidely gray and this is accentuated all about town, especially in the large buildings by the use of a peculiarly gloomy stone of a disagreeable yellowish gray color that catches and absorbs much of the smudge carried on the winds." He compared the facade to a lady's dress and the vermilion highlights to "a brilliant stone in your satin cravat." The building was built around a large and handsome light court clad in white tiles. The original cornice has been removed. The building is part of one of the most imposing groups of older buildings in the downtown area in the section of Market Street that runs from Fourth Street to the west side of Fifth.

A

M73 MAP V
825-833 Market Street
Commercial Building
Lewis Hobart
1908

Built on the site of G. W. Percy's Romanesque California Academy of Sciences Building (1887) whose partial reinforced concrete interior was demolished after the fire. The present building is a three part vertical composition with Renaissance/Baroque ornamentation. It is distinguished by terra cotta eagles at the mezzanine level and garlands and balconies in the upper zone. The building is of major significance as part of the majestic wall of buildings along this part of Market. Steel frame construction.

B

M74 MAP V
835-865 Market Street
The Emporium
Albert Pissis and Joseph Moore
1896, 1908

Built for the Parrott Estate in 1896 and entirely rebuilt behind the original facade after the fire. The original building housed commercial enterprises behind the 2-story glass base, with other functions above, including the California Supreme Court on the third level. Thus, like so many others in San Francisco's retail district, and contrary to the beliefs of Modern critics, the building did indeed reflect interior function in its exterior composition. However, it did so in a more complex manner than Modernists comprehended, one that incorporated urban and symbolic values in its understanding of function.

The composition is a three part vertical block with a giant order in the shaft and Renaissance/ Baroque ornamentation. Its facade is clad in gray sandstone, painted pink. Steel frame construction. The huge interior dome (once incorrectly reported in the *Architect and Engineer* as the largest dome in the U.S.) was created for the rebuilt structure of 1908. As designed, the building was an early and notable example of what was called neo-classical architecture in San Francisco. The building is a major element in this magnificent section of Market Street, and it relates powerfully to the Flood Building across the street, also by Pissis. In an article by Pissis, the *Architect and Engineer* once referred to "the calm magnificence of the Emporium."

A

M75 MAP V
838 Market Street
Sommer and Kaufmann
Kem Weber and Albert Roller
1930

The only downtown San Francisco design by the important Los Angeles Moderne architect, Kem Weber. The April 1930 *Architect and Engineer* said that it was attracting the attention of art critics and was considered one of the finest examples of "Modern architecture" in the U.S. Conceived as "a merchandising machine for the purpose of selling shoes," the building was an early and innovative example of the totally designed department store, with every aspect serving some retailing function. The facades were designed to provide adequate street level display space, to admit light to upper sales floors, and to function as a "dignified" advertisement for the merchandise. The interior was divided into atmospheric "salons" with peripheral storage areas. Exterior ornamentation was self-consciously without reliance on historical precedent. Bas relief green terra cotta panels were designed by Meyer Krieg. Monel metal signage, including the "Shoes" pylon, now removed, was streamlined Moderne in style. A "fireproof" steel frame building with facades on both Market and Ellis streets. The ground level has been entirely remodeled and the interior is vacant above the ground floor.

A

M76 MAP V
840 Market Street
Hart, Schaffner, and Marx Clothes
Building
Albert Roller; Bliss and Fairweather
1930

Another through-the-block Moderne store, designed at the same time as Sommer and Kaufmann's next door. Albert Roller was associated with both designs. In composition, the building is expressed as a vertical sign with a deep cutaway bay decorated in a black and gold geometric pattern. The original Hart, Schaffner, and Marx sign has been removed from the top of the facade and the ground floor has been remodeled. Steel frame construction clad in white California Yule marble.

B

M77 MAP V
870-898 Market Street
gore at Market and Powell
James Flood Building
Albert Pissis
1904

San Francisco's most monumental office building, located at one of the key intersections of the city and forming a powerful relationship with the magnificent group across Market, particularly with the Emporium Building. Almost completed at the time of the fire, the building was damaged but repairable. In composition, it is a stacked vertical block with Renaissance/Baroque ornamentation. Bold decorative detail is focused at the middle tier, reflecting the design of the Emporium Building. In an article on Pissis, the *Architect and Engineer* referred to the "florid grandeur" of the Flood Building and said that the two buildings imparted a "touch of grandeur to Market Street." The building is a steel frame structure with brick curtain walls clad in gray Colusa sandstone. It was built by James Flood, the son of the Comstock silver millionaire whose house still sits on Nob Hill, now occupied by the Pacific Union Club.

A

Flood Building, ca. 1906.

M78 MAP V
901-919 Market Street
SW corner Fifth
Hale Brothers Department Store
later J. C. Penney's
Reid Brothers
1912

Now sadly vacant, this handsome reinforced concrete department store building, originally built for Hale Brothers, is extremely important for several reasons. In its massing, scale, and detail, it is the last building in the major group on Market Street that begins at the Pacific Building at the corner of Fourth, and it is part of another group that extends down Fifth to the old Mint. It also is a fine example of department store design, simplifying the old compositional formula of mixed-use predecessors such as the City of Paris, the Emporium, and the Butler Building.

In composition, it is a two part vertical block over a glass base with a giant order in the upper zone and a deeply rusticated mezzanine. Ornamentation is Renaissance/Baroque. The interior is lit by broad modified Chicago windows and the upper floor was originally designed with a columned, skylit court. In construction, the building is reinforced concrete throughout, including decorative details, and incorporating a number of innovative and otherwise progressive construction details. Most interesting is the cantilevering of the walls 10 feet beyond the first row of columns in order to leave the base free for unbroken plate glass display windows. The building was constructed in the rapid time of five-and-one-half months.

A

M79 MAP V
923 Market Street
Taylors
architect unknown
1907

A two part small commercial block with the second level over an enframed 2-story base. Very restrained use of Renaissance/Baroque ornamentation. The "Taylors" sign dates from the 1930s. The cornice has been removed. Brick construction.

C

M80 MAP V
925 Market Street
architect unknown
1910

A two part small commercial block with skeletal expression on the facade and restrained Renaissance/Baroque ornamentation. Brick construction.

C

M81 MAP V
929 Market Street
National Dollar Store
architect unknown
1939

M82 MAP V
931-933 Market Street
National Dollar Store
architect unknown
1939

A pair of buildings, each with a two part vertical composition and Moderne ornamentation. They result from the remodeling of two 1907 brick buildings.

C

M83 MAP V
934-936 Market Street
NW corner North Fifth
The Gap
Bull, Field, Volkmann, Stockwell
1974

NOT RATED

M84 MAP V
938-942 Market Street
Garfield Building
Reid Brothers
1908

A three part vertical composition with Renaissance/Baroque ornamentation. Built by Mrs. Elsie Drexler for lease to the Brittain Hardware Co. It is an important supportive structure to the old Mechanic's Savings Bank Building (M86) next door. Reinforced concrete construction.

C

M85 MAP V
943 Market Street
architect unknown
1909

An enframed window wall with remodeled window openings. All that is left of the original Renaissance/Baroque ornamentation is the cornice. The Morrison's storefront remodel of about 1930 is an excellent example of an Art Deco design. Brick construction with wood posts.

C

M86 MAP V
948 Market Street
NE corner Mason
Mechanic's Savings Bank Building
L. B. Dutton
1907

A three part vertical composition with Renaissance/Baroque ornamentation and a distinctive curving facade intended to create a continuous frontage from Market to Turk Street. The distinctiveness of this treatment was appropriate to the function of the Market Street intersections as visual focuses. In 1943 the lower floors were remodeled for the Pepsi-Cola Service Center, a "furlough station" for men and women in the armed services, by the important New York firm of Harrison, Fouilhoux, and Abramovitz, in association with Morris Ketchum and Gardner Dailey. The rusticated piers and Ionic columns of the base were removed and replaced by stripped classical Moderne details. The interiors of the lower four floors were also remodeled in what was, at the time, an extremely modern design. The large spaces of the Pepsi-Cola Service Center have since been remodeled again and some of the exterior details have been removed. Steel frame construction.

B

M87 Empress Theater, ca. 1910.

M87 MAP V
949-961 Market Street
St. Francis Theatre
originally The Empress
John Galen Howard
1910

Originally a very large version of an enframed window wall composition with a great deal of stained glass, now almost entirely covered by a chaotic patchwork of signs. Handsome Renaissance/Baroque ornamentation is still visible, primarily in the cornice. The old Empress Theater was entered through the westernmost bay which was surmounted by a dome.

B

M88 MAP V
950-964 Market Street
gore of Market and Turk at Mason
Dean Building
architect unknown
1907

A 2-story flatiron remodeled about 1940. The new design strongly resembles contemporary remodels by Bliss and Fairweather, for example Grodins, at 790 Market (M69). A two part composition with formal treatment of the upper zone in Moderne details. Brick composition with terra cotta facing.

C

M89 MAP V
966-970 Market Street
architect unknown
1907

A two part small commercial block with formal treatment of the upper zone. Ornamentation is Renaissance/Baroque. Brick construction.

C

M90 MAP V
972 Market Street
architect unknown
1912

A two part small commercial block articulated by two projecting bay windows. Renaissance/ Baroque ornamentation. Brick construction.

C

M91 MAP V
973-977 Market Street
Wilson Building
architect uncertain
1908

The first in the fine group of Market Street loft structures characterized by skeletal facade articulation and modified Chicago windows. The history and authorship of this building is full of conflicting information, it being variously attributed on good authority to Henry Schulze, Willis Polk, and Henry Meyers, and variously dated as a pre-fire and post-fire structure. It is nevertheless a handsome skeletal design with extremely rich decorative terra cotta panels. A three part vertical composition with Sullivan- esque/Byzantine ornamentation. At the ground level it is the long-time home of the Palm Garden Grill. Steel frame construction.

A

M92 MAP V
979-989 Market Street
Hale Brothers Department Store
now Walgreen's
Reid Brothers
1902, 1907

The earliest of two remaining Hale Brothers stores in this block of Market. It is a pre-fire design whose facade alone was saved in a re- markable engineering feat. Originally the terra cotta facade had been attached to a steel frame at the front of a brick structure which was almost completely destroyed. In the reconstruc- tion the facade was held up by means of guy lines stretched across Market Street while a new steel framework was erected behind. The original design was a three part vertical block crowned with an entablature floor of giant round windows. Before the fire this floor had been replaced by a 2-story giant order identi- cal to the tier below it. In the 1930s the glass base and rusticated mezzanine were replaced with a smooth marble base that respected the fenestration of the original. Part of the Market Street loft group.

A

M93 MAP V
980 Market Street
Crest Theater
now Egyptian
architect unknown
ca. 1935

A 1910 theater building which was remodeled as the streamlined Moderne Crest about 1935. The stepped pylons of the Crest's facade were painted alternately orange and yellow and out- lined in neon. The facade has recently been painted a solid red and the building named the Egyptian. The original Egyptian Theater was across the street (M109) at 1067–1071 Market (now Pussycat). Said to be a reinforced con- crete shell inside older brick walls.

B

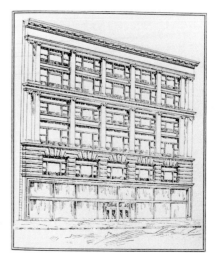

Right: Hale Brothers. Proposed remodeling, 1906.

M94 MAP V
982-998 Market Street
NE corner Taylor
Fox Warfield Theater
originally Loew's Warfield
G. Albert Lansburgh
1921

Part of a major group of theaters in this area, dominated by this building and the Golden Gate Theater. Like the Golden Gate by the same architect in the same year, this was built as a theater and office building. The office slab is located along Market Street, giving greater definition to the street and greater mass in relation to the Golden Gate. The slab turns as Golden Gate Avenue branches off Market, making a gesture of deference to the more prominently sited Golden Gate Theater. This is one of the last remaining big theaters in San Francisco which has not been seriously altered inside. In composition, a two part vertical block with differentiated end bays and Renaissance/Baroque ornamentation. Steel frame construction clad in terra cotta.

A

David Hewes Building, ca. 1920. Before remodeling.

M95 MAP V
995-997 Market Street
SE corner Sixth
David Hewes Building
Reid Brothers
1908, remodeled ca. 1960

Underneath that miserable and removable veneer is the David Hewes Building, probably intact except for its broad projecting cornice. The original design is a three part vertical composition with a rusticated mezzanine over a glass base, a smooth shaft, and an elaborate capital with a giant order over a transitional story. A piece of the original design is visible at the rear on Stevenson Street. In its pleasing proportions and rich detail, and the characteristically excellent work of these architects, it was undoubtedly an "A" group building before the remodeling, and probably could be again.

NOT RATED

M96 MAP VI
1000-1026 Market Street
gore of Market and Golden Gate at Taylor
San Christina Building
architect unknown
1913

A small flatiron building with a projecting cornice, located at an important Market Street intersection. A two part vertical block with Renaissance/Baroque detail. Brick construction with a smooth finish.

B

M97 MAP VI
1001-1005 Market Street
SW corner Sixth
Delger Building
architect unknown
1908

A small reinforced concrete office building clad in brown brick. It functions as a corner anchor to a group of smaller buildings on Market. In composition, a two part vertical block with differentiated end bays. Ornamentation is Renaissance/Baroque.

C

M98 MAP VI
1007-1009 Market Street
architect unknown
1911

A two part small commercial block with skeletal expression of the upper facade which has been covered by a large sign. The windows are framed in a handsome terra cotta molding. Modified Renaissance/Baroque ornamentation. Reinforced concrete construction.

C

M99 MAP VI
1019-1021 Market Street
Eastern Outfitting Co. Building
George A. Applegarth
1909

An astonishing example of an enframed window wall with giant Corinthian columns carrying an entablature and framing a very large bay window. The *Architect and Engineer* called it "an example of a simple monumental design adapted to the practical requirement of a commercial business." The design was considered economical because glass and copper were relatively inexpensive facade materials. Despite appearances, this is a brick building with wood posts. When this building was refurbished a few years ago, it was referred to as a leader in the expected rejuvenation of this part of Market, following the Market Street Beautification project. Unfortunately, little else has followed its lead. Part of the Market Street loft group.

A

M100 MAP VI
1023 Market Street
architect unknown
1907

A two part small commercial block with formal treatment of the upper zone. Gothic ornamentation. Brick construction.

C

M101 MAP VI
1025 Market Street
architect unknown
1909

A two part small commercial block with skeletal expression of the facade. Reinforced concrete construction.

C

M102 MAP VI
1028-1056 Market Street
Bijou Theater
previously Pompei and Regal
architect unknown
1907

A modest, small scale theater with commercial and office space. A two part small commercial block in composition with formal treatment of the upper zone. Very restrained Renaissance/Baroque ornamentation. Brick construction.

C

M103 MAP VI
1035 Market Street
Hyman and Appleton
1933

M104 MAP VI
1043-1045 Market Street
Hyman and Appleton
1933

Despite the remodeling of these two older buildings as one facade, their scale and fenestration relate them to the Market Street loft group. The smaller building at 1029 Market is also a part of this new facade. Both 1035 and 1043-1045 are two part vertical compositions. Reinforced concrete construction.

C

M105 MAP VI
1049 Market Street
Sterling Building
architect unknown
1907

Although its fenestration is more traditional, the simplicity of the facade and its scale and proportions make it an important member of the Market Street loft group. In composition, a two part vertical block with Renaissance/Baroque ornamentation. Brick construction with wood posts.

C

M106 MAP VI
1053-1055 Market Street
Forrest Building
MacDonald and Applegarth
1908

A very fine member of the Market Street loft group with a simple skeletal facade and modified Chicago windows. In composition, a two part vertical block with Renaissance/Baroque ornamentation. The facade was originally enframed by a string of light bulbs. In its original design the building bore a strong resemblance to Frank Lloyd Wright's Luxfer project. As built, the resemblance is still evident but less strong. Brick construction.

A

M107 MAP VI
1059-1061 Market Street
Ede Building
William E. Knowles
1910

Another fine member of the Market Street loft group, this one with a very distinctive ornamental treatment derived in part from the Viennese Secession movement. In composition, the building is an enframed window wall with skeletal articulation of the facade. The piers and slightly gabled entablature recess in slight layers to the plane of the facade. The piers are crowned by open globes. Brick construction with wood posts and a terra cotta front.

A

M108 MAP VI
1063 Market Street
architect unknown
1909

A two part small commercial block with skeletal articulation of the facade and Renaissance/ Baroque ornamentation. Brick construction.

C

M109 MAP VI
1067-1071 Market Street
Lippert Building/Pussycat Theater
originally Egyptian
architect unknown
1924

Another building without Chicago windows but which, in scale, proportion, and extent of window area, is an important member of the Market Street loft group. The Pussycat Theater at the ground level was originally known as the Egyptian. A two part vertical composition with differentiated end bays and Gothic ornamentation. Paired thin Gothic ribs leave very narrow slit windows between larger plate glass openings. Steel frame.

B

M110 MAP VI
1072-1098 Market Street
NE corner Market and Jones
Crocker Bank
originally Anglo California Trust Co.
H. H. Winner
1911

A City Beautiful era building which is clearly inspired by the Renaissance/Baroque classicism of the Hibernia Bank across the street and is intended to complement that design rather than compete with it. A two part vertical composition with a giant order in the upper zone that frames bays of modified Chicago windows. The interior has been remodeled. The Crocker Bank recently painted the base a garish orange, a change from its former respectful gray. Steel frame construction.

B

M111 MAP VI
1083-1087 Market Street
Federal Hotel
William Curlett
1912

A building which in its proportions and scale supports the character of the Market Street loft group, but which is more traditional in its fenestration. A three part vertical composition with Renaissance/Baroque ornamentation. Steel frame construction.

B

M112 MAP VI
1095-1097 Market Street
SE corner Seventh
Grant Building
Newton Tharp
1905, 1906

A very handsome office building with a distinctively and richly textured facade that suffers from the loss of its cornice. The building serves as a major anchor to its Market Street block; it forms an imposing pair with the Odd Fellows Building (M208) across Seventh; it is a suitable neighbor to the Seventh and Mission Post Office next door; and it terminates the view from the U.N. Plaza and the Civic Center.

In composition, a three part vertical block with differentiated end bays. Ornamentation is modified Renaissance/Baroque. The complex facades are rusticated in horizontal bands that cross recessed enframed bays. One of the few remaining examples downtown of architect Tharp's work. Steel frame construction clad in brick and terra cotta. The building was restored after the fire.

A

M113 MAP VI
1100-1112 Market Street
gore of Market and McAllister at Jones
Hotel Shaw
H. A. Minton
1926

A very important building at a major Market Street intersection which also includes the Hibernia Bank (M24) and the Crocker Bank (M110). Like many of the best of the traditionally designed office blocks, this building adds a rich texture to the street with its brick facades and the variety of colors in its brown walls with light terra cotta trim and a copper cornice. In composition, a three part vertical block. Ornamentation is Renaissance/Baroque. The present building is a 5-story addition and total remodel of the 2-story remains of the pre-fire Callaghan Building by Albert Pissis. Steel frame construction.

B

M114 MAP VI
1115-1117 Market Street
architect unknown
1920

A two part small commercial block with skeletal articulation of the facade and Gothic ornamentation. Reinforced concrete with wood posts.

C

M115 MAP VI
1125 Market Street
Embassy Theater
originally the Bell, later the American
Reid Brothers
1905, 1907

A pre-fire vaudeville theater, rebuilt with slight modifications to the fenestration. In composition, a two part vertical block with a giant order. Ornamentation is Renaissance/Baroque. The Starlight Room signs which flash yellow lights around the perimeter of the building are whimsical survivals of the 1920s or 1930s. Brick construction.

B

M116 MAP VI
1127 Market Street
Strand Theater
architect unknown
1917

A potentially handsome skeletal frame obscured by painted window areas. A curious two part composition with modified Chicago windows set in vaguely Sullivanesque frames at the second floor and casement windows above. Renaissance/Baroque ornamentation. Reinforced concrete construction with a steel truss roof.

C

M117 MAP VI
1169 Market Street
SE corner Eighth
Trinity Plaza
originally Towne House Motel
architect unknown
1960

If this building were in Miami Beach with a green lawn and palm trees in front it wouldn't look so bad. As it is, it is grotesquely out of place, breaking the long, continuous Market Street wall by setting far back from the street among parking lots, and possessing a style which bears no relationship to the city around it.

To make matters worse, its white and aqua colors have recently been painted "earth tones," thereby denying the building whatever integrity it had.

NOT RATED

M118 MAP VI
1182 Market Street
gore of Market, Grove, and Hyde
Orpheum Theater
originally Pantages
B. Marcus Priteca
1925

A large theater and office building. It has an extremely ornate main facade, derived from the ornamentation of the Cathedral of Leon, and an absolutely blank rear wall. The back of the building was designed in its form and massing to relate to the Civic Center, and plans were originally drawn up to clad its reinforced concrete walls appropriately. Confusion over whether the theater company or the City was to pay for this work resulted in its permanent postponement. A very large *trompe l'oeil* mural of a classical design could solve the problem.

The front facade is in a two part vertical composition with variable skeletal articulation.

Generally long narrow bays are defined by thin concrete colonettes culminating in finials. The entrance bay is of particularly elaborate ornamentation. Built for the Pantages Theater Company, the building became the Orpheum in 1929. Its auditorium was modified for Cinerama in 1953 and its rich Churrigueresque interior ornament was painted a flat pink. After falling on hard times in the 1960s, the theater was revived in the mid-1970s for musical productions. Steel frame construction with reinforced concrete curtain walls.

A NRD, CL

M119 MAP II
400-418 Mission Street
NW corner Fremont
architect unknown
1907

A two part vertical block with Renaissance/
Baroque ornamentation. Reinforced concrete
construction.

C

M120 MAP III
425 Mission Street
Transbay Transit Terminal
**Timothy Pfleuger, Arthur Brown, Jr., and
  John J. Donovan, consulting architects**
1939

The functional successor to the Ferry Building.
When electric trains began arriving here over
the Bay Bridge, use of the Ferry Building
dropped to almost nothing overnight, and the
Transbay Transit Terminal took over as the primary gateway to the city. This terminal also had
the advantage over the Ferry Building of a more
central location. According to the *Architect and
Engineer* in January 1939, "Convenience to
passengers was the governing motive in the
design of the terminal. To this end the structure
was developed less as a typical railroad station
than as a system of enclosed ramps and stairs
so arranged as to provide minimum walking."

The Terminal Building is an 870-foot long flat
slab with a 230-foot long central pavilion. The
construction is reinforced concrete, faced with
California granite. It is extremely simple in design and without ornament except for aluminum trim. Its most extravagant features are the
seven handsome 2-story windows which extend
across the front of the building. In composition,
the building is an enframed pavilion with end
bays, wings, and a base. Inside, it consists of a
basement garage, street level waiting room, a
mezzanine and tracks on a third level. The
tracks were removed as electrified trains gave
way to buses in the late 1950s. San Francisco
has long-range plans for replacing this building
with a larger one.

B

M121 MAP II
440-454 Mission Street
NE corner First
Terminal Plaza Building
originally C. C. Moore Building
Meyer and Johnson
1920

A two part vertical block that serves as a handsome backdrop to the open space in front of
the Transbay Terminal. The skeletal expression
of the reinforced concrete structure is lightly ornamented in Gothic details.

B

M122 MAP III
500-506 Mission Street
NW corner First
Brandenstein Building
architect unknown
1907

A reinforced concrete office building in a two
part vertical composition with Renaissance/
Baroque ornamentation.

C

M123 MAP III
511-519 Mission Street
architect unknown
1906

A two part small commercial block with formal
treatment of the upper section. Restrained Re-
naissance/Baroque ornamentation. Brick construction with iron posts.

C

M124 MAP III
516-520 Mission Street
Printing Arts Building
A. H. Knoll
1921

A 1907 brick structure with a new facade in
1921. In composition, a three part vertical block
with Renaissance/Baroque ornamentation. The
cornice has been removed. A strong supportive
structure to the larger building next door.

C

M125 MAP III
526 Mission Street
NE corner Ecker
Western Pacific Railroad Co. Building
Edward Bolles
1920

A handsome reinforced concrete loft structure.
A steel frame addition at the top and a walled-
in ground floor mar the character of the original. The skeletal facade is treated with Gothic
ornamentation.

C

M126 MAP III
532-536 Mission Street
NW corner Ecker
Golden Gate University
architect unknown
1923

A reinforced concrete loft in a two part vertical
composition with skeletal articulation and
Renaissance/Baroque ornamentation. Now
occupied by Golden Gate University.

C

M127 MAP III
535-539 Mission Street
SE corner Shaw
Goodyear Building
MacDonald and Kahn
1918

Designed as a reinforced concrete warehouse
and sales building, but built in brick with wood
posts. A two part vertical block with restrained
Renaissance/Baroque ornamentation.

C

M128 MAP III
540-552 Mission Street
Golden Gate University
William D. Podesto, architect; T. Y. Lin International, structural engineer
under construction 1978

NOT RATED

M129 MAP III
545-547 Mission Street
SW corner Shaw
Henry A. Schulze
1906

The only confirmed downtown building by this one-time partner of Arthur Brown, also the designer of the Olympic Club swimming pool. A three part vertical composition with Renaissance/Baroque ornamentation, notably in the rustication of piers and spandrels. The cornice has been removed. Brick construction with wood posts.

C

M130 MAP III
549-551 Mission Street
architect unknown
1905

A handsome example of a two part small commercial block with a skeletal brick facade and inset iron window framing. Restrained Renaissance/Baroque ornamentation. Brick construction with wood posts. The pre-fire date of this structure, from a usually reliable source, should be confirmed.

B

M131 MAP III
553 Mission Street
architect unknown
1906

A two part small commercial block, skeletal in construction, with restrained Renaissance/Baroque ornamentation.

C

M132 MAP III
554-560 Mission Street
Daziel Building
architect unknown
1907

Once the home of the *Daily Pacific Builder* and the *Building and Industrial News*. A three part vertical composition with restrained Renaissance/Baroque ornamentation. Brick construction with steel columns. The building relates in scale and articulation to its neighbor at 562–572 Mission Street.

C

M133 MAP III
562-572 Mission Street
Golden Gate University Law School Library
architect unknown
1919

A reinforced concrete loft building with extremely early use of mushroom column drop panel construction, an important breakthrough in reinforced concrete design that is still utilized today. There is no other known use of this technique prior to the year in which this building was built. In composition, the building is a two part vertical block with restrained Renaissance/Baroque ornamentation.

B

M134 MAP III
565-567 Mission Street
architect unknown
1907

A two part small commercial block with formal treatment of the upper zone. Ornamentation is restrained Renaissance/Baroque. Brick construction.

C

M135 MAP III
571-573 Mission Street
architect unknown
1910

A two part small commercial block with skeletal facade expression and limited use of Renaissance/Baroque ornament. Brick construction.

C

M136 MAP III
575-579 Mission Street
architect unknown
1912

A three part vertical block, skeletal in articulation with restrained use of Renaissance/Baroque ornament. Brick construction with wood posts.

C

M137 MAP III
583-585 Mission Street
Stoll and Sonniksen Building
architect unknown
1906

A two part small commercial block, skeletal in expression with Renaissance/Baroque ornamentation. The original ground floor is intact. Brick construction.

C

M138 MAP III
589-591 Mission Street
architect unknown
1907

A two part vertical composition, skeletal in expression, with restrained use of Renaissance/Baroque ornamentation. The original ground floor is intact. Brick construction.

C

M139 MAP III
602-606 Mission Street
Atlas Building
John V. D. Linden
1931

Originally built in 1904 to the design of Frank S. Van Trees, and rebuilt after relatively minor damage in the fire. The original was a very fine three part vertical composition with a giant order in the top zone; at the mezzanine level was Atlas with the world on his shoulders flanked by large lion caryatids, all in cast iron. At the time of the remodeling in 1931, the *Architect and Engineer* wrote, "In times of depression, when the building industry is at a low ebb and when property owners are too conservative to

invest in new structures, arguments for modernizing old buildings have a responsive appeal, and the opportunities for an architect to develop his business loom encouragingly. If he can convince the owner how he may place his property on a paying basis, the architect is certain of a commission that will at least tide him over until bigger things develop." The building today is in a weak two part composition in pink terra cotta with Moderne references. Steel frame construction.

C

M140 MAP III
609 Mission Street
SW corner Second
Stevenson Building
originally J. S. Morgan Building
E. J. Vogel
1907

A post-fire reconstruction, with variations, of the 1902 Morgan Building whose design was exhibited in the San Francisco Architectural Club show of that same year. The design is one of many which was derived from McKim, Mead, and White's Phoenix Building. It is a three part vertical block with restrained Renaissance/Baroque ornamentation. An important corner building on both Mission and Second streets.

C

M141 MAP III
617-623 Mission Street
SE corner New Montgomery
Koracorp Building
originally Crellin Building
Walter J. Mathews
1908

A simplified post-fire reconstruction of a 1902 design which was also by Mathews. In composition, a three part vertical block, skeletal in articulation with restrained Renaissance/Baroque ornamentation. Brick construction with steel posts and girders. An important corner building and part of the cohesive New Montgomery Street group.

C

M142 MAP III
641-643 Mission Street
architect unknown
1907

A two part small commercial block with formal treatment of the upper section and restrained use of Renaissance/Baroque ornamentation. Brick construction.

C

M143 MAP III
647-649 Mission Street
Veronica Building
architect unknown
1907

A compact example of a three part vertical composition with differentiated end bays. Renaissance/Baroque ornamentation includes flat arches, rusticated piers, and abstracted capitals. Brick construction with wood posts.

C

M144 MAP IV
652-654 Mission Street
architect unknown
1909

A two part small commercial block with skeletal articulation of the upper floor and a recessed ground level storefront behind two giant iron columns. Limited ornamentation is vaguely Renaissance/Baroque. Brick construction with interior wood posts.

C

M145 MAP IV
657 Mission Street
McLaughlin Building
William Koenig
1907

A two part vertical composition, skeletal in expression. Originally with modified Renaissance/Baroque ornamentation, but now stripped of all decorative detail. An early, large example of reinforced concrete construction.

C

M146 MAP IV
658-664 Mission Street
NE corner Annie
Graphics Building
previously Textile Building
architect unknown
1906

A post-fire reconstruction, with variations, of a 1902 design which was referred to in *Town Talk* as "the finest office furniture building in the West." Originally a 6-story building in a three part composition without the mezzanine level pediments; the present building is a two part composition. Ornamentation is Renaissance/Baroque. The mezzanine level pediments are designed, whether ingeniously or unconsciously, to read alternatively as swags that cross the piers. Brick construction with wood posts.

C

M147 MAP IV
663-671 Mission Street
Grant Building
Crim and Scott
1909

Originally the home of the Munich Art Glass Co. and later of Roberts Manufacturing. In composition, a two part vertical block with enframed bays and restrained Renaissance/Baroque ornamentation. Brick construction with wood posts.

C

M148 MAP IV
666 Mission Street
NW corner Annie
architect unknown
1922

A handsome two part small commercial block, skeletal in articulation with Renaissance/ Baroque ornamentation. The storefronts have shallow pointed arches. A concrete building with wood posts.

C

M149 MAP IV
674-676 Mission Street
Gallatin Building
architect unknown
1907

A small three part vertical block with differentiated end bays and Renaissance/Baroque ornamentation. The second story plate glass window is an alteration. Brick construction with wood posts.

C

M150 MAP IV
700 Mission Street
NW corner Third
Aronson Building
later Mercantile Building
Hemenway and Miller
1903

A fine example of a three part Sullivanesque composition, designed by a little-known firm which also did the excellent original design for the building now known as the old French Bank (R226). The Aronson Building consists of a glass base with a massively skeletal shaft, vertically articulated. The design culminates in a richly embellished arcade and a 2-story capital that includes small round windows in reference to such Sullivan skyscrapers as the Guaranty and Wainwright buildings. Renaissance/Baroque ornamental details are overscaled to be legible and to enhance the massiveness of the top. The glass base relates the design to the San Francisco type with glass commercial areas under "architectural" office floors. The building serves as a powerful corner anchor, although the buildings which it once anchored have all been demolished for Yerba Buena Center.

The Aronson Building achieved a measure of notoriety in the post-fire report of the U.S. Geological Survey on the condition of San Francisco buildings. It was the report's featured example of supposedly fireproof construction that met with disaster. Its tile clad steel columns failed, while concrete clad columns in other structures withstood the fire. The building was built by Abraham Aronson, a major real estate investor of the period and an active member of the Jewish community in San Francisco. Since the 1930s, when the Aronson family sold the building, it has been known as the Mercantile Building. Once scheduled for demolition as part of Yerba Buena Center, it is now included in YBC plans.

A   NRp

M151 MAP IV
756 Mission Street
St. Patrick's Church
architect unknown
1872

The last remnant of the large Irish community which was once located in the South of Market area. The church has survived subsequent eras dominated by manufacturing establishments and residential hotels, and most recently it has suffered the demolition of almost everything around it for Yerba Buena Center. The structure was gutted in the fire but rebuilt by architects Shea and Lofquist in 1909, minus the great steeple. Its stained glass is very fine. In composition, a basilica with a tower and Gothic ornamentation. The nave is flanked by buttressed wings and lit by clerestories. The tower culminates in spires at the corners. Presently isolated among parking lots, St. Patrick's will be incorporated in Yerba Buena Center.

A   NRp; CL

M152 MAP IV
760 Mission Street
St. Patrick's Rectory
architect unknown
ca. 1926

A reinforced concrete rectory for St. Patrick's Church next door. Also one of the last buildings in the large area cleared for Yerba Buena Center. The rectory building will remain along with the church. The composition is dominated by a large central projecting bay which overhangs a ground floor entrance. Gothic ornamentation.

C

M153 MAP IV
1 Montgomery Street
NW corner Post at Market
Crocker Bank Building
originally First National Bank
Willis Polk
1908

A "combination bank and office building" with one of the most lavish banking interiors in the city, but also with an unfortunately remodeled tower above the banking hall facade. The tower was remodeled about 1960 by Milton Pfleuger after the old sandstone facing appeared to be in danger of falling off. The original design was a three part vertical composition with a giant order in the upper zone. In 1921 the banking hall and its arcaded base were extended to the north in an exact copy of the original design. This extension made a grand interior even grander with its sumptuous marble furnishings, fluted columns, and coffered ceilings, but it incurred a characteristically flamboyant reaction from Polk who sued the architect, Charles E. Gottschalk, for plagiarism.

Up until the time of its remodeling, the building occupied a key position in what must have been one of the finest intersections of monumental buildings in America. Across Post Street and occupying the Market Street gore was A. Page Brown's flatiron Crocker Building, across Montgomery was Clinton Day's Union Trust Co. Building, and across Market were the Mer-

Ca. 1910. Before remodeling of tower.

chant's National Bank Building (M53) and the Palace Hotel (M54), still standing. The tower of the Hobart Building (M45) was visible over the Union Trust. Despite tremendous losses in the immediate area, the Crocker Bank is still an extremely important building at its location. Its arcaded base and columned entrance vestibule form rich street facades in contrast to the newly prevailing sterility of the area. And the tower, despite its remodeling, still displays in its form a knowledge of how to fill a space at an important intersection.

Crocker Bank is presently planning to remove the tower above the grand banking hall and build a new highrise west of Lick Place. A shopping arcade would front on Lick Place and a tower would rise in the southwest corner of the block, displacing the Lick Garage, the Foxcroft Building (R148), the Thompson and Ortman Building (R92), and the Lyons Building (R93). Architects of the project are Skidmore, Owings, and Merrill.

A

M154 MAP IV
2-44 Montgomery Street
NE corner Market at Post
Wells Fargo Building
John Graham
1966

On the site of Clinton Day's Union Trust Co. Building. The low pavilion on Market opens up the blank wall of the Hobart Building which was hidden by the old Union Trust.

NOT RATED

M155 MAP IV
17-29 New Montgomery Street
NE corner Stevenson
architect unknown
ca. 1906

A 1-story commercial block with a curious cut-away corner defined by a cornice. Renaissance/Baroque ornamentation. Brick construction.

C

M156 MAP IV
39-63 New Montgomery Street
Sharon Building
George Kelham
1912

A handsome steel frame, brick clad office building with what must be the city's broadest projecting cornice and a narrow ell that fills the New Montgomery Street frontage. It was one of the many buildings constructed for the estate of William Sharon in these years. Sharon was a colorful pioneer who was once William Ralston's partner in the Palace Hotel and who later was United States Senator. In composition, the building is a three part vertical block with Renaissance/Baroque ornamentation and terra cotta details at the base and capital. Both Webster Cigars and the House of Shields retain their original interiors. The building was being constructed under a general contract at a time when old methods of bidding and contracting with individual trades were being challenged. It is a steel frame structure with reinforced concrete curtain walls, and is "thoroughly fireproof." In both its structure and the process of construction, this building was considered to be a model in its day. Appropriately, the original occupation was largely by architects and the building trades. This building is a major element on New Montgomery Street.

A

M157 MAP IV
74 New Montgomery Street
SW corner Jessie
Call Building
Reid Brothers
1914

A richly clad facade in a two part vertical composition with an attic and a giant order in the shaft. The rusticated piers of the base are surmounted by a mezzanine with pulvinated rustication and a fluted Corinthian order, all creating a design of variously textured and articulated levels. The design of the New Montgomery Street end of the building is repeated at the rear on Annie Street. Constructed entirely of reinforced concrete. Originally built as headquarters of the San Francisco *Call* newspaper; from 1929–1940 it headquartered the *Call-Bulletin*. Now occupied by Crocker Bank as an office building.

A

M158 MAP III
79 New Montgomery
SE corner Mission
Crossley Building
addition by Mel I. Schwartz
1907, 1920

A 1907 reinforced concrete structure with a major 3-story addition (1920) that dominates the character of the building. In its present form, a two part vertical composition with vaguely Renaissance/Baroque ornamentation. The ground level has been walled-in, but the upper section of the building forms a good background element in the New Montgomery Street wall. Now occupied by Crocker Bank.

C

M159 MAP III
111-121 New Montgomery Street
NE corner Minna
Standard Building
architect unknown
1907

A two part vertical block with Renaissance/Baroque ornamentation. Steel frame construction. Part of the New Montgomery Street wall.

C

M160 MAP III
116 New Montgomery Street
SW Corner Mission
Rialto Building
Meyer and O'Brien/Bliss and Faville
1902/1910

A pre-fire building by Meyer and O'Brien, rebuilt by Bliss and Faville to the original design in 1910. This is the earliest San Francisco example of a facade expression that is used again in the Monadnock (M56) and Galen (R246) buildings, also by Meyer and O'Brien. It also represents an early and uncommon use of the U-plan with a light court at the front. The facade treatment was related to the innovative interior plan which was the result of a trip to Chicago by architect Meyer. Large offices were undivided until rented, at which time they could be arranged to suit a variety of needs. All wood and brick mullions were wide enough "to receive a dividing partition," and the great number of windows ensured that any interior arrangement would be amply lit.

In composition, the building is a three part vertical block. Ornamentation is Renaissance/Baroque. The steel frame structure is clad in brick and terra cotta with a massive wooden entrance arcade at the base of the light wall, rusticated and painted to look like granite. The marble lobby has paired Corinthian pilasters, a paneled ceiling, and ornate metal elevator doors. The building forms a major part of the New Montgomery Street wall.

A

M161 MAP III
134-140 New Montgomery Street
Pacific Telephone and Telegraph Co.
Building
Miller and Pfleuger; A. A. Cantin
1925

One of San Francisco's finest skyscrapers of any period and one of only two illustrated in Francisco Mujica's 1929 *History of the Skyscraper.* Mujica wrote: "The Telephone Building of San Francisco marks the end of the preparatory and experimental stage in skyscraper architecture," in reference to its original and entirely ahistorical ornamentation, and its reliance on Eliel Saarinen's Tribune Tower Competition design as a precedent. Apart from its broader historical importance, the building has had tremendous influence locally. The Shell Building (F8), the Pacific National Bank Building (now demolished), and the old William Taylor Hotel (100 McAllister Street), all followed its lead as a gracefully stepping back tower. And many others followed as well in its inventive use of ornament and expression of verticality.

It is a steel frame building, originally planned in an E shape, but built as an F, and designed to be seen from all sides. The New Montgomery side appears quite massive, while the rear is broken up in wings, each suggesting the main facade at a smaller scale. The fine terra cotta ornamentation, speckled like granite, has the quality of Gothic detail at times but is entirely original in reference. The lobby is a superb example of Moderne design with black marble walls, fantastic "Chinese" stenciled ceilings, and bronze elevator doors. At the time it was built, it was the largest corporate office building on the Pacific Coast.

A

M162 MAP III
137-159 New Montgomery Street
architect unknown
1907

Originally a two part vertical block, now a cumbersome 2-story addition from the 1930s. The building still succeeds as a part of the New Montgomery Street wall. Ornamentation is Renaissance/Baroque. Brick construction.

C

M163 MAP III
170-180 New Montgomery Street
NW corner Howard
Furniture Exchange
architect uncertain
1920

Originally built as the Furniture Exchange Building. Now occupied by the Telephone Company, and like too many of their buildings, this one has suffered the walling-in of the ground floor. The original design is tentatively attributed to MacDonald and Applegarth, but has been remodeled, primarily through the removal of decorative detail. A two part vertical composition with very limited Renaissance/Baroque ornamental references remaining. The building still serves as a part of the New Montgomery Street wall. Reinforced concrete construction.

C

M164 MAP II
2 Pine Street
NW corner Davis at Market
Oceanic Building
originally Tillman and Bendel
George A. Applegarth
1919

Originally the Tillman and Bendel Building of 1908 by MacDonald and Applegarth, re-modeled with the addition of three stories by George Applegarth alone in 1919. A three part vertical composition with a giant order in the upper zone and a small tower on the roof. Or-namentation is Renaissance/Baroque.

The construction of the building is one of the best documented of any in downtown San Fran-cisco, with detailed coverage by the *Architect and Engineer* of the initial construction in 1908 and the addition in 1919. The reinforced con-crete columns of the original were enlarged for the extra load of the addition by pouring new concrete through holes in the floor slabs into new forms around the old columns. In 1919, the *Architect and Engineer* said, "The building is con-sidered one of the best built and most attractive office structures in the down-town section of San Francisco." Site of the proposed Itel Building by Houston developer Gerald Hines, to be de-signed by Philip Johnson.

B

M165 MAP V
1 Powell Street
at Hallidie Plaza
Bank of America
originally Bank of Italy
Bliss and Faville
1920

Originally a corner structure partly hidden from Market Street by buildings on an intervening gore, but now forming a handsome backdrop to Hallidie Plaza. The design is the result of a competition entered by eleven invited competi-tors, and won by Bliss and Faville. Most entries were variations on the winning theme or were otherwise orthodox designs. The exception was the entry of E. T. Foulkes, which according to the *Architect and Engineer*, "broke away from the complacent six-story idea so apparently laid down in the programme with a mighty tower that sucked up all but the two lower floors with it, like a huge stone waterspout."

The existing building is a faithful execution of the winning design. In composition, it is a stacked vertical block with Renaissance/Baroque orna-mentation. Its resemblance to McKim, Mead and White's University Club in New York resulted in a lengthy essay in the *Architect and Engineer* on "the line between inspiration and plagia-rism," attributing it finally to inspiration and calling it "a building of unusual distinction, ably composed and proportioned, noble in scale, detailed with fine taste, and executed with beautiful perfection." The equally fine interior has lost some of its fine ornamental metal work but is largely intact. The sculptural group over the entrance is by John Portonova. The building

is a steel frame structure with a granite base and terra cotta cladding above.

A

M166 MAP II
1 Sansome Street
NW corner Sutter at Market
Crocker Bank Building
originally London Paris National Bank,
    later Anglo California National Bank
Albert Pissis/George Kelham
1910/1921

One of the city's finest banking temples, designed in two stages by two of the city's most
important architects. It was built for the London
Paris National Bank which became the Anglo
California National Bank and later merged with
Crocker Bank. In composition, the building is a
modified temple without a pediment. Ornamentation is derived from classical antiquity
with a Doric order superimposed over an arcade on the original Sutter Street facade. As
extended, the Sansome Street facade consists
of a colonnade at the street line with arched
pavilions flanking a recessed entrance porch.
Ornamental detail is carved in granite on a
steel skeleton. The major interior banking hall
is finished in artificial marble and bronze with
a coffered ceiling and a large central oval
skylight. A smaller space that continues the
banking hall to the north, in a complementary
manner, is actually carved out of Kelham's Standard Oil Building of 1924 at 225 Bush Street (F11).

The building is an important element in one of
the downtown area's finest rows on Sansome
Street in the blocks stretching from Market past
California. It is also part of the diminished but
still fine group on lower Sutter whose major
members are the Flatiron (M37) and Chancery
(M42) buildings on Market, 560 Market (M41),
and the Holbrook Building (F140) on Sutter. The
building is currently threatened by a proposed
35-story office structure to be developed by
J. Patrick Mahoney.

A

M167 MAP III
39-49 Stevenson Street
SW corner Ecker
architect unknown
1909

A handsome brick warehouse structure converted for commercial and office use in a
cohesive neighborhood of similar structures.

C

M168 MAP III
53 Stevenson Street
architect unknown
1908

A two part small commercial block with skeletal
treatment of the facade and Renaissance/
Baroque ornamentation. Brick construction.

C

M169 MAP III
55 Stevenson Street
Standard Varnish Works
architect unknown
1910

Built for the Standard Varnish Works with a
ground floor sales office, upper floor storage
rooms, and a testing laboratory under the roof.
In composition, a two part small commercial
block with mid-19th century treatment of the
upper section. The building has a mansard roof
with a dormer. Brick construction with heavy
timber framing, clad in iron.

C

M170 MAP III
71 Stevenson Street
Stevenson Garage
architect unknown
1923

A reinforced concrete parking garage with
bands of industrial sash windows.

C

M171 MAP III
77 Stevenson Street
San Francisco Municipal Railway Co.
    Substation
architect unknown
ca. 1910

Formerly a Muni Substation and now vacant. A
reinforced concrete warehouse-type structure
with steel trusses carrying the roof.

C

M172 MAP III
83 Stevenson Street
California Farmer
originally U.S. Post Office
Willis Polk
1908

A hybrid composition with a loggia treated as the base of a pedimented temple front. Renaissance/Baroque ornamentation includes an iron eagle at the peak of the pediment. The structure was designed by Willis Polk as a speculative building for L.M. Hoefler and was originally used as a Post Office. Brick construction.

B

M173 MAP IV
111-127 Stevenson Street
Palace Garage
O'Brien Brothers
1921

Another excellent example of a garage designed to resemble an office building, in this case as a two part vertical block with Gothic ornamentation. The very fine neon "enter" and "exit" signs seem suspended in air when lit at night. Reinforced concrete construction.

B

M174 MAP V
1 Stockton Street
NW corner Ellis at Market
Great Western Savings
Skidmore, Owings, and Merrill
1973

NOT RATED

M175 MAP V
2-16 Turk Street
NW corner Mason at Market
Oxford Hotel
originally Hotel Glenn
William H. Weeks
1911

A richly ornamented hotel building with a particularly prominent cornice that functions as a focal point at a major Market Street intersection. The curving facade of the old Merchant's National Bank Building (M86) turns the wall of the street from Market to the Oxford Hotel, emphasizing the latter as a strong visual anchor. In composition, the building is a three part vertical block with Renaissance/Baroque ornamentation. Its construction is steel frame with brick clad concrete curtain walls and terra cotta ornament at the base and capital. The building is the best downtown San Francisco work of an important northern California architect whose designs were mostly done in smaller cities and towns.

B

M176 MAP VI
1 United Nations Plaza
C. A. Meussdorffer
ca. 1935

A tiny triangular building which manages to hold its own in the monumentally scaled Civic Center by a lighthearted reinterpretation of classical elements in the fashionable style of the time, the Moderne. The upper facade consists of narrow, abstract pilasters alternating with bold faceted copper bays. As originally designed, the light colored pilasters (the receding spaces between columns) and dark bays (treated as projecting columns with cornices), suggested a reversal of the orthodox classical pattern. Unfortunately, the recent remodeling, with its blue paint and overscaled awning, obscures these relationships. The building is of reinforced concrete construction in a two part vertical composition. The unusual shape is rumored to be the result of the original owner's attempt to block access of the building behind it to what was then Fulton Street.

B   NRD

M177 MAP II
9-15 First Street
SE corner Market
Sheldon Building
Benjamin G. McDougall, architect;
   John B. Leonard, consulting engineer
1907

One of the first large reinforced concrete buildings in the city. Both the architect and the consulting engineer were important early designers of reinforced concrete structures in San Francisco. The structure is clad in terra cotta and has recently been painted bright yellow. The original highly decorative base and cornice have been stripped of detail. In composition, the building is a three part vertical block with differentiated end bays and Renaissance/Baroque ornamentation. According to an article in the *Architect and Engineer* in November 1906 by the architect, "the exterior is treated in a style that has evolved for office buildings in this country—and which lends itself well to a structure that must have abundance of light." The building occupies the site of a structure which was destroyed in 1906, also called the Sheldon Building.

B

M178 MAP II
38-40 First Street
SW corner Stevenson
architect unknown
1908

A two part vertical block with restrained Renaissance/Baroque ornamentation. Brick construction.

C

M179 MAP II
41 First Street
Blake, Moffitt, and Towne Building
Willis Polk
1911

A reinforced concrete office building built for the Regents of the University of California and originally occupied by Blake, Moffitt, and Towne, a long-time San Francisco paper distributing company. The terra cotta clad structure is designed in a two part composition with a giant order and an attic story. The ornamentation is Renaissance/Baroque.

B

M180 MAP II
51-63 First Street
Golden Gate Building
architect unknown
1907

A distinctive design, particularly in the wavy corbeled division between the upper two tiers that recalls the Hiram Sibley warehouse in Chicago (1882). In composition, the building is a stacked vertical block with loosely interpreted Renaissance/Baroque ornamentation. It is a brick building with steel posts at the ground level and wood posts above.

C

M181 MAP II
62 First Street
SW corner Jessie
Neustadter Brothers Building
Sylvain Schnaittacher
1917

A three part vertical block with restrained Renaissance/Baroque ornamentation, built of reinforced concrete.

C

M182 MAP II
76-80 First Street
Marwedel Building
architect unknown
1908

A simple two part vertical block with modified Renaissance/Baroque ornamentation. Brick construction.

C

M183 MAP II
82-84 First Street
architect unknown
1908

An L-shaped brick building which fronts on both First and Mission streets, with a two part composition and restrained Renaissance ornamentation. It recalls the commercial Italianate style of the late 19th century.

C

M184 MAP III
110 First Street
O'Brien Brothers
1922

A reinforced concrete loft structure in a two part vertical composition with Gothic ornamentation.

C

M185 MAP III
116 First Street
Bonestell Building
Joseph L. Stewart
1921

An unusual design with giant pilasters and arched windows, originally built for the Moss Glove Company. In composition, an enframed window wall with modified Renaissance/Baroque ornamentation. The arched marquee with clock dates from the 1930s. Reinforced concrete construction.

C

M186 MAP III
118-124 First Street
NW corner Minna
architect unknown
1907

One of many downtown San Francisco buildings whose design derives from McKim, Mead, and White's Phoenix Building of 1882 (New York) in the enframement of bays. A three part vertical composition with modified Renaissance/Baroque ornamentation. Brick construction with wood posts.

C

M187 MAP IV
20-28 Second Street
Schwabacher Building
architect unknown
1914

A reinforced concrete loft building with handsomely proportioned windows and a minimal skeletal facade. Two part vertical composition with Renaissance references.

B

M188 MAP IV
30 Second Street
NW corner Stevenson
architect unknown
1917

A two part small commercial block with skeletal articulation of the facade and restrained Renaissance/Baroque ornamentation. Reinforced concrete construction.

C

M189 MAP III
36-40 Second Street
SW corner Stevenson
Morgan Building
William D. Shea
1907

A three part vertical block with differentiated end bays along Stevenson and restrained Renaissance/Baroque ornamentation. Brick construction.

C

M190 MAP III
39-47 Second Street
SE corner Stevenson
Wentworth-Smith Building
originally Cunningham Building
Reid Brothers
1907

A large brick building with iron posts throughout. In composition, a two part vertical block with a giant order and restrained Renaissance/Baroque ornamentation.

C

M191 MAP III
42-46 Second Street
architect unknown
1907

A two part small commercial block with a handsome formal upper story and Renaissance/Baroque ornamentation. Reinforced concrete construction.

C

M192 MAP III
48-50 Second Street
Kentfield and Esser Building
architect unknown
1907

Built as a 4-story brick loft structure for the Kentfield and Esser Co., a supplier of surveying and drafting equipment, to accommodate offices, workrooms, repair rooms, and showrooms. A two part vertical block with skeletal articulation and Renaissance/Baroque ornamentation.

C

M193 MAP III
52-54 Second Street
architect unknown
1907

A two part vertical block with Renaissance/Baroque ornamentation. Brick construction.

C

M194 MAP III
60-64 Second Street
NW corner Jessie
architect unknown
1906

A three part vertical block with Renaissance ornamentation. Brick construction.

C

M195 MAP III
70-72 Second Street
SW corner Jessie
architect unknown
1907

A handsome two part small commercial block with deep-set windows; it recalls the 19th century commercial Italianate. The cornice has been removed. Renaissance ornamentation and brick construction.

C

M196 MAP III
71-85 Second Street
NE corner Mission
Wells Fargo Building
Meyers and Ward
1902; rebuilt 1907

Originally built for the Wells Fargo Express Company offices, and now occupied by Pacific Telephone. The building was damaged but not destroyed in 1906, and rebuilt with an additional two stories. The steel frame, clad in cinder concrete on a galvanized wire fabric, is a good example of what was considered to be fireproof construction in the period before the fire. Immediately after the fire, the top floor was occupied by the California Supreme Court. The building is a three part vertical block in composition, with restrained Renaissance ornamentation. The 2-story base is clad in granite.

A

M197 MAP III
76 Second Street
architect unknown
1908

A two part small commercial block with modified Renaissance/Baroque ornamentation. Note the sunburst capital of the ground floor pilasters. Brick construction.

C

M198 MAP III
84-88 Second Street
architect unknown
1907

Now occupied by the Trust for Public Land which spruced up a drab facade with a mural of a tree. The building's principal importance is in the contribution of its scale and texture to the block front. In composition, a two part small commercial block with vague Renaissance/Baroque references. Brick construction with wood posts.

C

M199 MAP III
90-96 Second Street
NW corner Mission
architect unknown
1907

A two part small commercial block with restrained Renaissance/Baroque ornamentation. Brick construction.

C

M200 MAP IV
17-29 Third Street
NE corner Stevenson
architect unknown
ca. 1910

A two part small commercial block with formal treatment of the upper stories and 18th century English ornamentation. Brick construction.

C

M201 MAP IV
51 Third Street
Hearst Parking Center
T. Y. Lin, Kulka, Yang and Associates
1970

A recent reinforced concrete garage which succeeds on several levels. As in the first downtown parking garages which had no model to follow for the appearance of a parking garage, it resembles an office building and manages to maintain the visual character of the street as part of an office district. The building respects the lot lines of its neighbors and provides a successful and attractive recessed shopping area at the ground level. The beautiful concrete work is typical of the quality of the engineering and design of T. Y. Lin.

NOT RATED

M202 MAP IV
71-77 Third Street
SE corner Jessie
Breen's Fine Food
architect unknown
1908

Important for both its design and as the long-time home of Breen's Fine Food. Located at this spot since 1912, Breen's is one of the last places that retains some of the character of the South of Market neighborhood demolished for Yerba Buena Center. Its carved wooden bar belongs to that group of bars reputedly brought around the Horn during the Gold Rush. The building, a two part vertical composition with Renaissance/Baroque ornamentation, has lost its cornice but retains its fine, almost quaint, old signs. The design of both building and signs is similar to those at 201–219 O'Farrell (R135). Brick construction. Now threatened by Yerba Buena Center.

B

M203 MAP IV
81-85 Third Street
architect unknown
ca. 1910

A two part small commercial block with modified Renaissance/Baroque ornamentation. Brick construction. Threatened by Yerba Buena Center.

C

M204 MAP IV
87-97 Third Street
NE corner Mission
Grace Building
Shea and Lofquist
1907

A once handsome loft structure with an unfortunate top story addition. It is located at what was formerly one of the prime downtown intersections. In composition, a two part vertical block with skeletal articulation and modified Renaissance/Baroque ornamentation. Reinforced concrete construction. Threatened by Yerba Buena Center.

C NRDp

M205 MAP IV
101-107 Third Street
SE corner Mission
Williams Building
Clinton Day
1907

This steel frame office building is one of only three remaining downtown commercial structures by Clinton Day, and the only one which is entirely his design. Day was one of the best and most prolific local architects of the decade prior to 1906. In composition, an elaborate three part vertical block with differentiated end bays and Renaissance/Baroque ornamentation. The building is notable for its excellent and inventive brick work, and for its environmental role at what was once one of the prime corners in downtown San Francisco. With the demolition of the Luning Building across Third Street (for

Yerba Buena Center), the Williams and Aronson (M150) buildings, diagonally across the intersection, are of added significance. Now surrounded by vacant lots and threatened by Yerba Buena Center.

B NRDp

M206 MAP IV
49 Fourth Street
Apparel Center Building
later Veterans Administration Building
Ashley and Evers
1925

An 11-story steel frame office loft with a 5-story rear addition. Its three part vertical composition with differentiated end bays and vaguely Gothic ornamentation is distinguished by a light skeletal articulation. From 1951 to 1973, the building was owned by the United States Government and known as the Veterans Administration Building. Today it stands vacant on Yerba Buena Center property, and is threatened by a proposed $56 million federal office building.

B

M207 MAP V
9-41 Fifth Street
SE corner Market
Lincoln Realty Building
D. H. Burnham and Co.
1908

An immense two part composition with a giant order of simple pilasters that stretches for 14 bays along Market Street. Ornamentation is Renaissance/Baroque. The design was prepared by the San Francisco office of the Chicago based D. H. Burnham and Co. As head of the local office, Willis Polk was in charge of this design. Originally three stores at the ground level, the building was remodeled inside as one large department store (Grayson's) in 1944. According to *Architectural Forum*, the remodeling was designed "to suit the expanding wartime business of a single firm of women's clothiers," reflecting the increasing importance of women in the local economy in those years. Since then the single store has been cut up again into ten separate stores whose variously shaped signs obscure part of the facade. The building is part of one of the most important and imposing stretches of Market Street.

B

M208 MAP VI
6-26 Seventh Street
SW corner Market
Odd Fellows Temple
architect unknown
1909

An unsophisticated but richly detailed steel frame structure which recalls the days when fraternal groups, such as the Odd Fellows, played a major role in American cultural life. Unlike the Bohemian Club, Olympic Club and other wealthier clubs west of Union Square whose buildings were entirely devoted to club uses, the Odd Fellows Hall is built above three floors of rentable commercial space.

In composition, it is a two part vertical block with differentiated end bays over a three story glass base (now partially obscured). Its dominant ornamentation is Renaissance/Baroque with elements of fraternal symbolism, notably in the stained glass of the upper bays. The clutter of commercial signs and remodeling around its base detract from the building's stature as a major Civic Center area landmark. It occupies a critical position at the end of United Nations Plaza, at a major Market Street corner, and at one end of the Seventh Street block which includes the Post Office and the Adam Grant Building (M112).

A

M209 MAP IV
Yerba Buena Center
originally Redevelopment Area D
planning begun ca. 1953

A large Redevelopment project occupying most of the blocks bound by Market, Harrison, Third, and Fourth Streets. Following complicated beginnings, in the late 1950s, private demolition began of buildings in an area along Howard Street. In 1963 the boundaries of the present Yerba Buena Center were established and in 1966 the Board of Supervisors approved a plan that involved clearance of two and a half blocks and called for a convention center, sports arena, and apparel mart, among its major elements.

Most of the buildings in Yerba Buena Center were cleared in the years 1966-1970. The area consisted of many fine buildings, mostly hotels and light industrial buildings, with office buildings along Mission Street. More important than the individual buildings was the handsome character of the area as a whole, and its many prospering businesses and vital street life. After years of delay, during which plans for demolition of the PG&E Substation at 222–226 Jessie Street, and the Aronson Building at Mission and Third were dropped, and housing developments were begun, construction began last year for a convention center. Plans for the rest of the area are still up in the air.

NOT RATED

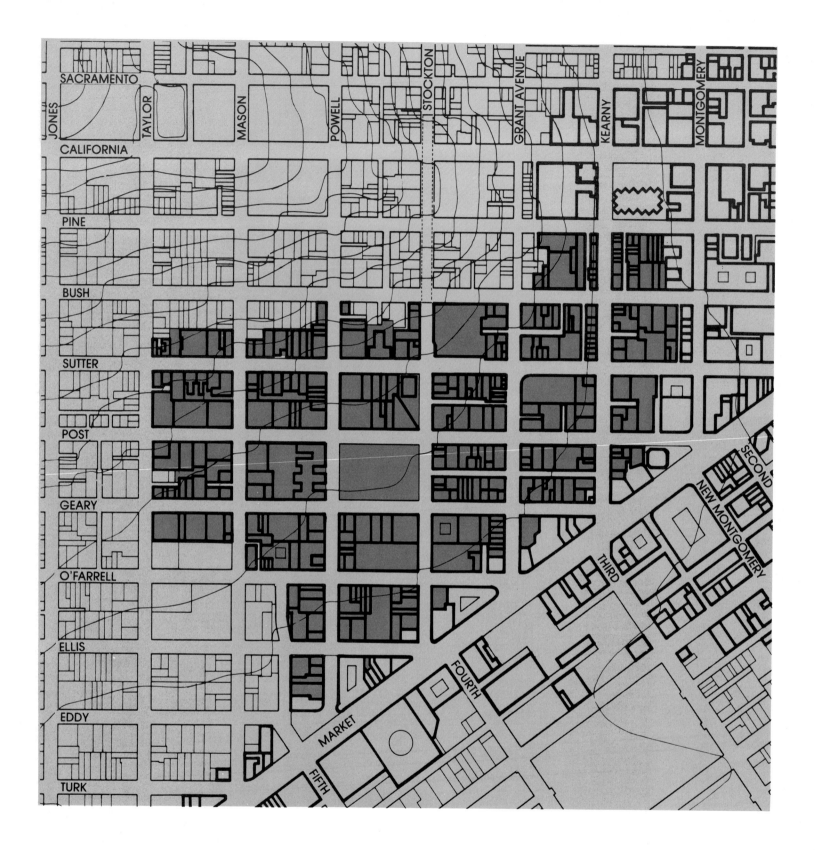

Retail District

BUSH

SUTTER

POST

GEARY

TAYLOR

MASON

POWELL

STOCKTON

271 273 270 267 265

209
207
257
253
255
254
253

208
252
225
224
251
223
247

272 271 269 266
275 268

264 262 258 256 206
128 260
205
204
203
202

201 250 249 248
222

276 178

276 178 176 175 173 200
174

172 171 170

182 181 180 179 127

177

169

125 199

53 51

65 64 63 62 60 59 57 56 54
61

126

MAP I

117

MAP II

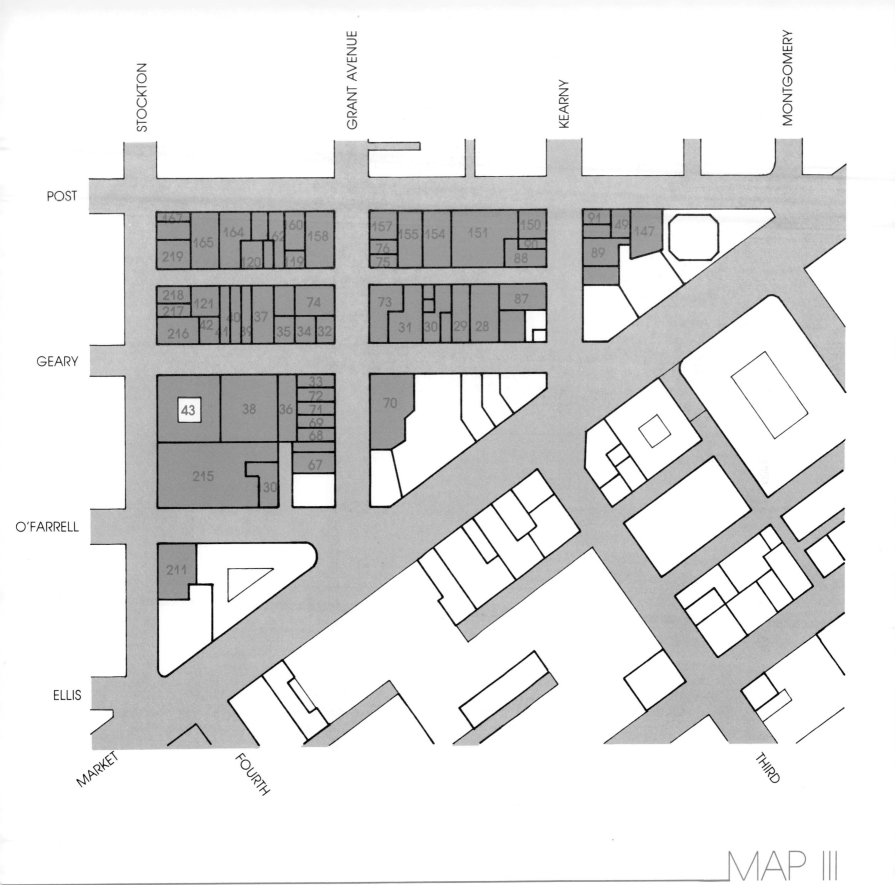

MAP III

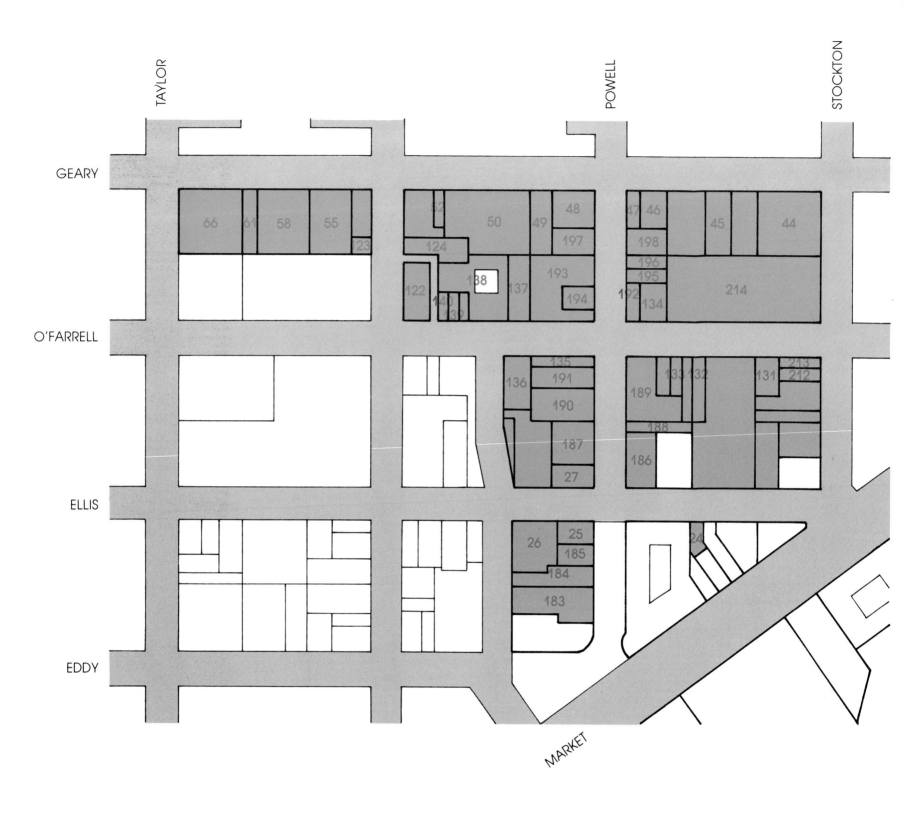

GEARY

TAYLOR

POWELL

STOCKTON

66 61 58 55 23

52 50 49 48 47 46 45 44
124 197 198
122 138 137 193 196 214
140 194 195 192
139 134

O'FARRELL

135
136 191 133 132 131 213
190 189 212
188
187 186
27

ELLIS

26 25
185
184
183
24

EDDY

MARKET

MAP IV

R1 MAP II
28 Belden Street
between Bush and Pine
architect unknown
1908, remodeled ca. 1926

A small brick structure remodeled about 1926 to conform to the other new Mission Revival style buildings on the alley. Part of a group of modest buildings which form a quiet, small scale street at the edge of the financial district. An enframed window wall with Mission Revival ornamentation.

C

R2 MAP II
40 Belden Street
between Bush and Pine
architect unknown
1926

The first Mission Revival building on the alley. The building jogs as the street width changes and consequently has the appearance of two buildings. In composition, a pair of parallel enframed window walls with Mission Revival ornamentation. Reinforced concrete construction.

C

R3 MAP II
52 Belden Street
between Bush and Pine
architect unknown
1922

A two part small commercial block, stripped of original ornamentation. Reinforced concrete construction. An important part of the Belden Street group.

C

R4 MAP II
334 Bush Street
T. Paterson Ross
1916

R5 MAP II
344 Bush Street
T. Paterson Ross
1923

A pair of very similar small commercial buildings designed at one time by the same architect but built seven years apart. Both buildings are enframed window wall compositions with Renaissance/Baroque ornamentation. Brick construction.

C

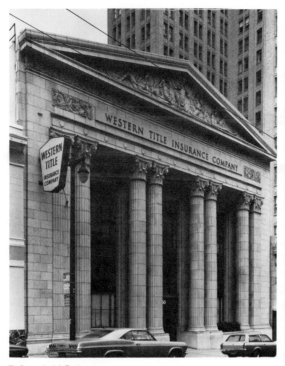

R6 MAP II
350 Bush Street
San Francisco Curb Exchange
originally San Francisco Mining
 Exchange, now Western Title Insurance
Miller and Pfleuger
1923

Originally the San Francisco Mining Exchange, and known as the San Francisco Curb Exchange from 1928 to 1938. Remembered as a symbol of the stock market crash of 1929. Partially remodeled inside in 1938 and now occupied by the Western Title Insurance Company. In composition, the building is a modified temple front with ornamentation derived from ancient Greek and Roman models. The terra cotta facade includes a sculptural group in the tympanum by Jo Moro. Despite its remodeling there is still a large interior space with thin pilastered walls and a large central skylight. A steel frame carries large steel trusses which span the exchange space. This is an early and uncharacteristic design by Miller and Pfleuger who are better known for their less literally historical work, particularly in the Moderne style.

A

R7 MAP II
355 Bush Street
Financial Center Garage
Powers and Ahnden
1925

Despite appearances, this is not an office building remodeled as a garage—but a garage designed to look like an office building. When this was built the parking garage was still a new building type and no one knew what it was "supposed" to look like. Rather than present a functional exterior which would have been considered out of place and disruptive to the character of the business district, the design was disguised so that it would blend into the background. Rather than "dishonest," as modern architecture would come to view such an approach, it was considered good manners and good sense to hide the ugly and disruptive, but often necessary, utilitarian structures of the city. In composition, a two part vertical block with restrained Renaissance ornamentation. Reinforced concrete construction with a brick curtain wall on the front facade. Entrance used to be through the ground floor arches where a restaurant is now located, but moved to the side in 1967 when the modern garage addition was built.

B

R8 MAP II
364 Bush Street
NE corner Belden
Sam's Grill
William F. Helbing
1907

A two part small commercial block with second story fenestration reminiscent of the forms of the late 19th century. Renaissance/Baroque ornamentation. Brick construction with wood and iron posts. Home of a long-time San Francisco institution, Sam's Grill, since 1946. It was originally built for J. M. McGee of Oroville. The building forms a corner to important groups of small scale buildings on both Bush and Belden streets.

C

R9 MAP II
380 Bush Street
NE corner Kearny
Shasta Hotel
E. P. Antonovich
1913

A three part vertical block with differentiated end bays and Renaissance/Baroque ornamentation. The cornice has been removed. Reinforced concrete construction.

C

R10 MAP II
381-383 Bush Street
SE corner Kearny
Alto Building
originally J. E. Adams Building
M. J. Lyons
1902, 1907

Built as the J. E. Adams Building in 1902 and rebuilt after the fire to exactly the same design in 1907. A three part vertical block with Renaissance/Baroque ornamentation. A good example of the common downtown building type designed for commercial uses on the two lower floors with offices above, and expressed in extensive use of plate glass on commercial floors with an implied masonry wall for offices. An important corner building on both Bush and Kearny.

B

R11 MAP II
410 Bush Street
NW corner St. George
Westinghouse Building
now Commercial Union Assurance
Albert Roller
1946

A 1915 reinforced concrete building remodeled in 1946 by Albert Roller.

NOT RATED

R12 MAP II
415 Bush Street
SW corner Claude
architect unknown
1908

A three part vertical block with Renaissance/Baroque ornamentation. Brick construction.

C

R13 MAP II
429-431 Bush Street
SE corner Mark
architect unknown
1908

A three part vertical block with Renaissance/Baroque ornamentation. Brick construction.

C

R14 MAP II
430 Bush Street
Pacific Telephone Building
Bliss and Faville
1924

A two part vertical office block with Renaissance/Baroque ornamentation in brick and terra cotta. Steel frame construction. Built on the site of the California Theater.

C

R15 MAP II
445 Bush Street
SW corner Mark
**Pacific States Telephone and
 Telegraph Building**
A. A. Cantin
1905

A pre-fire Telephone Company building by A. A. Cantin, who would later collaborate with Miller and Pfleuger on the famous New Montgomery Street Telephone Building in 1925. This building was relatively unharmed by the earthquake and fire of 1906 due to extensive fireproofing including a concrete clad steel skeleton and rolling steel shutters over wire glass in metal frames. The handsome brick and terra cotta design on the front facade is in a three part composition with Renaissance ornamentation.

A

R16 MAP II
447 Bush Street
Hansa Hotel
architect unknown
1914

A reinforced concrete residential hotel with Gothic ornamentation that culminates in a fanciful vaulted cornice.

C

R17 MAP II
453-455 Bush Street
Le Central
architect unknown
1906

A well-known French restaurant in an enframed window wall with vague Renaissance ornamental references. Its most noteworthy feature is the elegant neon restaurant sign. Brick construction.

C

R18 MAP II
461-463 Bush Street
Manufacturing Jeweler's Building
architect unknown
1907

A two part vertical brick loft structure with restrained Renaissance/Baroque ornamental detail.

C

R19 MAP II
466 Bush Street
Station 2, San Francisco Fire Department
Newton J. Tharp, City Architect
1909

An excellent example of civic architecture on a small scale, and an example of the effect of the City Beautiful Movement on the design of utilitarian structures. This was the first "thoroughly fire proof" structure erected by the City after the fire. As such it represented the new sense of responsibility felt by the city in erecting honest, safe, and attractive buildings, following the corruption of the Ruef period (symbolized by the collapse of the old City Hall during the earthquake). This hybrid composition with Renaissance/Baroque ornamentation everywhere includes overscaled details that simultaneously make it appear smaller than it is and more prominent than buildings that are actually much bigger. The skill with which this is achieved and the scarcity of surviving buildings by Tharp underscores the loss to the city caused by his early death in the same year this was completed. Tharp was City Architect at the time. Steel frame construction with a Vancouver granite front.

A

R20 MAP II
507 Bush Street
SW corner Grant
St. Charles Hotel
architect unknown
1907

A three part vertical block with differentiated end bays and Renaissance/Baroque ornamental references. The end of the Grant Avenue retail group.

C

R21 MAP II
515-519 Bush Street
Terbush Building
Wright, Rushforth, and Cahill
1907

A reinforced concrete building originally described as a "Bachelor's Hotel." A two part composition with a vaguely Gothic cornice.

C

R22 MAP II
585 Bush Street
Stockton-Sutter Garage
John Lord King/Sokoloff, Hamilton, and Bennett
1960/1977

NOT RATED

R23 MAP II
44 Campton Place
between Grant and Stockton
Vasilis
architect unknown
1907

Reputedly built as a steam room for Shreve's at the end of the alley. A fine remodeling inside and out by Donald Clever about 1970 with large metal sculptural forms. In composition, originally a vault. Brick construction.

C

R24 MAP IV
61-65 Ellis Street
Historic John's Grill
architect unknown
1910

A two part small commercial block with formal treatment of the upper story and modified Renaissance/Baroque ornamentation. The over-scaled window in the top story is nicely detailed. The ground floor has been remodeled. Brick construction.

C

R25 MAP IV
111 Ellis Street
SW corner Powell
Powell Building
architect unknown
ca. 1912

A two part vertical office block with Renaissance/Baroque ornamentation. A fine background building whose rusticated facades serve a double function as elements in the building composition and as important pieces in the street walls of Powell and Ellis. Brick construction.

C

R26 MAP IV
119-139 Ellis Street
SE corner North Fifth
Continental Hotel
Coxhead and Coxhead
1907

One of the few executed commercial designs of the Coxhead office, distinguished by an exuberant cornice. In composition, a three part vertical block with differentiated end bays and modified Renaissance/Baroque ornamentation. Like so many buildings in this area, the building functions well as a part of the urban fabric. Brick construction.

B

R27 MAP IV
120 Ellis Street
NW corner Powell
The Misses Butler Building
Albert Pissis
1909

A three part vertical block with Renaissance/Baroque ornamentation. A large brick structure with deep reveals that add character to an important corner building.

C

R28 MAP III
28-36 Geary Street
Rosenstock Building
Albert Pissis
1908

A stacked vertical composition with tiers of terra cotta pilasters on Geary and brick pilasters at the rear of the building on Maiden Lane. The tiers are stacked in a progression of orders from Doric to Ionic to Corinthian. The *Architect and Engineer* commented on the "graceful decorum" of this composition. Ornamentation is derived from Renaissance sources. Steel frame construction.

B

R29 MAP III
46 Geary Street
St. Paul Catholic Book and Film Center
architect unknown
1907, facade ca. 1950

Remodeled as one facade on Geary Street about 1950, the rear consists of the simple but handsome brick facades of two small buildings on Maiden Lane.

C

R30 MAP III
66 Geary Street
Hotel Graystone
architect unknown
1906

A residential hotel in a three part vertical composition with Renaissance/Baroque references. The shaft consists of arched bays with deep reveals, partially filled by bay windows. Brick construction.

C

R31 MAP III
88 Geary Street
Cailleau Building
now part of Livingston Brothers
architect unknown
1907

The rear section of Livingston Brothers department store, but built earlier as an independent building. In 1939 the ground floor was remodeled as one design with 100 Grant. A two part vertical composition with skeletal articulation and restrained Renaissance/Baroque references. An early example of a large reinforced concrete building.

C

R32 MAP III
100 Geary Street
NW corner Grant
Granat Brothers
architect unknown
1909

A long-time San Francisco specialty department store with strong skeletal expression and handsome decorative details, some of which have been removed. The sculptural masks beneath the cornice and the corner clock are particularly notable. The clock is discussed in the Urban Design section of this volume. In composition, a two part vertical block with Renaissance/Baroque ornamentation. The end of a very fine group on Geary Street.

C

R33 MAP III
101-111 Geary
SW corner Grant
Paragon Building
architect unknown
1907

A two part vertical composition with strong skeletal expression and vague Renaissance/Baroque references. The top story has been added and the cornice removed.

C

R34 MAP III
108-114 Geary Street
Marion Building
architect unknown
1909

R35 MAP III
120 Geary Street
E. Simon Building
architect unknown
1909

Evidently built as a pair and part of a very fine row of buildings on this block. Each is a two part terra cotta clad brick structure with Renaissance/Baroque ornamentation. A classic example of the retail district type consisting of an enframed window wall at the base for retail purposes, surmounted by an office shaft expressed as such.

B

R36 MAP III
125-129 Geary Street
architect unknown
1908

A two part vertical composition with skeletal articulation and richly detailed Renaissance/Baroque ornamentation that includes foliated spandrel panels and masked pier capitals. Brick construction with steel columns, clad in terra cotta.

C

R37 MAP III
132-140 Geary Street
Sachs Building
George Applegarth
1908

A three part vertical composition with Renaissance/Baroque details. The facade is clad in white terra cotta with green details, and is unusually richly decorated with spandrel panels, keystones, capitals, and lions' heads. The story above the cornice was added in 1913 by G. Albert Lansburgh. The building is a major element in the fine group in this block of Geary Street, and its unusual green and white color scheme relates to the facade of the Whitney Building and the City of Paris on this block. Steel frame construction with reinforced concrete curtain walls.

B

R38 MAP III
133-153 Geary Street
Whitney Building
J. R. Bowles Co.
1909

An unusual example of a downtown building entirely designed by an engineer, which demonstrates in many of its details the major concerns of engineers in the post-fire period, and expresses the less fettered response of the engineer to certain economic and functional requirements related to developing building types. The design and construction of the building was the subject of thorough coverage in the architectural journals. The building was designed to carry four additional floors on its deep concrete foundation and specially designed steel frame which was covered in concrete. The steel frame followed the innovative bracing system developed by the same firm for the Whittell Building across the street.

The building was planned for department store use on the three lower floors and offices above. The two sections of the building were served by separate elevators. All offices opened onto the street or to light courts. Light courts and the street facade were clad in a specially designed glazed tile veneer which served two important purposes: it reflected light in typically dingy light courts, and it was lighter in weight than traditional cladding materials. The light material was easily, safely, and quickly attached, leading to savings in construction time and structural steel which would ordinarily be needed to carry a heavier material. The build-

ing was equipped with all the most advanced mechanical systems for heat, water, and lighting. In composition, the building followed the traditional three part vertical formula with differentiated end bays. Its green and white coloring related to the Sachs Building and the City of Paris on this block.

B

R39 MAP III
146 Geary Street
architect unknown
1907

A two part vertical composition with skeletal articulation and Renaissance/Baroque ornamental references. Brick construction.

C

R40 MAP III
152 Geary Street
architect unknown
1907

A two part small commercial block with skeletal articulation and modified Renaissance/Baroque ornamental references. The most distinctive feature of the building is its second floor cast iron window framing in the form of an arcade, with elaborate cartouches in the spandrels. As the location for several years of Welton Becket's office, an illustration of the now common observation that rather than work in the type of large office buildings many architects build, modern architects typically choose small-scaled, richly textured old buildings which are the antithesis of their own designs.

C

R41 MAP III
156 Geary Street
architect unknown
1907

A two part small commercial block with skeletal articulation and Renaissance/Baroque ornamental references. Brick construction.

C

R42 MAP III
166 Geary Street
Whittell Building
Shea and Shea
1906

A distinctive early skyscraper, small in plan and with a hip roof, which has long been a landmark on the city's skyline and from Union Square. Under construction at the time of the earthquake, its little damaged open steel skeleton was one of the most prominent landmarks in the city in the period after the fire. Within a month after the fire, plans were announced to complete the building by sheathing it in steel plates for additional fire and earthquake proofing. It was to have been, according to the *Architect and Engineer*, "the first steel building erected in the world." Presumably because there were delays due to a shortage of steel and at the same time a premium on rapid completion of buildings, these plans were dropped. As built, the building was a three part vertical shaft clad in brick in 18th century "English treatment." Its successful passage through the earthquake was attributed to a variety of engineering features designed by J.B.C. Lockwood of the J.R. Bowles Co., and in particular to its deep foundation which extended to hardpan and functioned as a single massive unit. Its steel frame was the earliest in the city to employ spandrel plate girders at each floor for wind bracing. The steel frame was erected in the extremely short time of eleven weeks, due in large part to the use of pneumatic tools, an innovation at the time.

A

R43 MAP III
199 Geary Street
SE corner Stockton
City of Paris
originally Spring Valley Water Works
    Co. Building
**Clinton Day/rebuilt by Bakewell and
    Brown with Louis Bourgeois**
1896/rebuilt 1908

Designed by Clinton Day in 1896 and rebuilt after the fire by Bakewell and Brown with Louis Bourgeois. The exterior of the building is Day's design except for the cast iron store fronts of the bottom two stories and the wonderful sign on the roof. It was originally built for the Spring Valley Water Works Co. as an office building with retail space for the City of Paris Dry Goods Co. at the lower levels. The City of Paris store was established in 1850 in a ship bearing that name, and was located in many places before it occupied the present building. After the fire, the interior of the building was entirely remodeled for use by the City of Paris, to include for the first time a great central skylit space. In composition, the building is a stacked vertical block with modified Renaissance/Baroque ornamentation. The composition itself is modified by the articulation of a central pavilion on Geary and an end pavilion on Stockton. The building was an early example in San Francisco of an orderly design with Renaissance/Baroque orna-

mentation. This new style followed the example of the Chicago World's Fair in 1893, and was in contrast to the prevailing Romanesque and eclectic designs of the period. With the exception of the Hibernia Bank, the building is the earliest downtown building remaining which represents this extremely important change not only in style but in attitude toward design for the city. Apart from its great interior space with its superbly detailed columns and stained glass dome, the real importance of the building is in its relationship to Union Square, to Geary and Stockton streets, and to the architecture of the retail district.

Following the example of the success of the Chicago World's Fair as a triumph of urbanism, the articulation of the facade, the large but subsidiary glass area, the stylistic references of its details, and the colors and textures of its materials all relate to the city around it. The buildings around the City of Paris, all of which were

built later, relate to each other not so much out of a conscious effort to do so, but rather out of a shared attitude toward design and toward the urban function of a building on a street. The building is presently threatened by a Philip Johnson design for a new Neiman Marcus store which fails to understand the urban importance of the existing building. A new design which recognized these values would find less resistance in the community.

A   NR

Butler Building in 1907. Before remodeling as I. Magnin's.

R44 MAP IV
233 Geary Street
SW corner Stockton
I. Magnin and Co.
Pfleuger and Pfleuger
1946

Originally the Butler Building of 1905 by the Reid Brothers, the current I. Magnin store is a 1946 remodel on a pre-fire steel frame. The taller proportions of the two lowest ranks of windows are derived from the proportions of that existing steel frame. The flush fenestration and severe facades, often referred to as among the earliest truly modern designs in the Bay Area, have been described by Michael Goodman, a designer in the Pfleuger office, as the result of the owner's desire to "pigeon proof" the building.

NOT RATED

R45 MAP IV
251-259 Geary Street
Werner Building
architect unknown
1910

A two part vertical composition with restrained Renaissance/Baroque ornamentation that recalls John Reid, Jr.'s 1913 design for the Hind Building at 230 California Street (F19). Both buildings are dominated by shafts with thin piers, large glass areas, and pedimented windows at the bottom floor of the shaft. The removal of the cornice of this building during the course of the survey further destroys the character of the south facade of Union Square which is already dominated by solid walled structures. Brick construction with iron posts at the ground level and wood posts above.

C

R46 MAP IV
285-291 Geary Street
St. Paul Building
now Union Square Building
architect unknown
1909

One of the last old buildings on the severely eroded south side of Union Square which retains its character. A three part vertical composition with Renaissance/Baroque ornamentation. Brick construction with concrete columns.

C

R47 MAP IV
293-299 Geary Street
SE corner Powell
Lincoln Building
now Lufthansa Building
architect unknown
1907

A building which plays an important role on both Union Square and Powell Street. It is one of the last intact older buildings on the south side of the Square and forms part of the almost continuously fine street facade on Powell. A three part vertical block with restrained Renaissance/Baroque references. The principal ornamental and textural feature of the building is the keystone over each window. The high waisted remodeling of the base detracts from the quality of the whole. Brick construction.

B

R48 MAP IV
301 Geary Street
SW corner Powell
Elkan Gunst Building
G. Albert Lansburgh
1908

An important building on Union Square with major facades on both Geary and Powell and a rounded corner that helps enclose the space of the square. It is massive enough to fill its corner position and its overscaled details, particularly its cornice, enhance the definition of the building and its legibility from Union Square. It was originally designed with a mansard roof and domed corner that were never built. In composition, a three part vertical block with skeletal articulation and Renaissance/Baroque ornamentation. Reinforced concrete construction clad in terra cotta. The characteristic ground floor remodeling by Casual Corner is terrible.

B

R49 MAP IV
333 Geary Street
Lefty O'Doul's
Cunningham and Politeo
1916

Designed as a theater by one of the Bay Area's best theater architectural firms, but converted to other uses after only one year. The unusual facade consists of two massive piers linked by an arched center and ornamented in modified Renaissance/Baroque details. Reinforced concrete construction.

B

R50 MAP IV
347-373 Geary Street
Hotel Stewart
Cunningham and Politeo
1907, 1913, 1917

A long-time San Francisco hotel in a two part composition with a remodeled base, an awkward shaft of bay windows and fire escapes, and Art Nouveau decorative detail concentrated at the cornice. The building was constructed in stages but with a continuous facade. Its original interior which was the subject of an article in the *Architect and Engineer* in 1909, was partially remodeled in 1916 by Louis Christian Mullgardt. The lobby and shops have since been remodeled again. Steel construction.

B

R51 MAP I
366-374 Geary Street
Rosebud's English Pub
architect unknown
1917

A simple but attractive and well-maintained brick structure with a recent copper awning and stained glass transoms. A two part small commercial block with formal treatment of the upper zone and restrained Renaissance ornamental details.

C

R52 MAP IV
381 Geary Street
architect unknown
1922

A two part small commercial block with formal treatment of the upper zone and Renaissance/Baroque ornamentation. Reinforced concrete construction.

C

Hotel San Marco.
Before addition and remodeling.

R53 MAP I
386 Geary Street
NE corner Mason
Hotel Rafael
Stone and Malloy
1939

Originally built by MacDonald and Applegarth in 1909 as the 8-story Hotel San Marco, remodeled as a 12-story Moderne hotel in 1939, and now in its third incarnation with a superficial application of evidently removable metal awnings and spandrel panels. Reinforced concrete construction.

C

R54 MAP I
400-414 Geary Street
NW corner Mason
architect unknown
1916

A two part small commercial block with skeletal articulation and restrained Renaissance/Baroque ornamental references. Brick construction.

C

R55 MAP IV
415 Geary Street
Geary Theater
originally Columbia Theater
Bliss and Faville
1909

Since its opening as the Columbia Theater, the building has been a center of theater arts in the Bay Area. The original two building complex (including the Annex at 333 Mason—R123) has grown to include 450–456 (R59) and 458–466 (R60) to accommodate its growing importance as a center for training young actors. The main building is a steel frame and reinforced concrete structure clad in brick and terra cotta. In composition, it is an enframed pavilion, with Renaissance/Baroque ornamentation. Its central pavilion consists of three arches on rich polychrome columns set between pairs of Corinthian orders. The ground level is sheltered by an ornate metal and glass marquee. The decorative treatment of the exterior is carried inside to the lobby and the hall, with its three seating levels and giant proscenium arch. The interior is finished in Utah Caen stone and Tennessee marble. The building was constructed by the Ransome Concrete Co., one of the pioneers of reinforced concrete and "fireproof" construction in America.

A   NR; CL

R56 MAP I
418-432 Geary Street
Paisley Hotel
William H. Weeks
1911

A hotel building in a three part vertical composition with 18th century English ornamental references. Major bays are framed in cream terra cotta surrounded by red brick walls. Brick construction.

C

R57 MAP I
436-440 Geary Street
Somerton Hotel
originally Metcalf Hotel
Righetti and Headman
1912

Designed in a three part vertical composition with differentiated end bays—a classic example of the type. Ornamentation is Renaissance/Baroque. Reinforced concrete construction.

C

R58 MAP IV
445 Geary Street
Curran Theater
Alfred Henry Jacobs
1922

A more restrained design than the Geary Theater, but handsomely executed in fine materials, and a fine neighbor to its predecessor next door. The architect was Alfred Henry Jacobs about whom little is known other than that he studied at M.I.T. and the Ecole des Beaux-Arts and that he completed designs for at least one other major theater, the California at Fourth and Market. In composition, the Curran is an enframed pavilion with end bays and adjoining wings. Ornamentation is Renaissance/Baroque. The central pavilion is defined by three central arches, each embellished with a masked keystone and swags, and each arch is filled with elaborate metal window framing. Like the Geary, the Curran has a handsome metal marquee over the entrance. The facade is capped by a copper mansard with finials. The building is of reinforced concrete construction. It was built by Homer Curran.

A

R59 MAP I
450-456 Geary Street
Sussex Building
architect unknown
1922

R60 MAP I
458-466 Geary Street
architect unknown
1922

Built as a pair and nearly identical to 459-465 Geary (R61) across the street, all in the same year as the Curran. These reinforced concrete loft structures provide storage, rehearsal, office, and study space for the American Conservatory Theater. Handsome two part vertical blocks with skeletal articulation and limited use of Renaissance/Baroque ornamentation.

B

R61 MAP IV
459-465 Geary Street
architect unknown
1922

Part of a nearly identical group of three, including 450-456 (R59) and 458-466 (R60) Geary, all built in 1922. A two part vertical block with skeletal articulation and limited use of Gothic ornament. This structure is one bay narrower than its companions across the street. Reinforced concrete construction.

B

R62 MAP I
468 Geary Street
architect unknown
1920

A two part small commercial block, skeletal in articulation, with a curious, evidently altered design of Renaissance/Baroque derivation over the window. The ground floor has been remodeled with 476-480 Geary next door. Brick construction.

C

R63 MAP I
476-480 Geary Street
Hotel David
originally Hotel Cosmos
architect unknown
1911

Originally the Hotel Cosmos whose painted advertisement is faded but still visible on the west side of the building. A three part vertical composition with differentiated end bays and Renaissance/Baroque ornamentation. Reinforced concrete construction.

C

R64 MAP I
484-486 Geary Street
architect unknown
1910

A small reinforced concrete residential hotel with overscaled cornices above each bay window. A two part vertical composition with modified Renaissance/Baroque ornamentation.

C

R65 MAP I
490-498 Geary Street
NE corner Taylor
Maryland Hotel
Righetti and Headman
1912

A handsome residential hotel at an important corner location. In composition, a variation of a three part vertical block with differentiated end bays. Ornamentation is Renaissance/Baroque. Each part of the composition is set off by a projecting minor cornice. The facade is distinguished by shallow squared bay windows. The arcaded upper tier is crowned by a broad projecting cornice. Remains of the once elegant lobby are still visible as part of the Tudor galleries. Reinforced concrete construction.

C

R66 MAP IV
491-499 Geary Street
SE corner Mason
Clift Hotel
MacDonald and Applegarth/
Schultze and Weaver
1913/1926

The elegant Clift Hotel was designed for lawyer Frederick Clift in 1913 by MacDonald and Applegarth to accommodate visitors to the 1915 P-P.I.E. It was enlarged in 1926 in the manner of the original by the important New York firm of Schultze and Weaver. The design has been marred by the removal of the cornice. In composition it is a three part vertical block with Renaissance/Baroque ornamentation. Its steel frame is sheathed in light colored brick curtain walls. The famous Redwood Grille (now the Redwood Room) was originally designed by G. Albert Lansburgh and Anthony Heinsbergen in 1935 and was restored in 1977. In 1978 the interior of the hotel was refurbished by architect Fred Schmitt of Los Angeles.

B

R67 MAP III
17-23 Grant Avenue
Zobel Building
now Grant Avenue Building
architect unknown
1909

An excellent example of an enframed window wall surmounted by an implied masonry office shaft, in a three part vertical composition with Renaissance/Baroque ornamentation. The glass base and "masonry" shaft correspond to commercial and office floors, respectively. This is the characteristic building type of the retail district. Together with the Kohler and Chase Building (20-26 O'Farrell), the Zobel frames the Security Pacific Bank at the corner and presents a fine view from Market Street. A steel frame building with reinforced concrete curtain walls.

B

R68 MAP III
39-41 Grant Avenue
Fisher Building
architect unknown
1909

A two part vertical block, skeletal in articulation, and stripped of ornamental reference by the loss of its cornice. Built on the site of a pre-fire structure by Frederick H. Meyer also called the Fisher Building.

C

R69 MAP III
45 Grant Avenue
Timothy Pfleuger
1939

A 1909 brick building, remodeled in 1939. One of several retail area remodels of this type, following the old compositional type of the enframed window wall, but with Moderne references. The marquee, ground floor, and signage have been altered.

C

R66   Clift Hotel. Interior, ca. 1913.

R70 MAP III
50 Grant Avenue
SE corner Geary
Liebes Building
once I. Magnin's, later Ransohoff's
**William Mooser/Frederick H. Meyer/
Bliss and Fairweather
1912/1917/1929**

A building which has been enlarged twice by different architects, but still retains the character of the original design by William Mooser. In 1917 two stories were added to the original and fenestration was changed by Frederick H. Meyer, and in 1929 the rear tower was added by Bliss and Fairweather. The unfortunate loss of the cornice is more recent. Along with its physical changes the building has been variously known as I. Magnin's (until 1946) and as Ransohoff's until its closing a few years ago. It is now vacant. In composition, the building is a three part vertical block with restrained Renaissance/Baroque references. Its skeletal articulation, industrial sash, and minimal ornamentation resemble many strictly functional industrial buildings in the city and, as such, render it close to the stated ideal of many early spokesmen for the Modern Movement. A steel frame building clad in white glazed terra cotta.

B

R71 MAP III
51-55 Grant Avenue
Eleanor Green Building
architect unknown
1909

A two-dimensional version of the Eastern Outfitting Co. Building at 1019–1021 Market (M99) by George Applegarth. In composition, a pair of stacked enframed window walls with Renaissance/Baroque ornamentation. Rather than the more common retail area type that expresses a mixture of commercial and office spaces in the composition, this mixes two types of commercial loft spaces. Brick construction with an iron and terra cotta front.

B

R72 MAP III
59 Grant Avenue
architect unknown
1929

A two part vertical composition with mixed historical references. Reinforced concrete clad in terra cotta.

C

R73 MAP III
100 Grant Avenue
NE corner Geary
Livingston Brothers
G. Albert Lansburgh
1920

Functionally joined with 88 Geary as Livingston's Department Store but designed and built independently. A two part vertical composition which has suffered the loss of its cornice. Its base was remodeled as one with 88 Geary by Miller and Pfleuger in 1939. Brick construction with concrete and wood posts.

C

R74 MAP III
117-129 Grant Avenue
SW corner Maiden Lane
Saks Fifth Avenue
Burke, Kober, and Nicolais
1955

A remodel of a 1908 design for the George A. Moss Glove House Building by MacDonald and Applegarth.

NOT RATED

R75 MAP III
140 Grant Avenue
NE corner Maiden Lane
architect unknown
1909

A two part small commercial block with 18th century English ornamentation. Reinforced concrete construction.

C

R76 MAP III
166 Grant Avenue
architect unknown
1908

A two part vertical block with a giant order in the shaft and Renaissance/Baroque ornamental references. The totally remodeled ground floor was probably originally an enframed window wall. Brick construction.

C

R77 MAP II
201 Grant Avenue
NW corner Post
Shreve Building
William Curlett
1905

Completed in 1905 and rebuilt after the fire.
Steel frame construction with brick curtain walls
sheathed in Colusa sandstone. In composition,
a variation of the three part vertical block with
differentiated end bays, having expanded
transitional sections at the base and capital.
Renaissance/Baroque ornamentation. Together
with the Head Building (R158) across the street,
also by Curlett, the Shreve Building is the tallest
building on Grant Avenue. Centrally located
between Market Street and the Chinatown Gate,
it punctuates the skyline at just the right place,
defining the historic heart of the retail district.
The quality of its materials and its carved detail
enhance the prominence it achieves by its size,
location, and function as a focal point. The two
lower floors are occupied by Shreve's monumental salesroom with black marble Ionic columns and fine bronze entrances. The marquees
at the entrances have been removed.

A

R78 MAP II
220-228 Grant Avenue
Phoenix Building
George A. Applegarth
1908

One of the best of several retail area buildings
characterized by a facade of immense square
windows. Each window consists of a single
large sheet of glass in a hinged casement that
is framed in dense moldings and sits in an undifferentiated skeletal wall. In composition, a two
part vertical block with restrained Renais-
sance/Baroque ornamentation. The ground
floor occupant, Podesta Baldocchi, is a well-
known local florist. Reinforced concrete with
curtain walls.

B

R79 MAP II
233 Grant Avenue
NW corner Campton
architect unknown
ca. 1907

A characteristic response to the small lots and high property values in this area reflected in the tall narrow shape of the building. A two part vertical composition with a rusticated facade and ornate decorative treatment of the cornice. Ornamentation is derived from Renaissance/Baroque sources. The rusticated wall characteristically provides a good supportive texture for the street facade and for more significant designs such as the Shreve Building. Brick construction.

B

R80 MAP II
251-253 Grant Avenue
NW corner Tillman Place
architect unknown
1907

A two part commercial block with 18th century English ornamental references. The cornice has been removed. Brick construction.

C

R81 MAP II
255 Grant Avenue
architect unknown
1907

An important supportive structure to Sutter's Corner next door (R237). A two part small commercial block with freely interpreted Renaissance/Baroque ornamentation. Brick construction.

C

R82 MAP II
301-305 Grant Avenue
NW corner Sutter
Myers Building
architect unknown
1905

A handsome composition for a thin tower at an extremely important location. The three part vertical composition resembles a design by Oliver and Foulkes for the Gaffney Building (now demolished), with its enframed bay on each facade and Renaissance/Baroque ornamentation including the prominent cornice. The small scale of the tower relates to its neighbors on both Sutter and Grant, and yet as a tower it manages to hold the corner with just the right degree of authority. At the same time, it functions as part of the much larger Grant Avenue group. A steel frame building of 1905, rebuilt after the fire.

B

R83 MAP II
311-319 Grant Avenue
Abrahamsen Building
architect unknown
1909

Another very fine example of the retail area type characterized by a facade of immense square windows. Buildings of this type are among the few in downtown San Francisco which would have been considered progressive by early proponents of Modern architecture. In composition, a two part vertical block with skeletal articulation and Renaissance/Baroque ornamental references, notably in the cornice. Although smaller than its neighbors, the building plays an extremely important role in the simultaneously lively and controlled Grant Avenue street facade. The building is occupied by the Frank Lloyd Wright Foundation and the offices of Aaron Green. Reinforced concrete construction.

A

135

R84 MAP II
321-323 Grant Avenue
SW corner Harlan
Hotel Baldwin
Ross and Burgren
1910

A three part hotel building with differentiated end bays. It was raised two stories in 1912, accounting for the peculiar cornice and finials at the eighth floor. Ornamentation is modified Renaissance/Baroque. Steel frame construction.

C

R85 MAP II
333 Grant Avenue
NW corner Harlan
Pacific Telephone and Telegraph Co.
originally Home Telephone Co.
Coxhead and Coxhead
1908

Although superficially in the style of other urban buildings of the period, this stands apart from most in its self-conscious, mannered treatment of ordinary details. Most of San Francisco's downtown buildings use historical ornament in a purposefully ''correct'' way, in a way designed to achieve contextual objectives, as a decorative veneer, or unconsciously, merely as the prevailing style of the time. Few attempt the sort of assertively, intelligently ''incorrect'' use of detail achieved in this building. The oversized details and the unexpected juxtapositions of the scale of parts of the facade result in a complexity of design that manages to be successful in several ways at once—from its function as a part of the urban fabric to its interest as an isolated object. In composition, the building is a three part vertical block surmounted by an attic, with a giant order in the shaft. Its ornamentation is Renaissance/Baroque. It is a steel frame structure clad in Colusa sandstone. The rich plaster lobby ceiling is hidden by a drop ceiling, but is still intact. This was one of at least three designs by Coxhead for the Home Telephone Co., for which this was originally the headquarters building.

A

Left: Home Telephone Co. Building. Detail.

R86 MAP II
334-352 Grant Avenue
SE corner Bush
Beverly Plaza Hotel
originally Washington Hotel
Frederick H. Meyer
1912

Originally the Washington Hotel, built for Mortimer Fleishhacker. A two part vertical composition with an attic above a copper cornice. Ornamentation is restrained Renaissance/Baroque. The fine ornamental metal entrance marquee has been replaced. Steel frame construction.

C

R87 MAP III
25-33 Kearny Street
SW corner Maiden Lane
O'Bear Building
now Baldwin Building
Milton Lichtenstein
1909

A handsome composition executed in fine materials on both Kearny Street and Maiden Lane. A three part vertical composition with enframed bays. Renaissance/Baroque ornamentation includes polychrome terra cotta work. Part of an important group of similarly scaled structures on lower Kearny. Steel frame construction.

B

R88 MAP III
45-47 Kearny Street
NW corner Maiden Lane
Oscar Luning Building
Nathaniel Blaisdell
1907

A three part vertical composition with a rusticated shaft on both Kearny Street and Maiden Lane which serves as a fine textural background on both block fronts. Renaissance/Baroque in ornamentation. Reinforced concrete construction.

B

R89 MAP III
48-52 Kearny Street
Maskey Building
Havens and Toepke
1908

A three part vertical composition with Renaissance/Baroque ornamentation, referred to as French Renaissance in the *American Builder's Review*, and verging on Art Nouveau. The steel frame structure is clad in a particularly fine quality of white glazed terra cotta. Transom windows of the ground floor stores are largely intact, as is the original interior of the store now occupied by the Tie Rack. The building occupies an important Kearny Street location. It has recently been refurbished.

B

R90 MAP III
49 Kearny Street
Roullier Building
Albert Pissis
1908

One of three twenty-foot wide skyscrapers in the downtown area, this one is a curious hybrid composition with a skeletal shaft surmounted by an enframed window wall and a dormered mansard. The scale of the building is strongly supportive of its neighbors. Reinforced concrete construction. The ground floor has been remodeled as one with the Luning Building as part of Brooks Cameras.

B

R91 MAP III
60 Kearny Street
SW corner Post
Bullock and Jones Co. Building
Julius E. Krafft
1907

One of several good designs for the Bullock and Jones Co. in the early years of this century. A three part vertical composition with Renaissance/Baroque ornamentation, particularly at the mezzanine and capital levels of the design. The cornice has been removed. Located at an important corner.

B

R92 MAP II
110-116 Kearny Street
NE corner Post
Thompson and Ortman Building
now Insurance Building
Meyer and O'Brien
1908

A curiously fenestrated building that results from two clients with two separate needs pooling their resources for a less expensive single building. The south end of the building with its small double hung windows was designed for doctors' offices. The north end, with its large horizontal window openings, was designed for undifferentiated loft space. A two part vertical composition with restrained Renaissance/Baroque references. The ground floor was remodeled in a typically insensitive fashion by Stone and Malloy in 1939. Now called the Insurance Building. This building would be replaced by the proposed new Crocker Bank tower.

C

R93 MAP II
120-130 Kearny Street
SE corner Ver Mehr
White Building
now Lyons Building
architect unknown
1908

A three part vertical composition with elaborate Renaissance/Baroque ornamentation, particularly in the arcaded capital section. The height of the building and the articulation of its facade contribute to the consistent wall of the street. An unsuccessful attempt was made in the remodeling of the ground level to be compatible with the upper part of the building. Steel frame construction.

B

R94 MAP II
123-133 Kearny Street
Young Building
architect unknown
1910

Part of a fine group of three that extends to the Sutter Street corner. The three buildings step up successively to the corner Eyre Building, the articulation of their facades becomes progressively less skeletal, and there is progressively less glass. At the same time the overall impression is of a skeletal, glass walled group. This building is a two part vertical block with minimal Renaissance/Baroque ornament at the cornice. Steel frame construction clad in unglazed terra cotta.

B

R95 MAP II
153 Kearny Street
Bartlett Doe Building
now Dubbs Building
Havens and Toepke
1909

An L-shaped building that wraps around the Eyre Building with frontages on both Kearny and Sutter. Part of a fine group that extends from the Young Building (R94) next door to the corner. A two part vertical composition, skeletal in articulation with limited use of Renaissance/Baroque ornamentation. A steel frame structure clad in terra cotta.

B

R96 MAP II
161 Kearny Street
SW corner Sutter
Eyre Building/Sherman Clay and Co.
  Building
now Argonaut Building
L. B. Dutton
1907

A fine building in an extremely important location that has important relationships both to its immediate neighbors and to the larger street facades of Kearny and Sutter Streets. Designed in the office of L. B. Dutton by George Applegarth and variously known as the Eyre Building, the Sherman Clay and Co. Building, and the Argonaut Building. In composition, a three part vertical block with an attic. Ornamented in Renaissance/Baroque details, notably with a giant Ionic order in the upper level beneath an exuberant cornice. Steel frame construction, clad in terra cotta.

B

R97 MAP II
200 Kearny Street
NE corner Sutter
architect unknown
1908

Another example of the characteristic retail area type with large square windows in a simple but elegant facade. A two part vertical composition with Gothic ornamentation, particularly in the hanging cornice which foreshadows that of the Hallidie Building two doors down Sutter Street. The details of the facade are superbly rendered in glazed terra cotta. Apart from its architectural excellence the building is an extremely important member of groups on both Kearny Street and Sutter Street. Most importantly, it is at the end of the Hallidie Building block which steps up from this building to the California Pacific building at the Montgomery Street corner, and in its present state involves a complex play of color, material, ornamental treatment, and structural expression. A steel frame building.

A

R98 MAP II
201 Kearny Street
NW corner Sutter
architect unknown
1910

An important building in its context, tall enough to anchor the corner, with a skeletal facade that relates to its neighbors in its large glass area. In composition a two part vertical block with limited use of Renaissance/Baroque ornament. The recent use of mirror glass in some of the windows is a disturbing alteration which changes the character of the design. Steel frame construction.

B

R99 MAP II
209 Kearny Street
architect unknown
1907

A two part small commercial block with formal treatment of the top section. Renaissance/Baroque ornamentation. Brick construction.

C

R100 MAP II
215-217 Kearny Street
architect unknown
1907

A two part small commercial block with formal treatment of the top section and Renaissance/Baroque ornamentation. Brick construction.

C

R101 MAP II
219-225 Kearny Street
architect unknown
1907

A two part vertical block with only vague Renaissance/Baroque references now that the cornice has been removed. Brick construction.

C

R102 MAP II
220-226 Kearny Street
SE corner Hardie Place
Robins Building
T. Paterson Ross
1907

The small original corner structure was enlarged on both facades with an L-shaped addition. A two part vertical block, skeletal in articulation, with restrained Renaissance/Baroque ornamentation. Brick construction. Part of an important group on this side of the street.

C

R103 MAP II
227-231 Kearny Street
architect unknown
1908

A more interesting design than most of the similar buildings of this type with mannered rustication of the piers that encroaches on the recessed, enframed window area. A two part small commercial block with modified Renaissance/Baroque ornamentation. Brick construction.

C

R104 MAP II
237-241 Kearny Street
architect unknown
1907

A two part small commercial block with a typically 19th century treatment of the upper section. A curious remodeling of the interior spaces has evidently changed the floor levels and added a third story where there were only two before. Brick construction.

C

R105 MAP II
240-244 Kearny Street
NE corner Hardie Place
Marston Building
Meyer and O'Brien
1906

A curious stacked composition with loosely interpreted Renaissance/Baroque ornamentation. Originally designed in 1905 and quickly rebuilt after the fire. As the tallest building on the block it appropriately punctuates a good row of generally smaller buildings. Steel frame construction.

B

R106 MAP II
243 Kearny Street
McKay Building
architect unknown
ca. 1940

A remodel of a 1908 brick building in a classicized Moderne manner that still manages to relate to the older small scaled buildings on the street. A two part small commercial block.

C

R107 MAP II
246-250 Kearny Street
Hotel Stanford
architect unknown
1908

A good illustration of the effect of irregular lot lines and economics on the shapes of downtown buildings. This has frontages of different widths on both Kearny and Bush streets, and backs up on Hardie Place in an irregular T-shape. A three part vertical block with loosely interpreted Renaissance/Baroque ornamentation. Brick construction with steel posts and girders on the first floor.

C

R108 MAP II
251-255 Kearny Street
SW corner Bush
Charleston Building
originally Charles H. Schmidt Building
Albert Pissis
1908

A straightforward design for an office building by one of the city's most important Beaux-Arts designers. A two part vertical composition with an attic. Skeletal articulation which maximizes the glass area for office lighting predominates over restrained Renaissance/Baroque ornamentation. As a big corner building it anchors two blocks and at the same time relates in scale to the larger buildings up and down the south side of Bush. The original cage elevator is intact. Steel frame composition with brick curtain walls.

B

R109 MAP II
260 Kearny Street
architect unknown
1908

A two part vertical block with an enframed bay and Renaissance/Baroque ornamentation. Brick construction.

C

R110 MAP II
315 Kearny Street
architect unknown
1907

A two part small commercial block with an enframed bay and modified Renaissance/Baroque ornament. The walling-in of the windows on the south half of the facade and the gross remodeling of the ground floor as part of the design of the corner building are unfortunate but easily reversible. Brick construction.

C

R111 MAP II
325-329 Kearny Street
architect unknown
1907

A two part small commercial block with skeletal expression of the upper section and modified Renaissance/Baroque ornamentation. Brick construction.

C

R112   *MacDonough Building. Proposal, 1906.*

R112 MAP II
333-343 Kearny Street
MacDonough Building
William Curlett
1907

A large and important early example of reinforced concrete construction which was thoroughly covered in the local architectural press. The structural design was by the important local engineer, John B. Leonard, who did a great deal of the first wave of reinforced concrete design in the city. The facade is finished in a stucco of marble dust, cement, and sand in a three part vertical composition with modified Renaissance/Baroque ornamentation.

B

R113 MAP II
334 Kearny Street
architect unknown
1906

A two part small commercial block with a characteristically 19th century treatment of the upper section. Renaissance ornamental references. Brick construction.

C

R114 MAP II
344 Kearny Street
Harrigan Weidenmuller Co.
architect unknown
1927

An excellent and nearly unique example of an enframed window wall. The parapet is embellished with an elaborate carved design derived from Renaissance/Baroque sources. The name of the company is crisply inscribed in the facade. The large interior space is carried on giant pilasters. The reinforced concrete structure is ornamented in cast concrete decorative details and the window is set in an iron frame.

B

R115 MAP II
346-350 Kearny Street
architect unknown
1907

A two part small commercial block with unusually rich ornamentation for a building of its size, type, and location. Part of a fine group of small scale structures on this block. Ornamentation is Renaissance/Baroque with rusticated piers, swags in the spandrels, and a modillioned cornice with antefixae. Its thoroughly remodeled ground floor includes the "Eye" store, a fine period piece of the late 1960s, which has been vacant since a recent fire. The store was entered through a black tube with small showcase windows displaying surreal white styrofoam heads wearing glasses. The store itself was like a slick cave at the end of a tunnel, walled in chrome and plastic. The easy accommodation of such a design in a building like this illustrates the recognition by the architects of so many downtown buildings that the ground level would change as styles and functions changed.

From a broader perspective it illustrates the appropriateness of an urban architecture that took such possibilities into account. Most buildings with a commercial ground floor were simply designed at that level, so that alterations there would not mar the whole design. The commercial base was crowned by a cornice or molding beneath which almost anything was acceptable, but above which almost anything

was not. The serious upper facades offered an image of stability while the ground levels provided vitality in the continuously changing and continuously up-to-date commercial storefronts and interiors. Although these changing storefronts are essential to the dynamic nature of a thriving commercial area, it is a shame that a few of the better ones, like the "Eye," could not be retained for new uses.

B

143

R116 MAP II
353-359 Kearny Street
SW corner Pine
Kearny-Pine Building
architect unknown
1907

A two part vertical office block with Renaissance/Baroque ornamentation. Brick construction.

C

R117 MAP II
358 Kearny Street
architect unknown
1908

A reinforced concrete building in a two part small commercial composition with vague Renaissance/Baroque ornamentation.

C

R118 MAP II
362-364 Kearny Street
SE corner Pine
Maybeck, Howard, and White
1908

An excellent example of its type with handsomely framed windows and a simple cornice. A two part small commercial block with 19th century treatment of the upper section. The windows of the Pine Street facade are pulled apart, suggesting two buildings, each in a scale more in keeping with the area as it was built than a single long facade. The end of a fine group of small scaled buildings on Kearny. This is the only known building by the Maybeck office surviving in downtown San Francisco. Brick construction.

B

R119 MAP III
118-124 Maiden Lane
between Grant and Stockton
Lloyd Building
architect unknown
1909

A three part vertical composition with differentiated end bays and restrained Renaissance/Baroque ornamentation. Brick construction. It is the texture of the brick wall that is important in the context of Maiden Lane (rather than the composition which is difficult to perceive in so narrow a place).

C

R120 MAP III
140 Maiden Lane
Helga Howie Boutique
originally V. C. Morris Store
Frank Lloyd Wright
1949

A superb example of a brick building in a narrow alley of anonymous buildings, and comparable, as an example of a type, to Willis Polk's P. G. & E. substation at 222 Jessie Street (M23). The Morris Store manages to be both a compatible element in its mundane context and a powerful, if small, architectural focus. The great arched entrance tunnel serves as an invitation to come inside for the real drama. Altogether it is an eloquent comment on what such a building can be. Proof that at least one aspect of Modern Architecture could be both sensitive to its context and individually expressive—and be more complex and interesting than an architecture which is only one or the other, or neither.

NOT RATED   CL

R121 MAP III
177 Maiden Lane
between Grant and Stockton
architect unknown
1907

A two part small commercial block with skeletal expression of the facade and slight Renaissance/Baroque references in the corbeled brick cornice. Brick construction.

C

R122 MAP IV
300-324 Mason Street
NE corner O'Farrell
Hotel Virginia
Frank S. Van Trees
1908

A three part vertical block with Renaissance/Baroque ornamentation. An important corner anchor on two streets. Brick construction.

C

R123 MAP IV
333 Mason Street
Geary Theater Annex
Bliss and Faville
1909

A handsome brick structure, attached to the rear of the Geary Theater, with a light-colored mortar that gives greater definition to the individual bricks, and with its original small-paned, wood-framed windows. A three part vertical block with a giant order. Renaissance/Baroque ornamentation.

B

R124 MAP IV
334-336 Mason Street
NE corner Elwood
King George Hotel
architect unknown
1912

A three part vertical block with Renaissance/Baroque ornamentation including a broad projecting cornice. Reinforced concrete construction.

C

Native Sons Building, ca. 1911.

R125 MAP I
414-430 Mason Street
Native Sons Building
Righetti and Headman; E. H. Hildebrand
1911

A fine example of a three part vertical composition with extremely rich polychrome terra cotta ornamentation. Designed by a firm which was active in the San Francisco Architectural Club and its influential exhibitions. At the base are bas relief panels of early California scenes by Jo Moro. The upper zone of the composition is a balconied loggia with paired columns under a heavy bracketed cornice. The brick shaft is enriched with diapered brick work. A large ground level banquet hall was designed with an immense steel truss carrying the floors above in order to be column-free. The *Architect and Engineer* called the truss the largest on the Pacific Coast at the time. The banquet hall has since been converted for use as a theater with a marquee that obscures some of the terra cotta outside. The building still houses the offices and lodge rooms of the Native Sons of the Golden West.

A

R126 MAP I
425 Mason Street
NW corner Derby
San Francisco Water Department
Willis Polk and Co.
1922

A reinforced concrete office building with a stone base, originally designed for the Spring Valley Water Co. A three part vertical composition with Renaissance/Baroque ornamentation. The business office inside is decorated with murals by Maynard Dixon.

B

R127 MAP I
441 Mason Street
SW corner Post
Barrett Hotel
Mario Gaidano
1971

NOT RATED

R128 MAP I
542 Mason Street
St. Francis Apartments
Rousseau and Rousseau
1914

A typical Tenderloin/Nob Hill area apartment by one of the most prolific designers of such buildings. A two part vertical composition with Renaissance/Baroque ornamentation. Brick construction.

C

R129 MAP I
602 Mason Street
NE corner Sutter
Rousseau and Rousseau
1919

A residential hotel in a two part composition with projecting bay windows. Ornamentation is Renaissance/Baroque including the unusual molded metal cornice.

B

R125 Native Sons Building. Detail.

145

R130 MAP III
20-26 O'Farrell Street
NW corner Bagley
Kohler and Chase Building
Frederick H. Meyer
1909

A typically careful design by Frederick H. Meyer which is both individually interesting and an excellent piece of urban architecture. The building forms a backdrop for the domed Savings Union Bank at 1 Grant and it leads the eye down O'Farrell (unfortunately now to the blank wall of Liberty House) in a small realization of the hopes of the City Beautiful Movement. It is in a variation of a three part vertical composition with an unframed shaft area of dark spandrels and mullions set in a border of glazed cream terra cotta. Only the street end of the slab, designed as a tower, receives major architectural treatment. Ornamentation is Renaissance/Baroque.

The monumental banking space, originally a piano sales room, is partially remodeled and the ground floor is now totally glazed. The original second floor music hall is indicated on the outside by pedimented windows of a transitional story. The fine clock that once hung at that level has been replaced by the Home Federal Savings signs, and the extremely fine copper and glass marquee has been removed. Steel frame construction.

B

R131 MAP IV
107 O'Farrell Street
architect unknown
1909

A two part vertical block with differentiated end bays and Renaissance/Baroque ornamentation. Brick construction.

C

R132 MAP IV
165-167 O'Farrell Street
Downtown Center Building
architect unknown
1908

A brick residential hotel in a three part vertical composition with Renaissance/Baroque ornamentation. The importance of the building is diminished by its unsupportive neighbors.

C

R133 MAP IV
175-179 O'Farrell Street
architect unknown
ca. 1907

A two part small commercial block with formal treatment of the upper zone and Renaissance/Baroque ornamentation.

C

R134 MAP IV
180-190 O'Farrell Street
St. Moritz Hotel
architect unknown
1910

A residential hotel in a two part vertical composition. Modified Renaissance/Baroque ornamentation, rounded bay windows, and the overall facade treatment recall some of the work of Cunningham and Politeo, particularly the Hotel Stewart at 347–377 Geary (R50). Brick construction. The building functions visually as part of the Powell Street corridor.

C

R135 MAP IV
201-219 O'Farrell Street
SW corner Powell
Marquard's Little Cigar Store
architect unknown
1907

A cousin of Breen's at 71–77 Third Street in the rustication of its facade, the design of its now rare old sign, and even in the loss of its cornice. The building is in a two part vertical composition with Renaissance/Baroque ornamentation. Its rusticated light brown brick facades form part of the warm texture of the street walls on both Powell and O'Farrell streets. Its street level corner cigar and newsstand is one of the last of a type which was once almost synonymous with the vitality of urban American street life. Brick construction.

B

R136 MAP IV
235-243 O'Farrell Street
SE corner North Fifth
Hotel Barclay/Bardelli's
architect unknown
1910

A handsomely detailed residential hotel with a long-time San Francisco restaurant at the ground level. The building is in a two part vertical composition with rounded bay windows and unusual oversized cornice brackets that look like snails at the start of a race. Ornamentation is modified Renaissance/Baroque. The restaurant includes some of the finest stained glass in the city. The building is visually part of the cohesive Powell Street corridor. The design and ornamentation, like that of the St. Moritz Hotel at 180–190 O'Farrell, (R134), also recall the work of Cunningham and Politeo. Brick construction.

B

R137 MAP IV
238-242 O'Farrell Street
Spaulding Hotel
G. B. Ashcroft
1914

A red brick residential hotel in a three part vertical composition with differentiated end bays. Renaissance/Baroque ornamentation. Steel frame construction.

C

R138 MAP IV
250-260 O'Farrell Street
Handlery Motor Inn
Mario Gaidano
1965

NOT RATED

R139 MAP IV
272 O'Farrell Street
architect unknown
1909

A two part vertical composition, skeletal in expression with Renaissance/Baroque ornamentation. Brick construction.

C

R140 MAP IV
280 O'Farrell Street
NE corner Elwood
architect unknown
1911

A reinforced concrete residential hotel in a three part vertical composition with Renaissance/Baroque ornamentation. The facade is articulated vertically by two shallow square bay windows.

C

R141 MAP II
445 Pine Street
McDonald's
original architect unknown
1906

An excellent 1978 remodel of an old brick building which retained the original upper level treatment and invented a new but compatible one for the ground floor. Architects for the remodeling, including the handsome wood and copper interior, were Wudtke, Watson and Davis. Still a two part small commercial block with formal treatment of the second story. The original cartouche over the cornice displays a man in a suit holding a tray on his head.

C

R142 MAP II
453 Pine Street
Duffy's/Graziano's
original architect unknown
1906

Another tasteful restaurant remodeling, with handsome interiors by Jack Menzie, which has left the exterior ornamentation intact. The ground level is handled less successfully than the imaginative historical treatment of McDonald's down the street, but it could be improved by the simple addition of a molding between the floors. In composition, a two part small commercial block with formal treatment of the upper level. Renaissance/Baroque ornamentation. Brick construction.

C

R143 MAP II
469 Pine Street
Temple Hotel
architect unknown
1912

A brick residential hotel in a restrained three part vertical composition. Ornamentation is Renaissance/Baroque.

C

R144 MAP II
471-475 Pine Street
Saroyan Building
architect unknown
1911

A brick residential hotel in a two part vertical composition. Most of its ornamentation was removed along with its cornice.

C

R145 MAP II
485 Pine Street
SE corner Belden
architect unknown
1911

A two part small commercial block with formal treatment of the upper level and a hint of Renaissance/Baroque ornamentation. The supergraphic stripes date from about 1970. The building is part of the Belden Street group. Brick construction.

C

R146 MAP II
555 Pine Street
Pacific Telephone Co. Building
Aleck Wilson
1959, 1967

NOT RATED

R147 MAP III
57-65 Post Street
Mechanic's Institute
Albert Pissis
1909

One of the state's earliest educational institutions, located at this site since 1866, and an excellent example of a mixed use building whose internal functions are clearly expressed in the external design. The ground floor with its commercial space and monumental entranceway is surmounted by two floors of well-lit library floors, with offices above that. The composition is a three part vertical block. Ornamentation is Renaissance/Baroque. The marble elevator lobby is decorated with an Arthur Mathew's mural and is the endpoint of a very beautiful circular iron and marble stairway. The Mechanic's Institute itself occupies three floors, two of them housing the merged Mechanic's Institute and Mercantile libraries, and the third including one of the oldest chess clubs in America. The rest of the building is occupied by offices. It is a steel frame structure with brick curtain walls. The building is a major San Francisco cultural landmark.

A

R148 MAP II
68-82 Post Street
Foxcroft Building
Meyer and O'Brien
1908

A beautifully clad example of the unusual U-shaped office building type by one of the most important local post-fire architectural firms. Buildings on the open U or H plan make manifest the reality of large office buildings as designed in the days before air-conditioning and fluorescent lighting. Up until the post World War II period, almost every office building in downtown San Francisco was built with open courts for light and air. These were usually in the center or rear and they were often rather dingy, but they had the advantages of bringing fresh air into buildings in a city where air-conditioning is rarely needed for comfort (only for efficiency), and of breaking up floor plans into human dimensions. Almost every desk in these old buildings is either near an outside window or a light well.

The Foxcroft Building and a few others (the Rialto at 116 New Montgomery, M160, the Physicians' Building at 500-516 Sutter, R253, and the Kohl at 400 Montgomery, F86, to name the most prominent) make an aesthetic advantage out of these functional necessities. The light court opens on the street and is incorporated in the design so that the three part vertical composition appears as a pair of identical twins, narrowly separated. In the case of the Foxcroft, the dinginess of so many light courts was resolved in the use of a newly developed glazed white brick tile veneer which was reflective of light, and of such sturdiness and light weight that it could be attached directly to the frame of the building, without unduly increasing the load. The street facade of this steel frame building is clad in white glazed terra cotta with green spandrel panels. The green copper cornice was removed during the course of this survey. Ornamentation is Renaissance/Baroque, showing the influence of the Viennese Secession like much of Smith O'Brien's work, notably here in the ornament at the base of the light well. The building forms a strong edge of the cohesive retail area group on Post Street. It would be replaced by the proposed new Crocker Bank tower.

B

R149 MAP III
79 Post Street
Federal Savings Building
originally Strauss Building
William H. Weeks/Lewis Hobart/
remodel architect unknown
1911/1923/1935

Built as a 2-story structure, followed by a 3-story addition and complete remodeling in 1923, and a 2-story addition and partial remodeling about 1935. In its last two states it has been a two part vertical composition with differentiated end bays. Ornamentation was more strongly Renaissance/Baroque after the 1923 remodeling. Its cornice has been removed and its ground floor remodeled. Part of a continuous wall of older structures on Post.

C

R150 MAP III
101 Post Street
SW corner Kearny
Hastings
Burke, Kober, Nicolais, and Archuleta
1969

Although superficially compatible in style, this building displays about as much sensitivity to its neighbors as the Aswan Dam would in its place. There is no better example in downtown San Francisco of a building which illustrates the vapidity of most contemporary use of historical styles, and the failure of most present-day architecture, whether "traditional" or Modern, to relate to an urban setting.

The causes are partly rooted in the widespread lack of comprehension of the aims of the kinds of architecture which make up an area like downtown San Francisco. Architects of the early 20th century were not taught merely to imitate old styles for their own sake. Rather, they were taught a comprehensive view of an architecture which demanded structural, functional, and symbolic satisfaction of complex requirements, and which, at the same time, responded to context and to the strictly expressive abilities of the individual architect. In 1910, even the most insidious conspiracy of a greedy client and a bad architect would have produced a building on this site which would have at least generally matched the cornice heights of its neighbors and whose articulation, texture, and ornamental references would have, at worst, provided only a competent background building in a larger whole.

A better architect and a more civic-minded client (of which there were many) would have produced a taller building than its neighbors on either street and one more richly ornamented. If a store was only needed at the lower levels, then offices would have been stacked on top. The result, at its best, might have been a strong focal point which contributed to the rhythm and texture of the street without overwhelming it, and which was individually eloquent in the expression of its parts, and inspired (perhaps even inspiring) in its use of ornament. Historicist ornament would not have been "meaningless" as charged by Modernists but would have been used more or less freely for the expression of aesthetic or symbolic ends.

The Hastings Building does utilize historical ornament to express the traditional nature of its merchandise, but only in the most perfunctory, unimaginative, and minimal manner. As a work of urban architecture it is a total failure—wrong in its massing, wrong in its color and choice of materials, clumsy in its details, and offering almost completely solid walls in an area of skeleton and glass facades. In truth, Hastings is no worse than many others built in the downtown area in recent years; it is just built in a finer setting than most, a setting which was so rich in possibilities. It occupies the site of the old Koening Building.

NOT RATED

R151 MAP III
117-129 Post Street
O'Connor-Moffatt Building
Reid Brothers/A. H. Knoll
1910/1925

An unusually successful bit of urban architecture with a lengthy history. The single building we see today was built separately as two, in 1906 and 1908, and then remodeled as one 4-story department store structure in 1910 by the Reid Brothers for O'Connor-Moffatt. The 2-story addition in 1925, in the style of the existing building, was by A. H. Knoll. In 1929, O'Connor-Moffatt moved to a much larger new building at 101 Stockton which became Macy's in 1948.

As designed in 1910, the building was a two part vertical composition with a giant order in the upper zone and Renaissance/Baroque ornamentation. With its high, glazed, expressively commercial base it was very much in the tradition of the Reid Brothers' many fine downtown department stores, including the Rose Building (R231), the Butler Building (altered beyond recognition), and the Hale Brothers' two department stores on Market Street (M78, M92). At present, the building is a stacked composition with two tiers of Ionic pilasters framing large glass areas. The building is now occupied by smaller stores. Its rear facade on Maiden Lane repeats the piers of the front in brick.

B

R152 MAP II
126-130 Post Street
NE corner Robert Kirk
Rochat Cordes Building
Albert Pissis
1909

One of the very best and certainly most distinctive examples of urban architecture in downtown San Francisco by the architect of the Hibernia Bank Building at 1 Jones. Unfortunately, it has recently been made even more distinctive by the application of a garish mix of paint colors which denies many of the most important "urban" qualities of the design.

In composition, the building is a three part vertical block with a giant order in the upper zone. Renaissance/Baroque ornamentation is executed in terra cotta on a steel frame. The "architectural" composition rests on a glass commercial base. The facade curves and the design is carried a short way down a dark, narrow alley, the result being a powerful focal point on a relatively small mid-block building. There is a certain mystery about the way the facade turns down that alley as if it were going somewhere, or as if it were a much older building in a newer city which has obscured the structure's full glory.

The way in which the design is at once both a respectful piece of the street fabric and a highly unusual and interesting building by itself exemplifies the highest goals of the architects of the period. The massing, original color, and historical references of the ornament all participated in the aspect of the building which receded into the background. The destruction of this quality with its current paint job makes a complex design into a one-dimensional joke. Fortunately, it will have to be painted again sometime and can then be restored.

A

R153 MAP II
150 Post Street
NW corner Robert Kirk
Jewelers Building
Lewis Hobart
1908

A good example of the work of an important local architect, resembling his Commercial Building at 825–833 Market Street (M73). In composition, a three part vertical block with a shaft of enframed bays over what was originally a glass base. Ornamentation is Renaissance/Baroque. The steel frame of the pre-fire Sloane Building was used here, but with entirely new walls, floors, and layout. The first occupants after the fire were Morgan and Allen, jewelers. The building functions as an important element in the continuously fine group of buildings in this block.

B

R154 MAP III
165 Post Street
Rothchild Building
architect unknown
1908

A variation of a two part vertical composition with a single articulated end bay above the entrance that reflects the location of elevators, stairs, and fire escape. The facade is skeletal in expression with Chicago windows. Restrained use of Renaissance/Baroque ornamentation is concentrated at the cornice. Part of a particularly cohesive group of commercial structures in this block. Steel frame construction.

C

R155 MAP III
175-177 Post Street
Liebes Building
architect unknown
1908

Like the O'Connor–Moffatt Building down the street, a rich example of street architecture on both Post and Maiden Lane where its front facade is restated in brick. In composition, a three part vertical block with a high arcaded shaft over a glass base. Renaissance/Baroque ornamentation is focused at the tops of the arches. Steel frame composition with a terra cotta front.

B

R156 MAP II
180 Post Street
NE corner Grant
Hastings Building
Meyer and O'Brien
1908

One of the most richly and beautifully ornamented buildings in the retail area by one of the most important San Francisco architectural firms of the period. The skeletal facades are enlivened by extremely sculptural Renaissance/Baroque ornamentation that tends toward Art Nouveau, particularly in the female heads of the top floor. The original storefront piers with their equally sinuous capitals are intact and carry the orderly and finished design to the ground. Its composition is a two part vertical block. The building was erected by the Lent Estate and was long occupied as an annex by the White House department store.

A

R157 MAP III
185 Post Street
SE corner Grant
architect unknown
ca. 1955

NOT RATED

R158 MAP III
201-209 Post Street
Head Building
SW corner Grant
William Curlett and Sons
1909

Along with the Shreve Building across the street (R77), the tallest structure along Grant, and as such, a major event in one of the finest architectural groups in the downtown area. Considered on its own, it is somewhat less imposing than the Shreve Building, with which it is inevitably compared, but its relative simplicity and (in its original condition) its glass base made for an extremely handsome office and commercial building nevertheless. Its base was remodeled in 1959 by William B. Meyer for Brooks Brothers. In composition, the building is a three part vertical block with Renaissance/Baroque ornamentation. Its steel frame is sheathed in glazed terra cotta.

A

R159 MAP II
216-220 Post Street
Guggenheim Building
Herman Barth
1907

An altered version of the original which has sadly lost its spandrel decoration but has happily been graced with handsome modern awnings in a block where awnings are a major element in its distinctive urban character. Hopefully, the recent closing of Abercrombie and Fitch and the imminent takeover by Eddie Bauer will not adversely affect these relationships.

The building is in a two part vertical composition. Its originally more profuse Renaissance/Baroque ornamentation is now concentrated at the cornice. Its original Chicago windows have been altered with the introduction of large central mullions. The ground floor was originally leased to Hirsch and Kaiser, "opticians and dealers in photographic supplies." Brick construction.

C

R160 MAP III
225 Post Steet
S. Christian of Copenhagen
architect unknown
1908

A very pretty French Baroque facade with piers treated as Corinthian pilasters and typically large window openings treated as graceful French doors, slightly recessed behind little balconies. The cornice has been removed and the ground floor remodeled with a pair of clumsy columns in the wrong place. A two part vertical composition. Reinforced concrete construction. Part of a fine group in this section of Post Street.

B

R161 MAP II
228-240 Post Street
Gumps/Elizabeth Arden
architect unknown
1909

A rare example of the successful treatment of a single building as two, with each half in a different color and each with a different type of awning. In composition, a two part vertical block. Ornamentation is Renaissance/Baroque. Construction is of brick with iron posts at the ground level and wood posts above. An excellent background building on this block.

C

R162 MAP III
233 Post Street
Graff Building
E. P. Antonovich
1908

A steel frame structure in a three part vertical composition with Renaissance/Baroque ornamentation. Part of a cohesive group in this block.

C

R163 MAP II
246-268 Post Street
Gump's
Clinton Day
1908

An old San Francisco specialty store, first built in 1861 for Solomon Gump and remodeled after the fire by Clinton Day for A. Livingston Gump with the particular idea of providing a setting for Asian art work. The existing building is a handsome design which is still closer than most in appearance to mid-19th century San Francisco commercial buildings. In composition, it is a modified Renaissance palazzo. It is a brick building with wood posts and is clad along its main facade in Colusa sandstone. Its dark color, distinctive design, gabled parapet, and red awnings, all contribute to its importance as a major element along Post Street.

B

R164 MAP III
251-253 Post Street
Mercedes Building
Julius Krafft
1908

A two part vertical composition, skeletal in expression with Renaissance/Baroque ornamentation. It is a brick building with applied terra cotta ornamental details. Part of the Post Street group.

C

R165 MAP III
259 Post Street
architect unknown
ca. 1940

An elegant Moderne remodel of a 1909 reinforced concrete department store building
which received a 4-story addition in 1918, by G.
Albert Lansburgh. As it now appears, it is the
only San Francisco example of an aspect of the
Moderne which was most common in New York,
even down to its light gray stone veneer. At the
same time its facade treatment recalls that of
Sullivan's Carson Pirie Scott store in Chicago. Its
composition, left over from the original design,
is a three part vertical block, skeletal in articulation with broad Chicago windows. Its bronze entrance and window frames are very beautiful.

The building is a good example of the manner
in which many Moderne (as opposed to
Modern) designs, using the same materials,
compositional formats, and approaches to designing in an urban setting as more traditional
designs, were able to blend into the existing city
—expressive of their age, yet not disruptive.
Despite its ornamental base, wholly different
from its neighbors, an excellent street building.
This building was occupied by Ransohoffs from
1909 until 1973, when Ransohoffs moved to 50
Grant Avenue. Vacant since that time, it is
scheduled to reopen as The Limited in 1979.

B

R166 MAP II
272 Post Street
architect unknown
1909

A reinforced concrete commercial loft in a two
part vertical composition with skeletal articulation of the facade and Renaissance/Baroque
ornamentation.

C

R167 MAP III
275 Post Street
SE corner Stockton
Lathrop Building
architect unknown
1909

A handsomely detailed stacked vertical composition which presents facades to both Post
Street and Union Square. Its three story commercial base is divided into a 2-story glass
storefront and a mezzanine of Chicago windows framed in decorative terra cotta moldings. The proportions of the upper level office
windows are the same but are divided by solid
brick piers. Ornamentation is Renaissance/
Baroque. The light brick facades are set off by
dark window frames and a black cornice. The
ground level has been remodeled except for
an area around the Post entrance. Construction
is steel frame.

C

R168 MAP II
278-298 Post Street
NE corner Stockton
Joseph Frederick's and Co. Building
D. H. Burnham and Co.
1910

An outstanding example of the characteristic
retail area type with a glass commercial base
and offices above, located at an extremely important Union Square corner. The building was
designed by Willis Polk for D. H. Burnham and
Co. Because its glass base is largely intact this
building displays, better than most, the purposefully unconnected relationships of commercial base to "architectural" top by even the
best known and most respected of local architects. The simple glass base was designed to
display merchandise and was expected to be
remodeled. The "architecture," therefore, was
kept up a couple of stories, out of harm's way,
where it would survive countless changes of
fashion as the permanent expression of a timeless architectural tradition. It was literally above
the seasonal change of merchandise and
storefront remodelings.

In composition, this building is a two part vertical block with an attic and a giant order in the
upper zone. Its ornamentation is Renais-
sance/Baroque. It is of reinforced concrete construction. The building presents a rich and suitably monumental design to Union Square, and
bears an important visual relationship to the
City of Paris as a similar corner building in a
similar style. The open ironwork attic level
balcony appropriately suggests another level
of human activity (even when it isn't there) on
the city's most urban square.

A

R169 MAP I
333 Post Street
Union Square Parking Garage
Timothy Pfleuger
1942

"Built Down Instead of Up," the Union Square Parking Garage was the first in this country to be constructed underground with a landscaped park on the roof. It was also the first and best of several such structures in San Francisco (cf. St. Mary's Square Garage, Portsmouth Square Garage, and the Civic Center Plaza Garage). As an example of a sensitive urban "non-architecture" it is the closest thing in this city to the Oakland Museum.

Its original construction caused a great controversy and it was widely criticized when completed by people who felt that the best qualities of the park were lost in the change. The *Architect and Engineer* summed up many people's feelings: "The old park was a poet's, the new one is a mathematician's. The layout perfectly symmetrical, and formal. San Franciscans are not formal." The more important issue, however, was the accommodation of automobiles in the city. Given the recent completion of the two bridges and the related increase in the use of automobiles downtown, and the necessity of maintaining the competitive edge of Union Square as a shopping center over suburban developments, the Union Square Garage was an extremely sensitive and successful solution.

The garage and its landscaped roof were built at the site of the old Union Square (see Urban Design section). The structure was built by a private corporation which leased the ground under the park from the city following a test litigation in the state courts which also paved the way for subsequent garage/parks. The project was financed by $600,000 in private loans, and another $850,000 from the Reconstruction Finance Corporation. It is now owned by the City but operated by a private company. Encouragement and advice were initially solicited from "military experts" who counseled on the design of the structure as a bomb shelter and for other emergency uses. It contains enough ducts, outlets, and sump pumps, for example, that with air-conditioning, "the garage could be turned into a hospital having greater floor space than San Francisco's 33-story Russ Building." This civil defense value of the structure made it possible to obtain materials such as steel which were otherwise extremely difficult to come by during wartime.

Because of its soil conditions, close neighborhood of large buildings, and rooftop park, the structural design of the building was difficult and unusual. Bulkheading the walls against cave-ins during construction, ventilating the finished structure, and designing the roof to support a park that included trees, granite curbs, large crowds of people, and the 350 ton 90-foot Dewey Monument, were the most difficult problems.

At the same time, the rooftop had to "simulate the contours of a landscaped area," providing a central flat space and sloping up and down at its various sides in general conformity with the natural rise of the site to the northwest. It is in this sensitivity to the continuing function of the site as a park that the design must ultimately be measured—and in particular, in relation to later city projects which did not fare as well. Quite apart from the landscaping (by the City Park Department), the design of the structure provided a basis on which a naturalistic yet urban park could be developed, a basis not provided for other similar projects. The result is a "non-building" which satisfies its functional requirements and still respects the most important urban place in San Francisco.

B

R170 MAP I
340 Post Street
Bullock and Jones
architect unknown
1923

A reinforced concrete commercial building with an iron front, in a two part vertical composition over a glass base. The upper tier is treated with a giant order derived from Renaissance/Baroque sources. The overscaled detail on this building gives it a presence equal to many of its larger neighbors on Union Square. Built in 1923 by the Fitzhugh family, in the same year as the Fitzhugh Building up the street, it seems plausible that the Reid Brothers may have been the architects. This is one of several fine buildings for the Bullock and Jones Co. in downtown San Francisco.

B

R171 MAP I
350-360 Post Street
Qantas Building
Skidmore, Owings, and Merrill
1972

The height of this building matches that of the Fitzhugh Building next door because of the guidelines of the Urban Design Plan. The Saks store on the site of the Fitzhugh will not be required to go so high.

NOT RATED

R172 MAP I
364-384 Post Street
NE corner Powell
Fitzhugh Building
Reid Brothers
1923

A superior example of urban architecture, scheduled for demolition and replacement by a mediocre modern design which fails to respond to the tremendous possibilities of its location on Union Square. The most important function this building serves as a work of architecture is as a rich supportive structure to the St. Francis Hotel on one of the city's most important public spaces. In style, color, articulation, and massing it is an ideal neighbor—and at the same time is a handsome building when considered on its own.

In composition, it is a three part vertical block. Ornamentation is Renaissance/Baroque. It is a steel frame structure with reinforced concrete floors and terra cotta exterior. Built as a physicians' office building by William Fitzhugh,

plans for the site first went through several different stages under two owners and a number of architects including Ward and Blohme, Bakewell and Brown, and Weeks and Day. Earlier schemes included a theater and a department store. Today it is one of the last tall buildings of the Reid Brothers surviving intact.

The demolition of this building and the design of its replacement have been the subject of great controversy in San Francisco. Heritage has offered detailed proposals for reuse of the building together with a modern rear annex, and the City Planning Department has forced changes in the new design. As of this writing, however, demolition is proceeding, to the great impoverishment of Union Square.

A   NR

R173 MAP I
438 Post Street
St. Andrew Hotel
George A. Applegarth
1907

A typical residential hotel in a three part vertical composition, distinguished by the rare surviving interior of John Howell Books at the ground level. The bookstore was designed by William C. Hays in 1924, at the suggestion of Bernard Maybeck, and was intended to have the quality of an English gentlemen's library, transported to a busy urban location. It is furnished in dark-stained wood bookshelves, desks, and chairs, with Craftsmen lamps and hardware. Exterior ornamentation is Renaissance/Baroque. The building is of reinforced concrete construction. This is the third location of John Howell Books since its establishment in 1912.

B

155

R174 MAP I
442-444 Post Street
Chamberlain Building
Arthur Brown, Jr.
1925

One of three 20-foot wide skyscrapers in downtown San Francisco, and the one which is most directly expressive of the land values which made such structures economically feasible. The building is in a two part vertical composition with the barest skeletal expression of the facade behind its light and beautiful decorative metal fire escape. This fire escape is one of the very few in a San Francisco building which is treated as an aesthetic element. The building is of reinforced concrete construction. It was built for Selah Chamberlain, an important post-fire real estate developer.

B

R175 MAP I
450-460 Post Street
Elks Club
Meyer and Johnson
1924

One of the largest and most richly decorated of San Francisco's many fine downtown club buildings, designed by one of the best and most important firms of the period—and one which consistently produced superior decorative work. Frederick Meyer and Albin Johnson were assisted by Anthony Heinsbergen in the design of the interior. The exterior is a three part vertical composition with a high stacked base that reflects major interior spaces. Exterior ornamentation is Gothic, including a balcony, lancet windows, and pair of squat towers flanking a central gabled parapet.

Inside, the entrance lobby is predominantly Spanish Gothic in inspiration. The richly ornamented swimming pool with its extensive tile mosaics is modeled after the Sistine Chapel. Other major decorative interior spaces include the auditorium, buffet and card room, billiard room, game room, dining room, and lounging room. Above these communal spaces are hotel rooms for visiting Elks. This wealth of eclectic decorative interiors, characteristic of Heinsbergen, who specialized in theater design, was the subject of articles in the contemporary architectural press including ten pages in the inaugural issue of *Architectural Digest*. The building is of steel frame construction with reinforced concrete curtain walls clad in light tan brick.

This building succeeded the old building at 540 Powell as local headquarters of the Elks organization.

A

R176 MAP I
470 (490) Post Street
NE corner Mason
Medico-Dental Building
George Kelham; William G. Merchant,
  associated architect
1925

A handsome medical office building, characteristic in design of Kelham's work. It was noteworthy at the time of its construction for its reliable mechanical systems. According to the *Architect and Engineer* this structure was designed as a model of mechanical reliability for all medical office buildings.

In composition, it is a two part vertical block, its top story functioning as part of the cornice rather than a separate capital section. Ornamentation is attenuated Romanesque with narrow bays culminating in round arches, and a corbeled brick cornice. The existing design is a change from an earlier published sketch which was Renaissance/Baroque in ornamental derivation. The building was constructed by a corporation of tenant stockholders.

B

R177 MAP I
491 Post Street
SE corner Mason
First Congregational Church
Reid Brothers
1913

A monumentally scaled church which, although physically smaller than its neighbors, manages to hold its own in a dense urban setting. Designed by one of the city's most important early century architectural firms. The location of this very fine building recalls the time when each Protestant denomination had a "main" church downtown. The congregation today appears to be a largely neighborhood one. First Congregational was established in San Francisco in 1849 and has been at this location, in only two different buildings, since 1879.

In composition, the present building is an enframed pavilion with end bays and wings. The pavilions consist of Corinthian colonnades. The main Post Street facade is entered on a broad stairway through four fluted columns, to a rich foyer. The interior with its coffered ceiling, three-sided balcony, and proscenium arch is well lit by arched windows at the balcony and clerestory level, and by a very large skylight. Ornamentation is "Italian Renaissance" rather than the usual Gothic or Romanesque, and the plan follows the traditionally more egalitarian pattern of New England Congregational churches, being less hierarchical in its spacial arrangement than most denominations. The building is of reinforced concrete construction, finished in cement.

A

R178 MAP I
524 Post Street
Olympic Club
Paff and Baur
1912

One of the handsomest of the downtown area's many fine private club buildings, and home of the Olympic Club, said to be the oldest private athletic organization in the nation. A pre-fire building on this site was replaced in 1906 by a temporary structure and a permanent, enclosed, skylit swimming pool, still standing at the east end of the property. The pool was designed by Henry Schulze and was originally intended to be part of a larger 6-story complex, also by Schulze. However, in 1909 a competition was held for the design of a permanent club house. The competition was won by Paff and Baur, with Sutton and Weeks, Coxhead and Coxhead, and MacDonald and Applegarth all receiving awards for their designs.

As executed, the building is a three part vertical composition with differentiated end bays, an arcaded mezzanine level, and Renaissance/Baroque ornamentation. The facade is one at the base level with the pool structure. It is a steel frame building with a light sandstone base, brown brick shaft, and a rich polychrome terra cotta capital and cornice. The Doric entrance porch is modeled after the Palazzo Massimi in Rome. Statues in the porch are by Haig Patigian. Inside there are clubrooms and a gymnasium in addition to the pool. In its formal configuration, its tiled ceiling, and use of art glass in the dome, the pool is one of the most magnificent interior spaces in the city. In 1930, the *Architect and Engineer* published a drawing of a 26-story Moderne "New Olympic Club Building" by Arthur Brown, John Baur, and John Bakewell, with a high set-back shaft rising from the rear of a 10-story base. This was never built. In 1934 the Olympic Club was thoroughly renovated by Douglas Dacre Stone.

A

R179 MAP I
545 Post Street
Hotel Cecil
architect unknown
1913

A steel frame residential hotel in a two part vertical composition with pairs of projecting angled bay windows and an old "Hotel Cecil" sign. Ornamentation is Renaissance/Baroque.

C

R180 MAP I
555 Post Street
Press Club of San Francisco
originally Union League Club
T. Paterson Ross
1922

A unique variation of a three part vertical composition, originally built for the Union League Club. After the Union League Club merged with the Pacific Club as the Pacific Union and moved to the Flood mansion on Nob Hill, the Press Club moved from its old building at 449–465 Powell to this location. This building has a rusticated base with a high mezzanine of immense plate glass windows, set off by giant Ionic pilasters. Ornamentation is restrained Renaissance/Baroque, executed in brick on a steel frame.

B

R181 MAP I
569 Post Street
Post-Taylor Garage
also Musto Garage
Frederick H. Meyer
1922

An L-shaped reinforced concrete garage with frontages on both Post and Taylor streets. One of a group of early downtown parking structures designed to look like office or commercial buildings, and thereby more successful as urban architecture than many of their Modern successors. Composition here is a two part small commercial block with formal treatment of the upper level. Ornamentation is Renaissance/Baroque, suggestive of the Spanish Colonial Revival.

C

R182 MAP I
593-599 Post Street
SE corner Taylor
architect unknown
ca. 1910

A reinforced concrete residential hotel built and still owned by the Joseph Musto Estate Co. The building was evidently built in two stages, but in a consistent style, with wide bays at the corner and narrow bays next to the Musto Garage next door on Post. Composition is a three part vertical block with bays enframed in mannerist quoins. Ornamentation is Renaissance/Baroque. The remodeled ground level includes a restaurant and bar, a rare Polynesian period piece called Tiki Bob's (1955) by Gardner Dailey.

C

R183 MAP IV
17-23 Powell Street
Powell Hotel
architect unknown
1910

A reinforced concrete residential hotel in a three part vertical composition with differentiated end bays. It plays a particularly important role in the streetscape, supportive of the taller Bank of America, and forming a part of the consistent wall of buildings on Powell. Ornamentation is Renaissance/Baroque.

B

R184 MAP IV
35-41 Powell Street
Powell Cinema
architect unknown
1909

An early reinforced concrete theater building in the compositional form of a two part small commercial block with skeletal expression of the facade. Ornamentation is Renaissance/Baroque.

C

R185 MAP IV
45-49 Powell Street
architect unknown
1909

A brick residential hotel in a three part vertical composition, with a 2-story commercial base and a top story fire escape treated as a balcony. Ornamentation is Renaissance/Baroque. The cornice has been removed. The building is part of a cohesive district of brick buildings along Powell Street.

C

R186 MAP IV
100-118 Powell Street
Hotel Golden State
architect unknown
1908

A suitably massive corner structure with rusticated bays in a cohesive brick district. It is a residential hotel in a three part vertical composition with differentiated end bays. Ornamentation is Renaissance/Baroque. Brick construction. One of the fine mosaics at the entrance was recently removed.

C

R187 MAP IV
111-133 Powell Street
Bernstein's Fish Grotto Building
architect unknown
1910

A two part small commercial block with formal treatment of the upper section and a partially remodeled ground floor that includes a unique original storefront for Bernstein's Fish Grotto. Bernstein's is a landmark San Francisco restaurant established in 1907 which has occupied this building since its completion in 1910. The restaurant is entered through a ship's prow and is treated inside in the manner of a ship's cabin. Bernstein's recalls the early San Francisco Gold Rush days when many commercial establishments were literally carved out of abandoned ships. This building forms a pair with a similarly massed building at 135–149 Powell (R190) and is part of the cohesive larger Powell Street corridor in its upper brick facade and its originally distinctive ground level.

B

R188 MAP IV
120 Powell Street
architect unknown
1909

A reinforced concrete residential hotel in a three part vertical composition. Ornamentation is restrained Renaissance/Baroque. This is a narrow and nondescript building which is nevertheless an essential part of the wall of buildings along Powell Street.

C

R189 MAP IV
134-168 Powell Street
Elevated Shops Building
architect unknown
1907

A handsome skeletal corner building with modified Chicago windows and a spiky cornice of modified Renaissance/Baroque origins. In composition, the building is a three part vertical block. Its ground floor has been compatibly remodeled by Japan Airlines.

C

R190 MAP IV
135-149 Powell Street
architect unknown
1909

A two part small commercial composition with a distinctive and unusually ambitious formal treatment of the upper story. A central Ionic colonnade is terminated by large rusticated piers, each of which contains an ornamented window opening. In its massing the building forms a pair with 111–133 Powell (R187) and in composition, despite its low profile, it is a focal point on this block. It is a brick structure with iron columns and Renaissance/Baroque ornamentation executed in terra cotta.

B

R191 MAP IV
151-161 Powell Street
Hotel Herbert
architect unknown
1909

A brick residential hotel in a three part vertical composition with differentiated end bays. Ornamentation is Renaissance/Baroque. By virtue of its size and ornamental details it is a prominent element along the Powell Street corridor.

C

R192 MAP IV
200-216 Powell Street
SW corner O'Farrell
Omar Khayyam's
architect unknown
1933

In its 1933 remodeling, one of the finest examples of Moderne shop design in San Francisco—recently altered through the shaving off of its parapet projections and the loss of its signs. The building was originally designed by Salfield and Kohlberg in a "Spanish Design" but was remodeled inside and out in 1933. The basement level Omar Khayyam's Restaurant, with its Moderne decorative details in several materials, its custom designed furniture, and its many murals, was designed by William P. Day. Omar Khayyam's was originally built and operated by the late George Mardikian, widely known for his civic generosity. In composition, the building is a two part small commercial block with formal treatment of its upper level. Angled glass bays alternate with fluted piers. The bays were designed as windows in bronze frames with peaked terra cotta parapets (now flat-topped). The piers were designed with abstracted sunburst capitals (now removed). Despite the recent unnecessary mutilations to the building it is still a visual landmark in its distinctive color and what remains of the design.

A

Before recent alterations.

201 Powell Street
NW corner O'Farrell
Manx Hotel
architect unknown
1908

A large and unusually shaped brick residential hotel which wraps around the Howard Building, resulting in two Powell Street facades. In composition, it is a three part vertical block with differentiated end bays. Ornamentation is Renaissance/Baroque. In its size it is a major element in the cohesive Powell Street corridor. Baron's bar at the corner is a good example of a Moderne interior, slightly altered.

C

R194 MAP IV
207-217 Powell Street
Howard Building
architect unknown
1906

A steel frame residential hotel in a three part vertical composition. Ornamentation is Renaissance/Baroque. An important element in scale and articulation along Powell Street.

C

R195 MAP IV
222 Powell Street
Lew Serbin Co./World of Fabric
architect unknown
ca. 1935

A circa 1935 Moderne remodel of a 1906 brick structure, remarkable in the original character of its facade and signs. A two part small commercial block with formal treatment of the upper level. This is a building whose entire design recognizes the commercial character of Powell Street.

C

R196 MAP IV
226-230 Powell Street
architect unknown
1910

A two part small commercial block with formal treatment of the upper level. Limited ornamentation is Renaissance/Baroque. Brick construction. In scale and articulation, part of the cohesive Powell Street corridor.

C

R197 MAP IV
235-245 Powell Street
architect unknown
1910

A reinforced concrete residential hotel in a three part vertical composition. Ornamentation is Renaissance/Baroque. In scale, articulation, and quality of detail, an important element along Powell Street.

C

R198 MAP IV
236 Powell Street
Hotel Stratford
Glenn Allen and Charles Young
1908

A steel frame residential hotel in a three part vertical composition by the important Stockton architectural firm of Allen and Young. Ornamentation is Renaissance/Baroque. An important element along Powell Street.

C

R199 MAP I
301-345 Powell Street
St. Francis Hotel
Bliss and Faville
1904, 1907, 1913

Architecturally, historically, and in context, one of the major monuments of the city. It was originally built with two wings of three bays each facing Union Square at the south end of the present site. Gutted in the fire, it was rebuilt with a third wing, also of three bays, in 1907. A tower was planned at the southwest corner of Post and Powell to complete the frontage of the building on Union Square, but in 1913, the old building, as we know it today, was completed by enlarging the third wing of the building by four bays. The result is a large E-shaped building with two light wells open to the Square above the ground level.

In composition, the building is a three part vertical block. Ornamentation is Renaissance/Baroque. The building is steel frame in construction with a granite base, gray Colusa sandstone walls, a copper cornice, and giant Ionic marble columns at the base of each light well. Elsewhere, the ground level is articulated by large arched windows in a rusticated wall. The building is entered through the columns at the base of the original light well. Some of its several grand columned interior spaces have been remodeled but enough remain, including the entrance lobby, to recall the magnificence of the original. Other quieter spaces like the Borgia Room, the English Grill, and smaller bars and meeting rooms are also intact.

Today the ground level connects at the rear to the new lobby of the St. Francis Tower, a major 32-story addition designed by William Pereira Associates in 1972. The new lobby is typical in its ersatz magnificence of so many recent interiors —and it completely misses the quality of the original. Among the finest of the old St. Francis interiors which has subsequently been lost was Timothy Pfleuger's cocktail lounge of 1941 with its black patent leather walls and lucite ceiling. In its texture, color, broken massing, and detail, the old St. Francis establishes the character of Union Square, the city's most important public space. Long pictured in postcards and travel literature, almost as much as any other building, it serves as the architectural image of the city of San Francisco.

A

R200 MAP I
421 Powell Street
NW corner Post
United Airlines Building
originally Argonaut Club
Sylvain Schnaittacher
1909, 1920

A brick club building, originally designed as a modified Renaissance Palazzo, with a later attic addition and a sensitive recent ground level remodeling by Arthur Gensler and Associates. The building was originally occupied by the Argonaut Club which later merged with the Concordia Club and became the most prestigious Jewish men's club in San Francisco.

B

R201 Sir Francis Drake Hotel. Perspective rendering, 1927.

R201 MAP I
432-462 Powell Street
SE corner Sutter
Sir Francis Drake Hotel
Weeks and Day
1928

Along with the Mark Hopkins, the Sir Francis Drake is one of the city's two truly elegant hotels of the 1920s, both designed by Weeks and Day. It is an amalgam of stylish images, both inside and out, on a set-back skyscraper form that culminates in a spiky gabled top. The *Architect and Engineer* described it as "Italian in character, of late Gothic influence, simple in mass, residential in spirit." Its lobby and mezzanine level "lounge," with a sweeping split stairway connecting them, are an extremely effective pair of spaces, as monumental through less bombastic means as the St. Francis or Fairmont lobbies.

The steel frame was unusually heavily braced against wind and was built on a foundation of deep concrete piles. It is clad in pink Tennessee marble with iron and bronze storefront trim at the base, and in brick and terra cotta above. In 1947, the upper level of the tower was altered when Louis Lurie's penthouse apartment was remodeled by Thomas and Meret as the "Starlight Roof" with its exterior ribbon windows. Published preliminary studies of the massing of the building suggest that the client opted for a more traditional image than the architect proposed—characterized by its Gothic ornamentation, its multiple gabled silhouette, and its hip roof. The building is highly successful at both the street level and the skyline, in its ornamental use of rich materials around storefronts at the base, and its distinctive set back tower massing.

A

R202 MAP I
433 Powell Street
Chancellor Hotel
Rousseau and Rousseau
1914

A steel frame hotel building, distinguished both by its handsome traditional facade and by the difficulty of seeing that tall narrow facade on a narrow street. The blank walls of the sides and rear are as prominent as the "architectural" front from almost any angle—a fact which incurred the criticism of the *Architect and Engineer*. While the criticism still holds, the building, with all its faults, has an additional interest today as an illustration of the way in which so many of the downtown area's buildings were designed. Most were fortunate enough to be surrounded by comparable masses, hiding blank sides, but many looked like this when they were erected and many, like the Merchant's Exchange, were criticized for it.

In composition, this building is a three part vertical block. Its Renaissance/Baroque ornamentation is executed in tan brick and terra cotta. In 1937, the mezzanine level of the lobby was remodeled by Hertzka and Knowles as the "Chancellor Clipper Ship," a very fine Moderne bar with a 360-degree mural of the city and strong airplane imagery. Some of its furniture is new but the room is intact and well maintained.

B

R203 MAP I
435 Powell Street
architect unknown
1907

A 6-story brick building with the unusual arrangement of a commercial front for its full height and a residential hotel at the rear. The building is in a two part vertical composition, skeletal in expression, with restrained Renaissance/Baroque ornamentation. Its ground level hat store was remodeled with the building next door at 439 Powell (R204) by Williams and Grimes as Tiny's Waffle Shop in 1937. The space has been enlarged and partially remodeled since then as Sears Fine Foods.

C

R204 MAP I
439 Powell Street
architect unknown
1907

A two part small commercial block with formal treatment of the upper floor. A modified Chicago window is framed by pairs of Ionic pilasters carrying a high entablature with a balustraded cresting. In 1937, Goodfellows Grill was remodeled by Williams and Grimes as Tiny's Waffle Shop together with the ground level space of the building next door at 435 Powell (R203). This interior has been partially remodeled again for Sears Fine Foods. Brick construction.

C

R205 MAP I
445-447 Powell Street
architect unknown
1914

A small steel frame building in a two part small commercial composition with skeletal treatment of the upper level. Ornamentation is Renaissance/Baroque.

C

Poetz Building, ca. 1926.

R206 MAP I
449-465 Powell Street
SW corner Sutter
Poetz Building
originally Press Club
Frederick H. Meyer
1913

A three part vertical composition with its shaft treated as an enframed pavilion with end bays. The "architectural" composition is built above the ground level glass commercial base. Ornamentation is Renaissance/Baroque. The building was built for the Press Club of San Francisco which later moved to 555 Post after the Union League Club merged with the Pacific Club and moved to Nob Hill. The main public spaces of the club are at the third floor, articulated by the 2-story arched pavilions on the facades. In its texture and massing the building plays an important role at a crucial intersection. It is brick with terra cotta ornamental detail.

B

R207 MAP I
535 Powell Street
Harcourt's Gallery
originally Perine House, later Daroux
House
C. A. Meussdorffer
1911

A rare and very late example of a Second Empire Style house which would be notable anyplace in San Francisco and is particularly so as the only structure left downtown which was built as a single-family residence. It is entered through an ornate arched entranceway with carved garlands and volutes, its windows are capped by flat arches with massive stone voussoirs, and it is crowned by a mansard roof with a richly embellished Palladian dormer. Despite its size and original purpose, it ably holds its own on the street by virtue of its fine materials and assertive details. The house was originally built for George M. Perine. According to *Here Today*, it was then bought by Frank Daroux, a gambler and Republican political boss of the Tenderloin, for his bride Tessie Wall, "a prominent madam." Tessie, "who said she would rather be a lamppost on Powell Street than own all of San Mateo County," shot Frank in 1917 after they were divorced.

A

R208 MAP I
540 Powell Street
SE corner Anson
Elks Building
now Academy of Art College
A. A. Cantin
1909

A handsome but curious hybrid composition with a mixture of stylistic references. Built as a fraternal hall, it was vacated by the Elks upon completion of their new building at 450–460 Post (R175) in 1924. Since that time it has been occupied by a variety of tenants including the Museum of Erotic Art. The building consists of an enframed pavilion over a high arched base, with Corinthian columns on pedestals in the pavilion, all dervied from Renaissance/Baroque sources. The parapet is treated in the Mission Revival Style with vestigial hip-roofed towers at the corners and a central shaped gable. Florid moldings above ground level arches and a tiled pent roof cornice have been removed but the handsome metal entrance marquee is intact.

B

R209 MAP I
545 Powell Street
SW corner Bush
Family Club
C. A. Meussdorffer
1909

A small but very handsome club building with fine use of materials and comparatively literal use of the Renaissance Palazzo as a model. It is a dark red brick structure with cream colored terra cotta ornamentation and a broad (probably metal) cornice. The building is on a rusticated base which slopes down the hill.

A

R210 MAP I
560 Powell Street
SE corner Bush
Chesterfield Apartments
architect unknown
1911

A steel frame residential hotel in a richly textured variation of a three part vertical composition. Giant pilasters frame projecting angled bay windows. These are pedimented at the upper level beneath an elaborately bracketed, modillioned, and denticulated cornice. Shaft and capital sections are divided by a prominent mannerist molding. The entrance is sheltered by a cantilevered metal marquee. The facades are unusually plastic for a San Francisco residential hotel. Because of its prominent corner location this building is more successful than the very similarly treated design at 427–439 Stockton Street (R225).

B

R211 MAP III
46-68 Stockton Street
SE corner O'Farrell
Joseph Magnin
originally Newman and Levinson
Lansburgh and Joseph
1909

A handsome steel frame skeletal department store with large glass areas and a curving corbeled cornice. The building is in a three part vertical composition with minimal Gothic ornamental references. Before its base was remodeled, the glass areas grew progressively smaller from bottom to top, with plate glass at the base, four part bays in the shaft, and arched five part bays in the capital. The articulation of the facade and the large glass areas contribute to the light structural character of the street facades of the area, and are particularly handsome at a prominent corner of a block of major buildings. This is an unusually uncluttered design for the work of Lansburgh and Joseph who are best known for their elaborate ornamented movie theaters.

B

R212 MAP IV
55-59 Stockton Street
architect unknown
1906

A two part small commercial block, skeletal in expression, with Gothic ornamentation. The ground level "Eppler's Bakery" sign is a handsome survivor of the late 1930s. Brick construction.

C

R213 MAP IV
65 Stockton Street
SW corner O'Farrell
Imperial Realty Building
G. Albert Lansburgh
1931

A 1931 remodel of a 1910 structure, in what the *Architect and Engineer* called "Modernism, adopted with a degree of restraint." The two part vertical composition reflects the design of the earlier building in its system of structural bays. In 1931, the building was a "soft yellow" with gray and green highlights and custom designed aluminum spandrel panels. Showcase windows for its ground level shop, the Unique, had zigzag corners. The sidewalk at the entrance was of inlaid terrazzo in several colors. Neither the ground level remodeling nor the single paint color at the upper level is irreversible.

B

R214 MAP IV
101 Stockton Street
NW corner O'Farrell
Macy's
originally O'Connor-Moffatt
Lewis Hobart
1928, 1948

Originally built in 1928 for the O'Connor-Moffatt Department Store, the building, now known as Macy's, was enlarged along O'Farrell Street in 1948 in a compatible manner with the original. The store has expanded to the north into the old building at 239 Geary and the newer one (1968) at 281 Geary, both fronting on Union Square. The latter structures both have blank brick facades and are totally unresponsive to their superb setting.

The original building is a three part vertical block in composition. Terra cotta Gothic ornamentation includes major and minor piers culminating in finials and tracery. The 1948 addition is similar but without the upper level ornamental elaboration. An innovative commercial design, it included, when built, automated merchandise handling, flexible mechanical systems, express elevators, and interstore communications systems, and was designed to

accommodate expansion. Natural light was originally considered an asset with windows occupying large amounts of wall area.

The recent change in merchandising methods and its devastating effect on the street is evident both in Macy's Geary Street extensions and in the Liberty House building across the street—both with blank walls to provide for open floor areas with peripheral storage space. The compromise solution of painted glass (as in the White House, R233, or the Hasting's Building, 180 Post, R156) or hanging curtains (as in Joseph Magnin's at 46–68 Stockton, R211) and maintaining traditionally articulated fenestration would seem to be a solution that has not been considered.

B

R215 MAP III
120 Stockton Street
NE corner O'Farrell
Liberty House
Morganelli, Heunann
1974

A totally inappropriate, blank-walled, suburban shopping center department store located one-half block from Union Square. It replaces the Shiels Estate Building of about 1912 by Ross and Burgren.

NOT RATED

R216 MAP III
200-212 Stockton Street
NE corner Geary
Colson Building
architect unknown
1908

An interesting and distinctive example of an early reinforced concrete building expressed as such in its skeletal facade with polygonal columns and smooth spandrels. Straight-sided polygonal columns were less expensive and more easily realized than round columns in the early days of reinforced concrete construction because of the difficulty of making round formwork. This building is a two part vertical composition with restrained use of Renaissance/Baroque ornamentation. It forms part of the only intact older block front on Union Square (other than the St. Francis Hotel).

C

R217 MAP III
216 Stockton Street
George A. Schastey
1930

A Moderne addition and remodeling, for Foster and O'Rear Confectioners, of a one-and-a-half story reinforced concrete building originally built in 1909. The building is in a two part small commercial composition with formal treatment of the upper level. Second floor fenestration is an abstracted Palladian motif, with lozenge topped, almost Art Nouveau side lights—all partially obscured by a clumsily attached fire escape. The skeletal third story is glazed in industrial sash. Wall areas are clad in black granite with a dripping aluminum scalloped frieze and cornice. The building is a valuable period piece in a city where Moderne shop fronts are comparatively rare. The design with its arched cornice neatly bridges the gap between its two larger neighbors. It is part of a diverse but cohesive group of older buildings on the east side of Union Square.

B

R218 MAP III
218-222 Stockton Street
SE corner Maiden Lane
A. M. Robertson Building
A. B. Foulks
1908

A two part vertical composition with 18th century English ornamentation, built as a 3-story structure in 1908, and later enlarged by one story. An article in the *Architectural Record* in 1912 on "The New San Francisco" stated, "the bookstore of A. M. Robertson is worthy of remark as a very discreet example of the small shop which solicits attention by being modestly but somewhat self-consciously different from its neighbors and prototypes."

The Town and Country Club, a prestigious women's club located on the upper floors, was designed by Willis Polk in 1909. The current rooftop Pan Am sign is entirely appropriate to its Union Square location. The building is located at the crucial juncture of Maiden Lane and Union Square.

B

R219 MAP III
234-240 Stockton Street
NE corner Maiden Lane
Schroth Building
Cunningham and Politeo
1908

A scaled-down version of an 18-story skyscraper proposed just before the fire, a victim of the height limit imposed afterwards. In composition, a hybrid of a three part vertical block stacked above a two level commercial base. Ornamentation is Renaissance/Baroque including a heavily rusticated floating "base" level, mannerist window surrounds, and strong horizontal courses between tiers of the composition.

Its cornice was removed in the late 1930s and the parapet remodeled with Moderne ornamentation—a far more sensitive way of dealing with a sometimes unavoidable problem than merely stripping the cornice, as has typically been done in recent years. The building is a large and early example of reinforced concrete construction. In its size, texture, and ornamentation, it is an important element on Union Square.

B

R220 MAP II
334 Stockton Street
NE corner Campton
Wilson Building
now Hotel Drake-Wiltshire
W. L. Schmolle
1910

A reinforced concrete brick clad structure originally designed as a "bachelor's hotel" and now functioning as an annex to the Hotel Drake-Wiltshire. It is in a three part vertical composition with Renaissance/Baroque ornamentation, and is distinguished by square window openings and banded rustication at the mezzanine and capital levels.

C

R221 MAP II
340 Stockton Street
Hotel Drake-Wiltshire
MacDonald and MacDonald
1916

Remodeled in 1916 with a Spanish Colonial Revival treatment of the facade for Charles H. Crocker, the Drake-Wiltshire was originally constructed in 1909. In 1916 the Spanish Colonial Revival was extremely stylish, having been popularized only the year before at the 1915 San Diego Exposition.

It is a steel frame structure with reinforced concrete curtain walls. The building appears to have been enlarged by three stories in 1916 and by one more, more recently. Its 1916 facade is in a three part vertical composition with a shaft of square windows, and a balcony dividing the shaft and capital. Its cornice was evidently removed at the time of the most recent top floor addition. The tall narrowly shaped building nicely punctuates the Stockton street facade.

B

R222 MAP I
345 Stockton Street
NW corner Post
Hyatt Union Square Hotel
Skidmore, Owings, and Merrill
1972

One of the best examples in San Francisco of urban architecture in the Modern idiom. Its handsome shaft is crisply detailed, enlivened by the use of color, and crowned by a vaguely historical "roof" that brings the high building to a more satisfactory conclusion than the typically abrupt termination of Modern highrises. The tower is respectfully set at the rear of the lot behind a low triangular pavilion that maintains the dominant massing of the Square and simultaneously opens up a small mid-block pedestrian area. Height levels and important lot lines are maintained at the same time pedestrians are accommodated by a network of paths through the complex. The famous fountain in the mid-block plaza is by San Francisco sculptor, Ruth Asawa.

NOT RATED

R223 MAP I
415 Stockton Street
architect unknown
ca. 1907

A very small, 1-story glass front building with a handsome entablature.

C

R224 MAP I
417 Stockton Street
Navarre Guest House
Oliver and Foulkes
1907

According to the *American Builders Review*, an example of a residential hotel in the "Mission Colonial" style. In composition, it is a three part vertical block. Today we would refer to its ornamentation as a mixture of Renaissance/Baroque and Mission Revival. Brick construction.

C

R225 MAP I
427-439 Stockton Street
architect unknown
1911

A residential hotel in a three part vertical composition that strongly resembles that of the Chesterfield Apartments at 560 Powell (R210), also of 1911. In ornamentation, notably bays, piers, and cornice, and in the rich plastic quality of the facade, it is clearly by the same architect. The building is of steel frame construction with reinforced concrete curtain walls.

C

R226 MAP II
108-110 Sutter Street
NW corner Trinity
French Bank Building
originally Bullock and Jones
Hemenway and Miller/E. A. Bozio
1902, 1907/1913

An extremely fine early San Francisco skyscraper with a somewhat cloudy history, originally designed in a skeletal Chicago School manner by an important but little-known firm and remodeled with an overlay of Beaux-Arts details by a (presumably) French architect.

In 1902, the architectural supplement to the San Francisco periodical *Town Talk* called the original design "A modern, superbly appointed, fire proof building, now in the course of construction." It was designed for the Bullock and Jones Co., who occupied the lower two floors, with offices above. At that time it was a two part vertical composition, strongly skeletal in expression with the principal differentiation between the 2-story base and the shaft being the color of the decorative tile cladding. The shaft was terminated in a frieze punctuated by small round windows recalling Sullivan's Guaranty and Wainright buildings, among others. Ornamentation was Renaissance/Baroque, applied in a purely decorative manner except in the traditional cornice and cresting. Unfortunately the tile cladding of the steel frame failed in the fire and the exterior was badly damaged. In 1907, it was apparently rebuilt to its original design.

At some point after 1907 the building was taken over by the French American Bank. In 1913, it was enlarged and remodeled by E. A. Bozio for the French Bank. As remodeled, although the facade was still skeletal, its composition and ornamentation became even more elaborate and its base and columns were treated as rusticated masonry. Piers were clad in gray Colusa sandstone; spandrels and cornice were copper. The design and placement of the decorative iron grilles above the spandrels are taken directly from Ernest Flagg's first Singer Building in New York, of 1904, as is a certain quality of the overall conception, albeit in miniature. The building was extended for three bays down Trinity Street and is fully ornamented for the length of that alley facade. Although part of that facade is hidden by the California Pacific Building, much of it is visible above the low buildings on Montgomery Street. The small but sumptuous marble banking hall, with its coffered ceiling, has been partially remodeled. In composition, the present building is a three part vertical block.

Apart from its great architectural value, the French Bank (now the French branch of the Bank of America) is extremely important as a supportive structure to the Hallidie Building and as a part of one of the finest rows of buildings in downtown San Francisco in this block of Sutter (and extending west another block to Grant). The block can be viewed as a capsule history of downtown San Francisco architecture which has come together in an aesthetically highly successful group. This building represents both the skeletal, Chicago-derived aspect of the city's buildings and the influence of the Ecole des Beaux-Arts, and also serves as an integral element in the progressively taller buildings on the block whose cornices change in design and color at every step.

A

R227 MAP II
126 Sutter Street
architect unknown
1907

A small and inconsequential building on its own terms, but one which plays an extremely important role in this superb block. From Kearny Street to the Hallidie Building, each building in the group is of a related breadth. The last two buildings in the group, the French Bank and the California Pacific Building (105 Montgomery), are both tall slender towers.

For both these last two buildings the sense of mass, and hence of equality with the rest of the block, is enhanced by the quality of each as a freestanding tower. The California Pacific Building stands between Montgomery Street and Trinity alley, and the French Bank stands between Trinity alley and this building which is so small that it serves to space the building and allow it to stand free at its upper levels. This building is a two part small commercial block, skeletal in expression, with restrained Renaissance/Baroque ornamentation. It is of brick construction.

C

R228 MAP II
130-150 Sutter Street
Hallidie Building
Willis Polk
1917

More than "the world's first glass curtain walled structure," for which it is well-known, the Hallidie Building is a superb work of urban architecture. Like the best such architecture anywhere, it is drawn from its surroundings, and in turn, it speaks to and ennobles them.

Within a radius of two blocks, there are at least half a dozen earlier buildings which can be viewed either as prototypes or sources of inspiration for the Hallidie Building. Foremost among them is the Bemiss Building of 1908, at 266 Sutter (R235)—a glass front building in the bare minimum of an iron frame with a cantilevered historicist cornice. The Rose Building (W. & J. Sloane Co.) of 1908, at 216–220 Sutter (R231), is one of the best extant representatives of a once-common San Francisco compositional type which placed an implied masonry "archi-

tecture" above a 2- to 4-story glass curtain wall base. The best of the local architects, including the Reid Brothers, in the case of the Rose Building, and Polk himself, in the case of the Frederick's Building (278–298 Post, R168), had worked with this type. For the remarkable cantilevered Gothic cornice, Polk need have looked no further than 200 Kearny (at Sutter, R97), of 1908 in the same block, or the Flatiron Building of 1913 (540–548 Market at Sutter, M37). Moreover, the building is in the traditional three part compositional format with differentiated end bays, defined humorously by Gothic fire escapes.

The building responds to its environment by taking common elements in its neighborhood and recombining them in a new way which overwhelms the others in the intelligence of its

conception, but still relates to them in its constituent parts and in the working out of the idea. As it is executed here, with the glass curtain wall hung a foot beyond the reinforced concrete structure of the building, it is as beautifully and clearly expressed as any glass curtain wall built since. The composition is arranged like so many of its neighbors—which are also curtain walls, but whose implied masonry walls lend better visual support to the ever-present fire escapes and cornices. The unusually overscaled iron cornice, here, heightens the contrast of structure and ornament which is present everywhere in San Francisco—and heightens the joke.

While he makes fun, however, Polk simultaneously utilizes these same vernacular elements to relate the building to its neighbors in the traditional way. He recognizes the contradictions in the architecture he teases, but he also recognizes its strengths. As the last building built on the block, the Hallidie tied a diverse group together into a superb whole. In addition to the relation of its design to the architecture of the downtown area in general, it related specifically to its block in scale, massing, height, color, and structural expression in a complex dialogue. For all his outrageousness, Polk was too sensitive to the city and too much a part of the traditions of the day ever to have purposefully designed a building out of harmony with its setting. The building is very much related to the larger body of Polk's work, the best of which always responded to the vernacular in inventive ways—whether in shingled houses or traditional office buildings. The building is named after Andrew Hallidie, inventor of the cable car, and it was built by the Regents of the University of California.

A NR; CL

R230 MAP II
171 Sutter Street
SE corner Kearny
Sutter Hotel
L. B. Dutton
1911

A traditional hotel building in a three part vertical composition which serves as a solid anchor at a very important intersection. It is of steel frame construction with reinforced concrete floors and was described as "absolutely fireproof." The facades are pressed brick with a rusticated mezzanine, arcaded upper level of the shaft, and paneled capital under a galvanized iron cornice—all with reference to Renaissance/Baroque models. The *Architect and Engineer* wrote, "The exterior of the first story will be entirely of plate and prism glass, giving the utmost possible amount of light for stores, which are designed to occupy the entire first story." It was originally built for the Jacob Z. Davis Estate Co.

C

R229 MAP II
154 Sutter Street
Central Realty Building
Sylvain Schnaittacher
1907

A handsome skeletal commercial and office building which is strongly supportive of the Hallidie Building and is an integral member of its superb block. The building is in a two part vertical composition with a 2-story plate glass commercial base surmounted by a skeletal shaft of three part windows. Before the cornice was removed ornamentation was clearly Renaissance/Baroque. A textured round molding enframes the bays.

The original, entirely glass base was remodeled in the 1930s, maintaining its large glass areas but framing them in an Art Deco veneer of blue and green tiles—in a conscious gesture to the colors of the Hallidie Building. Like the other buildings in this block, this is an element in the progressively higher masses from Kearny to Montgomery and it is part of the diversely expressed structural and stylistic character of the group. A steel frame building clad in glazed brick and terra cotta.

B

R231 MAP II
216-220 Sutter Street
NW corner Claude
Rose Building
now W. & J. Sloane
Reid Brothers
1908

The finest extant example of the characteristic retail area type with a glass base and an "architectural" top. It also is a major element in the continuing Sutter Street group. In composition, a three part vertical block with a rusticated base/mezzanine, a shaft defined by a giant order, and a capital—all placed above a high, 2-story glass storefront.

Once again, the design accommodates the changing requirements of merchandising at the ground level where unencumbered showcase windows can be used to greatest advantage, or can even be remodeled without damaging the permanent character of the historicist, implied masonry top. This is a steel frame building clad in gleaming white terra cotta. The mezzanine level and sides of its glass base have been painted and its cornice removed without altering the character of the whole. The vertical "W. & J. Sloane" sign relates to those for Sherman Clay and the White House.

A

Left: Rose Building, 1910.

171

The White House, ca. 1958.

R232 MAP II
250-254 Sutter Street
Goldberg Bowen Building
Meyers and Ward
1909

Another example of the retail area type with a glass commercial base and an implied masonry office shaft. This building is notable for its superb terra cotta cornice of very full organic ornamentation—an appropriate image for the original ground level Goldberg Bowen delicatessen. In composition, the building is a two part vertical block. Apart from its cornice, its ornamentation is Gothic in the ribs of its shaft, paneled spandrels, and top floor relieving arches. The enframed window wall of the base has lost its first floor glass panes. The frame of this base still has sockets all around where incandescent bulbs once served as a forerunner of the neon sign, cheerfully drawing attention to itself. The building is of brick construction. It forms part of the very fine two blocks of Sutter between Montgomery and Grant.

A

R233 MAP II
255 Sutter Street
SE corner Grant
The White House
Albert Pissis
1908

A famous old San Francisco department store building which was converted to a parking garage about 1968. It was occupied by the Raphael Weill Co. (which had been established as a dry goods store in San Francisco in 1885) as the White House store from its opening until 1965. At its peak the White House occupied four other buildings in its block. Considering the high demand for parking in this area and the more common alternative of demolition for an outmoded structure, its use as a garage has been appropriate. In its central location, and as the largest building in the area, it was the only one which could have been successfully converted from a functional standpoint. The result has been maintenance of a very fine curving facade as one of the key elements in the retail area, built at the intersection of its most important streets. Use of the ground level for a variety of shops has maintained the vitality of the street. As built, it was a 4-story steel frame structure in a two part vertical composition with a glass base and a giant order in its upper tier. The attic story was a later addition, but is entirely sympathetic to the original. In its monumentality and its curving corner it is another example of the urban sensitivity which is always one of the strongest features in the work of Albert Pissis. The handsome old "White House" signs relate to those for Sherman Clay and W. & J. Sloane. The exterior is in need of maintenance.

A

Davis-Schonwasser Co. Building, ca. 1910.
Before remodeling for Hibernia Bank.

R234 MAP II
256-262 Sutter Street
Sather Building
architect unknown
1911

A reinforced concrete office building in a two part vertical composition above a commercial base and mezzanine. Ornamentation is restrained Gothic with a Renaissance/Baroque cornice. The structure is clad in a handsome imitation sandstone terra cotta. The fire escape is a rare example of one which is incorporated into the design, both by virtue of its ornamentation and its deployment. The building is an important element in a very fine block.

B

R235 MAP II
266-270 Sutter Street
Bemiss Building
architect unknown
1908

This glass walled structure of 1908, less than two blocks from the Hallidie Building, perhaps deserves the title of the "world's first." A stunningly simple and beautiful structure, it clearly contains the seeds of the Hallidie Building design, whether considered as a direct influence, or merely as the purest expression of a widespread local vernacular tradition to which the Hallidie responded. The Bemiss is in a two part vertical composition, purely structural in its skeletal facade expression, with iron crossbeams carrying three huge square plate glass windows at each floor. Its only ornamentation is its Renaissance/Baroque cornice.

Despite its uniqueness, as the logical extreme of a common local type it relates to its surroundings because it is a clear and direct outgrowth from them—like the Hallidie Building. The proportions of its facade and the size of its windows recur so often in the area that it seems quite probable that these windows were the largest standard size sheet of glass locally available.

A

R236 MAP II
290 Sutter Street
NE corner Grant
Hibernia Bank
Hertzka and Knowles
1958

A remodel of the 1908 Davis-Schonwasser Co. Building by MacDonald and Applegarth; a commercial building in a two part vertical composition with a glass base and a giant order in the upper tier. The building was a handsome and suitably monumental design at a very important intersection. It was distinguished by its "monolithic reinforced concrete" construction, reinforced by the Kahn system, one of the most technologically advanced of its day.

NOT RATED

R237 MAP II
301-303 Sutter Street
SW corner Grant
Sutter's Corner
architect unknown
1907

A commercial jewel box—small in scale yet rich in an exuberant and delightful ornamentation. The design takes maximum advantage of its important corner location, reaching out at the cornice, cresting, and entrance marquee levels to occupy more than its limited physical site. In composition, it is an enframed window wall over a 1-story base. The broad arches at each public facade of its top story are in tension with its prominent corbeled cornice. Gothic ornamentation includes foliated spandrel panels and very ornate crests at the top of each arch. A ceiling has been added in the ground level store, below the once open mezzanine level, obscuring the very fine ornate plaster ceiling (still intact). The building is small but well known and a public favorite.

A

R238 MAP II
307-309 Sutter Street
Orpheus
**original architect unknown/storefront by
    Gerard Benamou**
1909/ca. 1975

A 1-story small commercial block with Renaissance/Baroque ornamentation in its cornice and parapet. The storefront has recently been stylishly remodeled, respectfully leaving the cornice, but disregarding the overall impact of the new first floor design on the proportions of the whole. Brick construction.

C

R239 MAP II
310 Sutter Street
architect unknown
1909

A reinforced concrete commercial and office structure in a two part vertical composition with skeletal facade expression and restrained Renaissance/Baroque ornamentation. It is one of several vertical compositions on very narrow lots in this area, a situation which results in a diverse and vital streetscape.

B

R240 MAP II
312-318 Sutter Street
Nutall Building
architect unknown
1909

A three part vertical composition, skeletal in expression with Renaissance/Baroque ornamentation. The three part composition of office floors rests on a high glass commercial base. The building is of brick construction with iron posts. It is the last building in the continuous wall of fine buildings on the north side of Sutter, beginning at Montgomery Street.

B

R241 MAP II
315-317 Sutter Street
Newbegin Building
architect unknown
1909

A hybrid composition with two major cornices. The facade is largely skeletal in expression with limited use of Renaissance/Baroque ornamentation. Brick construction.

C

R242 MAP II
323-333 Sutter Street
Hotel Alamo
architect unknown
1909

A brick residential hotel in a two part vertical composition over a high commercial base and mezzanine. Ornamentation is Renaissance/Baroque.

C

R243 MAP II
345-353 Sutter Street
architect unknown
1910

A reinforced concrete structure in a two part small commercial composition with formal treatment of the upper level and Renaissance/Baroque ornamentation. The handsome and stylishly remodeled ground floor Ariston store is by Donald Clever (1973).

C

R244 MAP II
355-363 Sutter Street
originally Forbidden City Night Club
architect unknown
1910

Originally the Forbidden City Night Club, the building was converted for use as a movie theater about 1973. In composition, it is a two part small commercial block with formal treatment of the upper level. Modified Chicago windows are framed by pairs of pilasters beneath a full entablature. Ornamentation is Renaissance/Baroque. It is of reinforced concrete construction.

B

R245 MAP II
371-375 Sutter Street
Nathalie Nicoli Building
architect unknown
1907

A three part vertical composition, skeletal in expression with Renaissance/Baroque ornamentation including a fine corbeled cornice. The office shaft is built on a 2-story glass commercial base which has been partially remodeled. In scale, massing, articulation, and material, the building is a strong supportive structure to the Galen Building next door.

C

R246 MAP II
391-399 Sutter Street
SE corner Stockton
The Galen Building
Meyer and O'Brien
1908

A handsome, structurally expressed steel frame skyscraper located at an important corner that terminates continuous groups of older buildings on two streets. The building is a three part vertical composition with Renaissance/Baroque ornamentation. Its facade is the same as that first used by these architects in the Rialto Building (M160) in 1902, and repeated by them in the Monadnock Building (M56) in 1906. The facade is characterized by rusticated piers and plain spandrels designed to maximize glass areas for office lighting, and to accommodate a flexible interior plan. The first use of this facade on the Rialto Building was influenced by a visit to Chicago by Smith O'Brien.

B

R247 MAP I
400-406 Sutter Street
NW corner Stockton
McCloud Building
architect unknown
1907

A two part vertical block, skeletal in expression with restrained use of Renaissance/Baroque ornamentation. Brick construction.

C

R248 MAP I
431-437 Sutter Street
Skidmore, Owings, and Merrill
1972

An attractive "traditionally styled" structure designed at the same time as the Hyatt Union Square Hotel next door. It is a remodel of a 1909 brick structure.

NOT RATED

R249 MAP I
445 Sutter Street
Pacific Gas & Electric Co. Building
Frederick H. Meyer
1916

A typical, beautifully detailed office building by Frederick Meyer, exhibiting his characteristic mastery of textures and colors and fine use of terra cotta ornamentation. The steel frame building is in a three part vertical composition with a high commercial base (poorly remodeled) surmounted by a 5-story office shaft. The brick shaft is ornamented in decorative terra cotta spandrel panels and it culminates in a terra cotta segmental arcade and capital. An intricate black iron fire escape is utilized for its decorative and textural qualities, and the whole is capped by a sculptural dark brown cornice. The building is part of a very fine group of three, including the P. G. & E. Building at 447 Sutter (R250) and the Sir Francis Drake Hotel at 432–462 Powell (R201). This group provides a rich supportive setting for 450 Sutter (R251) across the street and is visually tied to the intersection of Powell and Sutter. The building was constructed as part of a pair of P. G. & E. office buildings, with 447 Sutter, in 1916.

A

R249, R250 445 and 447 Sutter, ca. 1910.

R250 MAP I
447 Sutter Street
Pacific Gas & Electric Co. Building
Ivan C. Frickstad
1916

Built as a fine pair with 445 Sutter (R249) for P. G. & E. in 1916, by a company architect who did a number of substations and office buildings based on prototypes by Willis Polk and Frederick Meyer. The building is also part of an excellent group of three (including the Sir Francis Drake at 432–462 Powell, R201) that provides a rich textural setting for 450 Sutter (R251). In composition, it is a three part vertical block over a glass base. Brick walls are richly detailed in Renaissance/Baroque terra cotta ornamentation. The capital is defined by arches enclosing paired arches, and the whole is crowned by a corbeled cornice. The glass base retains its original intricate iron frame and entrance arch. Steel frame construction.

A

R251 MAP I
450 Sutter Street
Medical-Dental Office Building
Miller and Pfleuger
1929

A highly innovative design when it was built, and still one of the finest skyscrapers ever constructed here. It was one of the earliest skyscrapers anywhere to display a particular interest in the "skin" of a tall building as opposed to its structural character—a quality which may partly account for its great current popularity. While it is this treatment of the skin which is most striking about the design, this is not accomplished without expression of traditional concerns of massing, verticality, and the structural frame, or without a very beautiful and original use of ornamentation.

Overall, the building is simple and clear in its T-plan and soft silhouette, but rich and complex in the use of materials and details. Its skin consists of horizontal bands of glass and terra cotta which bulge out between structural bays, emphasizing the lightweight non-structural quality of the curtain wall and simultaneously maximizing rentable floor area and access to natural light. This skin appears to be literally wrapped around the steel frame in its rounded corners and parapet. Spandrel panels are ornamented in Mayan inspired decorative motifs. The aluminum clad Mayan base and entrance, and the elevator lobby, with its dark marble walls and elaborate aluminum Mayan ceiling, are superb. Everywhere the Mayan detail is tempered by the Moderne quality of the whole and by the intention to create a suitable source of decoration for a modern American building. The building was an early and extremely important example of Modernist architecture in the Bay Area and it marked a significant step in the development of the

American skyscraper. The building was designed as an innovative mixed-use project which included a parking garage, shops, drugstores, office space, and other related medical and dental services. When it was built, 450 Sutter was the second tallest building in San Francisco, and was said to be the largest medical office building in the world.

A

R252 MAP I
480 Sutter Street
NE corner Powell
Holiday Inn Union Square
originally Westbury Hotel
William Tabler
1972

NOT RATED

R251   450 Sutter. Perspective rendering, ca. 1929.

R253 MAP I
500-516 Sutter Street
NW corner Powell
Physician's Building
now Sutter-Powell Building
Frederick H. Meyer
1914

The last of the distinctive U-plan office buildings by Frederick Meyer (see also the Rialto Building at 116 New Montgomery, M160, and the Foxcroft Building at 68–82 Post, R148); this one is typically richly ornamented, and is located at an extremely important intersection. The building is in a three part vertical composition with a glass commercial base and a 2-story arcaded capital. The attic is a 1932 addition by Kent and Haas. The steel frame is clad in brick with terra cotta ornamentation concentrated in the bays and capital. Ornamentation is Renaissance/Baroque. The building is a major element in the cohesive group along Powell Street, and it has a strong visual and textural relation to the group diagonally across the intersection—the Sir Francis Drake (R201) and the two P. G. & E. buildings at 445 and 447 Sutter (R249 and R250).

A

177

R254 MAP I
524 Sutter Street
Cartwright Hotel
N. W. Sexton
1913

A reinforced concrete hotel building in a three part vertical composition. Ornamentation is 18th century English. The cornice has been removed.

C

R255 MAP I
532-536 Sutter Street
Seventh Church of Christ Scientist
architect unknown
1910

A handsome structure in a two part small commercial composition with formal treatment of the upper level. It was altered for use by the Christian Science Church by Henry Gutterson in 1950. Gutterson's plans for the exterior, which were not realized, brought the columns of the second story loggia down to the ground, with decorative wood or metal window framing between. The simplicity of the classically derived wooden ornamentation and the relationship of materials recalls the kind of work done by Gutterson, and other Arts and Crafts Bay Regionalists, at the time this was originally built.

B

R256 MAP I
535-545 Sutter Street
Westphal Building
architect unknown
1921

Designed as a pair with 547–555 Sutter (R258) for Proctor and Chamberlain. Both are two part vertical compositions, skeletal in articulation, with Chicago-type windows and restrained Renaissance/Baroque ornamentation. Reinforced concrete construction.

C

R257 MAP I
540 Sutter Street
John Simmons
originally The Print Rooms of Hill
  Tollerton
William C. Hays
1916

A very unusual 1-story commercial building, designed by an important figure in Bay Area architecture in the early part of this century. Hays' only other known downtown area design is the Old First Presbyterian Church on Van Ness. The facade consists of a recessed storefront plane behind a pair of plain piers. The storefront consists of a Greek Doric order with irregularly spaced pilasters, and a parapet wall which originally bore the name of the building between flanking bas relief panels. This parapet wall has been remodeled. Brick construction.

B

R258 MAP I
547-555 Sutter Street
Lowell Building
architect unknown
1922

Identical to 535–545 Sutter. See R256 above.

C

R259 MAP I
550-556 Sutter Street
architect unknown
1909

A unique downtown design, now remodeled, which is set back in part behind a landscaped courtyard with a Doric column at the entrance gate. The original Renaissance/Baroque ornamentation has been stripped and the walls stuccoed smooth. The decorative iron fence is intact but the column capital and sculptural figure are gone.

C

559–565 Sutter, ca. 1921.

R260 MAP I
559-565 Sutter Street
Willis Polk and Co.
1921

An example of a two part small commercial block with a high glass base and a particularly well designed formal top. The glass wall of the mezzanine is still largely intact, although partially obscured by signs. The upper level consists of a Tuscan order in-antis with a full entablature. This upper part can be read alternately as a decorative design with short columns, or as a side view of a Tuscan temple stacked on top of a 2-story commercial base. It is of reinforced concrete construction. It was built for Chamberlain and Procter.

B

R261 MAP I
562-570 Sutter Street
Hotel Regent
Hemenway and Miller
1907

A richly ornamented example of a residential hotel in a three part vertical composition with differentiated end bays. Renaissance/Baroque ornamentation includes an ornate ground level entrance arch, a rusticated mezzanine with pedimented windows, terra cotta window surrounds, a paneled capital, and a projecting cornice on massive brackets. Fire escapes are treated as balconies and as part of the design. This is one of three known downtown-area designs by the important architects of the Aronson Building (M150) and the old Bullock and Jones Building (now remodeled and known as the French Bank, R226).

B

R262 MAP I
575 Sutter
architect unknown
1919

A reinforced concrete structure in a two part vertical composition, skeletal in articulation with restrained Renaissance/Baroque ornamentation. When the building was remodeled about 1970, its fenestration was altered and its ground level storefronts were recessed behind the plane of the front facade, creating an open entrance area with stairways to basement shops.

C

R263 MAP I
578-580 Sutter Street
architect unknown
ca. 1960

A remodeling of a 1916 brick building which was identified as being of interest in *Buildings of the Bay Area* (1960).

NOT RATED

R264 MAP I
595 Sutter Street
SE corner Mason
Francisca Club
E. E. Young
1919

A private women's club, designed as a modified palazzo in composition, with 18th century English ornamentation. It is of brick construction with red brick walls and white trim.

B

R265 MAP I
600-608 Sutter Street
NW corner Mason
architect unknown
1916

A two part small commercial block with formal treatment of the upper level. Ornamentation is Renaissance/Baroque. Brick construction with wood posts. It was once occupied by the Munson School for Private Secretaries.

C

R266 MAP I
609 Sutter Street
SW corner Mason
Marine's Memorial Club
originally Women's Club of
 San Francisco
Bliss and Faville
1927

A large private club building, originally designed for the Women's Club of San Francisco which lost it in the depression. It has been known in recent years as the Marine's Memorial Club. The Women's Club returned as tenants in 1952, as the Western Women's Club, and only disbanded in 1978. Plans for the building were under discussion at least as early as 1922 for the San Francisco City and County Federation of Women's Clubs. In 1923, a "Competitive Design" by O. R. Thayer was published in the *Architect and Engineer*.

The existing building by Bliss and Faville is a three part vertical block with differentiated end bays and Renaissance/Baroque ornamentation. Its finest ornamental feature is the projecting domed bay window over the entrance. The barrel vaulted lobby has been partially remodeled. Differing internal functions are reflected by changes in fenestration. The top story is a later addition. Steel frame construction.

B

R267 MAP I
620 Sutter Street
Y.W.C.A.
Lewis Hobart
1918

A three part vertical composition with differentiated end bays, designed for the Y.W.C.A. with both athletic and residential facilities. Ornamentation is 18th century English. The steel frame is clad in terra cotta at the base and brick with terra cotta trim above. The building forms a fine pair with the Metropolitan Club next door (R270).

B

R268 MAP I
625-627 Sutter Street
Academy of Art College
architect unknown
1921

A unique downtown San Francisco design in a three part vertical composition with a single, strongly articulated end bay. Ornamentation is Renaissance/Baroque in derivation with Churrigueresque detail at the end bay. In style, the building belongs to the Spanish Colonial Revival. Reinforced concrete construction.

B

R269 MAP I
635 Sutter Street
Hotel Beresford
architect unknown
1911

A brick residential hotel in a three part vertical composition. Ornamentation is Renaissance/Baroque. Part of a wall of similarly massed structures in this block.

C

R270 MAP I
640 Sutter Street
Metropolitan Club
originally Women's Athletic Club
Bliss and Faville
1916, 1922

A very handsome brick building with typically fine detailing and use of materials by Bliss and Faville. Originally only the three easternmost bays were constructed. When the building was enlarged, the entrance was moved in order to remain centrally located. In composition, the building is a modified Renaissance Palazzo. Its reinforced concrete structural frame is clad in red brick with terra cotta ornamental detail. The balconied arches of the fourth level are outlined in decorative brick bands. The upper tier is defined by a shallow colonnaded loggia. The building has a gabled roof and overhanging eaves. It forms a fine pair with the Y.W.C.A. next door (R267). Interior spaces include a swimming pool, gymnasium, guest rooms, and club rooms. Originally built for the Women's Athletic Club, it was taken over by the Metropolitan Club about ten years ago.

A

R271 MAP I
655 Sutter Street
architect unknown
1912

An ordinary brick residential hotel in a three part vertical composition with richly sculptural decorative terra cotta spandrel panels. These panels with their high relief figures recall those on the old Fireman's Fund Building at 233–241 Sansome (F128) by Weeks and Day. This ornamentation is Renaissance/Baroque in derivation.

C

R272 MAP I
679-683 Sutter Street
architect unknown
1922

A reinforced concrete apartment building in a two part vertical composition with differentiated end bays. Renaissance/Baroque ornamentation includes twisted columns, a corbeled cornice, and a red tiled false roof. The remodeled "Colonial Room" storefront is a rare survivor of an aspect of the late 1930s Moderne.

C

R273 MAP I
680 Sutter Street
C. A. Meussdorffer
1918

An unusual apartment house design with a narrow recessed entrance court and an elaborately bracketed gable roof. It is representative of the diverse body of work designed by the architect of the Family Club and the little building at 1 United Nations Plaza. Reinforced concrete construction.

C

R274 MAP I
690 Sutter Street
architect unknown
1919

A small and individually undistinguished reinforced concrete "flat and store" which serves as a link in the continuous street wall on this block. In composition, a two part small commercial block with formal treatment of the upper level. Ornamentation is restrained Renaissance/Baroque.

C

R275 MAP I
693 Sutter Street
SE corner Taylor
architect unknown
ca. 1935

A Moderne remodel by an unknown architect, of a 1922 steel frame office building by Mathew Politeo. In composition, a two part vertical block. Its skeletal Moderne facade has recently been painted in earth colors.

C

R277 MAP I
700 Taylor Street
NE corner Sutter
Edward Foulkes
1922

A reinforced concrete apartment building in a narrow slab shape and in a variation of a two part vertical composition. Its softly angled bay windows create a waving facade that almost rolls around the corner. The lightly applied Renaissance/Baroque spandrel panels and cornice frieze and the small paned casement windows enhance the lightness and prettiness of the design.

C

R276 MAP I
625 Taylor Street
NE corner Post
Bohemian Club
Lewis Hobart
1934

One of the city's most colorful and influential private institutions and a handsome classical Moderne club house. The present building replaces a George Kelham design of 1912 which was more literally reliant on traditional historical ornamental motifs but which was quite similar in feeling. This building is in a three part vertical composition with a high exposed base at the downhill end of Post Street, but no base at all on the uphill end. Bays are enframed by recessing layers of brick. The upper level is treated with abstracted fluted pilasters. The facades are ornamented with bronze and terra cotta panels by Carlo Taliabue, Haig Patigian, and Jo Moro. Interior spaces include meeting, lounging, and dining rooms, and upper level residential quarters. The interior is handsomely finished in the best materials and is decorated with the prolific art work of the club's members. The Bohemian Club, established in 1872 as a private men's club, can count among its past members many of the most creative and influential of San Francisco's citizens, including artists, writers, and politicians.

A

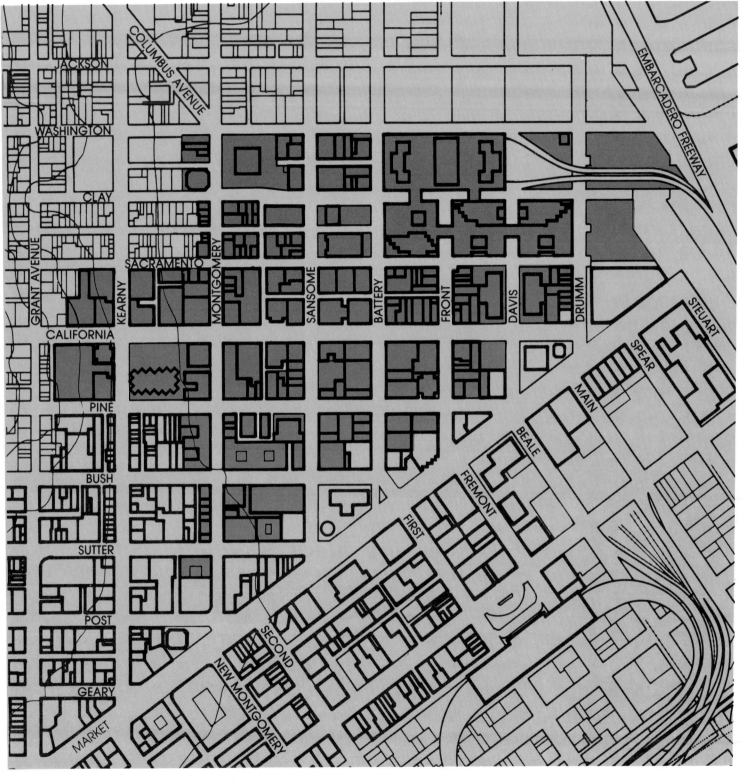

Financial District

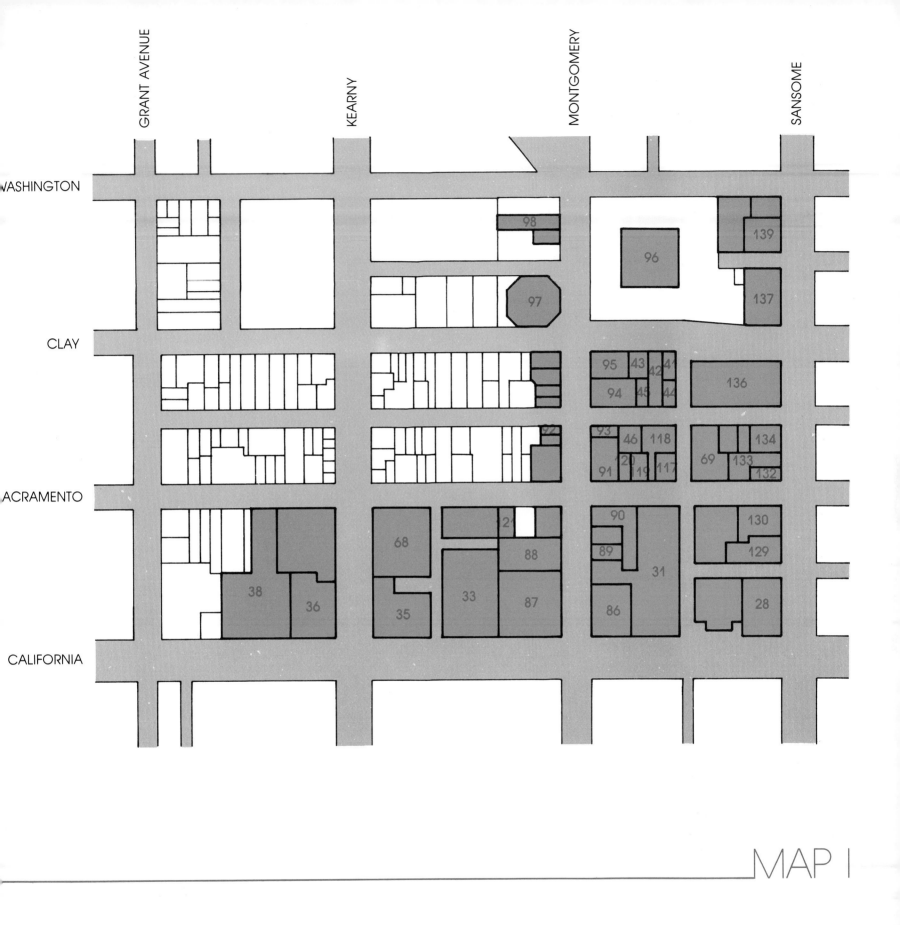

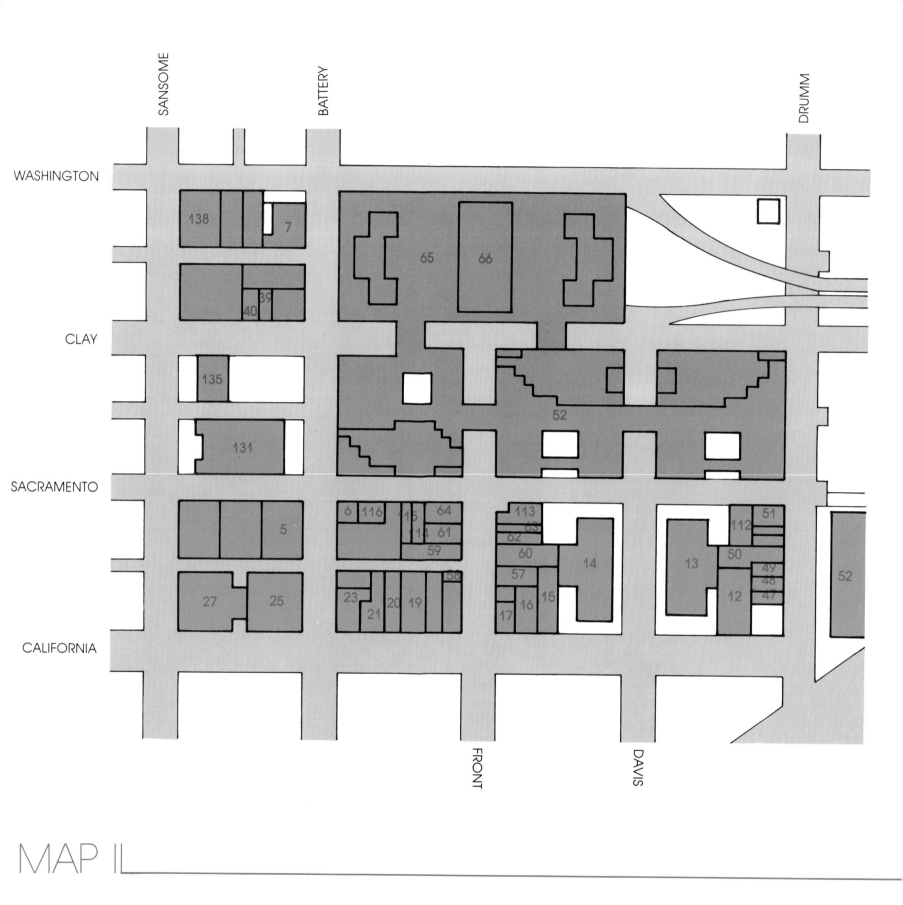

MAP IL

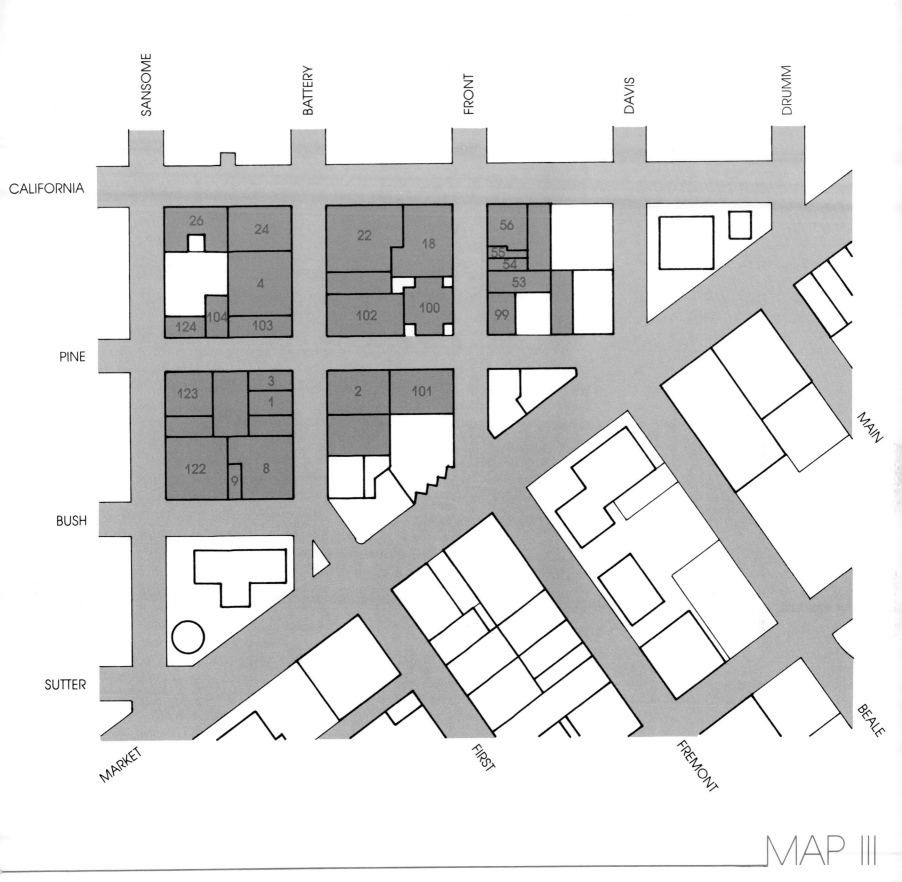

MAP III

187

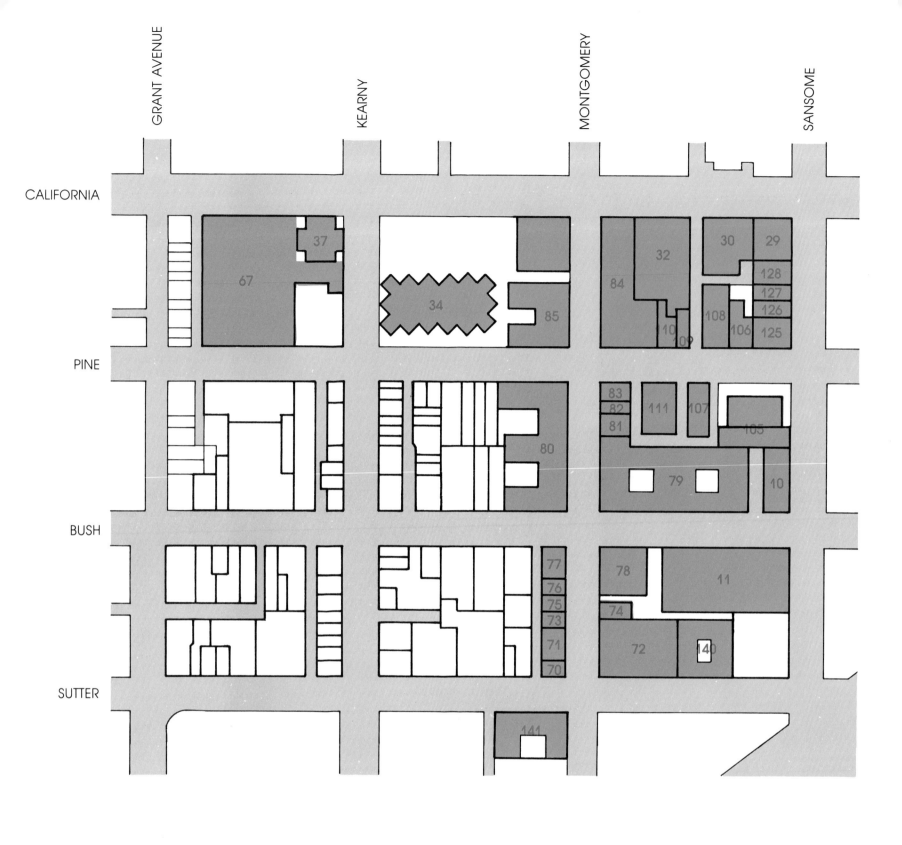

F1 MAP III
77 Battery Street
architect unknown
1907

Built as a reinforced concrete warehouse and now converted to office space. A two part vertical composition with modified Renaissance/Baroque ornamentation.

C

F2 MAP III
98 Battery Street
SE corner Pine
Levi Strauss Co. Building
Howard and Galloway
1907

A steel frame office building built for the Levi Strauss Co. by the important firm of Howard and Galloway. The building was originally constructed as two adjacent structures of identical design with a continuous facade along Battery Street. The three bays of the mid-block structure were demolished, except for the ground floor, in the 1930s and converted to a parking garage. The existing building is a three part vertical block in composition, with Renaissance/Baroque references in the ornamentation. This is another building which recalls McKim, Mead, and White's Phoenix Building in its facade treatment.

B

F3 MAP III
99 Battery Street
SW corner Pine
Donahoe Building
Ross and Burgren
1908

A 6-story steel frame office building with interior wood posts, built for the estate of Michael Donahoe. The original ground floor with its iron pilasters is, remarkably, intact, and it still houses a bank as originally intended. In composition, the building is a two part vertical block with Renaissance/Baroque ornamentation.

B

F4 MAP III
111-141 Battery Street
R. Stanley Dollar Building
MacDonald and MacDonald
1917

A reinforced concrete office building with a partial conversion to garage space in 1947. It is now tied into the Robert Dollar Building around the corner on California Street (F24) on several floors. Originally built for John A. Hooper but now known as the R. Stanley Dollar Building. In composition, a two part vertical block with restrained Renaissance/Baroque references.

C

F5 MAP II
241 Battery Street
SW corner Sacramento
Eastman Kodak Building
Bliss and Faville
1911, 1926

A distinctive design with modified Corinthian capitals banding faceted piers, built in two stages, and sadly altered with an insensitive third story. In composition, a loggia with modified Renaissance ornamentation.

B

F6 MAP II
280 Battery Street
SE corner Sacramento
White Investment Co. Building
Lewis Hobart
1908

A small but handsomely detailed brick and concrete building, originally designed for the White Investment Company. In composition, an enframed window wall with Renaissance/Baroque ornamentation. Details include an unusual fish and shell molding in the frieze and a large cartouche over the cornice.

B

F7 MAP II
447 Battery Street
NW corner Merchant
Jones Thierbach Coffee Co.
architect unknown
1907

A handsome post-fire brick warehouse building indistinguishable from much earlier buildings of the same type. Originally the Jones Thierbach Coffee Co. and recently refurbished as office space. In composition, a two part small commercial block with a strictly structural expression. A cornice has evidently been removed, and the walls may have been stuccoed originally.

B

F8 MAP III
100 Bush Street
NW corner Battery
Shell Building
George Kelham
1929

Described by the *Architect and Engineer* as having the Russ Building's central tower, the Telephone Building's penthouse, Gothic verticality, and its own distinctive treatment of the upper eight floors, the Shell Building also follows the model of Eliel Saarinen's Chicago Tribune Tower Competition entry. It is one of the city's best Moderne designs of the 1920s. The building is richly decorated in sepia glazed terra cotta with blue-green cast concrete spandrels. Ornament, described as "of Egyptian ancestry and with a modernistic flare," includes elaborately abstracted shell designs in reference to the building's owner. The upper part of the tower with its concentration of ornament was originally dramatically floodlit at night. Ornamental detail is carried inside to the building lobby, all elevator lobbies, and the executive offices. Office floors were designed with movable partitions. The building was built in "record breaking" time. Steel frame construction.

A

F9 MAP III
130 Bush Street
Heineman Building
now the Liberty Mutual Building
MacDonald and Applegarth
1910

Although not the only twenty-foot-wide tall building in downtown San Francisco (see the Chamberlain Building at 442–444 Post—R174, and the Roullier Building at 49 Kearny—R90), the Heineman Building is probably the most successful. Seen by itself it is a richly detailed hybrid composition with Gothic ornamentation executed in cream glazed terra cotta. The verticality of the tall narrow structure is ably expressed in the thin Gothic ribs of the shaft culminating in a heavy top story crowned by finials. A penthouse in the same style is set back behind the plane of the street. Seen in its context, as a narrow projecting bay between two much larger and flatter facades, it manages to more than hold its own without being disruptive to the texture and scale of the street. Steel frame construction. Now called the Liberty Mutual Building.

A

Left: Heineman Building. Perspective rendering, ca. 1909.

F10 MAP IV
200 Bush Street
NW corner Sansome
Standard Oil Building
Benjamin G. McDougall
1912, 1916

The oldest and best of four Standard Oil Company buildings now in downtown San Francisco, and one of the most sumptuous office buildings ever built in the area. Every detail of its construction and finishing is first rate. The building is as fireproof as it was possible to make it in 1912, with a steel frame, reinforced concrete floors, and metal window and door frames. The exterior is clad in a rich variety of materials, textures and colors—granite at the base, gray limestone for the first two floors, dark brown pressed brick in the shaft, cream terra cotta colonnades in the upper stories, and a green terra cotta cornice.

All corridors have ceramic tile floors and marble wainscoting, and all elevator fronts and the main stairway are of solid bronze. The ground floor entrance and elevator hallway, according to a 1916 article in the *Architect and Engineer*, "runs magnificently the whole length of the building. It expresses to a nicety the princely character of one of the world's wealthiest corporations and it impresses the visitor most profoundly with the importance, the perfection, and the power of this most efficient and most successful of all America's business organizations." This space was sensitively transformed for use by California Federal Savings in 1976 by Bull, Field, Volkmann, Stockwell.

In composition, the building is a three part vertical block with differentiated end bays and Renaissance/Baroque ornamentation. The upper two floors were added in 1916 and were successfully integrated into the original design. The building plays an important role as part of fine street groups on both Sansome and Bush.

A

F11 MAP IV
225 Bush Street
SW corner Sansome
Standard Oil Co. Building
George Kelham
1922

The second oldest Standard Oil Co. building in San Francisco, located across the street from the older building at 200 Bush. The front facade is modeled after York and Sawyer's widely publicized winning competition design for the Federal Reserve Bank of New York. The more interesting view of this building, however, is from the rear where the wings, stair tower, and corbeled cornice provide a picturesque view from Market Street. The originally L-shaped building was completed as a U in a 1948 addition by Harry Thomsen which exactly matches the original. In composition, a two part vertical block with an attic and Renaissance ornamentation derived from a Florentine palace. Steel frame construction.

B

F12 MAP II
24-26 California Street
Marvin Building
C. A. Meussdorffer
1908

A three part vertical office block, skeletal in articulation with Renaissance/Baroque ornamentation. Its steel frame is clad in glazed terra cotta, recently cleaned and painted. Ornamental detail chiefly consists of oversized brackets beneath undersized cornices. An important supportive structure to the corner building and a rare element of textural and decorative interest in a largely new area. It is visible from Market Street.

B

F13 MAP II
50 California Street
NE corner Davis
Union Bank Building
Welton Becket and Associates
1972

NOT RATED

F14 MAP II
100 California Street
NW corner Davis
old Bethlehem Steel Building
Welton Becket and Associates
1959

Follows the example of Skidmore, Owings, and Merrill's Inland Steel Building, in Chicago (1957), with exterior framing.

NOT RATED

F15 MAP II
130-138 California Street
architect unknown
1907

An insensitive remodeling of the ground floor detracts from an otherwise nicely detailed two part small commercial block with formal treatment of the upper story in Renaissance/Baroque details. Brick construction with wood posts.

C

F16 MAP II
150 California Street
Walter H. Ratcliff
1919

The only downtown San Francisco building by the important Berkeley architect, Walter H. Ratcliff. Compositionally unique in the downtown area, and one of only a few in the Mission Revival idiom. Brick construction with handsome iron columns in the ground floor retail space.

C

F17 MAP II
158 California Street
NE corner Front
Marine Building
architect unknown
1908

A three part vertical composition with Renaissance/Baroque ornamentation. Distinguished by its high rusticated base, handsome window frames, and projecting cornice. An important corner structure at the end of blocks of small scaled, generally less imposing buildings on both California and Front streets. Brick construction.

B

F18 MAP III
201 California Street
SW corner Front
Hibernia Bank Building
Arthur Gensler and Associates
under construction 1978

In composition, a three part vertical block with differentiated end bays. The first brick walled structure built downtown in many years.

NOT RATED

F19 MAP II
230 California Street
Hind Building
John Reid, Jr.
1913

The only known downtown building by John Reid, Jr., one of the designers of the Civic Center, and, as the long-time City Architect, designer of many public schools. A three part vertical composition with Renaissance/Baroque details, distinguished by an unusually large amount of glass for a financial district office building. The lower floor of the otherwise simply treated glass shaft is crowned by pedimented spandrels. Steel frame construction clad in brick and terra cotta.

B

F20 MAP II
240-242 California Street
Tadich Grill
Crim and Scott
1909

Previously Chris's Cafeteria and now the Tadich Grill, this building has long been a landmark restaurant and retains an interior that dates at least as far back as the 1920s. Tadich's has been in existence in San Francisco since 1865 at two previous locations. One of the finest buildings of its type in the city; in composition, it is an enframed window wall with Renaissance/Baroque ornamentation. The handling of materials and colors is superb. Although easily mistaken for copper and bronze, all but the bronze window frames is actually terra cotta. Although the architect is unconfirmed, the design has been attributed to the firm of Crim and Scott. This firm designed a strikingly similar building for the Landry C. Babin Co. at 423 Kearny Street, also built in 1909, now demolished. Reinforced concrete construction.

A

F21 MAP II
244-256 California Street
Welch Building
architect unknown
1908

A richly detailed variation of the standard three part vertical composition. In an unusual re-arrangement of the typical relationship between shaft and capital, the capital is almost as tall as the shaft. The facade forms a handsome element in the fabric of the street, supportive of the Newhall Building and relating to the Hind Building down the street. The distinctive composition recalls that of the Orient Building at 332 Pine (F106) by Charles Paff. Steel frame construction.

B

F22 MAP III also Market MAP I
255 California Street
SE corner Battery
John Hancock Building
now Industrial Indemnity
Skidmore, Owings, and Merrill
1959

A building which was given a great deal of publicity when it was completed for its success as a Modern design that took special care to respect its environment. Its ground floor shops are overhung by the warm wooden undersides of the second story balcony, the windows and solid wall areas of the shaft are articulated at a human scale, and its second level employee cafeteria and conference rooms open out on a garden.

NOT RATED

F23 MAP II
260 California Street
NE corner Battery
Newhall Building
Lewis Hobart
1910, 1917

One of Lewis Hobart's best designs, displaying a rich sense of color and detail in the ornate cream terra cotta decoration and red brick piers. The ornamentation is highlighted by terra cotta eagles in the spandrels of the top floor. Enlarged by two bays to the north by Hobart in 1917. In composition, a three part vertical block with Renaissance/Baroque detail. Steel frame construction. In its color, scale, and articulation, the building is an extremely important element on California Street.

A

F24 MAP III
301-333 California Street
SW corner Battery
Robert Dollar Building
Charles McCall
1919

Originally designed in 1910 by W. S. Schmolle as a 5-story reinforced concrete structure, this building was greatly enlarged and entirely remodeled by Charles McCall in 1919 as the headquarters building of the Robert Dollar Steamship Lines. It was one of the first big buildings in the city to be constructed after World War I and was identified by the *Architect and Engineer* as inaugurating the boom that carried into the early 1920s. The building is a three part vertical block with Gothic references in its ornamentation. The terra cotta cladding of its predominantly steel frame includes representations of the company flag, marine life, and ship details. Despite the removal of its cornice, the building is an important element in a nearly continuous wall of older structures on California Street. The ground floor banking rooms of the Bank of Nova Scotia (Parkin Architects) and the Bank of Montreal (Hugh Stubbins and Rex Allen) were stylishly remodeled in the early 1970s.

B

Robert Dollar Building, 1921.

320 California Street
NW corner Battery
Cahill Building
Meyer and Evers
1946

NOT RATED

Balfour Building, ca. 1942.

F26 MAP III
341 California Street
SE corner Sansome
J. Harold Dollar Building
originally Balfour Building
George Kelham
1920

Built as the Balfour Building and now known as the J. Harold Dollar Building as part of the fine group of Dollar Lines buildings on this block. Designed by George Kelham with a handsome brick facade over a carved limestone base in a two part vertical composition. Ornamentation is restrained Renaissance/Baroque outside and in the vaulted ground floor elevator lobby. The dark textured brick wall makes a superb material for street facades on both California and Sansome streets. Steel frame construction.

B

370 California Street
NE corner Sansome
California First Bank Building
Skidmore, Owings, and Merrill
1977

Except for the regrettable circumstance of its having replaced the Alaska Commercial Building on this site, this is one of the most successful of the recent downtown buildings, both in the quality of its design and in its relationship to the older buildings of the area, particularly the Bank of California. The sensitivity of the new design is ironic in view of its having replaced one of downtown San Francisco's most important and historic architectural landmarks. One may ask why that design sensitivity couldn't have gone into preservation of the old building together with a new tower, following the example of the Bank of California or Citizens Savings. The Alaska Commercial Building was an extremely handsome skeletal tower with some of the city's best and most distinctive ornamentation. The Alaska Commercial Company played a major role in the early history of Alaska. All that is left of the building today is a frieze of granite walruses near the entrance of the new Bank and at the rear. When the Bank opened, one of its giveaways to new customers was a plastic walrus head bank, perhaps an admission of some sort that their previously stated desire for a modern building with a modern image was not the best strategy after all.

NOT RATED

400 California Street
NW corner Sansome
Bank of California
Bliss and Faville
1907

The finest banking temple in a city of banking temples. Modeled after McKim, Mead, and White's Knickerbocker Trust Building in New York (now demolished). The *Architectural Record* wrote of the design in 1906 that it "promises to be one of the most imposing edifices in the United States devoted to banking purposes." The building is of steel frame construction with a carved granite exterior. In composition, it is a modified temple without a pediment, and its ornamentation is derived from classical antiquity. The building is treated on three sides with a giant Corinthian order highlighted with exquisitely carved capitals. The interior is a single great space with columns around the perimeter, a coffered ceiling, and a marble sculptural group by Arthur Putnam. In 1967 a sensitive modern tower by Anshen and Allen was joined to the Bank's west side, opening onto the roof of the old Bank building.

A   CL

425 California Street
SW corner Sansome
Great Western Savings Building
John Carl Warnecke
1968

NOT RATED

F30 MAP IV
433 California Street
SE corner Leidesdorff
Insurance Exchange Building
Willis Polk
1913

A very fine street building with a facade designed to relate to the Merchant's Exchange Building (F32) across Leidesdorff, also by Polk. A two part vertical composition with a giant order over a remodeled base, and a shaft consisting of courses of variously detailed terra cotta panels. Ornamentation is derived from Renaissance/Baroque sources. The giant order picks up the rhythm of the columns on the Merchant's Exchange and the Bank of California (F28), and the shaft improves on the textured wall of the Merchant's Exchange. The building exemplifies the aims of the City Beautiful Movement in its simultaneous success as urban architecture, achieved through form and composition, and as an individual building, achieved in the quality of its details. The handsome 2-story interior exchange space has been subdivided and remodeled. Steel frame construction.

A

Insurance Exchange, ca. 1920.

F31 MAP I
464 California Street
NW corner Leidesdorff
Wells Fargo Bank
originally American Trust Co.
Ashley, Keyser, and Runge
1959

NOT RATED

F32 MAP IV
465 California Street
SW corner Leidesdorff
Merchant's Exchange Building
D. H. Burnham and Co.
1903

Architecturally and historically one of the major landmarks of the city. Designed in 1903 by D. H. Burnham and Co.'s representative in San Francisco, Willis Polk, and rebuilt by Polk after the fire. One of the earliest big buildings of the great downtown building boom that began before the earthquake, and an extremely prominent building on the skyline for its first few years, until the city grew up around it. This is the third Merchant's Exchange Building in San Francisco's history and it has long played a central role in the commerce of the city. Messages of incoming ships were originally sent to the belvedere on the roof and relayed to the merchants in the great hall below who could then rush to the docks to meet them.

Architecturally the building represented the most up-to-date stylistic treatment from one of Chicago's most important architectural firms. Its design has served as one of the major prototypes for later downtown office buildings from the immediate post-fire period up to the mid-1920s. The Matson (M30), California Commercial Union (F85), Financial Center (F87), J. Harold Dollar (F26), Hobart (M45), and P. G. & E. (M2) buildings are among the most prominent whose designs follow the Merchant's Exchange in one or more major ways. It was the first San Francisco building to use a large textured curtain wall treated as rusticated masonry with single or paired windows. This distinctive wall treatment which was used over and over again downtown has been extremely successful as a consistent but variable element in downtown street facades. The ornamental belvederes on many later downtown buildings recall the original one on the Merchant's Exchange. The three part composition, with columns defining the base and capital, was followed with greater and lesser degrees of elaboration. The building provided a basic vocabulary for designing buildings which were simultaneously great urban designs and individually interesting.

The interior was just as fine as the exterior but unfortunately not as successful as a prototype. The building is entered through a marble lobby with exquisite bronze elevator doors. The lobby passes under a skylight open to a large central light court to the old Merchant's Exchange space. The great marble columns and superb murals by William Coulter have recently been restored for the Chartered Bank of London. Evidence that would confirm the widely held belief that Julia Morgan was the designer of the Exchange has been inaccessible to historians. Upstairs, the Commercial Club of 1916 was designed by Walter Ratcliff, and the Club Bar was designed by William P. Day in 1935. In construction, the building was an early San Francisco example of modern "fireproof" steel frame construction with Roebling system cinder concrete slab floors.

A

F33 MAP I
550 California Street
NE corner Spring
Occidental Life Building
Meyer and Evers; Ashley, Keyser,
and Runge
1960

Originally the Cahill Building, now with two stylish banking rooms on the ground floor: The Banco do Brasil (ca. 1970) by Tallie B. Maule and the Royal Bank of Canada (ca. 1973) by Environmental Planning and Research, Inc.

NOT RATED

F34 MAP IV
555 California Street
SW corner Montgomery
Bank of America World Headquarters
Wurster, Bernardi, and Emmons;
Skidmore, Owings, and Merrill;
Pietro Belluschi, design consultant
1968

In the separation of the tower and the banking hall, the Bank of America follows an early 20th century practice, popular among San Francisco bankers. It was considered more prestigious to build a separate banking hall, because to do otherwise was to admit that the bank needed the extra income from the rental of offices. Although out of scale with the city when it was built, and somewhat out of place in its dark color, this is certainly one of the most beautiful post-war buildings in San Francisco. The quality and richness of the materials and finishing is unsurpassed. The best view of this building is up the walkway between the 1921 California Commercial Union Building and the new banking hall to the tower. This building replaced the Clunie Building of about 1912, by Ross and Burgren and the very fine Pacific National Bank Building of 1930, by the O'Brien Brothers and Wilbur Peugh.

NOT RATED

F32   Merchants Exchange, ca. 1905.

F35 MAP I
580 California Street
NE corner Kearny
Fireman's Fund Insurance Co. Building
originally Home Insurance Co. Building
T. H. Englehardt; Meyer and Evers
1950

Originally built for the Home Insurance Co., the tower is reputed to be an exact replica of Independence Hall in Philadelphia. The building itself is of reinforced concrete.

NOT RATED

F36 MAP I
600 California Street
NW corner Kearny
Pacific Mutual Life Building
Wilbur D. Peugh
1954

One of the better 1950s International Style office buildings in the city.

NOT RATED

F37 MAP IV
601 California Street
SW corner Kearny
International Building
Anshen and Allen
1960

Built for American President Lines. A carefully scaled modern building which exhibits a welcome use of color.

NOT RATED

F38 MAP I
636-650 California Street
Hartford Insurance Building
Skidmore, Owings, and Merrill
1965

For a few years this was the tallest building in San Francisco.

NOT RATED

F39 MAP II
418 Clay Street
architect unknown
1911

A two part small commercial block with formal treatment of the upper story and Renaissance ornamental references. Brick construction.

C

F40 MAP II
432 Clay Street
architect unknown
1912

A two part small commercial block with skeletal articulation of the facade and Renaissance/Baroque ornamentation. Reinforced concrete construction.

C

F41 MAP I
553-557 Clay Street
SW corner Leidesdorff
architect unknown
1907

A two part small commercial block with formal treatment of the upper story and Renaissance/Baroque ornamental references. Brick construction.

C

F42 MAP I
559-561 Clay Street
architect unknown
1906

A two part vertical block with skeletal articulation and Renaissance/Baroque ornamentation. Brick construction.

C

F43 MAP I
565 Clay street
architect unknown
1907, remodeled ca. 1950 and 1977

Remodeled entirely in the 1950s, and again in 1977 at the ground floor level by Lambert Woods as Don Nunzio's restaurant.

NOT RATED

F44 MAP I
554 Commercial Street
NW corner Leidesdorff
architect unknown
1908

A superb example of an ordinary compositional type with polychrome brick walls. A two part small commercial block with a structural expression of the brick facade that has survived from the mid-19th century. It has Renaissance/Baroque ornamentation. Walls are laid in Flemish bond with dark red headers and light stretchers. The walls are set off by horizontal courses of red brick and by light quoins. This treatment has the visual effect of denying the structural importance of brick bearing walls, a particularly delightful fantasy in the interior of a block of predominantly dark brick structures.

A

F45 MAP I
564-566 Commercial Street
architect unknown
1907

A unique example of an enframed window wall treated as a single immense Gothic window. Currently occupied by Andrew Hoyem, Printer, one of the many widely recognized fine arts printers in the Bay Area.

B

F46 MAP I
569 Commercial Street
Pacific Gas & Electric Co., Station J
Frederick H. Meyer
1914

One of the best of many P. G. & E. substations in San Francisco and northern California which follow a prototype by Willis Polk. As part of the City Beautiful Movement these designs sought to beautify and pay respect to building types which had previously been considered beneath the concern of an architect. The task of the architect was to make an essentially blank wall interesting in a building which had no need for windows (skylights providing more useful lighting). Typically, ornament was concentrated at the entrance, as in this case with a giant linteled doorway and large ornate cartouche. In composition, a vault with Renaissance/Baroque ornamentation. Related in past use and design to 568 Sacramento (F119) located directly behind on the same lot.

A

F47 MAP II
17 Drumm Street
architect unknown
1912

F48 MAP II
25-29 Drumm Street
architect unknown
1912

A pair of two part small commercial blocks, each skeletal in articulation with restrained Renaissance/Baroque ornamental references. They differ only in color. Brick construction.

C

F49 MAP II
33 Drumm Street
architect unknown
1912

A two part small commercial block with formal treatment of the upper section and a ground floor which has been remodeled as one with 37 Drumm (F50) next door. Ornamentation is vaguely Secessionist. The upper facade is an unusually rich example of decorative brick work with an encircling zipper-like band that recesses in layers to the plane of the windows. Wall surfaces are treated in different brick patterns. Brick construction.

B

F50 MAP II
37 Drumm Street
architect unknown
1912

A two part vertical block with a giant order and Renaissance/Baroque ornamentation. Handsome brick and terra cotta details. Brick construction with wood posts.

C

F51 MAP II
91 Drumm Street
SW corner Sacramento
National Maritime Union
Albert C. Ledner
1966

A reinforced concrete union hall which shows the influence of Frank Lloyd Wright. Attributed to Albert C. Ledner on the basis of its strong stylistic resemblance to the National Maritime Union Building in New York.

NOT RATED

F52 MAP II
Embarcadero Center
John Portman & Associates
Built in phases since 1970

A rare example of a recent highrise group which is both built to the lot lines, maintaining the continuous fabric of the city's traditional street facades, and also is providing pedestrian interest and activity with shops along the streets. The design of this project was, in part, a response to the less successful first phase of the Golden Gateway Center which was built over two levels of parking.

NOT RATED

F53 MAP III
124 Front Street
architect unknown
1907

A two part vertical block with Renaissance/Baroque ornamentation. The cornice has been removed. Brick construction with iron posts on the ground floor and wood posts above.

C

F54 MAP III
136 Front Street
architect unknown
1907

A two part small commercial block with skeletal articulation and Renaissance/Baroque ornamental references. Brick construction.

C

F55 MAP III
140 Front Street
Isuan Building
architect unknown
1907

A two part small commercial block with formal treatment of the second story. Renaissance/Baroque ornamentation with a loggia on twisted colonettes between fluted Corinthian pilasters.

C

F56 MAP III
146-150 Front Street
SE corner California
Commercial Block
architect unknown
1908

A three part vertical composition in a U-plan. Modified Renaissance/Baroque ornamentation. Brick construction.

C

F57 MAP II
222 Front Street
Smith O'Brien
1918

A two part vertical block with skeletal articulation and vague Renaissance/Baroque ornamental references. The building is distinguished by its fine brick work. An article in the *Architect and Engineer* in 1919 stated that the building "shows what can be done with simple materials, intelligently handled." Originally built as a coffee and spice company warehouse, in 1967 the building was converted to office use by Whistler Patri. The original windows were removed and mirror glass recessed behind the plane of the building, creating open walkways. Brick construction with wood posts.

B

F58 MAP II
225-227 Front Street
SW corner Halleck
Fox Building
architect unknown
1907

A two part small commercial block with skeletal articulation and Gothic ornamentation. Reinforced concrete construction.

C

F59 MAP II
235-237 Front Street
NW corner Halleck
architect unknown
1909

A terra cotta clad brick building in a two part vertical composition with Renaissance/Baroque ornamental references. Now occupied by the Western Women's Bank.

C

F60 MAP II
236 Front Street
Schroeder's
architect unknown
1927

A reinforced concrete loft structure with a long-time San Francisco restaurant at the ground floor. The building is in a stacked composition of skeletal elements with modified Renaissance/Baroque ornamentation. The ground floor has been remodeled and the cornice removed.

C

F61 MAP II
239-249 Front Street
architect unknown
1907

A two part small commercial block with skeletal articulation and Renaissance references. Brick construction.

C

F62 MAP II
246 Front Street
architect unknown
1913

F63 MAP II
250-254 Front Street
architect unknown
1909

A pair of two part small commercial blocks, each with a formal second story and restrained Renaissance/Baroque references. They differ only in brick color. Brick construction.

C

F64 MAP II
251 Front Street
SW corner Sacramento
D. DeBernardi and Co. Warehouse
Righetti and Headman
1911

Built as a warehouse for D. DeBernardi and Co. and converted to office use with a ground floor restaurant and bar in 1972 by Ron Kaufman. A two part vertical composition with skeletal articulation and Renaissance derived ornamentation. Originally brick construction with wood posts, now reinforced with exposed interior steel bracing. The original cast iron ground floor storefront is intact.

B

F65 MAP II
Golden Gateway Center
Plan/Design and Development
Skidmore, Owings, and Merrill/Wurster,
Bernardi, and Emmons; DeMars and
Reay
1957/1959

F66 MAP II
1 Maritime Plaza
Alcoa Building
Skidmore, Owings, and Merrill
1964

A well-intentioned design, and sometimes attractive, but ultimately unsuccessful; typical of post-war planning. The project began with the premise that a new city could be created in the midst of the old by starting all over again, in effect, creating a little bit of country in the middle of the city. The key ingredients in the plan and the reasons for its failure were the alteration of the grid through the creation of "superblocks," and the manner of the separation of pedestrian from vehicular traffic. Rather than a design which enhances its urban site, this anti-urban scheme, with its raised pedestrian park, denies the character of its location at the edge of a major business district. Moreover, its two-level parking garage base, which cuts across the old city grid, is a blank wall which functions visually as a barrier. The plan is a descendant of LeCorbusier's city planning schemes of the 1920s. It is altogether a victory of style over rational planning based on an accurate understanding of the way American cities have developed. Fortunately, its overall scheme was amended and greatly improved in its extension as Embarcadero Center.

NOT RATED

F67 MAP IV
433 Kearny Street
St. Mary's Square Garage
John Jay Gould
1955

Following the example of the Union Square Parking Garage, but not following it well enough, this garage replaced St. Mary's Square without being sufficiently disguised and integrated into the landscape. The landscaped roof by Eckbo, Royston, and Williams is discussed in the Urban Design section of this volume.

NOT RATED

F68 MAP I
530-550 Kearny Street
SE corner Sacramento
Meyer and Evers
1957

NOT RATED

F69 MAP I
222 Leidesdorff Street
NE corner Sacramento
Pacific Gas & Electric Co., Station J
Ivan C. Frickstad
1923

The second Station J in this area (the first is now Paoli's), designed by a P.G.&E. company architect who did a number of substations following prototypes by Willis Polk. The entrance with its ornate cartouche is the principal decorative feature of the building. In composition, a modified vault with Renaissance/Baroque ornamentation. A steel frame and reinforced concrete structure.

B

F70 MAP IV
105 Montgomery Street
NW corner Sutter
California Pacific Building
Reid Brothers
1910

A fine example of the Reid Brothers' San Francisco skyscrapers, a building type for which they were nationally recognized. With the demolition of the Fitzhugh Building, the last such example in the city. More importantly, the building is a solid anchor of one of the architecturally finest and historically most important groups of buildings in the downtown area—the 100 block of Sutter Street. This group, the Hallidie Building block, functions as a kind of capsule history of downtown types and styles of the 20th century, with this building representing the implied solid masonry walled buildings characteristic of the Financial District, and following the model of New York (as opposed to Chicago) skyscrapers. Moreover, the group functions extremely well aesthetically, stepping up gradually from 200 Kearny (R97) to this building, with a different colored cornice on each building, employing a variety of rich facade materials, textures, and colors, spaced at pleasing intervals, and relating to the Hallidie Building (R228) by virtue of the latter's intelligent and complex references to its neighbors.

In composition, this structure is a variation of a three part vertical block with transitional zones at the base and capital. Ornamentation is derived from Renaissance/Baroque sources. The building is of steel frame construction with red pressed brick curtain walls, cream colored terra cotta ornamental detail, and a green copper cornice.

B

F71 MAP IV
109-123 Montgomery Street
architect unknown
1907

A two part small commercial block with formal treatment of the upper zone. Renaissance/Baroque ornamentation. Brick construction. The low horizontal mass of the building permits a view from Montgomery of the French Bank's fine side facade.

C

F72 MAP IV
120 Montgomery Street
NE corner Sutter
Equitable Life Building
Wilbur D. Peugh
1955

The stepping up of the Montgomery Street facade, the geometric increase in bays, and the "zigzag" pattern of the pressed metal spandrels constitute an attempt to relate this design to the same architect's much better building next door, the French Bank (F74) of 25 years earlier. The building is in a traditional two part composition with an articulated base and windows. The building is distinguished by expensive marble cladding and a time and temperature sign at the top.

NOT RATED

F73 MAP IV
125-129 Montgomery Street
Wilson Building
architect unknown
1907

A simple two part vertical composition with handsome Renaissance/Baroque details. Brick construction. This tallest mid-block building punctuates a varied and lively group of small commercial structures. One arch of its ground floor arcade is insensitively obscured by a sign.

C

F74 MAP IV
130 Montgomery Street
French Bank of California
originally Title Insurance Co. Building
O'Brien Brothers; Wilbur D. Peugh
1930

A fine example of a small Moderne office building, and one of the few in downtown San Francisco. In composition, a vertical sign with three
narrow dark bays over an abstracted classical
base whose treatment recalls an Egyptian
tomb. Bays are darkened with decorative copper spandrel panels and dark metal window
frames. The flat arched entrance consists of immense voussoirs and a giant keystone over
fluted columns, flanked by fine bas reliefs of
figures whose designs comment on the implied
structure of the building and on the modern
city. The best of the panels, of a man seeming
to hold the stones of the facade in place, recalling the 1915 P-P.I.E. poster, has been crudely
obscured with a sign and alarm box. The interior was stylishly remodeled in 1972 for the
French Bank of California by Michel Marx. Reinforced concrete construction with cast concrete "artificial stone" cladding. The French
bank is presently planning to leave this building
for the new one next door, now under construction.

B

F75 MAP IV
133-137 Montgomery Street
architect unknown
1919

A two part small commercial block with formal
treatment of the upper floor and an arcaded
base. Ornamentation is lightly Renais-
sance/Baroque. Part of a rare group of small
commercial buildings in the financial district
which adds needed variety and vitality to a
sometimes overly serious area.

C

F76 MAP IV
141-145 Montgomery Street
Steil Building
Weeks and Day
1921

An excellent facade design on a modest commercial building by an important local firm. The
two part vertical composition has been
respected in ground level remodelings which
have remained not only below the shaft, but
within the enframed storefront. Gothic ornamentation is executed in glazed terra cotta on
a reinforced concrete frame.

B

F77 MAP IV
149-157 Montgomery Street
SW corner Bush
Alexander Building
Lewis Hobart
1921

A steel frame tower in a three part vertical composition with Gothic ornamentation. The mass of
the building anchors an important corner, relating up and down both Montgomery and
Bush streets. Its warm brown brick curtain walls
reinforce the prevailing colors and textures of
the district.

B

F78 MAP IV
180 Montgomery Street
SE corner Bush
Corwin Booth
under construction 1978

Built on the site of G. Albert Lansburgh's E. F.
Hutton Building.

NOT RATED

F79 MAP IV
220 Montgomery Street
NE corner Bush
Mills Building and Tower
Burnham and Root/D. H. Burnham and
Co./Willis Polk/Lewis Hobart
1891/1908/1914, 1918/1931

An excellent example of Chicago School design by one of Chicago's most important firms during the heyday of the early skyscraper. Also, the earliest entirely steel frame building in San Francisco. The Mills Building was one of the tallest in the city at the time it was built and for many years afterwards. Seriously burned in the fire, it was rebuilt and enlarged in 1908 by D. H. Burnham and Co., with Willis Polk in charge. The building was extended again by Polk in 1914 and 1918. In 1931, the 22-story Mills Tower by Lewis Hobart was erected at the rear of the building in an excellent adaptation of the original design. In composition, the building is a three part vertical block with differentiated end bays. Ornamentation is Romanesque, including the very fine massive round entrance arch. Brick walls are ornamented in terra cotta, some of which has been replaced in recent years with stucco in a mutilation of the original. The base, including the arch, is clad in Inyo County white marble. Built around a large central light court, and with continuous corridors on each floor, the building represented the latest in efficient office building planning and was a model for later downtown construction. The building was built by Darius Ogden Mills, founder of the first bank in the West and later of the Bank of California. This is one of the major architectural landmarks of the city.

A NR; CL

F80 MAP IV
235 Montgomery Street
Russ Building
George Kelham
1927

Along with the Telephone Building (M161) by Miller and Pfleuger and A. A. Cantin, this is the only San Francisco building in Francisco Mujica's 1929 *History of the Skyscraper*. Although somewhat backward-looking for its day in its Gothic ornamentation, in its massing and use of ornament to express soaring verticality, it reflected the latest thinking about skyscraper design and was tremendously successful on its own terms. In 1927, the *Architect and Engineer* wrote, "In nearly every large city there is one building that because of its size, beauty of architectural design and character of its use and occupancy, has come to typify the city itself . . . Today the Russ Building takes this place in San Francisco. By its size and location and by the character of its tenants the building becomes indeed—'The Center of Western Progress.' "

Like the Telephone Building, the Russ Building follows the model of Eliel Saarinen's Tribune Tower competition design in the setting back of its tower. The tower rests on a massive base which entirely defines the street facade at the general height of existing buildings in the area. The glazed terra cotta ornament, the relation of piers and spandrels, and the central projection of the facade constitute a richly textured street wall. The ground level with its arched storefronts and entrances is superbly handled and has been unusually well maintained in its integrity. In plan, the building is a giant E with perpendicular wings from the base that create great numbers of well-lit offices. At the same time this presents a richer silhouette to the city which looks at its western side, while the sheer Montgomery Street facade maintains the street wall. Other important features of the plan were the 11th story "service floor" and the early incorporation of a parking garage in the building itself. The "matt" foundation and steel frame were designed by the important structural engineer, H. J. Brunnier.

The building is the latest in a series of Russ Buildings on the site, the first constructed in 1847. The present building was, according to the *Architect and Engineer*, the "first to apply the principal of public ownership in office building financing. The bonds and the entire equity in this outstanding real estate holding were offered without reservation to the investing public."

A

F81 MAP IV
240 Montgomery Street
Inecon Building
architect unknown
1914

A two part vertical block with 18th century English ornamental references. In texture and articulation part of the Montgomery Street wall. Brick construction.

C

F82 MAP IV
248-250 Montgomery Street
architect unknown
1907

A two part vertical block, skeletal in articulation with Renaissance/Baroque ornamental references. Part of the Montgomery Street wall. Brick construction.

C

F83 MAP IV
256 Montgomery Street
SE corner Pine
Barneson Building
architect unknown
1907

A three part vertical block with vaguely Renaissance/Baroque ornamentation that verges on Gothic in the thin clustered colonettes of the piers. Part of the Montgomery Street wall and the fine Pine Street group. Brick construction.

C

American National Bank Building, ca. 1940. Before remodeling and additions.

F84 MAP IV
300 Montgomery Street
old Bank of America Building
originally American National Bank
George Kelham/The Capitol Co.
1922/1941

An important building with monumental frontages on three streets in the form of Ionic colonnades at the ground level. The present appearance of the building is the result of a major addition and remodeling in 1941 by the Capitol Co. (L. J. Hendy, architect and L. H. Nishkian, structural engineer) for the new head offices of the Bank of America. The California Street and most of the Montgomery Street facade, the mezzanine levels and fenestration above them, all remain from the original George Kelham design. The rusticated shaft of the original two part composition had a very literal relationship to the Merchant's Exchange (F32) next door. This was replaced by a less literal but equally successful shaft with modernistic suggestions of vertical piers that culminate in a restrained cornice surmounted by an attic story.

The remodeling left the superb original banking hall largely intact at the north end of the building, and inserted a Moderne elevator lobby and bank at the south end. The original bank has recently been refurbished, including the re-marbelizing of its columns. The 1941 bank has been remodeled. Other interior features include art work by Maynard Dixon and Haig Patigian, some of it in upper level executive offices.

In 1942 in an article on the structural design of the addition, the *Architect and Engineer* wrote that ten years had passed "since the construction of tall steel frame buildings occurred with some frequency in San Francisco," and that the design of this building reflected structural engineering advances of the previous decade. These advances were not dramatic but indicated "psychological" changes: "the engineer now approaches his problems in a more realistic manner than in the 1920s." Certain "taboos" which had resulted from a more rudimentary understanding of developing structural techniques were discarded, resulting in more sophisticated designs that, for example, shifted some of the burden of the load, and of resistance to lateral forces, to concrete curtain walls. This building was among both the first and the last to reflect the particular structural changes of the period, as it was followed by another long period of building inactivity.

B

F85 MAP IV
315 Montgomery Street
NW corner Pine
**California Commerical Union Building
George Kelham and Kenneth
  MacDonald
1923**

A fine example of the generation of San Francisco office blocks of the early 1920s that, to a
greater or lesser degree, followed the type
established here by the Merchant's Exchange
(F32). Like the Merchant's Exchange, this is a
three part vertical composition with a dominant
brick shaft and a belvedere on the roof. The
shaft is the nicely textured brown brick wall with
paired windows that constitutes the standard
background material of downtown area street
facades. Renaissance/Baroque ornamentation
of the base and capital is executed in glazed
cream terra cotta. The base is defined by piers
and a mezzanine with a giant entrance arch.
The upper "capital" zone is an arcade
crowned by a cornice. The original entrance
and elevator lobby was a skylit basilica with
giant columns. Only the shallow entrance lobby
still exists, now housing the elevators.

The building is extremely handsome in its proportions and workmanship. It is a major piece of
the characteristic downtown fabric which forms
important elements in the streetscapes of both
Montgomery and Pine streets. As is so often the
case with juxtapositions of old and new, in this
instance this building with the Bank of America
(F34), the new is immeasurably enriched by its
proximity to the old. The pedestrian walkway
(formerly Summer Street) from Montgomery up
to the Bank of America tower that passes between the lower banking pavilion and the
California Commercial Union Building is one of
the finest such juxtapositions in the city.

California Commercial Union Building, 1923.

F86 MAP I
400 Montgomery Street
NE corner California
Kohl Building
originally Alvinza Hayward Building
**Percy and Polk/Willis Polk
1901/1907**

A handsome and important early San Francisco
skyscraper and the only one in the burned area
which at least partly survived without any fire or
earthquake damage. The building was first
built for Alvinza Hayward, an associate of
banker William Ralston; his last initial is possibly
the source of the unusual "H" shape of the
building. The original design was the result of
the short-lived association of George W. Percy
and Willis Polk, with Henry Meyers as supervising
architect. The building was burned below the
fourth floor and was rebuilt by Polk in 1907. In
recent years pieces of its cornice have been
removed.

It was an early and excellent example in San
Francisco of the more formal designs that later
came to characterize the city, relying on a
relatively restrained and "correct" use of Re-
naissance/Baroque ornamentation and the two
or three part compositional formula. It was also
an early example of "fireproof" construction,
the success of which can be measured in its
unique survival of the fire. It is a steel frame
building with reinforced concrete floors and
expanded metal reinforcing, hollow tile partitions, metal covered door and window frames,
and suspended ceilings of plastered expanded metal. Its brick curtain walls are clad in
Colusa sandstone, the favored building material for pre-fire prestige buildings. Ornamenta-

A

tion in this three part composition is concentrated in the upper tier with its mannerist giant order and carved garlands and animal heads. The remodeled base includes Skidmore, Owings, and Merrill's stylish and expensive Banco di Roma of about 1972. In an article entitled "The Local Architecture of San Francisco" in *Architect and Engineer* in 1909, the important critic B. J. S. Cahill referred to the Kohl as "one of the most beautiful buildings in San Francisco."

A

F87 MAP I
405 Montgomery Street
NW corner California
Financial Center Building
Meyer and Johnson
1927

The last and one of the best of the several downtown buildings which loosely followed the three part compositional type as established by the Merchant's Exchange, and a corner anchor for the entire financial district of the 1906-1920s period.

Medievalized Renaissance/Baroque ornamentation included rusticated terra cotta wall areas with arcades at the base and capital, and a handsome red brick shaft which provided a rich textural backdrop to the street. A giant entrance arch led to an elevator lobby about which architect Meyer wrote, "we frankly approached the problem with the idea of making it very colorful and awaited the removal of the scaffolding with fear and trembling, thinking that perhaps we had overstepped by transforming a sober business building entrance into a theatre lobby, but judging from the approval of the public, the decoration scheme is appreciated. The walls are of polished Botticini marble with the elevator openings in carved marble and doors of cast bronze. The overhead treatment represents a wood beam ceiling with set-in cast metal ornamental panels. The background is in rich tones of red, blue, and black." This lobby and the exterior base were remodeled in 1958 by Loubet and Flynn. The building occupies the site of the old Parrott Building, a solid granite structure of 1852 that survived the earthquake.

A

Financial Center Building, ca. 1949.

F88 MAP I
417 Montgomery Street
Kemper Building
originally Lurie Building
Wilbur D. Peugh
1936

Until recently, a good example of a Moderne office building, completely intact down to the ground level with its handsome entrance way and "streamlined" mezzanine. In 1975 the base was insensitively remodeled in flat travertine panels by Arthur Gensler and Associates for the Mitsubishi Bank. Although Moderne in style, it is a traditional two part vertical block in composition. The verticality of the shaft is expressed in uninterrupted vertical members that culminate in a streamlined cornice. Its small but stylish marble entrance lobby that followed Miller and Pfleuger lobbies at 450 Sutter (R251), the Telephone Building (M161), and the Stock Exchange (F105), was also remodeled in 1975. Its office floors were undivided until leased and requirements of individual tenants were known. The building was an early, and according to the *Architect and Engineer*, "an outstanding example of this new type of 'made-to-order' building." The building was also said to be the only office building put up in downtown San Francisco between the advent of the Depression and 1941, and the first in the United States since the start of the Depression. In construction, it is reinforced concrete clad in limestone.

C

F89 MAP I
440 Montgomery Street
Anton Borel and Co. Bank
Albert Pissis
1908

A dignified Corinthian banking temple, long since converted to other uses, by one of the city's most important and prolific designers of monumental banks. This belongs to the largest and best remaining group of these temples, but is separated from the rest of the group by one small remodeled building. It is in the heart of the financial district of the 1860s, and recalls that era by its maintenance of the traditional imagery of banking. In composition, the building is a modified temple without a pediment. Ornamentation is derived from classical antiquity. The minor (and reversible) alterations of signs, awnings, and entrances have changed the character of the design to a symmetrical temple front, from a segment of a colonnade without a pronounced central entrance. The granite face of this steel frame building is carved with consummate craftsmanship. Its bronze transom and window mullions are intact.

A

F90 MAP I
460 Montgomery Street
SE corner Sacramento
Sutro and Co.
originally Italian-American Bank
Howard and Galloway
1908

A fine granite banking temple in the heart of the last good group of monumental banks in San Francisco. Its most important relationships are to the old Borel Bank (F89) at 440 Montgomery and to the American Asian Bank (F91) across Sacramento in the establishment of a nearly continuous colonnade and a powerful concentration of temple images. This image is particularly strongly associated with San Francisco as an outgrowth of its long-standing importance as a financial center that began with the Gold Rush. Other American financial centers outside New York have not achieved such a unified and effective architectural image, and New York long ago lost most of its comparable buildings.

The design of this building went through several stages including one as a skyscraper with a bank at the ground level. The existing design is, in composition, a modified temple without a pediment. Ornamentation is derived from classical antiquity. The principal facades are each composed of a Doric order in-antis, with a recessed iron wall plane. The original interior, with its well crafted bronze teller's cages by T. J. Welsh, has been remodeled. The building is steel frame in construction, clad in concrete for fireproofing. A specially designed truss system carries the second floor, leaving the ground level free for a banking space.

A

F91 MAP I
500 Montgomery Street
NE corner Sacramento
American Asian Bank Building
originally Canton Bank
William Wilde and Otto Schiller
1918

Another columned banking temple at a major intersection in the heart of the Montgomery Street temple group, and a long-surviving representative of the early Chinese presence in San Francisco finance. The building's major visual importance is in its continuous colonnades that join 520 Montgomery to the temple group and relate to Sutro and Co. (F90) and the Borel Bank (F89) across Sacramento. In composition, the building is a modified temple without a pediment, with ornamentation derived from classical antiquity. It is a steel frame structure clad in glazed terra cotta.

B

F92 MAP I
520 Montgomery Street
SE corner Commercial
architect unknown
1920

The last building in the Montgomery Street temple group. In composition, a modified temple without a pediment. Ornamentation is derived from classical antiquity. The facades of fluted Corinthian pilasters carry the temple theme to its Montgomery Street conclusion, and provide an equally suitable element in the diverse but fine streetscape of Commercial. Apparently originally a bank, but now occupied by Joe Paoli's restaurant. Reinforced concrete construction with glazed terra cotta ornamentation.

B

F93 MAP I
527 Montgomery Street
SW corner Commercial
architect unknown
1906

A two part small commercial block with formal treatment of the upper story in a blend of Renaissance/Baroque and Mission Revival ornamental detail. The design resembles several by Frederick H. Meyer including one for the Swedish American Bank, now demolished. Brick construction. Built on the site of the bank of James King of William.

C

F94 MAP I
540-560 Montgomery Street
NE corner Commercial
Bank of America International Banking Center
H. A. Minton
1931

Built as an annex to the old Bank of Italy headquarters (F95) next door in a compatible but simplified Depression-era design. In composition, a three part vertical block with restrained Renaissance/Baroque ornamentation. The structural design of the steel frame building was by L. H. Nishkian.

C

F95 MAP I
552 Montgomery Street
SE corner Clay
Bank of America
old Bank of Italy
Shea and Lofquist
1908

An altered version of the winning design of a much publicized competition for a new Bank of Italy, predecessor of the Bank of America. The most interesting submittals in the limited competition were by Charles Paff and Co., for a more French design with a high base whose proportions recall those of Coxhead's Home Telephone Co. building of the same year, and by Loring P. Rixford who embellished his design with caryatids at mezzanine and capital levels.

The existing design is a variation of a three part vertical composition with a giant order transitional story beneath the capital. Ornamentation is Renaissance/Baroque. The steel frame structure is clad in granite at the deeply rusticated ground level, with terra cotta above. The ground floor banking hall was altered in 1921 by John H. Powers, and again in 1975 by Mario Gaidano. It remains an especially rich interior with fine marble furnishings and a coffered ceiling. Environmentally, the building is significant as the end of the post-fire financial district which, historically, gave way at this point to earlier buildings which either did not burn or were rebuilt. Recently, this adjacent area has changed from a pre-fire to a post-1970 area, strengthening the sense of this building as a bulwark of the old financial district. This corner is thought to be the landing place of Captain J. B. Montgomery in 1846, before Yerba Buena Cove was filled in.

A   NR

F96 MAP I
600 Montgomery Street
Transamerica Building
William Pereira and Associates
1971

The more big rectangular blocks are built downtown the better this looks.

NOT RATED

F97 MAP I
601 Montgomery Street
NW corner Clay
William Schuppel and Associates
under construction 1978

NOT RATED

F98 MAP I
643 Montgomery Street
architect unknown
1908

A two part small commercial block with formal treatment of the upper story. Fine brickwork is an abstraction of Renaissance/Baroque ornamentation. Brick construction.

C

F99 MAP III
64-70 Pine Street
NE corner Front
Kirkham Building
architect unknown
1917

A handsome three part vertical block, skeletal in articulation, with Renaissance/Baroque ornamentation. Reinforced concrete construction with brick curtain walls. The building recalls the Fuller Building (now demolished), and the Charleston Building at 251–255 Kearny (R108) both by Albert Pissis. This entire block is the site of the proposed Itel Building to be designed by Philip Johnson for Houston developer Gerald Hines.

C

F100 MAP III
100 Pine Street
NW corner Front
Pacific Insurance Co. Building
Hertzka and Knowles
1971

NOT RATED

F101 MAP III
111 Pine Street
SW corner Front
Mario Gaidano
1963

NOT RATED

F102 MAP III
160 Pine Street
NE corner Battery
Continental Insurance Co. Building
originally America Fore
Hertzka and Knowles
1956

One of the few interesting examples of 1950s Modernism in downtown San Francisco.

NOT RATED

F103 MAP III
216 Pine Street
NW corner Battery
Exposition Building
originally MacGregor Building, now
 Liberty Mutual Building
original architect unknown
1907

A large and early reinforced concrete office building built by the Ferrolite Co. for the Jean MacGregor Boyd Estate, and first known as the MacGregor Building. The building was later occupied by the Panama Pacific International Exposition Co. while the 1915 Exposition was being planned, and was known for many years as the Exposition Building.

Much of the exterior ornamental detail was stripped in a 1939 remodeling by Douglas Dacre Stone, and the decorative plaster lobby was mutilated by the installation of a hung ceiling. Since the late 1940s the building has been occupied by the Liberty Mutual Insurance Co. which remodeled the building again in 1973-74. Architects were Langdon and Wilson of Los Angeles. At that time the light well was enclosed, elevators moved, and exterior fenestration partially filled in. The original three part vertical composition with differentiated end bays is still intact. Rusticated piers and restrained cornices are all that remain of the Renaissance/Baroque ornamentation.

C

F104 MAP III
244 Pine Street
California Union Insurance Co. Building
Hertzka and Knowles
1957

Another of the few interesting examples of 1950s Modernism in downtown San Francisco, this one distinctly South American in inspiration.

NOT RATED

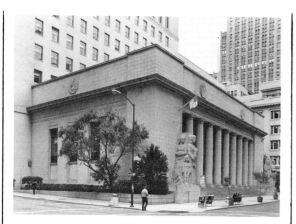

F105 MAP IV
301 Pine Street
SW corner Sansome
Pacific Coast Stock Exchange
originally U.S. Treasury Building
J. Milton Dyer/Miller and Pfleuger
1915/1930

An extremely fine design with a complex history, which in its present state, as one of Miller and Pfleuger's best works, was one of the major sources of Modernism in the Bay Area. The Pacific Coast Stock Exchange (formerly the San Francisco Stock Exchange) consists of two buildings, a lower trading hall and a twelve-story office tower (155 Sansome Street) behind it. The trading hall was originally built in 1915 as the United States Treasury (commonly known as the Sub-Treasury), the result of a competition won by J. Milton Dyer of Cleveland.

In 1928, in a separate and unconnected competition, Miller and Pfleuger were chosen to design a new San Francisco Stock Exchange at the corner of Montgomery and Summer (presently the site of the Bank of America banking pavilion). The winning design called for a traditional temple form with Moderne details and profuse bas relief panels and masks. Before work on the new building began, the Stock Market crashed and the U.S. government vacated the Sub-Treasury. In an economy measure the San Francisco Stock Exchange took over the Sub-Treasury.

With the existing building available on a new site, the winning competition designs were abandoned but Miller and Pfleuger were retained as architects for the conversion and construction of an adjacent office tower. The old Treasury building was redesigned by adding massive corners to the front facade terminating the existing Doric colonnade, adding a massive attic wall above the existing cornice, altering the fenestration of end walls, and placing two colossal sculptural groups by Ralph Stackpole on pedestals in front of the building. In composition, it retained the traditional form of an enframed pavilion with end bays, an attic, and a base. The interior space was left as a single great hall with new floor furnishings and a louvered screen under the skylight. The office tower behind was de-signed in a traditional three part vertical composition with a giant order in the capital. Limited exterior ornamentation in a blend of classical and Moderne styles is focused in a sculptural group over the door.

Inside, the black marble elevator lobby and two-story top level Stock Exchange Club were superbly designed in the most up-to-date Moderne manner, executed in the finest materials. It was these spaces more than any other aspect of the fine complex that were so extremely influential locally, in effect, introducing this latest New York-Paris approach to design which incorporated fine art and fine materials in an overall ahistorical scheme, to San Francisco. The finest individual art work in the building is the immense Diego Rivera mural in the stairwell of the two-level Stock Exchange Club, an ironic decoration by a socialist in a hot-bed of capitalism. Both buildings are of steel frame construction, clad in granite. The foundation of the old Sub-Treasury consisted of a forest of concrete pedestal piles, an innovation at that time.

A

F105   Sansome Street facade. Detail.

F106 MAP IV
332 Pine Street
Orient Building
now Associated Insurance
Charles Paff
1912

A nicely textured and detailed office building, by the architect of the Olympic Club, which forms an important element in the fine street facade along this block of Pine. In composition, a three part vertical block with a high capital and an attic. The composition recalls that of the Welch Building at 244–256 California Street (F21), architect unknown, with its low base, tall capital, and fine detailing. Ornamentation is Renaissance/Baroque. Construction is steel frame with a marble base, brick walls, and terra cotta ornamentation at the upper levels.

B

212

F107 MAP IV
333 Pine Street
SW corner Century, foot of Leidesdorff
**old San Francisco Chamber of
   Commerce Building**
architect unknown
1917

An important building by virtue of both its design and siting. In composition, a two part vertical block with Renaissance/Baroque ornamentation. Its massive piers establish its presence next to the old Sub-Treasury Building (now the Stock Exchange) while the layering of the piers adds a complexity to the relationship of the building's parts. The building is located at the foot of Leidesdorff on one of the central blocks of the old financial district. It is flanked by Century Alley on one side and a private alley on the other, setting the building off like the Sub-Treasury/Stock Exchange. Reinforced concrete construction, clad in imitation granite terra cotta.

B

F108 MAP IV
340-344 Pine Street
NE corner Leidesdorff
Selbach and Deans Building
Lewis Hobart
1928

In materials and texture, an integral part of this important Pine Street block, and the home since it was built of the California Canadian Bank (formerly Canadian Bank of Commerce). A two part vertical composition with Romanesque ornamentation. Its ground floor has been sympathetically remodeled.

C

F109 MAP IV
348-354 Pine Street
NW corner Leidesdorff
Dividend Building
S. H. Woodruff
1907

An early reinforced concrete office building in a three part vertical composition which has lost all its cornice moldings. The Doric columns of the ground floor are intact. Ornamentation is Renaissance/Baroque. The building is part of the important Pine Street group. Aptly, for its neighborhood, and optimistically named the Dividend Building.

C

F110 MAP IV
358-360 Pine Street
Phoenix Building
Bakewell and Weihe
1928

A three part vertical composition with 18th century English ornamentation. Its materials and texture contribute to the overall quality of this block. Steel frame construction.

C

F111 MAP IV
369 Pine Street
SE corner Petrarch
Exchange Block
architect unknown
1918

A handsome two part vertical block with restrained Renaissance/Baroque ornamentation. A reinforced concrete structure with a rusticated and arcaded base and a brick clad shaft. It is one of three adjacent buildings in this block set off from its neighbors by public and private streets or alleys and as such is part of a unique downtown streetscape.

C

F112 MAP II
119 Sacramento Street
architect unknown
1912

A brick warehouse with vaguely Secessionist ornamentation in the piers.

C

F113 MAP II
265 Sacramento Street
SE corner Front
Home Savings
Millard Sheets
1974

Probably the only metal modular building in downtown San Francisco and certainly the first one-story building in many decades. The fine tile mosaic by the entrance is also by Millard Sheets. If this didn't appear to be a temporary building it would be worthy of criticism for its small size and failure to fill its lot.

NOT RATED

F114 MAP II
325 Sacramento Street
architect unknown
1908

A two part small commercial block with 19th century treatment of the facade and very slight Renaissance/Baroque ornamental references. Brick construction.

C

F115 MAP II
333 Sacramento Street
architect unknown
1923

A reinforced concrete structure in a two part small commercial block composition with skeletal articulation of the facade and industrial window sash. Ornamentation is slightly Renaissance/Baroque.

C

F116 MAP II
353 Sacramento Street
Benjamin G. McDougall
1922

A handsomely detailed steel frame, brick clad structure which punctuates a block of smaller scale buildings. Originally designed as a 3-story building, either three stories were added later, or three stories were added when it was first built, simply by stacking elements on the old design without bothering to alter the original. In composition, a stacked vertical block. Ornamentation is Renaissance/Baroque.

B

F117 MAP I
558 Sacramento Street
NW corner Leidesdorff
architect unknown
1907

A modest example of a three part vertical block with differentiated end bays and restrained Renaissance/Baroque ornamentation. Brick construction. In texture, scale, and detail, part of the important small scaled group clustered around Leidesdorff and Commercial streets.

C

F118 MAP I
560 Sacramento Street
architect unknown
1909

An L-shaped brick structure which also occupies the southwest corner of Commercial and Leidesdorff and is an important part of the fine group clustered around those streets in its texture, scale, materials, and details. In composition, a three part vertical block. Ornamentation is Renaissance/Baroque.

C

F119 MAP I
568 Sacramento Street
Pacific Gas & Electric Co., Station J
now Paoli's
Frederick H. Meyer
1914

Built as a rear annex to the main Station J building on Commercial in the same monumental style that was the trademark of the P.G. & E. substations of the early years of this century. The elegant design of this building, a vault with Palladian entrance, suggests something much grander through very simple means. In addition to its historic and architectural relationships to two nearby substations, the building relates to others all over the city.

B

F120 MAP I
576 Sacramento Street
Potter Building
architect unknown
1907

A reinforced concrete office building with a giant ground floor order that relates the building to the cluster of columned banking temples in the area. In composition, a three part vertical block. Ornamentation is Renaissance/Baroque.

C

F121 MAP I
615 Sacramento Street
Jack's
architect unknown
1907

A long-time San Francisco restaurant in a handsome design, now standing by itself between a large post-war office block and a parking lot. The composition is a two part small commercial block with a mid-19th century upper level. Modified Renaissance/Baroque ornamentation shows the influence of the Craftsman movement in the clinker brick window surrounds set in a stucco wall. Brick construction.

B

F122 MAP III
114 Sansome Street
NE corner Bush
Adam Grant Building
Howard and Galloway
1908, ca. 1910

A very handsome steel frame office building with a skeletal, almost "Chicago school" facade, and an important link in the extremely fine group of major buildings along the north side of Bush Street. The building was built in two stages, the lowest six floors at least two years earlier than the rest, but evidently designed as one. The building went through several preliminary design stages as the Murphy Grant Building, none of them as restrained, unorthodox, or successful as the version that was built.

In composition, it is a three part vertical block with differentiated end bays. Its upper zone consists of a giant order over a transitional story with re-entrant corners. Renaissance/Baroque ornamentation is very restrained in deference to the structural expression of the facade and its handsome brick cladding. The original ornamented entrance has been remodeled but the rest of the ground floor treatment is intact.

A

F123 MAP III
160-180 Sansome Street
SE corner Pine
Hong Kong Bank Building
Hertzka and Knowles
1965

One of the most successful pieces of urban architecture of the post-war period in San Francisco. In composition (as a two part vertical block with differentiated end bays and an attic, over a strongly articulated base), color, and scale it is a perfect neighbor in an overwhelmingly much older area. And all this has been achieved without committing the ultimate sin against Modernism—use of historical ornamentation.

NOT RATED

F124 MAP III
200-206 Sansome Street
NE corner Pine
American International Building
originally Insurance Center Building
Powers and Ahnden
1927

A handsome slender tower in a three part vertical composition with Gothic ornamentation. It is a more successful version of a very similar design by Lewis Hobart for the Alexander Building, at 149-157 Montgomery (F77), a few years earlier. Its steel frame is clad in brick with terra cotta ornamental details. Part of a fine group on Pine and an important corner.

B

A two part small commercial block with formal treatment of the upper stories. Ornamentation is Renaissance/Baroque. Part of the continuous wall of older buildings in this block.

C

F125 MAP IV
201 Sansome Street
NW corner Pine
Royal Globe Insurance Co.
Howells and Stokes
1907

One of the richest of all downtown designs in its use of color, materials, and ornamentation; it also is an important building at a major corner and an integral part of the Pine and Sansome streetscapes. The building is in a three part vertical composition. Its 18th century English ornament is executed in white marble, red brick, and green and white terra cotta. The base, identical to a contemporary company building in New York, includes an extremely fine carved marble clock over the entrance with a lion and a unicorn. Doors in the elevator lobby are from a 17th century Italian palazzo. The recent replacement of a heavy upper level cornice molding with a copper substitute was an ingenious solution worthy of the generation of architects who designed the post-fire downtown with less interest in literalness than in effect. When the copper weathers to green it will pick up the existing green terra cotta highlights and amplify the rich play of colors which distinguishes this building. All these original exterior materials were brought from the East Coast.

The building is a steel frame structure with reinforced concrete floors and brick curtain walls. The walls were "earthquake proofed" by means of a mesh of iron rods which wrapped around the building and served as a nearly continuous reinforcement of the brick curtain walls. This system was designed by the New York architects and their engineers, Purdy and Henderson.

A

F127 MAP IV
231 Sansome Street
T. C. Kierulff Building
architect unknown
1925

A reinforced concrete office building in a two part vertical composition with 18th century English ornamentation. In 1917, a building was planned for this site for the same owner by architect Benjamin G. McDougall which was not built, presumably because of the interruption of World War I. The architect for the present building is unknown. The treatment of the ground floor recalls that of the Welch (F21) and Orient (F106) buildings, the latter by Charles Paff. A steel frame building with reinforced concrete floors, roof, and walls and brick and terra cotta cladding. Part of a fine group in this block of Sansome Street.

B

F128 MAP IV
233-241 Sansome Street
Fireman's Fund Insurance Co. Building
Weeks and Day
1924, 1929

Originally built as an office annex to the Fireman's Fund Insurance Co. Building at the corner of Sansome and California (now demolished). It was built in a three part vertical composition with Gothic ornamentation, but a major addition in 1929 changed the character of the facade to a stacked composition. Its steel frame is clad in a handsome modulated gray terra cotta, finely detailed, with a green cornice. Part of a harmonious group in this block of Sansome, now diminished by the replacement of the old Fireman's Fund temple by the Great Western Savings Tower at the corner.

B

F129 MAP I
343 Sansome Street
NW corner Halleck
Crown Zellerbach Building
Hyman and Appleton
ca. 1930

Built in 1908 as the 8-story Security Building by Howard and Galloway for Jacob Stern in a three part vertical composition. Entirely remodeled with a 5-story addition as a streamlined Moderne set-back office building about 1930. The building is now occupied by the Bank of California. Its terra cotta and bronze entrance and lobby follow contemporary precedents by Miller and Pfleuger. The building is part of a continuing older streetscape along Sansome. It is perhaps best viewed from the landscaped roof of the old Bank of California for which it forms part of an encircling wall of buildings. Steel frame construction.

B

F130 MAP I
345 Sansome Street
SW corner Sacramento
architect unknown
1931

An unusual 1-story Moderne office building, ornamented like a squashed skyscraper. Its oversized entrance surround and corner piers and the ribbed treatment of the facade are borrowed from a much larger and more logically vertical building. The "owl's eyes" ornamental motif is a familiar one in San Francisco. Reinforced concrete construction.

C

F131 MAP II
400 Sansome Street
NE corner Sacramento
Federal Reserve Bank of San Francisco
George Kelham
1924

A variation of a two part vertical composition with an attic—with upper and lower zones of about equal height and a giant order in each. The dominant element in the composition is the Ionic colonnade on a raised porch with free-standing eagles on the entablature. The building is making clear reference to San Francisco's tradition of temple form banks, and at the same time to the federal government's increasing association at the time with monumental architecture. The best features of this rather stiff design are the lobby and banking hall. The murals in the lobby are by Jules Guerin.

B

F132 MAP I
401-405 Sansome Street
NW corner Sacramento
Sun Building
originally National Building
architect unknown
1906

A small scale Mills Building in a three part vertical composition with an arcaded shaft. Ornamentation leans to Renaissance/Baroque rather than Romanesque. It forms a handsome pair with the L-shaped building at 407–411 Sansome (F133) which is next door on both streets. A strong corner anchor for the varied group of small scale structures in this area. Brick construction.

C

F133 MAP I
407-411 Sansome Street
architect unknown
1909

A three part vertical composition in an L-shape; it fronts on both Sansome and Sacramento streets, wrapping around 401 Sansome (F132) and complementing it in material and composition. Ornamentation is restrained Renaissance/Baroque. Part of a varied group of small scale structures. Brick construction.

C

F134 MAP I
415-429 Sansome Street
SW corner Commercial
Fugazi Building
originally Yokohama Specie Bank
W. L. Woollett
1908

Originally the Yokohama Specie Bank, ancestor of the major presence of Japanese banks in present-day San Francisco, and the only downtown building by W. L. Woollett, one-time California State Architect. In composition, a pavilion with flanking wings, unchanged on the outside but completely remodeled within. Ornamentation is Renaissance/Baroque. Part of a larger group of small scale buildings of this area which includes the city's major collection of banking temples.

B

F135 MAP II
450 Sansome Street
SE corner Clay
Hadley, architect
1967

This building has the largest blank, scaleless exposed back of any in San Francisco—in enameled metal panels, evidently awaiting an addition.

NOT RATED

F136 MAP I
475 Sansome Street
SW corner Clay
Albert Roller
1969

NOT RATED

F137 MAP I
505 Sansome Street
NW corner Clay
Pacific Mutual Building
William Pereira and Associates
under construction 1978

Site of the Niantic Building and the remains of the old ship Niantic, itself, which were found during excavation for this project. This will be the first downtown building in many years to have windows that open.

NOT RATED

F138 MAP II
532 Sansome Street
SE corner Washington
San Francisco Fire Department,
  Station 13
John Portman
ca. 1974

The odd circumstance of a John Portman fire station in San Francisco is the result of a deal made when a fire station was removed to make way for Embarcadero Center nearby. The city still needed a downtown fire station so the Embarcadero Center architect designed it.

NOT RATED

F139 MAP I
545 Sansome Street
NW corner Merchant
Willis Polk and Co.
1930

A reinforced concrete "printing and publishing building," now offices, designed by Willis Polk and Co. several years after Polk's death. As built, this was a handsome skeletal structure, neutral gray in color with slight Moderne detailing and an asymmetrical facade created by a bulkhead over the articulated elevator shaft. In later years the facade was made "symmetrical" by the addition of a penthouse at the opposite corner from the elevator housing, clad in a test panel for the Bank of California tower. More recently the industrial character of the raw concrete facade has been lost to a new "earth color" paint job.

C

F140 MAP IV
58-64 Sutter Street
Holbrook Building
MacDonald and Applegarth
1912

A steel frame, terra cotta clad office building with beautiful if somewhat underscaled detail, designed by one of the best post-fire commercial firms. It was built for Charles H. Holbrook (1830-1925), a Gold Rush pioneer whose firm of Holbrook, Merrill & Stetson became one of the city's major suppliers of specialized non-structural metal building material in the period after the fire. In his later years Holbrook attracted some attention as a long-time survivor of the Gold Rush era. The building is a crucial element in this deteriorated block of Sutter which is almost overwhelmed by modern highrises at 44 and 120 Montgomery. The building helps define the still impressive streetscape along with 1 Sansome (M166) next door and several buildings across the street. It is in a three part vertical composition with Renaissance/Baroque ornamentation that is richest at the upper columned and arcaded level and cornice. Steel frame construction.

B

Hunter-Dulin Building, ca. 1954.

F141 MAP IV
111 Sutter Street
SW corner Montgomery
Hunter-Dulin Building
Schultze and Weaver
1926

One of downtown San Francisco's finest and most distinctive skyscrapers by the important New York firm of Schultze and Weaver, architects of such landmarks as the Waldorf Astoria, Sherry-Netherland, and Park Lane hotels in New York, the Los Angeles Biltmore, and the Miami Breakers. Earl Theodore Heitschmidt was the supervising architect. The building was originally built for a Los Angeles investment firm.

The three part vertical composition was detailed in what, by 1926, was considered a rather backward looking stylistic mix of Romanesque and French Chateau ornamentation. Nevertheless, it is an extremely fine version and this city's only example of the type. The base and main office shaft, clad in a particularly fine glazed terra cotta, is designed in a rather attenuated version of the Romanesque. Above this is a set-back continuation of the shaft crowned by a high, red, dormered man-sard roof with copper cresting. It is this roof which is one of the richest features on the city's skyline. The giant ground level entrance arch leads into a richly detailed elevator lobby.

The steel frame was built on a reinforced concrete sheet piling system designed by the prominent local engineer, H. J. Brunnier. The foundation was laid by continuously pouring concrete for 44 hours, the object of which was to speed up construction by eliminating joints and delays between pours. The *Architect and Engineer* commented, "In the annals of construction a stupendous task has been accomplished in building operations." Built on the site of the old Lick Hotel.

A

219

Secondary Survey Areas

FINANCIAL

NOB HILL

RETAIL

MARKET STREET

TENDERLOIN

SOUTH OF MARKET EAST

CIVIC CENTER

SOUTH OF MARKET WEST

SAN FRANCISCO BAY

PRIMARY SURVEY AREA
SECONDARY SURVEY AREA

The following list of buildings includes all those in the secondary survey areas which were given summary ratings of 3, 4, or 5 in the 1976 Architectural Inventory of the San Francisco Department of City Planning. In addition, it includes other buildings identified as significant as a result of historical research for this inventory, and still others identified as visually significant following the findings of the more intensive survey of the primary areas. Where buildings are listed below which were not rated 3, 4, or 5 in the Department of City Planning (DCP) inventory, their lower rating is given whenever one exists, or they are identified as NOT RATED.

The Department of City Planning inventory was primarily a visual inventory of urban design quality and did not consider cultural qualities or qualities of architectural history to any great degree. Thus the summary scores of Its scale ranging from 0 (contextual significance) to 5 (great significance) do not correspond exactly to the final evaluation ratings of this inventory (A, B, C, and D).

The lists below, therefore, should not be considered comprehensive in the same sense that the inventory of primary areas is comprehensive. Additional research and systematic application of the criteria used in the primary areas would result in many more buildings on the lists below, particularly in the Nob Hill and Tenderloin areas. Indeed, the files of this inventory already contain a great deal of information which, with more time and money, could be used to that end.

SOUTH OF MARKET EAST

234–246 First Street
Phillips and Van Orden Printing Co.
Henry H. Meyers
1929

DCP-1

425 First Street
Union Oil Co. Building
Lewis P. Hobart
1941

DCP-4

650 First Street
Oriental Warehouse
architect unknown
ca. 1867

DCP-3   CL

121 Second Street
Rapp Building
originally Drexler Estate Building
Reid Brothers
1908

DCP-2

400–416 Second Street
California Blue Shield Co. Building
originally Pacific Coast Envelope Co.
  Building
William H. Crim, Jr.
1919

NOT RATED

698 Second Street
Fire Department Pumping Station
architect unknown
ca. 1920

DCP-3

625 Third Street
warehouse
architect unknown
ca. 1885

DCP-4

22 Fourth Street
The Apparel Mart
Whisler-Patri
under construction 1979

NOT RATED

360 Fourth Street
Senior Activities Center
architect unknown
1925

DCP-3   NRp

55 Fifth Street
Hotel Yerba Buena
originally Hotel Lankershim
Reid Brothers
1919

NOT RATED

155 Fifth Street
Crocker Data Center
Skidmore, Owings, and Merrill
1975

NOT RATED

32, 36, 40 Berry Street
Wilbur D. Peugh
ca. 1935

DCP-3

50 Berry Street
architect unknown
ca. 1935

DCP-3

60 Berry Street
architect unknown
ca. 1935

DCP-3

70 Berry Street
V. & W. Diversified
architect unknown
ca. 1935

DCP-3

185 Berry Street
China Basin Building
Bliss and Faville/Robinson and Mills
1922/1973

DCP-1

301 Brannan Street
Bancroft-Whitney Co.
architect unknown
ca. 1920

DCP-3

95 Center Place
Gran Oriente Filipino Masonic Temple
architect unknown
ca. 1960

DCP-3

166 The Embarcadero
YMCA
Frederick H. Meyer
1924

DCP-1

The Embarcadero
Pier 24
architect unknown
ca. 1920

DCP-3

The Embarcadero
Pier 42
Charles W. McCall
1930

DCP-3

611 Folsom Street
Pacific Telephone Co. Equipment
   Building
McCue, Boone and Tomsick
1972

NOT RATED

633 Folsom Street
Pacific Telephone Co.
J. C. Warnecke and Associates
1970

NOT RATED

666 Folsom Street
Pacific Telephone Co.
J. C. Warnecke and Associates
1968

NOT RATED

795 Folsom Street
Pacific Telephone Long Lines Building
Primiani and Weaver
1977

NOT RATED

2 Harrison Street
Hills Brothers
George Kelham
1933

DCP-4

101 Harrison Street
Hathaways
architect unknown
ca. 1900

DCP-3

450 Harrison Street
Sailors' Union of the Pacific
William G. Merchant
1950

DCP-4

657 Howard Street
office building
architect unknown
ca. 1925

DCP-3

820 Howard Street
architect unknown
ca. 1920

DCP-3

835 Howard Street
Dettner's Printing
Coxhead and Coxhead
1909

DCP-2

1–21 Mission Street
Audiffred Building
architect unknown
1889

DCP-3   CL

99 Mission Street
Rincon Annex Post Office
Gilbert Stanley Underwood
1940

DCP-3

301 Mission Street
W. P. Fuller Building
Albert Pissis
1909

NOT RATED

800 Mission Street
Community College Center
Rockrise, Odermatt, Mountjoy, and Amis
1979

NOT RATED

816 Mission Street
Hueter Building
Charles F. Whittlesey
1908

DCP-1

145 Natoma Street
office building
architect unknown
ca. 1968

DCP-3

147 Natoma Street
Underwriters Fire Patrol Headquarters
architect unknown
ca. 1910

DCP-3

158–160 South Park Avenue
architect unknown
ca. 1920

DCP-3

123–135 Townsend Street
The Townsend Building
Charles Lee Tilden
1907

DCP-3

178 Townsend Street
warehouse
architect unknown
ca. 1910

DCP-3

264 Townsend Street
Pacific Machinery and Mercantile Co.
architect unknown
ca. 1890

DCP-3

334 Townsend Street
Cudahy Co.
architect unknown
ca. 1935

DCP-3

350 Townsend Street
Paul Wood Warehouse
architect unknown
ca. 1905

DCP-3

88 Fifth Street
United States Mint
Alfred B. Mullet
1869-1874

DCP-5   NR

665 Sixth Street
warehouse
architect unknown
ca. 1900

DCP-4

99 Seventh Street
United States Post Office and
   District Court of Appeals Building
James Knox Taylor/George Kelham
1902-1905/1931

DCP-5   NR

345 Seventh Street
Ukranian Orthodox Church of St. Michael
S. Ardrio
1906

DCP-3

567 Seventh Street
architect unknown
ca. 1970

DCP-3

650 Seventh Street
Independent Paper Stock Co.
architect unknown
ca. 1890

DCP-4

700–768 Seventh Street
Baker and Hamilton
originally Miller, Sloss and Scott Building
Albert Pissis
1905

DCP-3

66 Eighth Street
P. G. & E. Substation
William G. Merchant
1947

DCP-2

599 Eighth Street
Blake, Moffitt and Towne
originally National Carbon Co. Building
Maurice C. Couchot
1917

DCP-2

165 Tenth Street
Peoples Laundry
originally Lick Baths
J. W. Dolliver
1906

DCP-3

1380 Folsom Street
Mark Morris Tires
architect unknown
ca. 1910

NOT RATED

1489 Folsom Street
warehouse
architect unknown
ca. 1880

DCP-4

1275 Harrison Street
architect unknown
ca. 1930

DCP-3

995 Howard Street
Hotel Orlando
architect unknown
ca. 1910

DCP-2

1035 Howard Street
Eng-Skell Co.
architect unknown
ca. 1935

DCP-2

1130 Howard Street
Koret of California
architect unknown
ca. 1935

DCP-2

1155 Howard Street
architect unknown
ca. 1910

DCP-3

1415 Howard Street
St. Joseph's Church
architect unknown
ca. 1910

DCP-3

1231 Market Street
P.S.A. San Franciscan Hotel
originally Municipal Building, later
   Hotel Whitcomb
Wright, Rushforth and Cahill
1911

NOT RATED

1275 Market Street
State Compensation Insurance Fund
   Building
J. C. Warnecke and Associates
1976

NOT RATED

1355 Market Street
Western Furniture Exchange
The Capitol Company, architects
1937

DCP-3

1455 Market Street
Bank of America Computer Center
Skidmore, Owings, and Merrill
1977

NOT RATED

1525 Market Street
Bank of America Building
Wurster, Bernardi, and Emmons
1960

NOT RATED

965 Mission Street
California Casket Co.
Albert Pissis
1909

DCP-2

1235 Mission Street
Mangrum and Otter, Inc.
Bliss and Fairweather
1928

DCP-3

1500 Mission Street
Coca-Cola Bottling Co.
originally White Motor Co.
Henry H. Gutterson
1927

DCP-3

150 Otis Street
Juvenile Court and Detention Home
Louis C. Mullgardt
1914

DCP-5

100 South Van Ness
Firestone Garage
architect unknown
ca. 1925

DCP-3

NOB HILL

564 Bush Street
Notre Dame des Victoires
Louis Brochoud
1913

DCP-3

815 Bush Street
apartment building
architect unknown
ca. 1910

DCP-3

820 Bush Street
Fanny's Market
architect unknown
ca. 1925

DCP-3

863 Bush Street
residential hotel
architect unknown
ca. 1910

DCP-3

972 Bush Street
apartment building
architect unknown
ca. 1915

DCP-3

1020, 1026 Bush Street
apartment buildings
architect unknown
ca. 1910

DCP-3

1040 Bush Street
Mary Elizabeth Inn
architect unknown
ca. 1915

DCP-3

1349 Bush Street
P. G. & E., Station D
Willis Polk
1912

DCP-2

790 California Street
Palazzo Goldenmar
originally Leesmont Apartments
Henry C. Smith
1916

DCP-2

851 California Street
Arcona Apartments
C. A. Meussdorffer
1912

DCP-2

905 California Street
Stanford Court
Creighton Withers/Curtis and Davis
1911/1972

DCP-2

999 California Street
Mark Hopkins Hotel
Weeks and Day
1925

DCP-1

1000 California Street
Pacific Union Club
old Flood Mansion
Augustus Laver/Willis Polk/George Kelham
1886/1912/1934

DCP-5   NR; CL

1001 California Street
Morsehead Apartments
Houghton Sawyer
1915

DCP-4

1021 California Street
Co. George Shastey
1911

DCP-3

1045 California Street
Nob Hill Center Garage
Anshen and Allen
1956

NOT RATED

1055 California Street
apartment building
Lewis P. Hobart and H. P. Merritt
1921

NOT RATED

1075 California Street
Huntington Hotel
Weeks and Day
1924

NOT RATED

1111 California Street
Masonic Memorial Auditorium
Albert F. Roller
1958

NOT RATED

1201 California Street
Cathedral Apartments
Weeks and Day
ca. 1930

DCP-1

1490, 1494 California Street
apartment buildings
architect unknown
ca. 1920

DCP-3

1660 California Street
Bank of America
Smith, Barker, and Hannsen
1969

DCP-3

1700 Franklin Street
Christian Science Church
Edgar A. Mathews
ca. 1910

DCP-3

625 Hyde Street
apartment building
J. F. Dunn
ca. 1910

DCP-3

647 Hyde Street
apartment building
architect unknown
ca. 1935

DCP-4

655 Hyde Street
apartment building
architect unknown
ca. 1910

DCP-3

827 Hyde Street
East Office Telephone Building
originally Hyde Street Station of
    Pacific Telephone and Telegraph
A. A. Cantin
ca. 1905

DCP-4

1005 Hyde Street
apartment building
architect unknown
ca. 1910

DCP-4

630 Leavenworth Street
Marchbank Apartments
J. F. Dunn
1917

DCP-4

1201–1219 Leavenworth Street
apartment building
architect unknown
ca. 1910

DCP-3

1202–1206 Leavenworth Street
apartment building
variously attrib. to Wyeth and McCall,
    and Julia Morgan
ca. 1911

DCP-3

831–849 Mason Street
townhouses
Willis Polk
1917

DCP-4

950 Mason Street
Fairmont Hotel
Reid Brothers/Mario Gaidano (tower)
1906/1962

DCP-4

1000 Mason Street
Brocklebank Apartments
Weeks and Day
1926

DCP-1

Meachem Street (end)
P. G. & E., Station S
Frederick H. Meyer
1913

DCP-3

903 Pine Street
apartment building
architect unknown
ca. 1910

DCP-4

930 Pine Street
apartment building
Beverly Willis
ca. 1972

DCP-3

1140 Pine Street
apartment building
architect unknown
ca. 1915

DCP-3

1144 Pine Street
apartment building
architect unknown
ca. 1968

DCP-3

1145, 1163, 1167, 1175, 1179 Pine Street
apartment buildings
architects unknown
ca. 1910

DCP-3

1201 Pine Street
apartment building
architect unknown
ca. 1915

DCP-3

1250 Pine Street
apartment building
architect unknown
ca. 1915

DCP-4

1529 Polk Street
Royal Theater
Miller and Pfleuger
1925

DCP-4

775 Post Street
Warrington Apartments
Frederick H. Meyer
1915

NOT RATED

800 Powell Street
University Club
Bliss and Faville
1912

DCP-3

830 Powell Street
apartment building
architect unknown
ca. 1915

DCP-3

850 Powell Street
Francesca Apartments
MacDonald and Couchot
1923

DCP-0

901 Powell Street
The Saint Elizabeth
architect unknown
ca. 1920

DCP-2

1100 Sacramento Street
Park Lane Apartments
Edward E. Young
1924

NOT RATED

1230 Sacramento Street
apartment building
Arthur Laib
1916

DCP-3

1298 Sacramento Street
Chambord Apartments
J. F. Dunn
1921

DCP-4

1409 Sacramento Street
apartment building
architect unknown
ca. 1906

DCP-3

1525 Sacramento Street
apartment building
architect unknown
ca. 1906

DCP-3

1551–1555 Sacramento Street
apartment building
architect unknown
ca. 1915

DCP-3

1751 Sacramento Street
Old First Presbyterian Church
William C. Hays
1911

NOT RATED

600 Stockton Street
Cogswell College
originally Metropolitan Life
LeBrun and Sons/Miller and Colmesnil/
    Miller and Pfleuger/Thomsen and Wilson
1909/1913/1929/1952

DCP-4

645 Stockton Street
H. C. Bauman
1928

DCP-2

795 Sutter Street
Belgravia Apartments
Frederick H. Meyer
1916

DCP-1

860 and 872 Sutter Street.

860 Sutter Street
apartment building
architect unknown
ca. 1920

DCP-2

872 Sutter Street
apartment building
architect unknown
ca. 1920

NOT RATED

930 Sutter Street
apartment building
architect unknown
ca. 1920

DCP-2

1047 Sutter Street
apartment building
architect unknown
ca. 1915

DCP-3

1335 Sutter Street
architect unknown
ca. 1915

DCP-4

1337 Sutter Street
architect unknown
ca. 1915

DCP-4

1350 Sutter Street
apartment building
architect unknown
ca. 1915

DCP-3

1051 Taylor Street
Grace Cathedral
Lewis P. Hobart (design);
    Weihe, Frick, & Cruse (completion)
1925; 1965

DCP-5

1051 Taylor Street
Cathedral House
Lewis P. Hobart
1912

DCP-3

1055 Taylor Street
Diocesan House
Lewis P. Hobart
1936

DCP-3

1100 Van Ness Avenue
Jack Tar Hotel
Thomas M. Price/Hertzka and Knowles
1960

NOT RATED

1320 Van Ness Avenue
Regency Theater
originally Scottish Rite Temple
O'Brien and Werner
1911

DCP-3

1699 Van Ness Avenue
Paige Motor Car Co.
Sylvan Schnaittacher
1924

DCP-2

TENDERLOIN

380 Eddy Street
Cadillac Hotel
Meyer and O'Brien
1909

DCP-3

711 Eddy Street
Eastern Park Apartments
Robert Batchelor
under construction 1979

NOT RATED

939 Ellis Street
Redevelopment Agency Building
John Bolles
1970

NOT RATED

505 Geary Street
Bellevue Hotel
architect unknown
1908

DCP-4

650 Geary Street
Alcazar Theater
T. Paterson Ross
1917

DCP-5

765 Geary Street
Rossmoor Apartments
Charles Peter Weeks
1916

DCP-1

825 Geary Street
Castle Apartments
architect unknown
ca. 1920

DCP-3

850 Geary Street
Alhambra Apartments
J. F. Dunn
1914

DCP-3

1117 Geary Street
Goodman Building
Rousseau and Son/
    Conrad W. Meussdorffer
1864/1906

DCP-3   NR; CL

50 Golden Gate Avenue
Riverside Apartments
C. A. Meussdorffer
1917

DCP-3

150 Golden Gate Avenue
Syufy Building
originally Knights of Columbus
Smith O'Brien
1913

DCP-2

450 Golden Gate Avenue
Federal Office Building
Albert F. Roller; Stone, Marraccini and
    Patterson; J. C. Warnecke
1959

NOT RATED

125 Hyde Street
Motion Picture Studio
architect unknown
ca. 1935

DCP-3

245, 251, 255, 259 Hyde Street
architect unknown
ca. 1935

DCP-3

201 Mason Street
Hilton Hotel
William Tabler/J. C. Warnecke (tower)
1964/1971

DCP-2

325 Mason Street
Downtown Center Garage
G. A. Applegarth
1954

DCP-2

411 O'Farrell Street
Columbia Hotel
Smith and Stewart
1914

DCP-1

450 O'Farrell Street
Fifth Church of Christ, Scientist
architect unknown
ca. 1910

DCP-3

580 O'Farrell Street
Hotel Hacienda
Charles Peter Weeks
1913

DCP-3

631 O'Farrell Street
The Hamilton
Albert H. Larsen
1929

DCP-3

750 O'Farrell Street
Cristobal Apartments
architect unknown
ca. 1910

DCP-3

601–625 Polk Street
German House Association Building
Frederick H. Meyer
1913

DCP-5

1001 Polk Street
Pierce Arrow Building
John Galen Howard
1915

DCP-3

142 Taylor Street
commercial building
architect unknown
ca. 1910

DCP-3

405 Taylor Street
Hotel Californian
Edward E. Young
1925

NOT RATED

420 Taylor Street
NBC Building (remodeled)
Albert F. Roller
1940

DCP-3

150 Turk Street
garage
architect unknown
ca. 1925

DCP-3

351 Turk Street
YMCA Hotel
Frederick H. Meyer
1926

DCP-3

381 Turk Street
apartment building
architect unknown
ca. 1915

DCP-3

901 Van Ness Avenue
Earle C. Anthony Packard Showroom
Powers and Ahnden/Bernard Maybeck,
    associated architect
1927

DCP-4

999 Van Ness Avenue
Ernest Ingold Automobile Display and
    Service Building
John E. Dinwiddie
1938

DCP-1

1000 Van Ness Avenue
Don Lee Building
Weeks and Day
1921

DCP-2

CIVIC CENTER

133 Golden Gate Avenue
St. Boniface Church
Brother Wewer
1900

DCP-4

99 Grove Street
Exposition Auditorium
John Galen Howard; Frederick H. Meyer;
    John Reid, Jr.
1914

DCP-5   NRD

101 Grove Street
Health Building
Samuel Heiman
1931

DCP-5   NRD

200 Larkin Street
San Francisco Public Library
George Kelham
1916

DCP-5   NRD

1390 Market Street
Fox Plaza
Victor Gruen and Associates
1966

NOT RATED

83 McAllister Street
Methodist Book Concern
Meyers and Ward
1906

DCP-4

100 McAllister Street
William Taylor Hotel and
    Temple Methodist Church
Miller and Pfleuger (basic design);
    Lewis P. Hobart (completion)
1930

DCP-1   NRp

350 McAllister Street
State Building
Bliss and Faville
1926

DCP-5   NRD

50 Oak Street
Young Men's Institute
William D. Shea
1914

DCP-4

50 United Nations Plaza
Federal Building
Arthur Brown, Jr.
1936

DCP-4   NRD

25 Van Ness Avenue
Masonic Temple
Bliss and Faville
1911

DCP-5

135 Van Ness Avenue
San Francisco Public Schools
    Administration Building
originally High School of Commerce
John Reid, Jr.
1927

DCP-2

309 Van Ness Avenue
War Memorial Opera House
Arthur Brown, Jr.; G. Albert Lansburgh
1931

DCP-5   NRD; CL

400 Van Ness Avenue
City Hall
Bakewell and Brown
1915

DCP-5   NRD; CL

459 Van Ness Avenue
War Memorial Veterans' Building
Arthur Brown, Jr.; G. Albert Lansburgh
1931

DCP-5   NRD; CL

Urban-Design Elements

The many non-architectural elements in the downtown area which have contributed to its historic character are treated in this section. While many of these elements are amenable to the same kind of evaluation utilized in the survey section of this volume, and are so evaluated, many others are not. Those which are not amenable to evaluation for the most part date from the period after World War II, or, as in the case of the streets and alleys, they are simply not objects in the same sense as a building or a public statue and therefore are not subject to evaluation by a system designed for objects.

STREET GRIDS/ALLEYS/INTER-BUILDING CIRCULATION

As in the rest of San Francisco, the street grid of the downtown area is one of the fundamental determinants of form. Its regular character north and south of Market Street, the variability of the intersections of its differently sized grids along the diagonal of Market, and the almost random location of its alleys help to give the area a distinctive pattern which is historically associated with its image and which establishes an essential framework of locational reference.

The regularity of the grids and the irregularity of their intersections with Market, together with the formerly universal practice of building to lot lines, historically resulted in walls of buildings which appeared to be square or rectangular. Until recently, these shapes generally gave way to triangular or other odd-shaped buildings at Market Street. The straight streets of the grid still terminate visually in views of the bay, the city's hills, or the buildings along Market. They provide an efficient and easily comprehensible circulation pattern for the pedestrian.

Within the regularity of the major grids, the randomly placed alleys provide elements of variation and surprise, both in their modulation of the grid and in their effect on the scale and design of buildings. The alleys serve variously as through streets for cars and pedestrians, as service roads, and as pedestrian "places," or, usually, in some combination of these functions. They help to give large city blocks a more intimate scale by physically breaking them up and by helping to maintain historic patterns of land parcelization and use.

When the street grid has been altered or alleys closed and the historic pattern of the city changed, the result has generally been disorienting. Post-war developments have closed a few streets, blocked views, particularly with large featureless new buildings along Market, and altered the historic unity of lot shapes and building shapes. Although street and alley closings have largely come to a stop in the 1970s, as long as very large buildings are built there will continue to be pressures to take over these spaces.

A few alley closings in recent years have had urbanistically beneficial results: the transformation of Summer Street to a pedestrian walk between the California Commercial Union Building and the Bank of America pavilion at Montgomery and California; the creation of Transamerica Redwood Park; and the wholly different but very successful three-level pedestrian shopping area in Embarcadero Center.

Among the alleys which remain, most are publicly owned, but a few are private. Most function primarily as circulation or service roads and are important for those reasons, but some stand out for their particular value or potential value as "places," or for some other scenic or historic qualities. The most important alleys and groups of alleys are described below.

Leidesdorff Street.

Alleys

Belden Street

Belden Street connects Bush and Pine Streets just east of Kearny. Like nearby Claude Lane and St. George Alley, its continuing existence helps maintain the small post-fire scale of the two blocks of Kearny between Sutter and Pine Streets. However, more than any other downtown alley except Maiden Lane, it is a successful urban "place" as well. In its slight removal from the busy streets around it, in its small shops and restaurants, and in its ample sunlight, this is a rare and valuable oasis at the edge of the highrise financial district. Belden alley began to take its present shape in 1926 when 40 Belden was designed as a Mission Revival commercial building, and 28 Belden was remodeled in the same manner. Like Maiden Lane, only more so, its individual buildings are undistinguished architecturally, but the quality of the whole is greater than the sum of its parts.

NOT RATED

Campton Place

Connects Grant and Stockton between Post and Sutter. In its location near Union Square and its ample sunlight, Campton is potentially as lively and attractive as Belden Street or Maiden Lane.

NOT RATED

Commercial Street

Historically one of the most interesting and important alleys in downtown San Francisco, with its small-scale, immediately post-fire brick buildings stretching down the hill from Chinatown to Sansome Street. Only one-half block from Portsmouth Square at one point, the street is the closest remaining approximation to what the city must have been like in the 1860s in the simplicity and unpretentiousness of its small buildings. The lower part of Commercial, and the only part within our survey area (from Montgomery to Sansome), contains a number of important small banks, power substations, and supportive brick buildings. The view down Commercial, now passing between the towers of Embarcadero Center, terminates at the Ferry Building. Like Belden Street, the importance of Commercial is enhanced by its proximity to the much larger and busier financial district, immediately present on three sides.

NOT RATED

Elmwood Street

An elbow-shaped alley which runs into both Mason and O'Farrell Streets, and with them circumscribes the Hotel Virginia at 300–324 Mason. It is well-lighted, its surface is paved in brick, and it provides entrance to La Bourgogne restaurant.

NOT RATED

First/Second/Market/Mission

This large south-of-Market block is crisscrossed by narrow alleys: Elim Alley, Stevenson and Jessie Streets going east-west, and Ecker and Anthony Streets going north-south. The alleys give a more comfortable scale to a large block and they provide easier and more direct pedestrian routes through the area. The block is characterized by brick and reinforced-concrete warehouse and industrial structures, and is the only such area left within the immediate downtown area.

NOT RATED

Leidesdorff Street

A very important three-block alley which stretches from Pine Street, in the middle of the historic financial district, to Clay Street. Although it crosses a middle block of newer buildings, the whole street is important as both a pedestrian and visual corridor. Near its northern end, Leidesdorff crosses Commercial Street, and is part of a very fine small-scale group focused at that intersection. At its southern end it terminates in a view of 333 Pine Street, and is part of a block which is characterized by the large number of public and private alleys which break its still cohesive streetscape.

NOT RATED

Lick Place

A private alley owned by Crocker Bank. It is one of a group of parcels for which a new Crocker headquarters highrise is planned. This alley provides the only head-on view of the Hallidie Building.

NOT RATED

Maiden Lane

A narrow, two-block alley whose overall quality is far greater than the sum of its architectural parts. Someplace else it might not have been noticed, but located next to Union Square, Maiden Lane provides a striking and satisfying contrast in its rough textures, small scale, and sense of enclosure. It is composed, for the most part, of the backs of buildings which face the major thoroughfares of Geary and Post, with only a few small buildings facing the alley. Some of the larger buildings have been purposefully designed to enhance the alley, either by wrapping fronts around to the side on corner buildings, or by reflecting terra-cotta or finished-brick front designs in rough, red industrial brick at the rear. Other more anonymous buildings have been adapted to their sites by converting ground levels into commercial space. If there is an architectural focus, it is on Frank Lloyd Wright's superb V. C. Morris store which manages to be both a suitable element in an anonymous brick alley and a powerful, if small, comment on what a brick building in an alley can be.

The alley was landscaped in 1958 by Donald Clever and Welton Becket, with trees, jogged sidewalks, and streetlights. In its quiet enhancement of the street, but its near invisibility as "landscaping," this was a perfect solution for Maiden Lane. Today the street is closed to automobiles at noon and cafe tables sometimes occupy the space.

NOT RATED

2 Petrarch Place and 343 Pine Street

Together with Petrarch Place itself, these privately owned parcels function as a ring of alleys around 369 Pine, and together with Century Street, they set off 333 Pine and 369 Pine as freestanding buildings. For that reason they are part of a unique streetscape in this block which is open and airy, and which, at the same time, manages to maintain the street wall that is so important to the character of the downtown area. These private alleys and Century Street are linked to the "interior sidewalk" that runs along the north side of the Mills Building.

NOT RATED

Second/Third/Market/Howard

Two large south-of-Market blocks are given a more comfortable pedestrian scale by New Montgomery Street and a network of smaller crisscrossing alleys. New Montgomery is intercepted by Stevenson, Jessie, Aldrich, Minna, and Natoma alleys, as well as by Mission Street, giving it a distinctive rhythm of similarly massed structures set slightly apart. The block north of Mission and west of New Montgomery is further cut north-south by Annie Street. This area is dominated by the Palace Hotel and the Call Building, both of which are architecturally "finished" at their sides and backs, giving a monumental quality to a delightfully open and quiet area which is at once centrally located and out of the way.

NOT RATED

Tillman Place

Located off Grant Avenue between Post and Sutter. The only one of the dead-end alleys which has been closed to vehicular traffic and fully utilized for commercial purposes.

NOT RATED

Inter-Building Circulation

A final element in the circulation system deserves mention here: the minor but important network of interior connections between adjacent buildings, and the use that these secondary systems make of alleys. The most important of these networks is focused at the Mills Building and the Merchant's Exchange. The Mills Building and Tower have entrances on Bush, Montgomery, Century, and Petrarch, which are tied together by means of a long and circuitous "interior sidewalk." The Merchant's Exchange has entrances on Montgomery and Leidesdorff and is connected directly to 300 Montgomery. Other important interior sidewalk systems are those that pass through the lobbies of the Palace, St. Francis, and Sir Francis Drake Hotels. A variation on these secondary circulation routes is on the mezzanine level of the Phelan Building.

233

PUBLIC SQUARES

As described above, downtown San Francisco's buildings have historically been built up to the lot lines, creating continuous walls interrupted only by the streets of the city's regular grid. Where the grid has been interrupted, for example along Market Street, buildings have assumed triangular or other odd shapes, as they have continued to be built up to lot lines. In this manner, the walls of the streets, once established, were always maintained by new construction until about 1960.

Historically, the only downtown exceptions to the blocks of street walls were the city's public squares, and they were always very few in number. As the city was first laid out, the only public park was Portsmouth Square. In 1850 Union Square and Washington Square were donated to the city and, after the 1906 disaster, St. Mary's Square and Huntington Park were acquired. But there was no park plan within the 1847 O'Farrell survey (east of Larkin), and additions to the park system in that area were small and spotty. As long as this area of the city was residential, the lack of parks was a social problem (as it continued to be outside the downtown area, but within the 1847 grid).

However, as the downtown area became an office and commercial district, this same lack of parks was an urban asset. Only Union Square and St. Mary's Square fall within the primary downtown survey area, and only Huntington Park, Civic Center Plaza, and South Park are in the secondary areas. The scarcity of parks enhances their importance as visual focal points and their quality as centers of urban life. Located within the grid of the city, these parks reinforce its regular pattern, but at the same time, in the contrast of solid street wall to open park, they provide focal points within it.

After the original Union Square was replaced by the underground Union Square Garage and its landscaped roof, St. Mary's Square, Portsmouth Square and Civic Center Plaza were all treated in the same manner. After the success of the original, the others have been notable failures, losing that crucial relationship of open green park to solid-walled city as blatantly landscaped roofs. While St. Mary's Square and Portsmouth Square are still heavily used, they have lost those qualities which would visually relate them to their surroundings, and they have lost that crucial aspect of naturalness which distinguishes a park from the surrounding hard edges of the city.

Aerial view of Union Square, 1922.

St. Mary's Square

Established in 1906 by the City after the fire disrupted the disreputable activities which had previously occurred on its site, St. Mary's Square was replaced by a partially submerged parking garage in 1955 (see 433 Kearny), whose roof was re-landscaped in 1960. Despite its very pleasant rooftop design by Eckbo, Royston, and Williams, and its exhilarating view of the financial district, the garage/park fails to fully respond to the potential of its site. Almost invisible from Pine and California Streets which border it, it presents the concrete walls of a parking garage to the city, rather than the inviting green open space which would provide visual relief from the densely built-up surroundings. Since the enlargement of the Telephone Co. Building across Pine Street at the south end of the Square, the landscaped area has been blocked from the sun for much of the winter months.

NOT RATED

Union Square

In its present form, Union Square is a landscaped garage roof which dates from 1942 (see 333 Post Street) when the old park was excavated and a four-story underground parking garage was built. Union Square was originally a gift to the city in 1850, along with Washington Square, from the first mayor of San Francisco, John W. Geary. At first it was only a sandy lot in an undeveloped area; it was surrounded by fashionable residences by the end of the 1850s, and later it gradually developed as the retail area which it is today. Its name is said to come from the pro-Union rallies held there before and during the Civil War. The 90-foot-high Dewey Monument in the center of the Square commemorates Admiral Dewey's victory over the Spanish at Manila Bay in 1898.

The informal pre-1942 park had its green lawns and mature trees and, in its early days, was crossed by worn dirt paths. Its current form, which is the result of the collaborative efforts of Timothy Pfleuger and the City Park Department (with $100,000 from the Union Square Garage Corporation) is more formal and harder-edged, but perhaps more suitable for a heavily used mid-city park. Although built on a concrete roof, the roof warps to suggest the contours of a natural landscape, and the ample planting of lawns, hedges, and palm trees sustains the lush image of a park.

In the relationship of the scale of the park to the scale of the solid walls of buildings on the streets around it, this is a superb urban space, enclosed by buildings large enough to give it definition but not so large as to block out the sun or overwhelm the Square in size. In their texture, articulation, materials, and colors, the buildings around the Square, dominated by the St. Francis Hotel, give it a richness and character which are inseparable from the quality of the Square itself. In its parts, Union Square contains a number of examples of an urban-oriented architecture which saw as its fundamental aesthetic mission a visual enhancement of the whole. After the St. Francis, the most important of these architectural elements are the Fitzhugh Building (364–384 Post), Bullock and Jones (340 Post), the Fredericks Building (278–298 Post), the City of Paris (199 Geary), and the Elkan Gunst Building (301 Geary). Sadly, the Fitzhugh Building is being replaced by a bland modern structure, and the City of Paris will probably also be demolished (for an elegant modern building, but one which nonetheless fails to understand its contextual responsibilities and how to satisfy them). Added to the grossly insensitive Macy's facades on the south side of the Square, and other modern buildings of the last 30 years which have altered its character, these additional changes threaten to finally transform Union Square into a rather ordinary place.

NOT RATED

PRIVATE AND PUBLIC PLAZAS/MARKET STREET

In the years since World War II the tremendous growth in highrise buildings downtown has created a corresponding demand for open space. This open space has been provided largely in the form of private "plazas" accompanying new highrises, and in the public "plazas" along the new Market Street. During the same years a powerful vision of a new kind of city has pervaded most large-scale planning and architectural efforts in American cities. The vision is best expressed in Le Corbusier's Voisin Plan of 1925, in which a vast part of the historic center of Paris was to be cleared, and sleek glass and steel towers surrounded by parkland were to be established in its place. Such planning was predicated on the assumption that a city was, or could be, entirely subject to rational design, like a machine.

This vision has been the progenitor of most government-sponsored Redevelopment projects of the last 30 years, including the Western Addition clearance, Yerba Buena Center, and Embarcadero and Golden Gateway Centers in San Francisco. Where clearance at such a scale as these projects required was not feasible, or for other reasons was not attempted, this vision of a new city and the "tower-in-the-park" skyscraper has been just as powerful as an ideal of architects and a goal of public planners.

In San Francisco, apart from the Redevelopment Areas, this vision has been realized in limited form in the many private plazas that surround modern highrises, and, to some extent, in the execution of the public Market Street Beautification Project.

From the 1959 construction of the Crown Zellerbach and Bethlehem Steel Buildings until very recently, this new image held sway among private developments in downtown San Francisco, reaching a peak between the years 1969-1973. Encouraged by planning and zoning policies, the historic cohesiveness of the traditional city began to be eaten away. Although some of the resultant new plazas have been successful for various reasons—as generators of street life, as places with dramatic views, as needed open space in an increasingly dense urban core, or even simply as beautiful places—their cumulative effect, particularly along lower California and Market Streets, has been monotony at a monumental scale. Intended to be open and sunny pockets of refuge in a dense city, the new plazas have all too often been lifeless, windy, cold, and shaded areas of pavement with sparse and uncomfortable furniture. They have been too much

Standard Oil Plaza.

the products of inflexible codes and abstract designing, and too little responses to the real, long-term needs of the city.

Even the better of these places, such as the Crocker Plaza at the foot of the Aetna Life Building (corner of Market and Post), suffer from a fundamental misconception about the nature of the city. Potentially successful when considered in isolation, these towers and plazas are rarely able to respond to the totality of their environments. The Crocker Plaza, for example, can attract activity to it, but the whole complex of which it is a part does not relate back to the city in a supportive manner. The siting of the tower breaks the continuous wall of buildings on Market Street, and its design is intended to be seen from a distance and fails to relate to its surroundings at the lower levels most visible from Market Street.

The plazas of the Market Street Beautification Project, although stylistically similar, have been somewhat more successful than the private plazas for the simple reason that they are not necessarily associated with new office towers and most have not been carved out of the existing city. The best of these, the Mechanic's Monument Plaza at Battery and Market, with its variable paving, ample sunlight, comfortable seating, and superb focal statuary, situated at the foot of the old Postal Telegraph Building, has the very real feeling of being surrounded by the city and of being a part of it.

Where the Market Street Beautification Project has fallen short is in the clearance mentality it shared with redevelopment-area planning and the tower-in-the-park architecture. It did incorporate the very fine and very important Path-of-Gold streetlights. But, like those other projects, it generally followed a vision of a new and rational city with a monolithic design scheme. For example, it insisted on a single graphically pleasing but uncomfortable street furniture design; a modern fountain at United Nations Plaza that relates to Market Street but not to the Civic Center; and a single kind of paving that covered everything in its path, including the several fine terrazzo sidewalk patterns of the 1930s.

As the shortcomings of these efforts have become widely apparent, different types of pedestrian-level amenities have begun to be incorporated in new highrise projects. One example is the large enclosed shopping atrium at the base of the new towers at 1 Market Plaza. The current large new crop of highrises hopefully will bring a variety of other solutions.

45 Fremont Street
rear
Stephen Bechtel Plaza
Skidmore, Owings, and Merrill
1977

NOT RATED

425 Market Street
Metropolitan Plaza
Skidmore, Owings, and Merrill
1973

Usually in the shade.

NOT RATED

525 Market Street
Tishman Building Plaza
Lawrence Halprin & Associates
1973

Sunlit and important as a pass-through to Ecker and Stevenson Streets.

NOT RATED

555-575 Market Street
Standard Oil Plaza
Theodore Osmundson and John Staley
1975

A very pretty garden, like a picture to look at. It was fenced off after being repeatedly vandalized.

NOT RATED

600 Market Street
gore of Market and Post at Montgomery
Crocker Plaza
Peter Walker
1969

One of the most heavily used of the modern plazas.

NOT RATED

345 Stockton Street
Hyatt Hotel Plaza
Skidmore, Owings, and Merrill
1972

A sheltered but frequently sunlit open space which is carefully sited behind a small triangular pavilion in order to maintain the hard definition of Union Square. Its diagonal paths and changes of level provide richness of texture and diversity of movement and its fountain by Ruth Asawa provides a cheerful focal point. One of the best modern plazas in San Francisco, and one of the few which is properly cognizant of its role in the total fabric of its area.

NOT RATED

535 Washington Street
Transamerica Redwood Park
Tom Galli
1971

A very pretty and well-used, forested park.

NOT RATED

Market Street

Public Plazas and Parks

Market Street from the Embarcadero to the Central Freeway
Market Street Beautification Project
Mario Ciampi, Lawrence Halprin and Associates, John Carl Warnecke and Associates
1971-1978

The result of a 24.5 million dollar bond issue approved by the voters in 1968. The trees and restored streetlights are very fine. The unified image expressed in the brick paving and consistently designed street furniture has been at the expense of the street's ability to respond to particular conditions along the way. Maintenance of the new street and its plazas has been poor.

The Market Street Beautification Project includes the following plazas:

- **Robert Frost Plaza**
  foot of California at Market
  1978

Designed by the City after the original joint venture plan, which called for relocation of the cable car tracks, was found to be too expensive and scrapped.

- **Mechanic's Plaza**
  gore of Battery and Market

- **Annie Plaza**
  foot of Annie Street at Market

The City and the Palace Hotel were unable to get together on a cooperative plan for landscaping all the space between the Palace Hotel and the Monadnock Building, hence the standard city sidewalk by the Palace.

- **Hallidie Plaza**
  foot of Powell and Eddy Streets

- **Powell Mall**
  first block of Powell

An extension of Hallidie Plaza.

- **United Nations Plaza**
  first blocks of Fulton and Leavenworth

The modern fountain, the hard edges of the Plaza's landscaping, and the graceless granite block lampposts are all totally out of character with the Civic Center. Moreover, the Plaza's overall planning, by an expensive and unnecessary process, has built into the Civic Center a situation which is likely to further erode its character, either by long remaining vacant or by leading to the demolition of two important structures.

The problems began with the shape of the plaza, which was long ago designed not merely to fill the available publicly owned street spaces, but which lopped off the southern edges of several privately owned parcels on Market Street as well. The parcels had to be bought, the buildings on them demolished, and the resulting useless L-shaped property that was left resold to the private sector. The result is that a piece of land which is extremely important to the definition and character of the plaza and the Civic Center is unlikely ever to be built upon unless it is assembled with the parcels at 79 and 83-91 McAllister for a single larger building. Those parcels are occupied by the Seventh and McAllister Building of 1906, and the Methodist Book Concern by Meyers and Ward of 1907, both handsome and historically important structures. Along with 1256 Market, they are all that is left of the pre-Civic-Center City Hall Avenue, occupying the two ends of that street which once fronted on the pre-fire City Hall.

It is interesting to note that this was precisely the kind of situation which the original planners of the Civic Center tried hard to avoid. In fact, it was largely because such conflicts were not present that the Civic Center was planned where it is, rather than at Van Ness and Market as proposed in the Burnham Plan.

NOT RATED

Blocks bound by Clay, Washington, Drumm, and Davis
Justin Herman Park
Mario Ciampi, Lawrence Halprin and Associates, John Bolles
1971

A lightly-used park that may find more activity as the waterfront (hopefully) revives, and as additional Golden Gateway Center housing (now under construction) is completed. Its brutally functional freeway ramps and delightful space frame gazebo are its major built features. Designed as part of the Golden Gateway Redevelopment Project.

NOT RATED

Foot of Market Street
Justin Herman Plaza
Mario Ciampi, Lawrence Halprin and Associates, John Bolles
1971

A bland plaza built as part of the Golden Gateway Redevelopment Project. The plaza is at its best when it is full of street artists. It is circumscribed by the Embarcadero Freeway. The controversial Vaillancourt Fountain is in one corner.

NOT RATED

CIVIC ART: OUTDOOR FOUNTAINS AND LARGE STATUARY

Large-scale outdoor civic art in downtown San Francisco is of a very high caliber, but there is surprisingly little for so large and important an area and one with so many fine sites. The pieces that exist represent every major period and type of patronage including late 19th-century private donations, public subscriptions, private corporate gifts, and government-sponsored works. Listed below are the fountains and large statues which are of greatest prominence on the streets, plazas, and squares of the downtown area. Works which are indoors or are strictly architectural embellishments are treated along with their buildings.

Under federal requirements for government-sponsored projects which set aside 1% of a total project cost for artwork, the Golden Gateway and Embarcadero Centers together have as many major pieces as the rest of the downtown area combined. However, because the relationship of that work to the character of the streets of the downtown area is very different from the kinds of civic art being talked about here, because it is relatively recent, because it is amply documented in other sources, and because the focus of this project is on older buildings and cultural resources, it seemed unnecessary to list these works again here.

For a much more complete listing of artwork downtown and in San Francisco as a whole, see the Art Commission's *A Survey of Art Work in the City and County of San Francisco* (1975.)

Juan Bautista de Anza
Justin Herman Plaza
Julian Martinez
1967

The discoverer of San Francisco Bay on horseback. Given to the City by the Governor of the State of Sonora, Mexico.

NOT RATED

Dewey Monument
Union Square
Robert Aitken, sculptor; Newton Tharp, architect
1901 (placed 1902)

Made in 1901, placed in 1902, and dedicated by Theodore Roosevelt in 1903, commemorating Admiral George Dewey's victory over the Spanish at Manila Bay in 1898. It consists of a bronze "Victory" on a giant granite Corinthian column. This monument performs a major function as a focal point in Union Square. Built by public subscription.

A

Earth's Fruitfulness and Man's Inventive Genius
301 Pine Street
Pacific Coast Stock Exchange
Ralph Stackpole
1931-1932

A pair of monumental granite sculptural groups, flanking the colonnade of the Stock Exchange Building. They were designed specifically for their site as part of one of the finest integrated ensembles of art and architecture in the city. Their scale and design has a presence which stands up well in an area of much larger buildings. They are beautifully carved and deeply expressive works.

A

Carlos III, King of Spain
Justin Herman Plaza
Federico Collau
1976

NOT RATED

Fountain
Crown Zellerbach Plaza
David Tolerton
1967

NOT RATED

Lotta's Fountain
**intersection of Kearny and Geary
   at Market**
Wyneken and Townsend
1875

One of the city's oldest and best known monuments. It was originally a gift to the City by Lotta Crabtree, a famous 19th-century entertainer who considered San Francisco her home. Among the numerous memorable events which have occurred here was a performance by the opera star Luisa Tetrazzini on Christmas Eve 1910, attended by many thousands of people. A plaque at the base by Haig Patigian commemorates the event. In 1915 the shaft of the cast-iron column was lengthened by eight feet to correspond more sympathetically to the height of the new streetlights on Market.

A   NR; CL

Mechanic's Monument
Mechanic's Plaza
gore of Battery and Market at Bush
**Douglas Tilden, sculptor; Willis Polk,
   architect**
1894 (placed 1895)

One of the city's finest pieces of heroic public statuary, designed by one of its best sculptors, with Willis Polk as architect of the granite base. It consists of a group of five men trying to punch a metal plate in a typically well-modeled and energetic composition by the artist. It was a gift to the City by James Mervyn Donahue in memory of his father, Peter Donahue, founder of the city's first iron foundry, street railway, and gas company. It is the focal point of the best of the Market Street plazas.

A

Native Sons Monument
foot of Post at Montgomery and Market
Douglas Tilden
1897 (placed 1977)

A granite column on a pedestal, supporting a bronze angel on top and an armed miner with an American flag at the base. This is another of several superb pieces of civic art by Douglas Tilden. It is a major pedestrian focal point at a prime downtown intersection. From 1897 to 1948, it stood at the intersection of Mason and Turk Streets. It stood in Redwood Memorial Grove in Golden Gate Park from 1948 until 1977 when it was moved to its present location as part of the Market Street Beautification Project.

A

San Francisco Fountain
345 Stockton Street
Hyatt Hotel Plaza
Ruth Asawa
1973

A very popular work which shows San Francisco as a panorama of people, buildings and activities.

NOT RATED

Sun Yat-Sen
St. Mary's Square
Beniamino Bufano
1937 (placed 1938)

The only downtown example of this important local sculptor's art, and a centerpiece of St. Mary's Square. It was commissioned by the Northern California Art Project, W.P.A. The statue is of stainless steel on a granite base with rose granite hands and head. The base bears the caption, "Father of the Chinese Republic and First President (1921-1922)—Champion of Democracy—Proponent of Peace and Friendship among Nations."

A

Transcendence
A. P. Giannini Plaza
Masayuki Nagare
1967 (placed 1969)

NOT RATED

United Nations Fountain
United Nations Plaza
Mario Ciampi, Lawrence Halprin and
Associates, John Carl Warnecke, and
Associates
1977

Totally out of character with its surroundings.

NOT RATED

Vaillancourt Fountain
Justin Herman Plaza
Armand Vaillancourt
1971

NOT RATED

STREETLIGHTS

While the City Beautiful Movement is typically thought of as a movement for "beautifica-tion," some of its more lasting achievements were practical as well, representing the most progressive thinking of the day about urban health, safety, and efficiency. Among the most important and widespread of these practical achievements was the placing of streetlights. Streetlights had, of course, existed before, but they became far more common as well as more "beautified" under the City Beautiful Movement. In addition, with improvements in electric lighting, there was greater attention paid to the effects of the light source, materials, and design on illumination of streets.

In San Francisco, improvements in the city's street lighting were called for by the Burnham Plan in 1905, and most of the great variety of ornamental streetlights in down-town San Francisco today were placed between that time and the first World War. After the second World War, many of the older streetlights were replaced by more efficient ones of modern design. Others have apparently been moved around so that some streets and areas have a mixture of types.

Ornamental standards with three lights
Path of Gold
Market Street
Willis Polk, architect; Arthur Putnam and
 Leo Lentelli, sculptors
1908, 1917

The history of the Path-of-Gold streetlights began in 1908 when ornamental standards with single lights were designed for United Railroads of San Francisco by D. H. Burnham and Co. Willis Polk was the architect-in-charge and Arthur Putnam designed the sculptural relief work. Fol-lowing the widely noted success of the electric lighting at the Panama-Pacific International Ex-position, the designer of the illumination system there, Walter D'Arcy Ryan, was hired to design an illumination system for Market Street. In 1917, following his recommendations for spacing, height, and arrangement, 143 of the existing 1908 streetlights were redesigned with three lights each by Willis Polk, Arthur Putnam, and Leo Lentelli. Putnam designed the bas-relief panels at the bases of the streetlights, entitled "The Winning of the West," and depicting ani-mals, Indians, and pioneers moving west.

These streetlights were called the "Path of Gold" because of their imitation bronze color-ing and gold glass (and not because of their light which was described as "warm white"). The system was financed and maintained by a

complicated arrangement involving the Down-town Merchants' Association, the Board of Har-bor Commissioners, the Pacific Gas and Electric Co., the City, United Railroads, and other pri-vate property owners. In the 1960s these street-lights were restored as part of the Market Street Beautification project.

A

Ornamental standards with two lights
Eddy, Ellis, Geary, Grant, Kearny, Mason,
 O'Farrell, Post, Powell, Stockton, and
 Sutter Streets
Willis Polk, architect; Arthur Putnam and
 Leo Lentelli, sculptors
1908, 1917

Although the history of these streetlights is not entirely certain, their current resemblance to the Path-of-Gold streetlights and their initial de-sign by Willis Polk of D. H. Burnham and Co. for United Railroads suggests that they also were remodeled in 1917 by Polk, Putnam, and Lentelli. They are shorter than the Path-of-Gold street-lights, they have only two lights rather than three, and their ornamentation is strictly deco-rative rather than representational. In silhouette, composition, and quality of modeling, casting, and materials, however, they are cousins of the Path-of-Gold streetlights.

A

241

Ornamental standards with two lights
Embarcadero type
The Embarcadero
designer unknown
1917

Along with the Path-of-Gold streetlights and those in Union Square and the Civic Center, these were designed according to a scheme for illumination by Walter D'Arcy Ryan following the inspiration of electric lighting for the Panama-Pacific International Exposition. Because they were designed along the Embarcadero, they were under the jurisdiction of the State Board of Harbor Commissioners which normally undertook its own design work. These resemble the Path-of-Gold streetlights in composition but not in detail. They are nevertheless compatible. They originally met the Path of Gold at the streetcar turnaround in front of the Ferry Building, but are now separated by the Embarcadero Freeway.

A

Simple standards with single lights
Union Square
designer unknown
1917

Like the Path-of-Gold streetlights and those along the Embarcadero, these were designed following the example of the Panama Pacific International Exposition. The illumination system was by Walter D'Arcy Ryan, but the designer of the standards themselves is unknown. Because they were restricted to Union Square and the Civic Center and served no double functions as trolley poles, they were probably designed by the City Architect's Office. Much simpler than the other designs, they are nevertheless very elegant, and suitable to their parklike settings.

B

Ornamental standards with single lights
St. Francis Hotel type
Powell and Post Streets
design attributed to Bliss and Faville
ca. 1910

Unusual and very fine streetlights around the St. Francis Hotel whose design is tentatively attributed to Bliss and Faville on the basis of their having designed the St. Francis, and on the resemblance of these streetlights to others designed by Bliss and Faville for Geary Street in 1908 (no longer there). The standards consist of fluted columns on pedestals with protruding disks beneath the capitals. The present lights are not original but they are appropriate to their setting.

A

Simple standards with cantilevered lamps
Battery, Front, Kearny, Main, McAllister,
Montgomery, New Montgomery,
Sacramento, Sansome, Stockton,
Sutter, Third, Fifth, Seventh, and
Eighth Streets
designer unknown
ca. 1920

An unassertive design for one of the downtown area's most common streetlight types. Although it appears in a few variations, the most common has a tapered iron shaft with concave facets, and a pointed top. The arching cantilevered lamp is always the same.

C

Simple standards with hanging lamps
Battery, Bush, Geary, Hyde, Mason,
Mission, Montgomery, Post, Sansome,
Taylor, Third, and Fourth Streets
designer unknown
ca. 1920

A common downtown area streetlight type in two principal variations: more commonly with a single hanging lamp, but also with two hanging lamps.

B

Miscellaneous single-light standards
Battery, Grant, and Mason Streets
designers unknown
ca. 1906-1920

While most downtown area streetlights are part of a consistent pattern of design, these vary considerably and appear to be individually brought from other areas.

C

Simple bracketed lamps
on trolley poles
Sansome and Sacramento Streets
designer unknown
ca. 1920

This type appears only twice downtown but is common over large areas of northern California and may have been a standard type that could be ordered from catalogs.

C

Ornamental cantilevered lamps
on trolley poles
Kearny, McAllister, Sacramento, Stockton, and Sutter Streets
designer unknown
ca. 1917

Lamps in the same style as those on Market, designed to attach easily to unornamented trolley poles. These are scattered thinly throughout the downtown area.

B

CLOCKS

Although the City Beautiful Movement was largely financed by public funds, and in fact derives some importance from being an early example of government involvement in American planning, one of its goals was to inspire complementary private "beautification." The private placement of ornamental clocks on public sidewalks and cantilevered from privately owned buildings in prominent locations was a conspicuous example of the City Beautiful Movement at work in the private sector. More recently placed clocks along Market Street have been less successful.

260 California Street
NE corner Battery
Newhall Building Clocks
designer unknown
ca. 1925 (placed 1960)

Two very fine clocks on each face of the corner pier of the Newhall Building. It is not known who designed them, but their abstracted Gothic quality tends to place them in the mid 1920s.

B

100 Geary Street
NW corner Grant
Granat Brothers Clock
designer unknown
ca. 1909

A very fine bronzed-iron and stained-glass clock, treated as a pedimented pedestal with a glass dome, and cantilevered from the Granat Brothers Building at a prominent retail-area corner. Each of the pedestal's four sides consists of two panels: a lower clockface, and an upper "Granat Bros." sign in stained glass.

A

623-631 Market Street
SE corner Market and New Montgomery
Bank of America Clock
originally Metropolis Trust and Savings
  Bank Clock
designer unknown
ca. 1907

A fine cantilevered clock at a prominent intersection which has been slightly altered with the "Bank of America" sign underneath. The clock itself is rectangular with four faces and a parapet of anthemions. The frame is iron and the faces are decorative metal and glass.

B

856 Market Street
Albert S. Samuels Clock
Albert S. Samuels and Joseph Mayer,
  designers and builders
1915

The largest, best known, and most prominently located of the city's clocks. It was originally located in front of the Lincoln Building across Market, but was moved to its present location in 1943 when Samuels Jewelry moved. The clock is in three parts, a pedestal with glass panels that reveal the clock's mechanism, a fluted Corinthian column, and a giant spherical head with four clockfaces. It is a major adornment on revitalized Market Street.

A   CL

278 Post Street
next to the Fredericks Building
Clock
designer unknown
ca. 1910

An unfortunately altered street clock with an original iron pedestal and fluted column. Its length has been extended with a thin, graceless column and crowned by a modern clockface.

C

201 Sansome Street
First American Title Insurance
  Companies' Clock
designer unknown
ca. 1907

An iron street clock with a graceful fluted Ionic column crowned by a round clockface and florid trim.

B

MISCELLANEOUS STREET AND PARK FURNITURE

California Theater Plaque
444 Bush Street
Jacques Schnier
1932

A bronze plaque on the site of the old California Theater, one of San Francisco's most important 19th-century cultural institutions. The theater was built by William C. Ralston in 1869. The plaque was commissioned by the Commonwealth Club and the Pacific Telephone Company.

C

Robert Frost Medallion
Robert Frost Plaza
foot of California
Francis Sedgewick
1964 (placed 1978)

NOT RATED

Fort Gunnybags Plaque
near 119 Sacramento Street
between Davis and Front
designer unknown
1903

An early and unusual commemorative plaque, at the site of the headquarters of one of the Gold-Rush era Vigilance Committees.

B

Gazebo
Justin Herman Park
Mario Ciampi, Lawrence Halprin and Associates, John Bolles
ca. 1974

NOT RATED

Hitching Post
California Street near Leidesdorff
designer unknown
ca. 1900

A rare surviving hitching post from pre-fire days, designed like a squat column with a base, paneled shaft, and peaked roof with a finial. Rings for tying up horses protrude from the mouths of lions.

A

Mail box, detail.

Mail Box
Grant Avenue near Market
designer unknown
ca. 1910

An iron mail box with classically derived moldings and handsome lettering. It rests on voluted feet and is crowned by a cornice. It may have been designed for the old Union Trust Co. (now a branch of the Wells Fargo Bank at 744 Market) by Clinton Day. It is a unique example of private embellishment of the streets during the City Beautiful Movement.

A

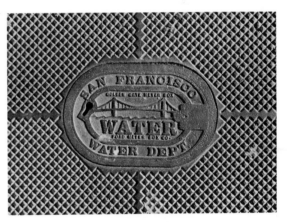

Manhole Covers/Utility Plates
various anonymous designers

Downtown San Francisco's numerous manhole covers and utility plates contain a wealth of handsome, anonymous designs, many of them dating back 50 years or more. Such objects are often simply labeled with the name of the manufacturer or the utility they serve, but frequently contain geometric or representational designs as well. Apart from their intrinsic interest, they contribute to the texture, variety, and character of the downtown area.

NOT RATED

Muni Bus Flower Stand
Jones Street
NE corner McAllister
designer unknown
ca. 1960

A whimsical design for a flower stand like a small trolley bus, complete with tires, windshield wipers, appropriate graphics, and trolley-wire connectors.

NOT RATED

Shoreline Markers
Market and First; Battery, Market, and Bush
designer unknown
1921

Three handsome bronze plaques placed in the sidewalk by the Native Sons of the Golden West, marking the old shoreline of Yerba Buena Cove.

B

CIVIL ENGINEERING

BART
under Market Street
Parsons-Brinkerhoff-Tudor-Bechtel
1965-1973

Downtown San Francisco stations were designed by different architects: Tallie B. Maule and Hertzka and Knowles designed the Embarcadero Station; Skidmore, Owings, and Merrill designed the Montgomery and Powell Street Stations; and Reid and Tarics designed the Civic Center Station.

NOT RATED

Cable Cars
Powell and California Streets
Andrew S. Hallidie, inventor
1873

The last remnant of America's first cable car system passes through downtown San Francisco. Invented here by Andrew S. Hallidie, they spread across the country in the 1870s and were part of one of the major episodes in the development of urban transportation in the United States. They were gradually replaced after the 1880s by electric streetcars, until only three lines still run in San Francisco.

A   NR

Embarcadero Freeway
The Embarcadero
California Division of Highways
1959

NOT RATED

The Embarcadero
The Seawall
T. J. Arnold for the State Board of
Harbor Commissioners
1872 (original design)

Modifications to the design resulted in early use of reinforced concrete.

NOT RATED   NRp

Stockton Street Tunnel
Bush to Sacramento
Michael O'Shaughnessy
1914

An example of a municipal improvement designed to facilitate movement to the Panama-Pacific International Exposition by City Engineer Michael O'Shaughnessy. The tunnel entrances, like triumphal arches, are excellent examples of the "beautification" of utilitarian works during the City Beautiful Movement. The southern entrance has been mutilated by an exit ramp from the Stockton-Sutter Garage.

A

Streetcars
Market Street

Like the cable car system, San Francisco's streetcar lines are representative of one of the great ages of urban transportation in the United States. One of the few systems to last into the 1970s, San Francisco's streetcars will shortly go underground downtown, and the cars themselves will be replaced by newer models. At the high point of the system at the end of World War II, San Francisco had one of the best public transportation systems anywhere. More than that, the routes of the system and the very nature of streetcar transportation were fundamental to the form and density of downtown San Francisco in the days before the automobile and BART.

A

Historic Districts

1. Powell Street Corridor
2. Retail-Shopping District
3. Kearny Street District
4. Financial District

5. Commercial-Upper Montgomery Street District
6. New Montgomery and Market Street District
7. Emporium Market Street Block
8. Market Street Loft/Theater District

HISTORIC DISTRICTS

Under the criteria of the National Register of Historic Places, there are eight areas in downtown San Francisco which appear to be eligible for listing as National Register Historic Districts, and four groups of buildings which appear to be eligible for listing as National Register Thematic Districts. Eligibility is established in relation to the published criteria of the National Register, but final determinations are made by the Secretary of the Interior following the recommendations of the State Historical Resources Commission.

A Historic District is a group of contiguous buildings or sites which meet the criteria of the National Register. It is not necessary that each building in a district be individually eligible, or that every building be a positive contributor, but that collectively they represent a unified ensemble that expresses a coherent image of a period in the history of a place or its architecture.

A Thematic District is a group of buildings or other cultural resources in a city or other defined area that meet the criteria of the National Register, but which are not necessarily on contiguous sites, and which represent a unified theme. For example, monumental banks in downtown San Francisco constitute a group of buildings that are not contiguous but which collectively contribute to the distinctive architecture and historic character of downtown San Francisco.

Listing as a Historic or Thematic District entails the same provisions and restrictions as individual listing on the National Register. Thus, similarly, Districts are afforded a degree of protection from federally licensed or funded projects that impinge on their integrity. More importantly, in downtown San Francisco, many buildings in Districts are subject to the provisions of the Tax Reform Act of 1976, and may be eligible for federal grants and loans for rehabilitation. Thus there are significant economic incentives to preservation of buildings in Districts.

Historic and Thematic District nominations have the advantage of being easier and quicker to prepare than individual nominations of the same number of buildings within a district. Thus, they are the most efficient manner in which a large number of properties might be listed and through which the property owners could take advantage of the Tax Reform Act.

Powell Street Corridor
(District 1)

An architecturally cohesive District that runs up Powell Street from Market to Bush, and includes Union Square and parts of cross blocks on Ellis, O'Farrell, Geary and Sutter. The District is in two parts, divided by Geary Street but linked historically and visually by the Powell Street cable car. The parts are further unified by a common view down Powell to the Lincoln Building and by the slope of the hill through the length of the District. The relative uniformity of the styles and heights of the buildings below Union Square on the lowest land, and the relative diversity of the same features above Union Square where the hill climbs more steeply, produce a visually satisfying streetscape.

The blocks below Geary Street are architecturally less distinctive but are unified by an exceptional harmony of materials and colors in the warm tones of brick facades above ground floor storefronts. Except for the remodeling of Omar Khayyams in 1933, and the continuous remodeling of ground floor storefronts, these blocks assumed their present appearance by 1910. A few of the ground floors are remarkable both for the quality of their designs and for simply having survived, notably Marquard's Little Cigar Store, Baron's Bar, the mural at the entrance to the Golden State Hotel, and the ship's hull at Bernstein's Fish Grotto. These blocks developed with a mixture of residential and office spaces above commercial ground levels, a rich combination of uses that has contributed to a vital street life.

Above Geary Street, there are several architecturally outstanding and otherwise more prominent buildings which at the same time remain part of a cohesive whole. The St. Francis Hotel is the focal point of the District and of Union Square. As the oldest building on the street it is the earliest example of the texture and rhythm that prevails elsewhere. Broken into bays, it retains the quality of the rhythm produced by several smaller buildings on similarly sized lots, yet as part of a unified composition it is simultaneously imposing enough to dominate Union Square. The Chancellor Hotel and the Sir Francis Drake, especially the latter, punctuate the otherwise roughly uniform height of the street, adding elements of variety within the fabric of color and materials of the surroundings.

At Sutter Street the District includes a wall of contiguous structures on the south side of Sutter, and 450 Sutter on the north side. The corridor culminates in a small group of architecturally distinguished buildings just below Bush including the old Elks Building, the old Frank Daroux-Tessie Wall house, and the Family Club.

The only significant intrusions in an otherwise cohesive District are the Holiday Inn at Sutter, and the new Saks store that will replace the Fitzhugh Building at Post on Union Square. The District meets the Emporium Market Street Block (District 7) at its south end and the Retail Shopping District (District 2) at the east side of Union Square.

Retail-Shopping District (District 2)

The finest of San Francisco's National Register Districts in the quality of its architecture and in the collective realization of the goals of the City Beautiful Movement. Centered on Grant and Sutter Streets, the District also includes blocks on Stockton, Kearny, Post, Geary, and Market Streets and generally occupies the area bound by Union Square and the financial district, Market Street, and Chinatown. It has been the principal shopping district of the city in its present form since the fire, and had begun to develop as such in the last decades of the 19th century.

The qualities of the District are best summed up along Grant Avenue from Market to Bush. This area is discussed in detail in the Reconstruction section of the Urban and Architectural Development essay in this volume. Briefly, it consists of an architecture, developed from the teachings of the Ecole des Beaux-Arts in Paris, which serves both symbolic and practical functions that are unusually well integrated. The basic building of this district consists of a glass commercial base of one or two stories and an upper section of offices, treated in a historicist imagery in brick, terra cotta, or, occasionally, stone. Thus, the glass commercial bases can change constantly with fashions, while the historicist upper levels remain as lasting images of the permanence of the city.

Although built by different architects and clients, Grant Avenue is also a remarkable example of the harmonious city that was a goal of the City Beautiful Movement. Its simultaneous unity and vitality is the result of a shared vision of architecture and the city which prevailed in the post-fire years when Grant Avenue took shape. When Grant had almost completely assumed its present form in 1909, the *Architect and Engineer*

called it the greatest architectural street in the world.

Other streets in the District, all dating largely from the same brief period, are almost as fine, notably Sutter Street in the two blocks from Grant to Montgomery. The north side of Sutter from Kearny to Montgomery, including the Hallidie Building, is one of the finest and most important short stretches of architecture in downtown San Francisco, functioning as not only a superb streetscape and as the setting for the Hallidie Building, but as a capsule history of the architecture of the area.

Still other notable groups are Maiden Lane; the two blocks of Post between Kearny and Stockton, with such urbanistically superior buildings as the Cordes Building, 117–129 Post, Gumps, and the Fredericks Building; Geary Street between Grant and Stockton with the City of Paris and the Marion, Simon, Sacks, and Whittell Buildings, and the consistent green detailing following the lead of the City of Paris; the blocks of Kearny above Market and below Sutter; and the intersections of Geary and Kearny with Market, with the architectural excellence of the former and the historical importance of the latter.

Less architecturally outstanding areas, such as the east side of Stockton between Geary and Post, facing Union Square, are equally important for the supportive setting they provide the better groups.

The Retail-Shopping District is unique among districts of American cities in its architectural cohesiveness, its urban vitality, and its freedom from visually destructive intrusions. Apart from a few scattered but relatively insignificant remodelings, the only weak spot in the District is at the corner of Post and Kearny, with Hastings at the southwest corner and Bonds at the northwest corner.

The District abuts the Powell Street District (District 1) at Union Square, the Kearny Street District (District 3) above Sutter, and the Market and New Montgomery Street District (District 6) at Market and Kearny.

Kearny Street District (District 3)

One of the few areas in downtown San Francisco which is still at a scale that prevailed in the years before the earthquake and fire. This District stretches along two blocks of Kearny from just north of Sutter to Pine Street and is partially bound on the east and west by Belden Street, St. George Alley and Claude Lane, three alleys that limit the depth of the lots on Kearny, thus contributing to the small scale of the lots and the buildings on them.

The buildings in the District were almost all built between 1906 and 1908, and, with a few promi-

nent exceptions, are mostly of three to five stories and brick construction. The result is an area which is unified in height, scale, materials and style, which shares a common history of growth, and which represents an earlier time by virtue of the physical attributes of its buildings and the layout of its streets and alleys.

The architecture of the district is ordinary for most of the individual buildings but as a group is a good illustration of one of the fundamental tenets of the establishment of historic districts—that the whole is greater than the sum of its parts. In this case the whole presents a streetscape that recalls an era most of whose remains were destroyed in 1906.

Several remodelings and missing cornices detract from the character and integrity of this District. Because its essential characteristics are questions of scale, however, these alterations would not appear to eliminate the area from eligibility for the National Register. The remodeled buildings should be considered primarily "sites of opportunity" (see Methodology section).

The Kearny Street District is contiguous with the Kearny Street section of the Retail-Shopping District (District 2) to the south.

Financial District (District 4)

In contrast to most of the other potential National Register Historic Districts, the Financial District is dominated in character by buildings from the 1920s. Also in contrast to other Districts, it contains a greater diversity of buildings of different sizes, styles, and periods, and it includes more recent buildings, most of which are compatible with the historic character of their surroundings. Nevertheless, despite this diversity, it is characterized by its cohesiveness and in this way is a testament to the success of the attitudes of the architects of the late 19th and early 20th centuries toward the city. From the Romanesque Mills Building of 1891 to the Renaissance-ornamented Merchants Exchange of 1903 to the slightly Gothic Russ Building of 1927, everything contributes to the underlying harmony of the area. Regardless of size or ornamentation, there is a similarity of color, composition, and treatment of the ground level that is part of a single evolutionary development of architecture in the area. Perhaps most important for this quality of cohesiveness is the repetition of the brick facade first used on the Merchants Exchange and later picked up throughout the District on buildings including the Financial Center, Balfour, and California Commercial Union Buildings, and most of the block of Pine between Montgomery and Sansome.

The Financial District includes parts of California, Pine, Bush, Sutter, and Market Streets, and also stretches of Battery, Sansome, and Montgomery. Its finest stretches are along California, Montgomery, and Bush, and its most cohesive is the block of Pine between Montgomery and Sansome. The north side of Bush from the Postal Telegraph Building at Battery to the Russ Building at Montgomery is the largest contiguous group of A-buildings in the survey area.

Unlike the other Districts, the Financial District is as distinguished from afar by its skyline as from the street. The Russ, Shell, Mills Tower, Standard Oil, and other buildings, although now partially obscured by new construction, are still visible and were long major elements in San Francisco's picturesque and widely known skyline.

Despite the changing nature of the area, many of the Financial District's oldest landmarks still recall the pre-fire era. The configuration of the District as a whole is large, but of the same general character as the city's financial area as long ago as the 1860s. The District thus also represents a continuity of development that is unusual in American cities. As it has been since the reconstruction of the city after the fire, the area is the unchanging heart of the city's financial district and thus representative of the traditional basis of its economy.

Commercial-Upper Montgomery Street District
(District 5)

A small, small-scaled and extremely important District for its multiple historic associations, its architecture, and its environmental value. The District encompasses three-quarters of the block bound by Montgomery, Clay, Sansome, and Sacramento Streets, and an additional half block south of the main area on Montgomery.

The larger block is crossed by Commercial and Leidesdorff Streets, breaking it into small blocks, each divided into small parcels. Commercial Street is the principal east-west spine of the District, and Montgomery Street is the major north-south street. Each of these two axes represents an aspect of the early historical development of the city. Although the single block of Commercial Street in this District is part of a much larger stretch of Commercial that runs down the hill from Chinatown (most of which is outside the survey area and therefore not considered here), its meeting with Montgomery Street is well integrated and the two streets are part of one District in this area.

With its small-scaled, simply detailed brick buildings, Commercial Street is little changed in appearance from the 1850s when, only a half block from Portsmouth Square at its closest point, it was one of the principal business streets of the Gold-Rush city.

The east side of Montgomery Street from Commercial to the middle of the block between California and Sacramento Streets, with its several small, classically ornamented banks, recalls the location of the city's first financial district. More than most other American financial centers, San Francisco's was always small and compact and characterized by references to classical temples in its architecture. Indeed, these buildings have long been a fitting symbol of the city itself. No other city has so many of them, and nowhere else in San Francisco are they so concentrated.

The most distinguished examples of the District's architecture are several fine financial temples, most notably the old Borel Bank and Sutro Co.; the three power substations on Commercial, Leidesdorff, and Sacramento; and 554 and 564 Commercial Street.

The importance of this small District today is enhanced by the contrast in its scale and character with booming modern office buildings around it, and by the views it preserves down both Commercial and Leidesdorff Streets.

New Montgomery and Market Street District
(District 6)

A cohesive District of office buildings that is largely representative of the post-fire city but which also contains significant buildings from other periods. The District stretches the entire length of New Montgomery Street from Market to Howard, and encompasses the south side of Market from Second to Third.

New Montgomery Street was originally laid out and developed in the 1870s. In the decade before the fire the construction of the Sharon, Crossley, and Rialto Buildings added to the prestige of the street and to its function, like its name says, as a "new" Montgomery Street. Only the Rialto Building survived the fire, however, and new Sharon and Crossley Buildings were erected, along with the new Palace Hotel, by 1912. The character of the street today is largely that of the reconstructed city, highlighted since 1924 by the superb tower of the Pacific Telephone Co. Building. It is a cohesive, architecturally distinguished grouping, given texture in the variety of materials and ornamental treatments that clad its facades, and rhythm in the regular interruption of the street by alleys that regulate the size of parcels. The warm brick walls of the Palace Hotel and Sharon Buildings and the broad cornice of the Sharon set the stage in the first block for the rest of New Montgomery Street.

The blocks of this District along Market Street are tied to New Montgomery largely by the Palace Hotel whose immense brick walls curve around the corners and provide a continuity of texture. The south side of Market between Second and Third also includes the pre-fire Monadnock Building and the Hearst Building at the historic intersection of Third, Market, and Kearny, and the several small buildings framed by the old

Metropolis Trust and Santa Fe Buildings opposite the intersection of Post, Montgomery, and Market. All along the Market Street section of this District, it faces the Retail-Shopping District (District 2) and several fine individual buildings.

The only intrusions in this otherwise extremely cohesive District are a low parking garage at New Montgomery and Mission, a vacant lot at New Montgomery and Howard, and a couple of buildings with ground floors walled in for computer and telephone equipment on New Montgomery.

Emporium Market Street Block (District 7)

The south side of Market from Fourth Street to the old Hale Brothers Department Store west of Fifth, together with the north side of Market, much of which is included in the Powell Street Corridor (District 1), is one of the most impressive groupings of monumental buildings in downtown San Francisco.

Although only the Emporium Building (and Flood Building on the north—outside this District) survives from before the fire, the character of the area is similar to that of the pre-fire period in its size, scale, and monumental ornamentation dominated by the Emporium. The other buildings in the District (the Pacific Building, the Commercial Building, the Lincoln Building, and the Hale Brothers Department Store) are all from the reconstruction period, and they represent the coalescence of a major retail center in the area. The Emporium, Lincoln Building, and Hale Brothers all contained major department stores, and the Pacific Building was the center of the garment business.

The major alterations to the District are the many signs on the Lincoln Building, which detract from its value as the terminus of the view down Powell Street, and the loss of the very fine marquee on the Hale Brothers Building.

The District could conceivably be extended down Fifth Street to the Mint, a possibility that was not considered here, because Fifth Street is outside the survey area.

Market Street Loft/Theater District (District 8)

An imposing but unfortunately rundown District that includes three major elements: a group of loft structures on the south side of Market, a collection of theaters, and two fine intersections on the north side of Market. These elements frequently overlap.

The lofts and their several supportive structures, most notably the Wilson Building, the Hale Building, the Eastern Outfitting Co. Building, the Forrest Building, and the Ede Building, are distinguished by the simplicity of their skeletal facades. They are among the few downtown San Francisco buildings that reflect the early Modernists' ideals of straightforward structural and functional expressiveness. At the same time many of them are treated with unusually fine ornamentation. Sadly, two of the central buildings in this group, the Forrest Building, and its neighbor, the Sterling Building, were recently burned in a fire. The Forrest Building, by MacDonald and Applegarth, bears a striking resemblance to Frank Lloyd Wright's Luxfer Project. Hopefully their owners will take advantage of the Tax Reform Act and rehabilitate these very fine buildings which form a centerpiece to an important potential Historic District.

The many theaters in the District, most of which began as vaudeville theaters, include the Warfield and Golden Gate at the intersection of Taylor, Golden Gate, and Market. Both fine examples of the extravagant picture palaces of the 1920s, they serve also as excellent elements in a complex and grand intersection.

The other notable intersection, at Jones, McAllister, and Market, has as its centerpiece the superb Hibernia Bank of 1891, by Albert Pissis.

Intrusions in the area are chiefly in the form of inappropriate signs and remodelings, most of which could be easily reversed. The St. Francis Theater Building (formerly the Empress Theater), for example, was originally a beautifully light skeletal structure, like the lofts around it, with immense areas of glass framed in terra-cotta clad steel. The terra-cotta is mostly intact, and the glass areas could be restored. Another example is the David Hewes Building at Sixth and Market, a very fine skyscraper by the Reid Brothers which was covered with a new veneer about 1960. Except for the broad projecting cornice, the original facade is almost certainly intact underneath.

THEMATIC DISTRICTS

Clubs

While most American cities have many private clubs, and some, like New York, are noted for them, in no other city have private clubs played such an important social and historical role. In the late 19th and early 20th centuries, membership in the right San Francisco clubs was almost prerequisite to business, political, and social advancement.

In the years after the fire, a district of men's clubs grew up in the area northwest of Union Square, and a few years later a district of women's clubs grew up in the same general area. The more exclusive clubs erected very fine buildings by the best architects (most of whom were members), but even more open organizations like the YWCA built handsome buildings in the area. Although the clubs tended to locate in one area, many were spread out. The following list is only of those clubs in the primary areas.

465 California Street	Commercial Club (Merchant's Exchange Building)
465 California Street	Exchange Club (Merchant's Exchange Building)
450-460 Post Street	Elks Club
524 Post Street	Olympic Club
555 Post Street	Press Club of San Francisco (originally Union League Club)
421 Powell Street	old Argonaut Club (now United Airlines Building)
449-465 Powell Street	old Press Club (Doetz Building)
540 Powell Street	old Elks Club
545 Powell Street	Family Club
155 Sansome Street	Stock Exchange Club
6-26 Seventh Street	Odd Fellows Hall
218-222 Stockton Street	Town & Country Club (Robertson Building)
595 Sutter Street	Francisca Club
609 Sutter Street	Marine's Memorial Club Building
620 Sutter Street	YWCA
640 Sutter Street	Metropolitan Club (originally Women's Athletic Club)
625 Taylor Street	Bohemian Club

Grand Hotels

Ever since the Palace Hotel of 1875, San Francisco has prided itself on its opulent hotels. Characterized by monumental lobbies or other interior spaces and conservative exterior imagery, these hotels have long been symbolic of the city itself. First the Palace, followed by the St. Francis and Fairmont, and later the Sir Francis Drake and the Mark Hopkins, the tradition continues up to the present with such popular buildings as the Hyatt Regency. Few other cities can boast of so many elegant hotels from the early years of this century.

Concentrated in two areas, around Union Square and on Nob Hill, only the grand hotels in the primary areas are listed below.

491-499 Geary Street	Clift Hotel
633-665 Market Street	Palace Hotel
301-345 Powell Street	St. Francis Hotel
432-462 Powell Street	Sir Francis Drake Hotel

Substations

Following the example of Willis Polk's Substation C at 222-226 Jessie Street, the Pacific Gas and Electric Co. became a national leader in that aspect of the City Beautiful Movement which "beautified" common industrial structures in its treatment of power substations in San Francisco. Scattered throughout the city, there are four in the primary areas alone, all readily identifiable by a similar imagery regardless of whether they were designed by Polk, Frederick H. Meyer, or the company architect, Ivan C. Frickstad.

569 Commercial Street	PG&E, Station J
222-226 Jessie Street	PG&E, Station C (Jessie Street Substation)
222 Leidesdorff	PG&E, Station J
568 Sacramento	PG&E, Station J Annex

Monumental Banks

Among American cities which have developed as financial centers, few have developed as coherent an architectural imagery to express that character, and none have retained it as thoroughly as San Francisco.

Banks and other financial institutions have taken two forms, both united by a common monumental, classically derived imagery. The small classical temple, epitomized by the Bank of California, was the preferred form among most early 20th-century bankers, but later constrictions of cost and space caused most to build office towers over monumental bases, as in the Crocker Bank at 1 Montgomery. A few were designed in a more unified exterior composition such as the old Bank of Italy at 552 Montgomery. All were originally provided with monumental interiors, some of which have been remodeled.

Downtown San Francisco has many of these buildings, the greatest concentration being on the east side of Montgomery for one block south of Commercial Street. A full list of San Francisco buildings in this category would include many outside the primary areas of this survey.

1 Grant Avenue	Security Pacific National Bank (originally Savings Union Bank and Trust)
1 Jones Street	Hibernia Bank
744 Market Street	Wells Fargo Bank (originally Union Trust Co.)
783–785 Market Street	Humboldt Bank Building
1072–1098 Market Street	Crocker Bank (originally Anglo California Trust Co.)
1 Montgomery Street	Crocker Bank (originally First National Bank)
1 Powell Street	Bank of America (originally Bank of Italy)
1 Sansome Street	Crocker Bank (originally Anglo and London Paris National Bank)
400 California Street	Bank of California
300 Montgomery Street	Security Pacific National Bank (originally American National Bank)
440 Montgomery Street	old Borel Bank
460 Montgomery Street	Sutro & Co. (originally Italian American Bank)
500 Montgomery Street	American Asian Bank (originally Canton Bank Building)
520 Montgomery Street	Joe Paoli's (origin uncertain)
552 Montgomery Street	Bank of America (originally Bank of Italy)
108 Sutter Street	Bank of America (formerly French Bank)
400 Sansome Street	Federal Reserve Bank
415–429 Sansome Street	Fugazi Building (originally Yokohama Specie Bank)

Appendix

Architectural Classifications Outline

For discussion of San Francisco's downtown architecture, the following matrix was devised and applied to each building:

Type
Massing
Period
Composition
Articulation
Ornamentation
Facade Material
Construction

The possibilities within each item of the matrix, which are outlined below, refer only to the variations found within downtown San Francisco today. Similar areas in other cities would probably have somewhat different possibilities, and other parts of San Francisco itself would also be different.

TYPE

A. Commercial building with retail space or show-rooms at ground level and offices or lofts above
B. Commercial building with major exchange space(s) (banking, insurance, etc.), at ground level and offices above
C. Commercial building with major exchange space(s) occupying majority of interior
D. Major hotel
E. Apartment house/residential hotel
F. Club
G. Governmental building (courthouse, post office, customs house, city hall, etc.)
H. Library
I. Theater
J. Firehouse
K. Garage
L. Utilities building
M. Mixed; e.g., retail below and club above
N. Warehouse
O. Transportation depot
P. Power substation

MASSING

A. Rectangular
B. U-shaped
C. L-shaped
D. H-shaped
E. Tower
F. Other

PERIOD

A. 1890–1925
B. 1925–1945
C. 1945–present

COMPOSITION

A. For commercial buildings:

1. *Enframed window-wall*
   Small commercial buildings primarily used for retail purposes. Facades are treated as a single bay with large glass areas framed by brick, terra cotta, or other solid materials at the sides and top. The type developed in the late 19th century with the availability of iron and steel which freed the front facade from its traditional structural role, and with the functional requirements of an evolving commercial architecture. Of three types:

a. Most commonly, one or two enframed stories and exclusively retail.

b. Less commonly, one to five enframed stories built above an all-glass base. In this case the upper stories might be lofts for a variety of commercial purposes.

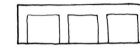

c. Infrequently, grouped in series. This type is common outside of the downtown area in less dense urban areas, notably in the strip commercial developments of the 1940s and 1950s.

d. A modification of (b), above, that occurred after 1925 with the advent of the Moderne. In this type the upper zone is still treated as an enframed bay but there is a predominance of solid frame over glass.

2. *Two-part small commercial block*
   Two-, three-, and occasionally four-story buildings with strong differentiation between ground-floor retail and upper loft or office levels. The origin of the type can be traced back to Roman antiquity, but it developed into its present form strictly for commercial buildings in the first half of the 19th century. From the mid-19th century onwards, the lower retail zone was frequently plate glass with mullions and expression of structural piers was reduced to a minimum. These buildings are most commonly constructed with brick bearing walls, but they are sometimes of steel-frame or reinforced-concrete construction.

a. Basically a hold-over from simple, mid-19th-century expression of the upper zone as a masonry wall punctured by windows at regular intervals. There are not many of these left in downtown San Francisco. The mid-19th-century commercial buildings in the Italianate mode, which are common in northern California, are typically of this type.

b. Common to the immediate post-fire period, with the upper zone treated as a formal, compositional unit, further enunciating the distinction between the "utilitarian" base and "architectural" top. In type (a), above, composition is seldom important. In this type composition is generally important in the upper zone only, which is to say that the whole does not read effectively as a unit. This type is a small building treated as a small building and could not be convincingly enlarged using the same treatment.

c. Strong expression of the structural frame of the facade where articulation assumes the role of composition in defining the building's form. The expression is a grid formed by structural posts and beams with plate glass forming most of the infill. In contrast to types (a) and (b), above, there is often little compositional differentiation between lower and upper zones.

3. *Stacked vertical block*

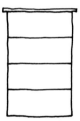

An infrequently used format found in large commercial buildings where the vertical mass is divided into three or more sections of generally two or three stories each. This arrangement was most frequently found in early tall office buildings of the 1870s and 1880s, but was still occasionally used after the turn of the century.

4. *Two-part vertical block*
   A compositional format common to sizable commercial structures such as office buildings, department stores, and some of the major apartment buildings and hotels. The vertical mass is divided into two principal zones where the analogy is made with the base and shaft of a classical column. The lower zone generally consists of one or two stories, sometimes with a one-story transitional area between lower and upper zones. The top story of the upper zone is sometimes slightly differentiated from those immediately below it in order to assist the cornice in providing a visual terminus to the composition. The lower zone is sometimes treated monumentally—rusticated wall, giant order, or arcade. Alternatively, the lower zone may be treated with large amounts of glass between structural piers, or on an all-glass base with no expression of piers. In this case a transitional zone between the lower and middle sections often helps define the base. The differentiation between glass base and upper zone usually corresponds to an in-

ternal differentiation between a commercial base and upper-level offices. A monumental base is more symbolically expressive of function and derived from architectural rather than functional requirements. The basic composition was developed for tall office buildings in the 1880s and 1890s in the United States. Sometimes a small building can be described as being in this type if it could be convincingly enlarged using the same treatment.

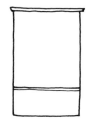

a. Basic division, as above.

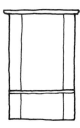

b. End bays differentiated to reinforce corner mass and hence visual stability. Heavier treatment of end bays was almost mandatory in the earliest San Francisco skyscrapers as long as the steel frame was diagonally braced—in order to hide the bracing both for fireproofing and aesthetic purposes.

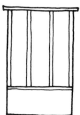

c. Use of a giant order as a major compositional device in the upper zone.

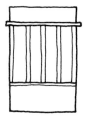

d. Any of the above variations with a one- or two-story attic zone above the principal cornice. Not to be confused with articulation of a "capital" as in the three-part vertical block, below.

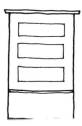

e. Like 2(c), above, a two-part composition with strong expression of the structural frame, but in this case, multi-story. Both 2(c) and this variation of the two-part vertical block are utilitarian in expression, and derived from Chicago examples.

5. *Three-part vertical block*
Like the two-part vertical block, a compositional format common to sizable commercial structures such as office buildings, department stores, and some of the major apartment buildings and hotels. The vertical mass is divided into three principal zones in an analogy with the base, shaft, and capital of a classical column. The lower zone generally consists of one or two stories, sometimes with a one-story transitional area between lower and middle zones. Similarly, there is sometimes a one-story transitional area between the middle and typically a one- or two-story upper capital zone. The three-part composition is normally terminated by a cornice. The lower zone is sometimes treated monumentally—as a rusticated wall, giant order, or arcade. Alternatively, the lower zone may be treated with large amounts of glass between structural piers, or as an all-glass base with no expression of piers. In this case a transitional zone between base and capital often helps define the base. The differentiation between glass base and middle zone usually corresponds to an internal differentiation between a commercial base and upper-level offices. A monumental base is more symbolically expressive of function and derived from architectural rather than functional requirements. The basic composition was developed for tall office buildings in the 1880s and 1890s in the United States.

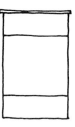

a. Basic division, as above.

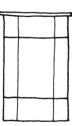

b. End bays differentiated to reinforce corner mass and hence visual stability. Heavier treatment of end bays was almost manda-

tory in the earliest San Francisco skyscrapers as long as the steel frame was diagonally braced—in order to hide the bracing both for fireproofing and aesthetic purposes.

c. Use of a giant order as a major compositional device in the middle zone.

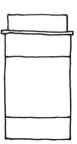

d. Any of the above variations with a one- or two-story attic zone above the principal cornice.
e. After 1925, in buildings which follow the model of Eliel Saarinen's Tribune Tower Competition entry, such as the Pacific Telephone and Russ Buildings, the three-part vertical composition is used for different reasons than before and three-dimensional massing and composition become more integral.

6. *Residential hotel*

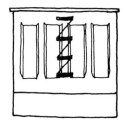

Format found on many apartment houses and residential hotels that follow the general two- and three-part divisions delineated above, but where projecting window bays and fire escapes frequently place the underlying compositional format in a subordinate role. The result becomes analogous to a quilt of patterns and forms with no one element or zone receiving pronounced emphasis. The format appears to have developed in the last quarter of the 19th century as buildings of this type emerged as major elements in the urban landscape. There were not enough of this type in the survey area to reach a more precise definition of its characteristics or variations.

7. *Others*
a. Loggia
b. Three-bay house
c. Hybrid—eccentric combinations of compositional types more commonly found alone.

8. *Miscellaneous*
   In addition to the compositional formats described above, a few structures could not usefully be described in terms of composition in this context. The one diner in downtown San Francisco follows the model of a railroad car. Several warehouses exist in which composition does not play a significant role. In addition, a few types appeared so infrequently as to defy classification in this context.

B. For civic and institutional buildings:

1. *Modified temple*
   A rectangular block, generally from two to four stories, the front elevation of which is derived from temple fronts of Greek and Roman antiquity. The form first gained widespread usage in Neo-Classical architecture and again became popular at the turn of the 20th century. During this latter period the front frequently consisted of a shallow, free-standing portico; however, engaged columns were sometimes used. On corner buildings the order was often carried around on the exposed side as engaged columns or pilasters.

a. Temple front

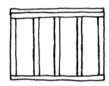

b. Temple front without pediment

c. Temple front surmounted by low dome. A composition derived from the Pantheon in Rome, and generally used for banks, churches, and central buildings such as libraries in institutional complexes.

2. *Enframed block*
   A long, rectangular mass, the majority of which is articulated by the use of a giant order or the suggestion of a giant order enframed by end bays of equal or almost equal heights. In the late 1920s and 1930s, the composition was often simplified to thin strips of the wall surface continuing vertically between tall bays of glass. The basic format developed in France during the 18th century and became popular in the United States in the late 19th and early 20th centuries for a wide variety of public and institutional buildings. Numerous variations

were developed; those present in the survey area include:

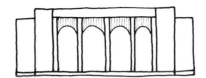

a. Colonnaded arcade with massive end bays and minor adjoining wings.

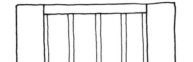

b. Colonnade with massive end bays.

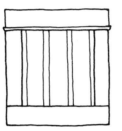

c. Colonnaded arcade and massive end bays with base and attic zones (frequently used for theaters and public office buildings).

3. *Central block with flanking wings*

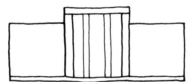

This format has the central section as the focal point, often taller and more elaborately articulated than the flanking sections which are treated as subordinate wings. The basic composition dates back at least to the mid-16th-century work of Palladio and became widely used for public and institutional buildings by the Neo-Classical period. It continued to be popular for large Victorian buildings. The central section can be treated as a temple front, have a colonnade, arcade, or simply contain larger and more elaborate elements.

4. *Vault*

A massive rectangular block with its fronts penetrated only by a greatly overscaled entrance and, on occasion, by small windows at the ground level. The principal source may be the elevation that rests behind the portico of antique temples. A few Neo-Classical buildings use this composition without the colonnade, but the format was not common

until the early 20th century. The vault was ideally suited to the taste for stripped classicism in the 1920s and 1930s. It primarily appears on banks and buildings housing heavy machinery where little natural light from the sides is needed.

5. *Modified palazzo*

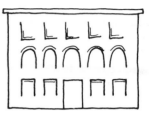

Long rectangular mass, generally divided into two or three horizontal zones with various small-scale openings articulating each. The basic composition is derived from Italian palaces of the 15th and 16th centuries. There is a considerable variety in the details of arrangement to be found in both the sources and their late 19th- and 20th-century adaptations. Sometimes 18th-century English models, based on the same prototype, are used. Frequently used for institutional buildings and clubs, as well as some large houses and moderate sized commercial buildings.

ARTICULATION

A. Skeletal
B. Vertical
C. Horizontal (created by piers and/or fenestration)
D. Balanced (found in masonry or implied masonry wall)
E. Combinations of above

ORNAMENTATION

A. Greek/Roman antiquity
B. Romanesque
C. Gothic
D. Renaissance/Baroque
E. 18th-century English
F. Art Deco/Moderne
G. Spanish Mission
H. Combinations of above
I. None

FACADE MATERIAL

A. Sandstone
B. Granite
C. Brick
D. Terra cotta
E. Concrete
F. Stucco
G. Combinations of above
H. Other

CONSTRUCTION

A. Steel frame
B. Reinforced-concrete frame
C. Brick load-bearing walls
D. Other

EXAMPLES

Hallidie Building
130–150 Sutter Street

Type: Commercial building with retail
                         ground level and office lofts
                         above

Massing:	Rectangular
Period:	1890-1925
Composition:	Three-part vertical block with differentiated end bays
Articulation:	Balanced
Ornamentation:	Gothic
Facade Material:	Glass and cast iron
Construction:	Reinforced-concrete frame with glass curtain walls

St. Francis Hotel
301–345 Powell Street

Type:	Major Hotel
Massing:	E-shaped (originally U-shaped)
Period:	1890-1925
Composition:	Three-part vertical block with differentiated end bays
Articulation:	Balanced
Ornamentation:	Renaissance/Baroque
Facade Material:	Colusa sandstone walls over granite base
Construction:	Steel frame with stone-clad brick curtain walls

Shell Building
100–120 Bush Street

Type:	Commercial building with retail ground level and offices above
Massing:	Tower with setbacks
Period:	1925-1945
Composition:	Three-part vertical block with differentiated end bays
Articulation:	Vertical piers
Ornamentation:	Art Deco/Moderne
Facade Material:	Terra cotta with reinforced-concrete spandrel panels
Construction:	Steel frame

Tadich Grill
240–242 California Street

Type:	Commercial
Massing:	Rectangular
Period:	1890-1925
Composition:	Enframed window-wall
Articulation:	Horizontal
Ornamentation:	Renaissance/Baroque
Facade Material:	Terra cotta and glass
Construction:	Reinforced-concrete frame

Bank of California
400 California Street

Type:	Commercial building largely given over to a major exchange (banking) space
Massing:	Rectangular
Period:	1890-1925
Composition:	Modified temple—temple front without pediment
Articulation:	Vertical colonnade
Ornamentation:	Greek/Roman antiquity
Facade Material:	Granite
Construction:	Steel frame

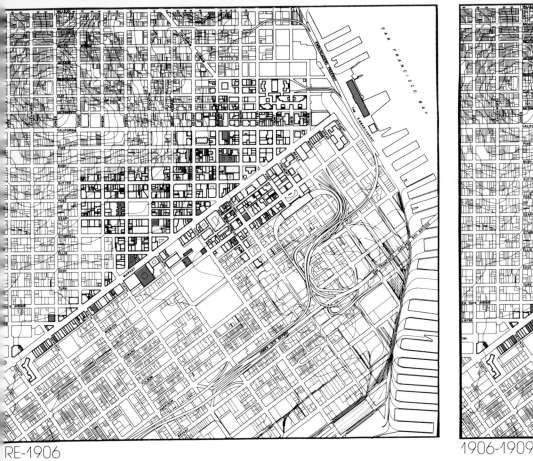

RE-1906

1906-1909

910-1918

1919-1930

Periods of Construction

1931-1945

1946-PRESENT

260

Bibliography

The following list is intended to provide reference to the major printed sources on downtown San Francisco's architecture, and to other sources which are useful in interpreting its architecture. There is no attempt to duplicate bibliographies on historic preservation, San Francisco history, or cultural geography, all of which were important in this project, but which are readily available elsewhere.

Allen, Glenn and Charles H. Young. *The Architecture of Allen and Young*. Stockton, 1926.

Alpern, Andrew. *Apartments for the Affluent: A Historical Survey of Buildings in New York*. McGraw Hill, 1975.

American Builders Review. San Francisco, August 1905–December 1907.

American Society of Civil Engineers, San Francisco Section. *Historic Civil Engineering Landmarks*. Edited by William A. Myers. The Pacific Gas and Electric Co., 1977.

The Architect (title varies: *The Pacific Coast Architect, The Building Review, California Arts and Architecture, Arts and Architecture*). Los Angeles, 1911–1945.

Architect and Engineer. San Francisco, May 1905–1945.

Architectural Association of the University of California. *Yearbook*. 1914.

Architectural Digest. John C. Brasfield, Los Angeles, 1926–1931.

Architecture and Allied Arts. Pictorial Publishing Co., San Francisco, 1930–1931.

Barth, Gunther. *Instant Cities, Urbanization and the Rise of San Francisco and Denver*. Oxford University Press, 1975.

Bowden, Martyn John. *The Dynamics of City Growth: An Historical Geography of the San Francisco Central District 1850–1931*. Ph.D. thesis, University of California at Berkeley, 1967.

Building and Industrial News. San Francisco and Oakland, 1911–1932.

Burnham, Daniel H. and Edward H. Bennett. *Report on a Plan for San Francisco*. Edited by Edward F. O'Day. San Francisco, September 1905.

Condit, Carl W. *American Building, Materials and Techniques from the First Colonial Settlements to the Present*. University of Chicago Press, 1968.

David, A. C. The New San Francisco: Architectural and Social Changes Wrought by Reconstruction. *Architectural Record* XXXI(1): 1–26, 1912.

Delaire, Emile. *Les Architectes élèves de l'Ecole des Beaux-Arts 1793–1907*. Paris, 1907.

Drexler, Arthur, ed. *The Architecture of the Ecole des Beaux-Arts*. The Museum of Modern Art, 1977.

Fitch, James Marston. *American Building, The Historical Forces that Shaped It*. Shocken Books, second edition, 1966.

Gebhard, David, et al. *A Guide to Architecture in San Francisco and Northern California*. Peregrine Smith, 1973.

Geerlings, Gerald K. *Metal Crafts in Architecture*. Scribners, 1929.

Geerlings, Gerald K. *Wrought Iron in Architecture*. Scribners, 1929.

Hansen, Gladys, ed. *San Francisco: The Bay and Its Cities*. Hastings House, 1973. Originally compiled by the Federal Writers Project of the Works Progress Administration for Northern California, 1940.

Himmelwright, A. L. A. *The San Francisco Earthquake and Fire, A Brief History of the Disaster*. Roebling Construction Co., 1906.

Kidney, Walter C. *The Architecture of Choice, Eclecticism in America, 1880–1930*. George Braziller, 1974.

Kirker, Harold. *California's Architectural Frontier*. Peregrine Smith, revised edition, 1973.

Kostoff, Spiro, ed. *The Architect: Chapters in the History of the Profession*. Oxford University Press, 1977.

Lockwood, Charles. *Suddenly San Francisco: The Early Years of an Instant City*. A California Living Book, 1978.

Mahony Brothers. *Illustrations of Buildings Built or Building During the Past 20 Months by Mahony Brothers of San Francisco*. F. L. Ebbets, 1908.

Modern San Francisco. Western Press Association, 1905–06 and 1907–08.

Moulin, Tom and Don DeNevi. *San Francisco, Creation of a City*. Celestial Arts, 1978.

Mujica, Francisco. *History of the Skyscraper*. Archeology and Architecture Press, Paris, 1929. Reprinted by DaCapo Press, 1977.

The Municipal Engineering Works of the City of San Francisco. Reprinted from *Engineering News*, the Pacific Coast number, 18 February 1915.

Noffsinger, J. P. *The Influence of the Ecole des Beaux-Arts on the Architects of the United States*. Washington, D.C., 1955.

Olmsted, Roger and T. H. Watkins. *Here Today, San Francisco's Architectural Heritage*. Sponsored by the Junior League of San Francisco. Chronicle Books, 1968.

Onderdonk, Francis S., Jr. *The Ferro-Concrete Style, Reinforced Concrete in Modern Architecture*. Architectural Book Publishing Co., 1928.

Philopolis: A Monthly Magazine for Those Who Care. San Francisco, 1906–1916.

Pomeroy, Earl. *Pacific Slope*. Knopf, 1965.

Powell, Edith Hopps. *San Francisco's Heritage in Art Glass*. Superior Publishing Co., Seattle, 1976.

Ransome, Ernest L. and Alexis Saurbrey. *Reinforced Concrete Buildings*. McGraw Hill, 1912.

Real Estate Atlas of San Francisco County, California. Real Estate Data, Inc., Miami, 1976.

Robinson, Cervin and Rose Marie Haag Bletter. *Skyscraper Style, Art Deco in New York.* Oxford University Press, 1975.

Roth Leland, ed. *A Monograph on the Works of McKim, Mead, and White 1879-1915.* Benjamin Blom, 1973. Reprinted by Arno Press 1977.

San Francisco. The Art Commission. *A Survey of Art Work in the City and County of San Francisco.* Joan Ellison, ed. New edition 1975.

San Francisco. Department of City Planning. *San Francisco Downtown Zoning Study.* December 1966.

San Francisco. Department of City Planning. *The Urban Design Plan for the Comprehensive Plan of San Francisco.* May 1971.

San Francisco Architectural Club. *Yearbook.* 1902, 1903-04, 1909, 1913, 1915.

Sanborn Map Co. *Insurance Maps of San Francisco.* Volume 1, 1963. Volume 2, 1961.

Scott, Mel. *The San Francisco Bay Area, a Metropolis in Perspective.* University of California Press, 1959.

Some Early Business Blocks in San Francisco. *Architectural Record* XX(1): 15-32, July 1906.

Stamp, Gavin. London 1900. *AD (Architectural Design)* XLVIII(5-6): 302-383, 1978.

Starrett, W. A. *Skyscrapers and the Men Who Build Them.* Scribners, 1928.

Svirsky, Peter S. San Francisco Limits the Buildings to See the Sky. *Planning:* 9-14, 12 January 1973.

Svirsky, Peter S. San Francisco: The Downtown Development Bonus System. In Marcus and Groves, ed. *The New Zoning.* Praeger, 1970.

Todd, Frank Morton. *The Story of the Exposition.* Knickerbocker Press, 1921.

Town Talk. San Francisco, X-XI, 1902.

United States Department of the Interior; Geological Survey. Bulletin #324. *The San Francisco Earthquake and Fire of April 18, 1906, and Their Effects on Structures and Structural Materials.* Government Printing Office, 1907.

United States Department of the Interior; National Park Service. National Register of Historic Places Inventory—Nomination Form for the San Francisco Civic Center. 1978.

Vance, James. *Geography and Urban Evolution in the San Francisco Bay Area.* Institute of Governmental Studies, University of California at Berkeley, 1964.

Wahrhaftig, Clyde. Downtown: A Petrographic Nature Walk Through the Financial District. *Mineral Information Service* XIX(11), November 1966.

Weisman, Winston. A New View of Skyscraper History. Edgar Kaufmann, Jr., ed. *The Rise of an American Architecture.* Praeger, 1970.

Woodbridge, John and Sally. *Buildings of the Bay Area.* Grove Press, 1960.

Photographs and Illustrations

Abbreviations are as follows: Top (T), Bottom (B), Left (L), Right (R), Center (C).

The Architect and Engineer. B33, BL34, TL40, BL43, 52, T53, T58, BR93, BC142, BC171, BC195, BC207

The Bancroft Library: T24, B24, 25, T26, B26, T27, C27, B27, TL28, TR28, B28, 29, T30, B30, B32, T33, BR34, B35, B37, B41, TR42, 49, TL54, TR54, B54, 55, L56, R56, B58, R59, 63, R83, BL85, B91, BL92, R129, BR132, R173, R190, R198

Bruce Judd Designs: R127

Burnham, D.H. and E.H. Bennett: *Report on a Plan for San Francisco:* BR31

Gabriel Moulin Studios, San Francisco: Title page, 17, T35, BR38, TR40, BR43, TR46, TL46, B47, TC145, R172, R195, B197, L206, B208, C219

The Pacific Coast Architect: B53

Stanley H. Page, Charles Hall Page Collection: 1, 21, BL31, T32, 36, T37, T41, 60, 234

John W. Procter, Florence M. Procter Collection: BL40, BR40, BL162, L163, BC177, R178

The San Francisco Architectural Club: T34

The San Francisco Public Library: BL38, B39, B46, C72, C94, R103, TL128, R176

Tribune Tower Competition: T38

United States Dept. of the Interior: Geological Survey. Bulletin #324: T31

All others by Charles Hall Page & Associates, Inc.: Jan Beecherl, Jack Schafer, staff.

Charles Hall Page & Associates, Inc.

Project Director:
Michael R. Corbett

Design:
Robin Thomas Sweet

Staff:
Jan Beecherl, Susan Harrison, Charles J. Hasbrouck, Jack Schafer

Office and Editorial:
Robert Bruce Anderson, Stephen Farneth, Lizabeth Gluck, Carolyn Jellinek, Bruce Judd, Ellen Lipsey, Charles Hall Page

This volume was researched, written and designed by the staff of Charles Hall Page and Associates, Inc. for Heritage. The office of Charles Hall Page and Associates, Inc. practices architecture and urban planning in the Western States, specializing in recycling older structures and revitalizing older cities and neighborhoods.

Typesetting by Sigmagraph, Inc., San Francisco.
Printed by Sinclair Printing Company.

The Foundation for San Francisco's Architectural Heritage

The Foundation for San Francisco's Architectural Heritage ("HERITAGE") is a publicly supported non-profit organization dedicated to the preservation of buildings and places important to San Francisco's architectural and historic character. Organized in 1971 and supported by more than 1,500 members, Heritage acts as an advocate for the preservation of significant buildings, provides technical and financial assistance, encourages city policies which recognize and protect architecturally and historically significant resources and neighborhoods, and sponsors public education programs designed to foster greater appreciation of San Francisco's built environment and the need to conserve it.

Heritage gratefully acknowledges the support of its members without whom this book would not have been possible. In particular, Heritage thanks the following donors who made substantial contributions to Heritage in the past year.

Bank of America Foundation
Catalyst Financial Corporation
Chevron, U.S.A., Inc.
Mr. and Mrs. Brook Clyde
Mr. and Mrs. Edward J. Conner
Mr. Newton A. Cope
S.H. Cowell Foundation
Catherine M. Davis Trust
T. Delaney Landscape Co., Inc.
Mr. and Mrs. David B. Devine
Emil Roy and Elizabeth Haas Eisenhart
Mr. and Mrs. Charles D. Field
Flack & Flack
James G. Gerstley
Mr. and Mrs. James M. Gerstley
Agnes H. Goss
Dr. Margot H. Green
Mr. and Mrs. Douglas W. Grigg
William Randolph Hearst Foundation
Mr. and Mrs. Austin E. Hills
Cecil Howard Charitable Trust
Mr. and Mrs. Reverdy Johnson
Kaplan/McLaughlin/Diaz
Mr. and Mrs. Marron Kendrick
Mrs. Charles B. Kuhn
Mr. and Mrs. Ernest Lilienthal
Cyril I. Magnin
Mr. and Mrs. Robert Magowan
Pettit & Martin
Charles E. Merrill Trust
Peter Z. Michael
Mr. and Mrs. Albert Moorman
National Endowment for the Humanities
Mrs. Ernst Ophuls
Mr. and Mrs. Charles Page
Mr. and Mrs. Charles Hall Page
Charles Hall Page & Associates, Inc.
Robinson, Mills and Williams
Christine H. Russell
Madeleine Russell
Alice Russell and Bill Shapiro
Security Pacific Charitable Foundation
Diana Bell Shore
Mr. and Mrs. Laurence C. Stein
Peter F. Supino & Partners
Richard and Helen Tavernetti
Francesca P. Taylor
Teevan Painting, Inc.
Robert and Jacqueline Young

Executive Director:
Robert Berner

Assistant Director:
Linda Jo Fitz

Program Coordinator:
Nancy Belden

Historian:
Randolph Delehanty